CULTURAL CRIMINOLOGY

⑤SAGE | 50 YEARS

SAGE was founded in 1965 by Sara Miller McCune to support the dissemination of usable knowledge by publishing innovative and high-quality research and teaching content. Today, we publish more than 750 journals, including those of more than 300 learned societies, more than 800 new books per year, and a growing range of library products including archives, data, case studies, reports, conference highlights, and video. SAGE remains majority-owned by our founder, and after Sara's lifetime will become owned by a charitable trust that secures our continued independence.

Los Angeles | London | New Delhi | Singapore | Washington DC | Boston

CULTURAL CRIMINOLOGY
AN INVITATION

JEFF FERRELL | KEITH HAYWARD | JOCK YOUNG

Los Angeles | London | New Delhi
Singapore | Washington DC | Boston

Los Angeles | London | New Delhi
Singapore | Washington DC | Boston

SAGE Publications Ltd
1 Oliver's Yard
55 City Road
London EC1Y 1SP

SAGE Publications Inc.
2455 Teller Road
Thousand Oaks, California 91320

SAGE Publications India Pvt Ltd
B 1/I 1 Mohan Cooperative Industrial Area
Mathura Road
New Delhi 110 044

SAGE Publications Asia-Pacific Pte Ltd
3 Church Street
#10-04 Samsung Hub
Singapore 049483

Editor: Natalie Aguilera/Amy Jarrold
Editorial assistant: James Piper/George Knowles
Production editor: Sarah Cooke
Copyeditor: Sharon Cawood
Proofreader: Nicola Marshall
Marketing manager: Sally Ransom
Cover design: Jennifer Crisp
Typeset by: C&M Digitals (P) Ltd, Chennai, India
Printed and bound by CPI Group (UK) Ltd,
Croydon, CR0 4YY

First edition published 2008. Reprinted 2011, 2012 and 2013.
This edition published 2015.

Library of Congress Control Number: 2014954247

British Library Cataloguing in Publication data

A catalogue record for this book is available from
the British Library

ISBN 978-1-44625-915-3
ISBN 978-1-44625-916-0 (pbk)

At SAGE we take sustainability seriously. Most of our products are printed in the UK using FSC papers and boards.
When we print overseas we ensure sustainable papers are used as measured by the Egmont grading system.
We undertake an annual audit to monitor our sustainability.

This book is dedicated to the memory of Jock Young –
friend, colleague, provocateur.

BRIEF CONTENTS

Detailed Contents

LIST OF PLATES

ABOUT THE AUTHORS

Jeff Ferrell is Visiting Professor of Criminology at the University of Kent, UK, and Professor of Sociology at Texas Christian University, USA. He is author of the books *Crimes of Style*, *Tearing Down the Streets*, and *Empire of Scrounge*. He is co-editor of the books *Cultural Criminology*, *Ethnography at the Edge*, *Making Trouble*, *Cultural Criminology Unleashed*, and *Cultural Criminology: Theories of Crime*. Jeff Ferrell is founding and current editor of the New York University Press book series *Alternative Criminology*, and one of the founding editors of the journal *Crime, Media, Culture: An International Journal* (winner of the Association of Learned and Professional Society Publishers' 2006 Charlesworth Award for Best New Journal). In 1998 he received the Critical Criminologist of the Year Award from the Critical Criminology Division of the American Society of Criminology.

Keith J. Hayward is Professor of Criminology at the University of Kent, UK and holds visiting positions at universities in Australia, Brazil, and the United States. He has published widely in the areas of criminological theory, spatial and social theory, visual and popular culture, and terrorism and fanaticism. As one of the leading figures in the field of cultural criminology, Dr Hayward is particularly interested in the various ways in which cultural dynamics intertwine with the practices of crime and crime control within contemporary society; as a consequence, he has written on everything from the role of documentary filmmaking in criminology to the existential allure of 'Jihadi cool'. He is the author, co-author, or editor of ten books, the most recent being, *Cultural Criminology* (2016), a four-volume edited collection for Routledge's Major Works series. Currently, Dr Hayward is completing a short (non-criminological) book on 'infantilization' and the life course.

Jock Young (1942-2013) was one of the world's pre-eminent criminologists. Over four decades, he shaped the nature and direction of the discipline and was at the forefront of almost every major development in the sociology of crime and deviance. He was the author of numerous influential monographs including *The Drugtakers* (1971), *The New Criminology* (1973, with Ian Taylor and Paul Walton), *The Exclusive Society* (1999), and *The Criminological Imagination* (2011). For many years he was Professor of Sociology at Middlesex University, before taking up a position at John Jay College of Criminal Justice, New York City in 2002. He later held positions at the University of Kent, UK and in 2009 was made Distinguished Professor of Criminal Justice and Sociology at the City University of New York's Graduate Center. His writings have been translated into 11 languages in 15 countries, and he was honoured for his research on many occasions. In 2008 he was awarded the American Society of Criminology's Sellin-Glueck prize for outstanding international contributions to criminology, and in 2012 he was the recipient of the British Society of Criminology's outstanding achievement award.

Acknowledgements

The existence of a book like *Cultural Criminology: An Invitation* suggests something of the collective project that cultural criminology has now become. Over the past decade or so cultural criminology has grown to include more and more students, scholars, and academic programmes in the United States, the United Kingdom, and elsewhere, and has become manifest in increasing numbers of books, articles, and conferences. While any book's list of those to be thanked and acknowledged is surely incomplete, then, this one seems especially so – and we apologize to all those participants in cultural criminology's collective project whom we have inadvertently omitted.

That said, we'll at least make an effort, and so for their generous contributions of ideas, information, and perspective, we thank Kester Aspden, Frankie Bailey, Carla Barrett, Nachman Ben-Yehuda, David Bradbury, Dave Brotherton, Phil Carney, Grey Cavender, Isaac Enriquez, Ruben Flores-Sandoval, Michael Flynn, Chris Greer, Mark Hamm, Philip Jenkins, Paul Leighton, Marilyn McShane, Vince Miller, Jayne Mooney, Wayne Morrison, Stephen Muzzatti, Ben Penglase, Jean Pockrus, Greg Snyder, Ken Tunnell, Tim Turner, Robert Weide, Iain Wilkinson, Trey Williams, Catriona Woolner, and Cecile Van de Voorde. Our thanks also to Joe Wilkes both for his advice regarding the filmography and for his inspiring music (www.joewilkes.co.uk) and also to 'writers' Colt 45 and Rasta 68 for their aesthetic assistance.

A special thank you is also due to Majid Yar for his careful reading of, and helpfully critical comments on, the book manuscript. Any errors or infelicities are, of course, ours alone.

Our editor at SAGE, Caroline Porter, has been a source of ceaseless intellectual encouragement and good will, and we thank her and the production team at SAGE for their professionalism and their dedication to scholarly work.

Acknowledgements for the second edition

In the years since the publication of the first edition of *Cultural Criminology: An Invitation*, the body of supportive scholars working in and around the field of cultural criminology has only grown. While we thank once again those we acknowledged in the first edition, then, we also thank Avi Brisman, Michelle Brown, Salo de Carvalho, Caroline Chatwin, Simon Cottee, Stuart Henry, Johnny Ilan, Paul Kaplan, Mitch Librett, Travis Linnemann, Roger Matthews, Cirus Rinaldi, Alvaro Oxley Rocha, David Redmond, Ashley Sabin, Frank van Gemert, Rene van Swaaningen, Marc Schuilenburg, and Damian Zaitch for their assistance with this second edition. We would also like to add a special thanks to Natalie Aguilera and the team at SAGE for their ongoing professionalism and support.

Jeff Ferrell and Keith Hayward, January 2015

PRAISE FOR THE NEW EDITION...

'Updating and expanding their path-breaking appreciation of the fundamentally cultural foundations of crime both as law enforcement target and as behaviour pursuing the charms of deviance, in their second edition, Ferrell, Hayward and the late Jock Young introduce "cultural criminology" within the long historical sweep of social thought on crime. Their far-reaching and generous appreciation of diverse contributions to the cultural criminology movement is heuristically explosive. On virtually every page their text will offer the keen reader multiple suggestions for taking research on crime and deviance in novel directions. As criminology faces a crisis of confidence, this rare work shows how a new generation of students can fit promising and practical investigations of crime and deviance under a single comprehensive canopy.'
Jack Katz, Professor of Sociology, UCLA

Praise for the first edition...

'This is not just a book on the present state and possible prospects of our understanding of crime, criminals and our responses to both. However greatly the professional criminologists might benefit from the authors' illuminating insights and the new cognitive vistas their investigations have opened, the impact of this book may well stretch far beyond the realm of criminology proper and mark a watershed in the progress of social study as such. This book, after all, brings into the open the irremediable unclarity, endemic contentiousness and the resulting frailty of the line dividing deviance from the norm of social life – that line being simultaneously a weapon and the prime stake in the construction and servicing of social order.'
Professor Zygmaut Bauman, Emeritus Professor, Leeds University

'*Cultural Criminology* offers a fresh new perspective on both criminality and criminal justice. It outlines the cultural hegemony of the powerful while also documenting the growing resistance to mindless criminalization and mass incarceration. Artfully written, the authors also document the work of those consciously

creating a new political space to challenge the increasingly global, security society that seems inextricably tied up with late capitalism.'
Meda Chesney-Lind, University of Hawaii at Manoa

'Beautifully written and superbly conceived, with illustrations and examples that combine theory and practice across a range of disciplines, *Cultural Criminology* should be read by anyone interested in crime, media, culture and social theory. Bravo to Ferrell, Hayward and Young on a tour de force that is at once cool and classic! *Cultural Criminology* will influence the field for a very long time to come.'
Lynn Chancer, Professor of Sociology, Hunter College, CUNY, USA

'Creative, challenging and controversial: a manifesto for mean times.'
Tony Jefferson, Visiting Presidential Scholar, John Jay College of Criminal Justice, USA

1

Cultural criminology: an invitation

In October 2011 at a demonstration organized by the protest movement Occupy, Julian Assange, the controversial Australian activist and long-time editor-in-chief of the whistle-blowing website WikiLeaks, appeared outside the London Stock Exchange in a stylized Guy Fawkes mask. Stark white, with pink cheeks, a wide smile and a rakish moustache, the Guy Fawkes visage has emerged as one of the most enduring icons of the many anarchist and protest groups that have sprung up in the wake of the 2008 financial crisis. The origins of the mask can be traced to the classic 1982 graphic novel *V for Vendetta* – a dark tale of one man's protest against a futuristic police state based loosely on the infamous Gunpowder Plot of 1605, when Catholic Revolutionaries attempted to overthrow the British Government by blowing up the House of Lords (Sauter, 2012). The anti-authoritarian story struck a chord with protestors, and after *V for Vendetta* was adapted into a movie in 2005, the Fawkes mask emerged as a ubiquitous symbol of contemporary political resistance; not least, it became the 'face' of the international hacker group Anonymous. But while the mask served the very practical purpose of hiding protestors' faces from the pervasive police surveillance that is now such a feature of political demonstrations, it also served the interests of an altogether different cultural group: the executives and shareholders of one of the world's biggest media conglomerates. As producers of *V for Vendetta*, the media giant Time-Warner owns the rights to the mask's image and is consequently paid a licensing fee with the sale of each unit. And the mask is big business. According to Harry Beige of Rubie's Costume, the New York-based costumier who produces the mask, sales are running at over 100,000 a year (Bilton, 2011). To make matters worse, it recently came to light that the masks are manufactured in non-unionized sweatshops in the impoverished backstreets of Brazil and Mexico.

Meanwhile, in Mexico, another clouded cultural relationship takes shape. For decades, the poor of Sinaloa in North West Mexico have paid homage to Jesus Malverde, a legendary 'Robin Hood'-style bandit who, according to local lore, stole from the rich and gave to the poor before the Federales eventually hanged him in 1909. More recently, however, Jesus Malverde has taken on a new, unofficial role as the patron saint of Mexico's drug dealers and border traffickers.

Dubbed the 'narco saint' by the Mexican press, Malverde was originally only popular in Sinaloa's capital Culiacán, but in recent years his familiar moustachioed face and black neckerchief have been seen in makeshift shrines everywhere from Tijuana to Mexico City. In the poor neighbourhoods where drug gangs thrive, Malverde has become not just a mythic symbol of crime, but a quasi-religious cult figure. Put simply, Malverde is the figurehead for what is known as 'narco culture' – the celebration and admiration of affluent drug lords and successful traffickers who, through skill or good fortune, beat the odds and avoid arrest. Today, narco culture is a veritable cottage industry which also includes the appropriation of the Mexican folk icon Santa Muerte (Saint Death or Holy Death), 'narco fashion' and the 'Chalinazo' subcultural clothing style, 'narco corrido' music and 'narco ballad' pop songs that recall the criminal exploits of legendary drug bandits (Lippman, 2005), and even a branch of the Mexican movie industry known as 'narco film'. Narco culture is even spreading into the Sun Belt cities of the United States and beyond (Ortiz Uribe, 2011). In Pico Rivera, California, partygoers flock to El Rodeo Night Club, one of many such narco corrido music clubs in the Los Angeles area that are at the forefront of this new form of Mexican-American cultural hybridization. Likewise, in recent years, Los Angeles gang members have started working as film extras in Tijuana's narco gangster movie industry. In all this, the startling truth is that narco culture bespeaks a certain acceptance of drug smuggling as a normal aspect of everyday life in the impoverished neighbourhoods that straddle the US–Mexican border; as one local teacher put it: 'To live in Culiacán is to be conversant with the legends of specific "narcotraficantes", whose names are as recognisable as those of great athletes or musicians' (Quinones, 1998: n.p.). And this narco culture is not without its dangerous digital echoes as well. Increasingly, citizens and 'cyber-guardians' use social media like Twitter, and websites and blogs like Wikinarco and Blogdelnarco, to track and warn of drug-related violence. In response, the Mexican authorities have made it a crime to use Twitter to 'undermine public order' or spread rumours, and the drug cartels, 'threatened by the decentralized distribution of the Web', have responded as well – in one case hanging two bodies from a bridge with the sign, 'this will happen to all the Internet snitches' (Cave, 2011: 5).

Each of these cases embodies fundamental issues for cultural criminology. Whether the symbolic dynamics of globalized street protest or the strange hybrid of criminality and religiosity associated with narco culture, both illustrate one of cultural criminology's founding concepts: that *cultural dynamics carry within them the meaning of crime*. Given this, cultural criminology explores the many ways in which cultural forces interweave with the practice of crime and crime control in contemporary society. It emphasizes the centrality of meaning, representation and power in the contested construction of crime – whether crime is constructed as political protest or stylized representation of drug culture, as ephemeral event or subcultural subversion, as social danger or state-sanctioned violence. In our view, the subject matter of any useful and critical criminology must necessarily move beyond narrow notions of crime and criminal justice to incorporate symbolic displays of transgression and control, feelings and emotions that emerge within criminal events, and public and political campaigns designed to define (and delimit) both crime and its consequences. This wider focus, we argue, allows for a new sort of criminology – a *cultural* criminology more attuned to prevailing conditions, and so more capable of conceptualizing and confronting contemporary crime and crime control. This cultural criminology seeks both to understand crime as an expressive human activity and to critique the perceived wisdom surrounding the contemporary politics of crime and criminal justice.

Thinking about culture and crime

Cultural criminologists understand 'culture' to be the stuff of collective meaning and collective identity; within it and by way of it, the government claims authority, the consumer considers advertised products – and 'the criminal', as both person and perceived social problem, comes alive. Culture suggests the collective search for meaning, and the meaning of the search itself; it reveals the capacity of people, acting together over time, to animate even the lowliest of objects – the homeless person's bedroll, the police officer's truncheon, the gang member's bandana, the Guy Fawkes mask – with importance and implication.

For us, human culture – the symbolic environment created and occupied by individuals and groups – in this way intertwines with structures of power and inequality. Culture is not simply a product of social class, ethnicity or occupation – it cannot be reduced to a residue of social structure – yet culture doesn't take shape without these structures, either. Both the cultural prowess of the powerful and the subcultures of acquiescence or resistance invented by the less powerful shape, and are shaped by, existing forms of patterned inequality. Cultural forces, then, are those threads of collective meaning and understanding that wind around the everyday troubles of social actors, animating the situations and circumstances in which their troubles play out. And for all the parties to everyday crime and criminal justice – for perpetrators, police officers, victims, parole violators and news reporters – *the negotiation of cultural meaning intertwines with the immediacy of criminal experience.*

As early work on 'the pains of imprisonment' demonstrated, for example, the social conditions and cultural dynamics of imprisonment form a dialectical relationship, with each forming and reforming the other. While all inmates experience certain pains of imprisonment, the precise extent and nature of these pains emerge from various cultures of class, gender, age and ethnicity – that is, from the lived meanings of the social lives that inmates bring with them to the prison. And yet these particular pains, given meaning in the context of pre-existing experiences and collective expectations, in turn shape the inmate cultures, the shared ways of life, that arise as inmates attempt to surmount the privations of prison life (Young, 1999; Fader, 2013). Facing common troubles, confronting shared circumstances, prison inmates and prison guards – and, equally so, street muggers, corporate embezzlers and criminal lawyers – draw on shared understandings and shape new ones, thereby investing troubles and their solutions with human agency.

As regards this human agency, cultural criminology builds from a foundational understanding as to the creativity of human action. From this view, people and their social groups create cultural meanings and craft their own cultural perspectives, albeit in a moral and material world not of their own making. To paraphrase Marx, they may not make their own history just as they please, but they do make history. Human behaviour is shaped by the actors themselves; it is not merely the unfolding of preordained essences somehow encoded in DNA sequences, psychoanalytical tendencies or the causal effects of a broken home or childhood trauma. Rather, moral careers are contingent on the present, with the past holding sway mostly to the extent that powerful actors reinforce notions of a fixed self and powerless subjects come to accept these narratives. Motives are, in this sense, cultural products – shared accounts and creative accomplishments – not simply individual essences revealed. In a hyper-plural society where a multitude of vocabularies of motive (Mills, 1940) circulate, individuals and groups may in fact pick among them – not willy-nilly, of course, but in relationship to their perceived problems. The individual self certainly remains, but less as an isolated entity and more as a centre of the human construction of meaning in a world riven by a plurality of options. To postulate that human beings operate as narrative creators, constantly writing and rewriting their personal stories, does not imply a lack of unity of the self, but rather the self as a unique constellation of constructed meanings (Presser and Sandberg, 2015).

Of course, none of this ongoing human creativity rules out dangerous or destructive meanings, bad faith decisions, or past decisions that over time take on the reified, mechanistic power of habituation. Nor does it preclude the common and dangerous human predicament of ontological insecurity, where various groups or sectors within the population come to sense that their social status is threatened and their identity disembedded. One cultural response to this problem is the process of 'othering', with actors actively embracing narratives about themselves and other groups that *deny* human creativity and imagine a world preordained and fated. Through othering, essentialist attributes are projected onto another and onto oneself so as to justify privilege and to stem feelings of deep insecurity. Ironically, this cultural strategy operates so as to erase culture itself. It promises fixed, essentialist lines of orientation in a late-modern world of increasing complexity and disorientation; seeming to guarantee set structures of superiority and inferiority, as encoded in binaries of gender or race, it is a guard against the vertigo of late modernity (J. Young, 2007).

A particularly potent version of this dynamic centres on crime and deviance; here the essentially 'normal' is contrasted with the inherently 'deviant', and the law-abiding cleanly set apart from the criminal. Here, virtue is contrasted with vice – and 'their' vice is seen to corroborate 'our' virtue. Such a process of othering allows vice to be seen as a lack of culture – that is, as a lack of values and assimilation into the moral order – and frequently this view forms the basis of a determinism that is presumed to propel the deviant actor. Layered onto this dynamic are social-psychological processes which add intensity and passion to the process of othering. Chief among these is a sense of moral outrage and indignation towards those others who are seen as cheating the rules of responsibility, sacrifice and reward. According to this cultural construction, 'deviants' live on the dole or irresponsibly parent children outside of marriage, while 'virtuous' citizens in contrast embrace their economic responsibilities and attend to their civic duties. This essentialist dichotomy is in turn exacerbated in situations where 'deviants' from immigrant groups or the underclass are seen as directly causing problems for the virtuous. Importantly, cultural criminologists argue that these psychodynamics are not determined by an individual's psychoanalytical past (e.g. Gadd and Jefferson, 2007) but instead result from current problems and pressures percolating in particular parts of the social structure. Amidst the current economic crisis, for example, corporate downsizing, the deskilling of work and chronic job insecurity are critical social problems in their own right – but when they are mixed with mistaken beliefs about their causes and racially charged ideologies of othering and essentialism, they can produce intensities of violent misperception that redouble their dangerous consequences. For cultural criminologists, then, psychosocial criminology operates most insightfully when existentially based and when grounded in the present structural and cultural problems of late modernity.

This shifting relationship between cultural negotiation, individual experience and social problem affirms another of cultural criminology's principal assumptions: that while crime and deviance constitute more than the simple enactment of essentialist traits, they constitute more than the enactment of a static group culture as well. Put simply, cultural criminologists understand culture to be not a product but a process – the sort of process through which Jesus Malverde's identity can continue to shift a century after his death. Here, cultural criminologists take issue with the tradition of cultural conflict theory, as originated with the work of Thorsten Sellin (1938) and as highlighted in the well-known subcultural formulation of Walter Miller (1958), where crime largely constitutes the enactment of lower working-class values. While such approaches do take note of 'the cultural', they do so in ways that tend to be simplistic and reductionist; Sellin's original formulation suggested that vengeance and vendetta among Sicilian immigrants led to inevitable conflict with wider American values. The danger of this approach can be seen today in, for example, the supposition that multiculturalism generates ineluctable cultural collisions. Yet, as we will argue, and as cultural criminologists like Frank Bovenkerk, Dina Siegel and Damian Zaitch (2003; Bovenkerk and Yesilgoz, 2004) have well demonstrated, cultures – ethnic and otherwise – exist as neither static entities nor collective essences. Rather, cultural dynamics remain in motion; collective cultures offer a heterogeneous mélange of symbolic meanings that blend and blur, cross boundaries real and imagined, conflict and coalesce according to dynamics of power and influence, and hybridize with changing circumstances. To imagine, then, that an ethnic culture maintains some ahistorical and essential tendency to crime (or conformity) is no cultural criminology; it's a dangerous essentialism, stereotypical in its notion of cultural stasis and detrimental to understanding the intricate dynamics that connect culture and crime.

In *Culture as Praxis*, Zygmunt Bauman (1999: xvi–xvii) catches something of this cultural fluidity and complexity. There he distinguishes two ways of thinking about culture, longstanding and seemingly diametrically opposed. The first conceptualizes 'culture as the activity of the free roaming spirit, the site of creativity, invention, self-critique and self-transcendence', suggesting 'the courage to break well-drawn horizons, to step beyond closely-guarded boundaries'. As we'll discuss further in the following chapter, culture of this first sort fits most easily into the tradition of subcultural theory as developed by Albert Cohen (1955) and others, where deviant or delinquent subcultures create collective responses to social inequality. Here, culture suggests the collective vitality of subversive social praxis, and the creative construction of transgression and resistance; in this sense, the illicit self-inventions of an outsider subculture can at times symbolically stand the social order on its head. As Bauman suggests, though, a second way of thinking about culture understands it as just the opposite: 'a tool of routinization and continuity – a handmaiden of social order', a symbolic universe that stands for 'regularity and pattern – with freedom cast under the rubric of "norm-breaking" and "deviation"'. Culture of this second sort is more the province of orthodox social anthropology, of Parsonian functionalism and of post-Parsonian cultural sociology. For these orientations, culture is the stuff of collective cohesion, the Durkheimian glue of social order and preservative of predictability, the *soi-distant* support of social structure. And if for the first conception of culture transgression signals meaningful creativity, for the second, transgression signifies the very opposite: an absence of culture, an anomic or even atavistic failure of socialization into collective meaning. For cultural criminologists, though, the two ways of understanding culture are not irreconcilable; both highlight the collective construction of shared meaning, if in different domains, and both suggest the ongoing, contested negotiation of morality and cultural identity. For some, this negotiation calls forth a collective *belief* in tradition, an emotional embracing of stasis and conformity, and the ideological mobilization of rigid stereotype and fundamental value. For others, it calls forth against this conformity a gnawing *disbelief* in the social order itself, and so a willingness to risk inventing collective alternatives. For cultural criminologists, both are of interest – and the moments when the two collide around issues of crime and justice form a significant subject matter for cultural criminology itself.

A cultural criminology that foregrounds human agency and human creativity, then, does not ignore those cultural dynamics that sometimes involve their renunciation. People, as David Matza (1969) famously pointed out, always have the capacity to transcend even the most dire of circumstances – but they also have the capacity to act 'as if' they are puppets unable to transcend the social order at all. If, in Dwight Conquergood's (1991) wonderful phrase, we are to view culture as a verb rather than as a noun, as an unsettled process rather than a *fait accompli*, then we must remember that this verb can take both the passive and the active tense. Culture suggests a sort of shared public performance, a process of public negotiation – but that performance can be one of acquiescence or rebellion, that negotiation one of violent conflict or considered capitulation. In this sense, cultural criminology, by the very nature of its subject matter, occupies a privileged vantage point on the everyday workings of social life. Its twin focus on culture and crime positions it at precisely those points where norms are imposed and threatened, laws enacted and broken, rules negotiated and renegotiated. Such a subject matter inevitably exposes the ongoing tension between cultural maintenance, cultural disorder and cultural regeneration – and so from the view of cultural criminology, the everyday actions of criminals, police officers and judges offer not just insights into criminal justice, but important glimpses into the very process by which social life is constructed and reconstructed. As we will see, this subject matter in turn reveals the complex, contested dynamic between cultures of control – that is, control agencies' downwards symbolic constructions of crime and deviance – and cultures of deviance and transgression whereby rule breakers construct their own alternative meanings upwards.

Cultural criminology old and new

Talk of culture, subculture and power evokes the rich tradition of subcultural theorization within criminology – and certainly cultural criminology draws deeply on subcultural research, from the early work of the Chicago School to the classic delinquency studies of the British Birmingham School. Likewise, cultural criminology is greatly influenced by the interactionist tradition in criminology and the sociology of deviance, as embodied most dramatically in labelling theory, and as taken up in the 1960s at the London School of Economics. Labelling theories, and the broader symbolic interactionist framework, highlight the conflicts of meaning that consistently animate crime and deviance; they demonstrate that the reality of crime and transgression exists as a project under cultural construction, a project emerging from ongoing negotiations of authority and reputation. In fact, these and other intellectual traditions are essential to the development of cultural criminology – and the following chapter will explore how cultural criminology represents perhaps their culmination and reinvention.

Yet, in addressing the question of 'whether cultural criminology really does represent a new intellectual endeavour rather than a logical elaboration of previous work on deviant subcultures' (O'Brien, 2005: 600; Spencer, 2011), we would firmly answer for the former. Cultural criminology actively seeks to dissolve conventional understandings and accepted boundaries, whether they confine specific criminological theories or the institutionalized discipline of criminology itself. In our view, for instance, existing subcultural and interactionist perspectives only gather real explanatory traction when integrated with historical and contemporary criminologies of power and inequality. Likewise, cultural criminology is especially indebted to theories of crime founded in the phenomenology of transgression (eg. Katz, 1988; Lyng, 1990; Van Hoorebeeck, 1997) – yet, here as well, our goal is to develop these approaches by situating them within a critical sociology of contemporary society (Ferrell, 1992; O'Malley and Mugford, 1994; Hayward, 2004).

Moreover, cultural criminology consciously moves beyond these orientations in sociology and criminology; as later chapters will show, it incorporates perspectives from social theory, urban studies, media studies, existential philosophy, cultural and human geography, anthropology, social movements theory – even from the historical praxis of earlier political agitators like the Wobblies and the Situationists. As much as cultural criminology seeks to ground itself in the best of existing criminology and sociology, it seeks also to reinvigorate the study of crime by integrating a host of alternative perspectives. Our intention is to continue turning the intellectual kaleidoscope, looking for new ways to see crime and the social response to it.

This strategy of reinvigoration is as much historical as theoretical; if we are to engage critically with the present crisis in crime and crime control, intellectual revivification is essential. Many of the perspectives just noted were forged from existing orientations during the political fires of the 1960s and 1970s, or in other cases out of the early twentieth-century blast furnace of industrial capitalism and working class upheaval. Developing what was to become labelling theory, for example, Becker (1963: 181) disavowed his work being anything more than the existing 'interactionist theory of deviance' – and yet his revitalized interactionist theory resonated with the uncertainties and inequalities of the

1960s, rattled the foundations of 'scientific' criminology and softened up criminology for still other radical remakings. So it is with cultural criminology today. We're not at the moment organizing the 1912 Lawrence cotton mills with the Wobblies or plastering Paris 1968 with Situationist slogans; we're working to make sense of contemporary conditions, to trace the emergence of these conditions out of those old fires and furnaces and to confront a new world of crime and control defined by the manufactured image, the constant movement of meaning and the systematic exclusion of marginal populations and progressive possibilities. To do so, we're pleased to incorporate existing models of criminological critique – but we're just as willing to reassemble these and other intellectual orientations into a new mélange of critique that can penetrate the well-guarded façades of administrative criminology, the shadowy crimes of global capitalism and the everyday realities of criminality today.

Crucial to cultural criminology, then, is a critical understanding of current times, which, for want of a better term, we'll call *late modernity*. Chapter 3 will provide a fuller sense of late modernity and of cultural criminology's response to it. For now, we'll simply note that cultural criminology seeks to develop notions of culture and crime that can confront what is perhaps late modernity's defining trait: a globalized world always in flux, awash in marginality and exclusion, but also in the ambiguous potential for creativity, transcendence, transgression and recuperation. As suggested earlier, human culture has long remained in motion – yet this motion today seems all the more moving and all the more meaningful. In late modernity, the insistent emphasis on expressivity and personal development, and the emergence of forces undermining the old constants of work, family and community, together place a premium on cultural change and personal reinvention. Couple this with a pluralism of values spawned by mass immigration and global conflict, and with the plethora of cultural referents carried by the globalized media, and uncertainty is heightened. Likewise, as regards criminality, the reference points which give rise to relative deprivation and discontent, the vocabularies of motive and techniques of neutralization deployed in the justification of crime, the very *modus operandi* of the criminal act itself, all emerge today as manifold, mediated, plural and increasingly global. And precisely the same is true of crime as public spectacle: experiences of victimization, justifications for punitiveness, and modes of policing all circulate widely and ambiguously, available for mediated consumption or political contestation.

Under such conditions, culture operates less as an entity or environment than as an uncertain dynamic by which groups large and small construct, question and contest the collective experience of everyday life. Certainly, the meaningful moorings of social action still circulate within the political economy of daily life, and in the context of material setting and need – and yet, loosened in time and space, they circulate in such a way as to confound, increasingly, the economic and the symbolic, the event and the image, the heroic and the despicable. If the labelling theorists of a half-century ago glimpsed something of the slippery process by which deviant identity is negotiated, how much more slippery is that process now, in a world that cuts and mixes racial profiling for poor suspects, pre-paid image consultants for wealthy defendants and televised crime personas for general consumption? If the subcultural theorists of the 1950s and 1960s understood something of group marginalization and its cultural consequences, what are we to understand of such consequences today, when globalized marginalization intermingles with crime and creativity, when national authorities unknowingly export gang cultures as they deport alleged gang members (Brotherton, 2011), when criminal subcultures are packaged as mainstream entertainment?

All of which returns us to contemporary phenomena like those Mexican drug gangs and British street protesters noted earlier, their violent images and symbols of resistance circling the globe by way of websites, news coverage and alternative media. In the next section, we consider some other contemporary confluences of culture and crime, focusing especially on the late-modern meanings of violence. In the chapter's final section, we explore politics and political conflict. There we'll make clear that we seek to revitalize political critique in criminology, to create a contemporary criminology – a cultural criminology – that can confront systems of control and relations of power as they operate today. There we'll hope to make clear another of cultural criminology's foundational understandings: that to explore cultural dynamics is to explore the dynamics of power – and to build the basis for a cultural *critique* of power as well.

.

Meaning in motion: violence, power and war

Amidst the fluid ambiguity of this late-modern world, violence might, at first glance, seem one of the few subjects of criminological inquiry whose solidity has not melted into air. Violence seems grounded in physicality and in the physics of force, damage and destruction. We know violence and its sad consequences when we see them: a human's body battered, a building broken into, an automobile wrecked. Certainly, violence may be interpersonal, a matter of one person physically dominating another, but it hardly seems the stuff of cultural uncertainty and mediated meaning. Yet, in the face of such physical violence, and its pervasive occurrence across many categories of crime, cultural criminologists like ourselves make a startling claim: violence is never only, perhaps never even primarily, physical. The dynamics of its occurrence and the damage that it causes are innately symbolic and interpretive – and this crucial process of symbolism and interpretation often continues long after the physicality of violence has ceased. As we see it, physical violence may start and stop, but its meaning continues to circulate. It also seems to us that most violence, maybe all interpersonal violence, involves drama, presentation and performance – especially dangerously gendered performance (Butler, 1999; Miller, J., 2001) – as much as it does bruises and blood. So, if we hope to confront the politics of violence – that is, to understand how violence works as a form of power and domination, to empathize with the victimization that violence produces and to reduce its physical and emotional harm – we must engage with the *cultures* of violence. Even this most direct of crimes – flesh on flesh, bullets and bodies – is not direct at all. It's a symbolic exchange as much as a physical one, an exchange encased in immediate situations and in larger circumstances; an exchange whose meaning is negotiated before and after the blood is spilt.

Sometimes such violence is even performed for public consumption, and so comes to circulate as entertainment. A televised pay-per-view title fight, for example, can be thought of as a *series* of performances and entertainments: before the fight, with the press conferences, television commercials and staged hostilities of the weigh-in; during the fight itself, with the ring rituals of fighter introductions, ringside celebrities and technical knockouts; and after the fight, with the press coverage, the slow-motion replays of punches and pain, and interviews with winner and loser. If a boxing commission inquiry happens to follow, or if a 'moral entrepreneur' (Becker, 1963) decides later to launch a crusade against pugilistic brutality, another series of performances may unfold – and another series of meanings. Now the fight's entertainment will be reconsidered as a fraud, or a fix, or as evidence of what used to be called 'man's inhumanity to man'. Now other press conferences will be staged, other moments from the fight rebroadcast in slow motion, and all of it designed to go another round in staging the fight and its implications. The immediate, vicious physicality of violence now elongates and echoes through video footage, legal charges and public perception. As it does, the linear sequencing of cause and effect circles back on itself, such that images of a physical altercation can come to be seen as crime, as evidence of crime, as a catalyst for later crime, even as the imitative product of existing mediated crime.

With the democratization of digital media, it's not only televised big-market violence that invokes this complex cultural dynamic; the proliferation of do-it-yourself fight videos – street fights, gang fights, 'bum fights' – call it into play as well. The widespread marketing and sale of these videos by way of digital media reveal the sort of pervasive leisure-time violence that Simon Winlow and Steve Hall (2006) have documented among young people who are increasingly excluded from meaningful work or education. They offer direct evidence of media technology's seepage into the practice of everyday life, such that kids can now stage and record, for good or bad, elaborate images of their own lives. Most troubling, they suggest the in-the-streets interplay between a mean-spirited contemporary culture of marketed aggression, an ongoing sense of manliness defined by machismo, violence and domination, and a world pervaded by cell phones and their cameras. Hunter S. Thompson (1971: 46) once said of a tawdry Las Vegas casino that it was 'what the whole ... world would be doing on Saturday night if the Nazis had won the war'. Yeah, that, and brutalizing each other on camera, uploading the image, selling it for a profit and watching it for entertainment.

Other sorts of violence demonstrate other dimensions of culture, power and inequality. As feminist criminologists have shown, domestic violence against women explodes not only out of angry situations, but emerges from longstanding patterns of interpersonal abuse and gendered expectation, and from the pernicious cultural logic by which men can somehow imagine that physical violence confirms their own possessive identities. As we'll discuss further in later chapters, various contemporary forms of violence as entertainment – prime-time police dramas, extreme fighting, war footage – each invoke particular social class preferences and political economies of profit, offering different sorts of flesh for different sorts of fantasies. As we'll also see, knuckles bruised and bloodied in pitched battles between striking factory workers and strike-breaking deputy sheriffs suggest something of the structural violence inherent in class inequality; so too do the knuckles of young women bloodied amidst the frantic work, the global assembly-line madness, of a maquiladora or south China toy factory (Redmon, 2015). As Mark Hamm (1995) has documented, young neo-Nazi skinheads, jacked up on beer and white power music and mob courage, write their own twisted account of racism as they beat down an immigrant on a city street or bloody their knuckles while attacking a gay man outside a suburban club.

Significantly for a cultural criminology of violence, episodes like these don't simply represent existing inequalities or exemplify arrangements of power; they *reproduce* power and inequality, encoding it in the circuitry of everyday life. Such acts are *performances* of power and domination, offered up to various audiences as symbolic accomplishments. A half-century ago, Harold Garfinkel (1956: 420) suggested that there existed a particular sort of 'communicative work ... whereby the public identity of an actor is transformed into something looked on as lower in the local scheme of social types', and he referred to this type of activity as a 'degradation ceremony'. Violence often carries this sort of communicative power; the pain that it inflicts is both physical and symbolic, a pain of public degradation and denunciation as much as physical domination. And in this sense, once again, it is often the *meaning* of the violence that matters most to perpetrator and victim alike. A wide and disturbing range of violent events – neo-Nazi attacks, fraternity hazing rituals, gang beat-downs, terrorist bombings and abduction videos, public hangings, domestic violence, sexual assaults, war crimes – can be understood in this way, as forms of ritualized violence designed to degrade the identities of their victims, to impose on them a set of unwanted meanings that linger long after the physical pain fades. To understand violence as 'communicative work', then, is not to minimize its physical harm or to downgrade its seriousness, but to recognize that its harms are both physical and symbolic, and to confront its terrible consequences in all their cultural complexity.

So violence can operate as image or ceremony, can carry with it identity and inequality, can impose meaning or have meaning imposed upon it – and in the contemporary world of global communication, violence can ebb and flow along long fault lines of war, terror and ideology. Among the more memorable images from the US war in Iraq, for example, are those photographs of prisoner abuse that emerged from Abu Ghraib prison in 2003–2004. Perhaps you still remember them: the hooded figure standing on a box with wires running from his hands, the pile of men with Lynndie England leering and pointing down at them, the prisoner on the leash held by England. If you remember, it's because those photographs have been so widely circulated as to become part of our shared cultural stockpile of image and understanding (see Carrabine, 2011). But before we go any further, a question: Do you remember whether a US soldier at Abu Ghraib ever sodomized a prisoner, murdered a prisoner, raped a prisoner? These things may well have happened, but if we've seen no photographic evidence of them, then they won't seem – can't seem – as real or as meaningful to us as those acts that were photographed. And so the suspicion arises: Was the 'problem' at Abu Ghraib the abuse or the photographs of the abuse? And if those photographs of abuse had not been taken and circulated, would Abu Ghraib exist as a contested international symbol, a public issue, a crime scene and the scene of a massive breakout in 2013 that freed senior al-Qaida leaders and hundreds of others – or would a crime not converted into an image be, for many, no crime at all (Hamm, 2007a)?

Those photos that *were* taken have certainly remained in motion since they were first staged, spinning off all manner of effects and implications along the way – including widespread imitation and digital recording of the 'Lynndie England pose', sometimes referred to as 'pulling a Lynndie'. Those photos didn't just capture acts of aggressive violence; they operated, as Garfinkel would argue, as a system of ritualized degradation in the prison and beyond, exposing and exacerbating the embarrassment of the prisoners, recording it for the amusement of the soldiers and eventually disseminating it to the world. For the prisoners and the soldiers alike, the abuse was as much photographic as experiential, more a staged performance for the camera than a moment of random violence. The responses of those outraged by the photos in turn mixed event, emotion and image: on the walls of Sadr City, Iraq, a painting of the hooded figure, but now wired to the Statue of Liberty for all to see; and in the backrooms of Iraqi insurgent safe houses, staged abuses and beheadings, meant mostly for later broadcast on television and the Internet (Ferrell et al., 2005: 9). And were we to reproduce those photos here – which we won't – the photos would be put in motion again, but in what direction? Toward educational edification, or the further objectification and degradation of those involved, now reduced to textbook illustration?

For those US soldiers who took the Abu Ghraib photographs, there was yet another sort of culture of the image: a sense that cell phone cameras, digital photographs emailed instantaneously home, self-made movies mixing video footage and music downloads, all seem normal enough, whether shot in Boston or Baghdad, whether focused on college graduation, street fights or prisoner degradation. Here, we see even the sort of 'genocidal tourism' that cultural criminologist Wayne Morrison (2004a) has documented – where World War II German police reservists took postcard-like photographs of their atrocities – reinvented in an age of instant messaging and endless image reproduction. And like street fight video makers, we now see soldiers, insurgents and jihadi terrorists who produce their own images of violence, find their own audiences for those images and interweave image with physical conflict itself.

Violence, it seems, is never only violence. It emerges from inequities both political and perceptual, and accomplishes the symbolic domination of identity and interpretation as much as the physical domination of individuals and groups. Put in rapid motion, circulating in a contemporary world of fight videos and newscasts, images of violence double back on themselves, emerging as crime or evidence of crime, confirming or questioning existing arrangements. From the view of cultural criminology, there is a *politics* to every moment of violence – to every eruption of domestic violence or ethnic hatred, to every body broken for war or profit or entertainment, to every nose bloodied in newspaper photos and Internet clips. As the meaning of violence continues to coagulate around issues of identity and inequality, the need for a *cultural* criminology of violence, and in response a cultural criminology of social justice, continues too.

The politics of cultural criminology

If ever we could afford the fiction of an 'objective' criminology – a criminology devoid of moral passion and political meaning – we certainly cannot now, not when every act of violence leaves marks of mediated meaning and political consequence. The day-to-day inequalities of criminal justice, the sour drift towards institutionalized meanness and legal retribution, the ongoing abrogation of human rights in the name of 'counter-terrorism' and 'free trade' – all carry criminology with them, willingly or not. Building upon existing inequalities of ethnicity, gender, age and social class, such injustices reinforce these inequalities and harden the hopelessness they produce. Increasingly crafted as media spectacles, consistently masked as information or entertainment, the inequitable dynamics of law and social control remain essential to the maintenance of political power, and so operate to prop up the system that produces them.

In such a world, there's no neat choice between political involvement and criminological analysis – only implications to be traced and questions to be asked. Does our scholarship help maintain a fraudulently 'objective' criminology that distances itself from institutionalized abuses of power, and so allows them to continue? Does criminological research, often dependent on the good will and grant money of governmental agencies, follow the agendas set by these agencies, and so grant them in return the sheen of intellectual legitimacy? By writing and talking mostly to each other, do criminologists absent themselves from public debate, and so cede that debate to politicians and pundits? Or can engaged, oppositional criminological scholarship perhaps help move us towards a more just world? To put it bluntly: What is to be done about domestic violence and hate crime, about fight videos and prison torture – and about the distorted images and understandings that perpetuate these practices as they circulate through the capillaries of popular culture?

We've already suggested part of the answer: critical engagement with the flow of meaning that constructs late-modern crime, in the hope of turning this fluidity towards social justice. In a world where, as Stephanie Kane (2003: 293) says, 'ideological formations of crime are packaged, stamped with corporate logos, and sent forth into the planetary message stream like advertising', our job must be to divert the stream, to substitute hard insights for advertised images. Later chapters will discuss this strategy of cultural engagement in greater depth, but first we turn to an issue that underlies it: the relationship of crime, culture and contemporary political economy.

Capitalism and culture

For us, that issue is clear: unchecked global capitalism must be confronted as the deep dynamic from which spring many of the ugliest examples of contemporary criminality. Tracing a particularly expansionist trajectory these days, late-modern capitalism continues to contaminate one community after another, shaping social life into a series of predatory encounters and saturating everyday existence with criminogenic expectations of material convenience (Hedges, 2009). All along this global trajectory, collectivities are converted into markets, people into consumers, and experiences and emotions into products. So steady is this seepage of consumer capitalism into social life, so pervasive are its crimes – both corporate and interpersonal – that they now seem to pervade almost every situation.

That said, it's certainly not our contention that capitalism forms the essential bedrock of all social life or of all crime. Other wellsprings of crime and inequality run deep as well; late capitalism is but a shifting part of the quagmire of patriarchy, racism, militarism and institutionalized inhumanity in which we're currently caught. To reify 'capitalism', to assign it a sort of foundational timelessness, is to grant it a status it doesn't deserve. Whatever its contemporary power, capitalism constitutes a trajectory, not an accomplishment, and there are other trajectories at play today as well, some moving with consumer capitalism, others moving against and beyond it. Still, as the currently ascendant form of economic exploitation, capitalism certainly merits the critical attention of cultural criminology.

And yet, even as we focus on this particular form of contemporary domination and inequality, we are drawn away from a simple materialist framework and towards a cultural analysis of capitalism and its crimes. For capitalism is essentially a *cultural enterprise* these days; its economics are decisively cultural in nature. Perhaps more to the point for criminology, contemporary capitalism is a system of domination whose economic and political viability, its crimes and its controls, rest precisely on its cultural accomplishments. Late capitalism markets lifestyles, employing an advertising machinery that sells need, affect and affiliation as much as the material products themselves. It runs on service economies, economies that marginalize workers while packaging privilege and manufacturing experiences of imagined indulgence. Even the material fodder for all this – the cheap appliances and seasonal fashions – emerges from a global gulag of factories kept well hidden behind ideologies of free trade and economic opportunity. This is a capitalism founded not on Fordism, but on the manipulation of meaning and the seduction of the image; it is a cultural capitalism. Saturating destabilized working-class neighbourhoods, swirling along with mobile populations cut loose from career or community, it is particularly contagious; it offers the seductions of the market where not much else remains.

As much as the Malaysian factory floor, then, *this* is the stuff of late capitalism and so the contested turf of late modernity. If we're to do our jobs as criminologists – if we're to understand crime, crime control and political conflict in this context – it seems we must conceptualize late capitalism in these terms. To describe the fluid, expansive and culturally charged dynamics of contemporary capitalism is not to deny its power but to define it; it is to consider current conditions in such a way that they can be critically confronted. From the Frankfurt School to Fredric Jameson (1991) and beyond, the notion of 'late capitalism' references many meanings, including for some a fondly anticipated demise – but among these meanings is surely this sense of a capitalism quite thoroughly transformed into a cultural operation, a capitalism inexplicable outside its own representational dynamics (Harvey, 1990; Hayward, 2004).

The social classes of capitalism have likewise long meant more than mere economic or productive position – and under the conditions of late capitalism this is ever more the case. Within late capitalism, social class is experienced, indeed constituted, as much by affective affiliation, leisure aesthetics and collective consumption as by income or employment. The cultural theorists and 'new criminologists' of the 1970s first began to theorize this class culture and likewise began to trace its connection to patterns of crime and criminalization. As they revealed, and as we have continued to document (Hayward, 2001, 2004; Young, 2003), predatory crime within and between classes so constituted often emerges out of *perceptions* of relative deprivation, other times from a twisted allegiance to consumer goods considered essential for class identity or class mobility (Hall et al., 2008). And yet, even when so acquired, a class identity of this sort remains a fragile one, its inherent instability spawning still other crimes of outrage, transgression or predation. If crime is connected to social class, as it surely is, the connective tissue today is largely the cultural filaments of leisure, consumption and shared perception.

Crime, culture and resistance

In the same way that cultural criminology attempts to conceptualize the dynamics of class, crime and social control within the cultural fluidity of contemporary capitalism, it also attempts to understand the connections between crime, activism and political resistance under these circumstances. Some critics argue that cultural criminology in fact remains too ready to understand these insurgent possibilities, confounding crime and resistance while celebrating little moments of illicit transgression. For such critics, cultural criminology's focus on everyday resistance to late capitalism presents a double danger, minimizing the real harm done by everyday crime while missing the importance of large-scale, organized political change. Martin O'Brien, for example, suggests that 'cultural criminology might be best advised to downgrade the study of deviant species and focus more attention on the generically political character of criminalization' (2005: 610; see also Howe, 2003; Ruggiero, 2005). Steve Hall and Simon Winlow (2007: 83–4) likewise critique cultural criminology's alleged tendency to find 'authentic resistance' in every transgressive event or criminal subculture, and dismiss out of hand forms of cultural resistance like 'subversive symbol inversion' and 'creative recoding' that cultural criminologists supposedly enjoy finding among outlaws and outsiders.

In response, we would note that cultural criminology doesn't simply focus on efflorescences of resistance and transgression; it also explores boredom, repetition, everyday acquiescence and other mundane dimensions of society and criminality (e.g. Ferrell, 2004a; Yar, 2005; Bengtsson, 2012; Steinmetz, 2015). Cultural criminology's attention to meaning and micro-detail ensures that it is equally at home explaining the monotonous routines of DVD piracy or the dulling trade in counterfeit 'grey' automotive components as it is the *sub rosa* worlds of gang members or graffiti artists. As cultural criminologists, we seek to understand all components of crime: the criminal actor, formal and informal control agencies, victims and others. In this book's later chapters, for example, we develop cultural criminology's existing focus on the state. For cultural criminology, attention to human agency means paying attention to crime and crime control, to emotion and rationality, to resistance and submission.

Then again, if you're a cultural criminologist, you might also pay particular attention to the ways in which new terms of legal and political engagement emerge from the fluid cultural dynamics of late modernity and late capitalism. To summarize some cultural criminological studies in crime and resistance: when gentrification and 'urban redevelopment' drive late capitalist urban economies, when urban public spaces are increasingly converted to privatized consumption zones, graffiti comes under particular attack by legal and economic authorities as an aesthetic threat to cities' economic vitality. In such a context, legal authorities aggressively criminalize graffiti, corporate media campaigns construct graffiti writers as violent vandals and graffiti writers themselves become more organized and politicized in response. When consumer culture and privatized transportation conspire to shape cities into little more than car parks connected by motorways, bicycle and pedestrian activists create collective alternatives and stage illegal public interruptions. When late capitalist consumer culture spawns profligate waste, trash scroungers together learn to glean survival and dignity from the discards of the privileged, and activists organize programmes to convert consumer 'trash' into food for the homeless, clothes for illegal immigrants and housing for the impoverished. When the same concentrated corporate media that stigmatizes graffiti writers and trash pickers closes down other possibilities of local culture and street activism, a micro-radio movement emerges – which is aggressively policed by local and national authorities for its failure to abide by regulatory standards designed to privilege concentrated corporate media (Ferrell, 1996, 2001/2, 2006a).

In all of these cases, easy dichotomies don't hold. These aren't matters of culture or economy, of crime or politics; they're cases in which activists of all sorts employ subversive political strategies – that is, various forms of organized cultural resistance – to counter a capitalist economy itself defined by cultural dynamics of mediated representation, marketing strategy and lifestyle consumption. Likewise, these cases don't embody simple dynamics of law and economy, or law and culture; they exemplify a confounding of economy, culture and law that spawns new forms of illegality and new campaigns of enforcement. Similarly, these cases neither prove nor disprove themselves as 'authentic' resistance or successful political change – but they do reveal culturally organized opposition to a capitalist culture busily inventing new forms of containment and control.

Most significantly, the cultural criminological analysis of these and other cases neither accounts for them as purely subjective moments of cultural innovation, nor reduces them to objective byproducts of structural inequality. Among the more curious claims offered by cultural criminology's critics is the contention that cultural criminology has abandoned structural analysis and 'criminological macro-theories of causality' in favour of 'subjectivist culturalism' (Hall and Winlow, 2007: 83, 86). In reality, since its earliest days, cultural criminology has sought to overcome this very dichotomization of structure and agency, of the objective and the subjective, by locating structural dynamics within lived experience. This is precisely the point of Stephen Lyng's (1990) 'edgework' concept, embodying both Marx and Mead in an attempt to account for the interplay between structural context and illicit sensuality. Likewise, Jack Katz's (1988) 'seductions of crime' are meant as provocative engagements with, and correctives to, 'criminological macro-theories of causality'. As Katz argues, a criminology lost within the abstractions of conventional structural analysis tends to forget the interpersonal drama of its subject matter – or paraphrasing Howard Becker (1963: 190), tends to turn crime into an abstraction and then study the abstraction – and so must be reminded of crime's fearsome foreground. Clearly, cultural criminology hasn't chosen 'subjectivist culturalism' over structural analysis; it has chosen instead a style of analysis that can focus structure and subject in the same frame (Ferrell, 1992; Hayward, 2004; Young, 2003). Perhaps some of our colleagues only recognize structural analysis when encased in multi-syllabic syntax or statistical tabulation, but structural analysis can be rooted in moments of transgression as well; it can show that 'structure' remains a metaphor for patterns of power and regularities of meaning produced in back alleys as surely as corporate boardrooms.

Commodifying resistance? Romanticizing resistance?

Engaging in this way with the politics of crime, resistance and late capitalism requires yet another turn as well, this one towards a central irony of contemporary life: the vast potential of capitalism to co-opt resistance into the very system it is meant to oppose, and so to transform experiential opposition into commodified acquiescence (Horkheimer and Adorno, 2002). This homogenizing tendency – glimpsed earlier in the corporate profits made from every Guy Fawkes mask – constitutes an essential late capitalistic dynamic and the most insidious of consumer capitalism's control mechanisms. The ability to reconstitute resistance as commodity, and so to sell the illusion of freedom and diversity, is powerful magic indeed (Heath and Potter, 2006). Because of this, a number of cultural criminological studies have explored this dynamic in some detail. Meticulously tracing the history of outlaw biker style, Stephen Lyng and Mitchell Bracey (1995) have demonstrated that early criminal justice attempts to criminalize biker style only amplified its illicit meanings, while later corporate schemes to incorporate biker style into mass production and marketing effectively evacuated its subversive potential. More recently, we have outlined the ways in which consumption overtakes experiences of resistance – indeed, most all experiences – within the consumerist swirl of the late capitalist city (Hayward, 2004). Likewise, Heitor Alvelos (2004, 2005) has carefully documented the appropriation of street graffiti by multinational corporations and their advertisers. And he's right, of course; as the illicit visual marker of urban hipness, graffiti is now incorporated into everything from corporate theme parks and Broadway musicals to clothing lines, automobile adverts and video games. When it comes to the politics of illicit resistance, death by diffusion – dare we say, impotence by incorporation – always remains a real possibility (see Hayward and Schuilenburg, 2014).

And yet again, a dichotomized distinction between authentically illicit political resistance and commodified market posturing does little to explain these cases, or the fluidity of this larger capitalist dynamic. From one view, of course, this dynamic would suggest that there can be no authentic resistance in any case, since everything – revolutionary tract, subversive moment, labour history – is now automatically and inescapably remade as commodity, re-presented as image and so destroyed. A more useful view, we think, is to see this dynamic as one of complexity and contradiction. As seductive as it is, the late capitalistic process of incorporation is not totalizing; it is instead an ongoing battleground of meaning, more a matter of policing the crisis than of definitively overcoming it. Sometimes the safest of corporate products becomes, in the hands of activists or artists or criminals, a dangerous subversion; stolen away, remade, it is all the more dangerous for its ready familiarity, a Trojan horse sent back into the midst of the everyday. Other times, the most dangerously illegal of subversions becomes, in the hands of corporate marketers, the safest of selling schemes, a sure bet precisely because of its illicit appeal. Mostly, though, these processes intertwine, sprouting further ironies and contradictions, winding their way in and out of little cracks in the system, often bearing the fruits of both 'crime' and 'commodity'.

A new generation of progressive activists born to these circumstances seems well aware of them, by the way – and because of this, well aware that the point is ultimately not the thing itself, not the act or the image or the style, but the activism that surrounds and survives it. So, anti-globalization activists, militant hackers, urban environmentalists and others throw adulterated representations back at the system that disseminates them, organize ironic critiques, recode official proclamations and remain ready to destroy whatever of their subversions might become commodities. Even within late capitalism's formidable machinery of incorporation, the exhaustion of meaning is never complete, the illicit subversion never quite conquered. The husk appropriated, the seed sprouts again.

Our hope for cultural criminology – that it can contribute to this sort of activism, operating as a counter-discourse on crime and criminal justice, shorting out the circuitry of official meaning – is founded in just this sensibility. We don't imagine that cultural criminology can easily overturn the accumulated ideologies of law and crime, but we do imagine that these accumulations are never fully accomplished and so remain available for ongoing subversion. In fact, the logic of resistance suggests that it is the very viability of crime control as a contemporary political strategy, the very visibility of crime dramas and crime news in the media, which makes such subversion possible and possibly significant.

In a world where political campaigns run loud and long on claims of controlling crime, where crime circulates endlessly as image and entertainment, we're offered a symbolic climate ready-made for a culturally attuned criminology – and so we must find ways to confound those campaigns, to turn that circulation to better ends. And as those in power work to manage this slippery world, to recuperate that meaning for themselves, we must remain ready to keep the meaning moving in the direction of progressive transformation.

This hope for social and cultural change, this sense that even the sprawling recuperations of late capitalism can be resisted, rests on a politics that runs deeper still. Certainly, the 'cultural' in cultural criminology denotes in one sense a particular analytic focus: an approach that addresses class and crime as lived experience, a model that highlights meaning and representation in the construction of transgression, and a strategy designed to untangle the symbolic entrapments laid by late capitalism and law. But the 'cultural' in cultural criminology denotes something else, too, something we suggested earlier – the conviction that it is shared human agency and symbolic action that shape the world. Looking up at corporate misconduct or corporate crime, looking down to those victimized or in revolt, looking sideways at ourselves, cultural criminologists see, again, that people certainly don't make history just as they please, but that, together, they do indeed make it.

For this reason, cultural criminologists employ inter alia the tools of interactionist and cultural analysis. In our view, notions of 'interaction' or 'intersubjectivity' don't exclude the sweep of social structure or the real exercise of power; rather, they help explain how structures of social life are maintained and made meaningful, and how power is exercised, portrayed and resisted. To inhabit the 'social constructionist ghetto', as some (Hall and Winlow, 2007: 89) have accused us of doing, is in this way to offer a radical critique of authorities' truth claims about crime and justice, and to unravel the reifications through which progressive alternatives are made unimaginable. That ghetto, we might add, also keeps the neighbouring enclave of macro-structural analysis honest and open; without it, such enclaves tend to close their gates to the ambiguous possibilities of process, agency and self-reflection. So an irony that appeals especially to 'ghetto' residents like ourselves: the categories by which serious scholars deny 'culture' and 'interaction' as essential components in the construction of human misconduct are themselves cultural constructions, shaped from collective interaction and encoded with collective meaning.

And further into the politics of cultural criminology and into some controversial territory indeed. Cultural criminology is sometimes accused of 'romanticism', of a tendency to embrace marginalized groups and to find among them an indefatigable dignity in the face of domination. As regards that critique, we would begin by saying … yes. A sense of human possibility, not to mention a rudimentary grasp of recent world history, would indeed suggest that human agency is never completely contained or defined by dominant social forces, legal, capitalist or otherwise. The Warsaw ghetto, the Soviet gulag, the American slave plantation – not even the horrors of their systematic brutality were enough to fully exhaust the human dignity and cultural innovation of those trapped within their walls. If, as someone once suggested, law is the mailed fist of the ruling class, then those hammered down by that fist, those criminalized and marginalized and made outlaws, carry with them at least the seeds of progressive opposition, offering at a minimum a broken mirror in which to reflect and critique power and its consequences. Marginalization and criminalization certainly produce internecine predation, but they also produce, sometimes in the same tangled circumstances, moments in which outsiders collectively twist and shout against their own sorry situations. From the Delta blues to Russian prison poetry, there is often a certain romance to illicit cultural resistance.

Or is there? In common usage, 'romanticization' suggests a sort of sympathetic divergence from reality; for some of our critics, it suggests that we create overly sympathetic portraits of criminals and other outsiders, glorifying their bad behaviour, imagining their resistance and minimizing their harm to others. Yet, embedded in this criticism is a bedrock question for cultural criminologists: What *is* the 'reality' of crime and who determines it? After all, a charge of romanticizing a criminalized or marginalized group implies a solid baseline, a true reality, against which this romanticization can be measured. But what might that be and how would we know it? As we'll demonstrate in later chapters, police reports and official crime statistics certainly won't do, what with their propensity for fraudulent self-invention and for forcing complex actions into simplistic bureaucratic categories. Mediated representations, fraught with inflation and scandal, hardly help. And so another irony: given the ongoing demonization of criminals and dramatization of crime in the interest of prison construction, political containment and media production values, it seems likely that what accumulates as 'true' about crime is mostly fiction, and that 'romanticism' may mostly mark cultural criminologists' diversion from this fiction as they go about investigating the complexities of transgression. As we'll show in Chapter 4, criminal acts are never quite so obviously little or large, never inherently inconsequential or important; they're made to be what they are, invested with meaning and consequence, by perpetrators, victims, lawyers, news reporters and judges, all operating amidst existing arrangements of power. Delinquents and death-row inmates, petty misdemeanours and high crimes all emerge from a process so fraught with injustice that it regularly confounds life and death, guilt and innocence – and so, again, this process must be the *subject matter* of criminology, not an a priori foundation for it. When urban gentrification is underway, little criminals like homeless folks and graffiti writers get larger, at least in the eyes of the authorities. When the United States Patriot Act passes, petty misdemeanours are reconstructed by some as terrorism and treason. With enough political influence, the high crimes of corporations can be made inconsequential, if not invisible. The key isn't to accept criminal acts for what they are, but to interrogate them for what they become.

Moreover, this sort of cultural criminological interrogation hardly necessitates that we look only at crimes made little or only affirmatively at crime in general. Mark Hamm's (1997, 2002, 2007b, 2013, 2015) extensive research on the cultures of terrorism, Phillip Jenkins' (1999) analysis of anti-abortion violence and its 'unconstruction' as terrorism, Chris Cunneen and Julie Stubbs' (2004) research into the domestic murder of immigrant women moved about the world as commodities, our own work on pervasive automotive death and the ideologies that mask it (Ferrell, 2004b) – the lens used to investigate such crimes is critical and cultural, sometimes even condemnatory, but certainly not affirmative. In fact, it would seem that these and similar studies within cultural criminology address quite clearly any charge of ignoring 'serious' crimes of political harm and predation.

Cultural criminology and the politics of gender

It's sometimes also argued that cultural criminology focuses inordinately on 'prototypically masculine, high-risk pursuits' (Howe, 2003: 279; Halsey and Young, 2006) – or more generally that cultural criminology is 'just boys studying boys', as a feminist criminologist once said to us – and that in this way cultural criminology ignores the politics of gender, crime and control. Certainly, many of cultural criminology's founding figures were male, and there have doubtless been various cultural criminological studies attentive to the risky cultures of largely male criminality. Yet we would hope, and would argue, that from the first, cultural criminology has engaged the politics of gender, and that this engagement has only grown as cultural criminology has matured.

As a starting point, consider the extent to which early North American cultural criminology was intertwined with feminist methodology and criminology. Ferrell's early article 'Criminological *Verstehen*: inside the immediacy of crime' (1997) set the tone not just for cultural criminology generally, but for a certain style of criminological ethnography – and with its confessional tales of male street adventure and arrest, it no doubt had something of a street-tough, 'blokey' feel to it. Yet, among the key orientations underpinning this immersive approach, as Ferrell made clear, were reflexive developments in feminist research methods, as embodied in Loraine Gelsthorpe's influential chapter 'Feminist methodologies in criminology' (1990) and Fonow and Cook's (1991) collection *Beyond Methodology: Feminist Scholarship as Lived Research*. Likewise, in the landmark collection *Cultural Criminology*, editors Ferrell and Sanders made it clear that the project was built from a synthesis of intellectual perspectives, including, importantly, feminist thought. Hence, they drew on the likes of Kathy Daly, Meda Chesney-Lind, Susan Caulfield and Nancy Wonders to argue that, 'as with cultural criminology's theoretical underpinnings, the methods of cultural criminology are thus "feminist" in their epistemological assumptions, their rejection of abstraction and universality, and their attention to the lived texture of culture and crime, whatever the gender of those who employ them or those they are designed to study' (1995: 323). A couple of years later, and Ferrell and Websdale's follow-up collection, *Making Trouble: Cultural Constructions of Crime, Deviance and Control* (1999), assigned a four-chapter section to the construction of gender and crime, including chapters by Meda Chesney-Lind and Adrian Howe. Around this same time, as we'll discuss in Chapter 8, Pete Kraska was reflecting on the gender dilemmas of the male ethnographer when researching hypermasculine research environments, and Stephanie Kane and Christine Mattley were undertaking reflexive ethnographic 'experiments in cultural criminology' in relation to sex and gender work, in Ferrell and Hamm's (1998) *Ethnography at the Edge*. Often forgotten as well is how much feminist thought was at the centre of another early work in the field – Cyndi Banks' (2000) *Developing Cultural Criminology: Theory and Practice in Papua New Guinea*. Looking back on this period now, none of this is particularly surprising. Indeed, given the extraordinary impact of feminist thought on the discipline, and especially the emergence in the 1980s of new research methods specifically attuned to gender dynamics and researcher reflexivity, the surprising thing would have been if this body of work had *not* in some way influenced cultural criminology as it developed in the 1990s.

This overlapping intellectual terrain between cultural and feminist criminology, in the domains of theory and method as well as in subjects of substantive inquiry, has grown alongside the more general growth of cultural criminology itself. Alison Young's (2010) use of aesthetics and visual cultural criminology to inter-rogate cinematic violence against women, Elaine Campbell's (2013) deployment of Judith Butler to enhance cultural criminology's interpretation of space, Fiona Measham's (2004) research on drugs, alcohol and gender, Jeanine Gailey's (2009) research into pro-anorexia subcultures, Rie Alkemade's (2013) account of the role of women in the Japanese Yakuza, Maggie O'Neill's (2004, 2010; O'Neill and Seal, 2012) ongoing action research among female sex workers and women migrants, Valli Rajah's (2007) work on women's response to intimate violence, Lizzie Seal's (2013) insights into feminist political protest – these and other research projects have all been undertaken under the rubric of cultural criminology and in engage-ment with its key concepts, and have built on and developed earlier methods and theory. To be honest, though, we have little interest in making either the sex of the researcher or the researcher's subjects a special virtue or a measure of cultural criminology's gender politics. For us, the real question is the degree to which any research illuminates human experience and creates critical possibilities for pro-gressive change in human circumstances – and for us, the answer to that question forms around the dynamics of culture. Put differently, the progressive politics of gender are no more rooted in essentialist traits than are the politics of crime; they're shaped by the power to construct cultural roles and their consequences, the power to hide such construction inside ideologies of essentialism and inevitability, and the willingness on the part of progressive criminologists to confront such arrangements of power. It is for this reason that we haven't set out to create a specifically feminist cultural criminology. Instead, cultural criminology has, since its inception, defined itself as an open, inclusive and invitational intellectual domain. As we stated in the first edition of this very book: 'From the first we've conceptualised cultural criminology as a free intellectual space from which to launch critiques of orthodox criminology and criminal justice, and in which to develop humane alternatives. We invite you into this space' (2008: 210). Few criminological perspectives embrace such invitational openness, nor find themselves sometimes criticized for it, by the way (Carlen, 2011).

The subject of openness poses a further question: with which further elements of contemporary feminist thought might cultural criminology productively engage? Here, we encounter a dilemma in what we might call the contemporary culture of feminism and critical gender studies. Feminist thought has always been commendably broad and multifarious, characterized as much by schism and debate as pat consensus. In recent years, however, as second-wave feminists have been challenged (or augmented, depending on your position) by their third- and fourth-wave counterparts, the concept of feminism itself has become a newly contested space. It is a line of argument intelligently explored by Nina Power (2009: 8) in her book *One Dimensional Woman*. Power argues that if 'feminism' today can mean pretty much anything, from behaving like a man (so-called 'raunch culture') to being pro-life or even pro-war (a la the 'Tea Party feminism' of Sarah Palin or Liz Cheney), 'then we may simply need to abandon the term, or at the very least, restrict its usage to those situations in which we make quite certain we explain what we mean by it'. For Power and other feminists like Ariel Levy (2006), if the legacy of feminism is reduced to gender-enhanced self-actualization, rather than the historical struggle for women's emancipation, then 'the political imagination of contemporary feminism is at a standstill' (Power, 2009: 3). Such contested claims for sovereignty inevitably surface in any discipline; feminist thought is no different. Indeed, one could argue that this type of internal debate is much needed if disciplines are to remain vibrant and vital, but it does pose a challenge for scholars wishing to continue to converse and co-evolve with feminism as an intellectual project.

Fortunately, the more specialist field of feminist criminology offers a corrective to this trajectory. Feminist criminology has steered a productive path through some of the more opaque aspects of post-structural feminist thought, whilst at the same time maintaining the healthy pluralism associated with early feminism (something exemplified in the term 'feminist *criminologies*'). In no small part because of this, tremendous gains have been made over the past few decades in reorienting criminology to issues of gender and crime, and to feminist theory and methodology, as Frances Heidonsohn (2012) has elegantly summarized. The positive rebalancing of criminology to better accommodate gender perspectives will, of course, continue, but what's equally clear – to us and to many feminist crimi-nologists – is that this issue should not remain the sole ontological base on which feminist criminology moves forward. Instead, feminist criminologists will continue to pursue other, newer directions of travel, whether through a reimag-ining of earlier principles or the development of alternative ones. Thankfully, this process is already well underway, and it is this more diverse, less essentialist, culturally pluralistic feminist criminology that resonates particularly well with similar orientations within cultural criminology.

The subject of gender in a rapidly changing global context offers a useful example – with feminist and cultural criminologies finding common ground amidst the particular challenges of late modernity. For Nancy Wonders (2013) and others, the relationship between globalization and gender remains woefully under-theorized (see also Fleetwood, 2014). In particular, conceptualizations of gender formulated in the 1960s and 1970s are 'too static' to make sense of the many new challenges that currently face feminism – everything from transna-tional flows and border and migration issues to the ways that historical dimensions of feminism have been subsumed by corporations that use ironic sexism as a technique to promote women's consumerist identities. Wonders argues that we must go beyond framing gender as an *individual identity or accom-plishment* and focus instead on 'the privilege and inequality that inevitably accompanies the construction of gender categories' (Wonders, 2013) under neo-liberal capitalism and, more widely, patriarchal cultures. This type of approach is important for a number of reasons. First, because globalized feminist theory is capable of constructing a systemic, even networked critique of meaning – a cri-tique demanded by the very depths at which gendered assumptions are embedded in the everyday dynamics of crime and justice – it offers more possibilities for theoretically integrating gender into all aspects of criminology (Walby, 1997). Second, unlike the mode of feminism associated with what some feminists now call the 'bourgeois women's revolution' of the 1960s and '70s (Eisenstein, 2010; Saur and Wöhl, 2011), globalized feminist theory is focused on developing 'gen-der projects' (Wonders, 2013) that transcend the identity concerns of 'well-educated women in the North' (Saur and Wöhl, 2011: 110). In place of these identity issues, these theorists proceed from the position that 'gender equality is strongly related to the quality of life for everyone in every country' (Peterson and Runyan, 2010: 14); a sensibility that, as Wonders states, is better suited to breaking down international barriers and allowing women to act collectively to build a new kind of feminist future. Third, as will be seen throughout the following chapters, this approach begins to integrate cultural and feminist criminologies across the land-scape of late modernity and so to suggest new sorts of critical engagement.

Transnational flows of populations and popular cultures, corporate appropria-tions of cultural resistance, ongoing instabilities of work and identity, insinuations of legal control and symbolic violence into everyday life, contested cultures of the body and its appearance – this is the shared subject matter of feminist and cultural criminology, perhaps the necessary subject matter of any viable criminology, under the conditions of late modernity. As we hope to demonstrate throughout this book, this subject matter brings with it new possibilities for critical analysis and critical intervention. For cultural criminologists, feminist criminologists and others, mediated meaning and mediated representations – of criminals, of women, of immigrants, of policing – emerge as an essential area of interrogation, and as much so a potential field of activism. The ability to locate the global in the local and the everyday, to see the shifting shape of the world in little moments of neighbourhood policing or public disorder, equals in importance the mastering of theoretical paradigms. A willingness to deconstruct official definitions, to take apart what we're meant to be sure of and to explore instead the shifting uncertainties of late modernity, now becomes its own kind of disorienting orientation. In fact, in the book's conclusions we'll argue that this is the emerging shape of critical thought, the contemporary contribution offered by any viable criminology – and the critical thread connecting cultural criminology to feminist criminology and to other progressive and critical approaches.

At the end of each chapter, we have included a list of film and television sources that we hope will enhance your understanding of some of the various theories and concepts employed in the book. Those readers interested in using this dual approach to interpreting and understanding criminological theory through a filmic lens should also explore the chapters in Nicole Rafter and Michelle Brown's book *Criminology Goes to the Movies* (2011). Using a well-known movie to explain a particular criminological theory (e.g. Martin Scorsese's (1976) *Taxi Driver* as a vehicle for introducing social disorganization theories), Rafter and Brown provide a good introduction to the relationship between popular culture and academic criminology.

For a more general collection of essays on cultural criminology and visual culture, take a look at Keith Hayward and Mike Presdee's (2010) book, *Framing Crime: Cultural Criminology and the Image*.

A selection of films and documentaries illustrative of some of the themes and ideas in this chapter

We Steal Secrets: The Story of WikiLeaks, 2013, Dir. Alex Gibney

A documentary about the controversial website, WikiLeaks, which facilitated the largest security breach in American history. Providing an interesting history of computer hacking and online whistle-blowing, Gibney's film adopts an even-handed

(Continued)

(Continued)

approach to WikiLeaks and its controversial founder Julian Assange. A good primer on the subject of digital activism.

The Pervert's Guide to Ideology, 2012, Dir. Sophie Fiennes

The sequel to Fiennes' 2006 documentary, *The Pervert's Guide to Cinema* (see Chapter 6), *The Pervert's Guide to Ideology* once again sees the highly caffeinated Slovenian philosopher Slavoj Žižek transplanted into the scenes of famous movies like *A Clockwork Orange* and *The Sound of Music*; this time his goal is to unpack the prevailing ideologies that undergird cinematic fantasy.

Kamp Katrina, 2007, Dirs David Redmon and Ashley Sabin

An achingly poignant documentary about the trials and tribulations of a group of New Orleans residents who, left homeless by Hurricane Katrina, attempt to rebuild their lives in a small tent village set up by a well-intentioned neighbour. This is no alternative utopia, though, and very soon the frailties of humanity become all too apparent. See also Spike Lee's hard-hitting 2006 documentary *When the Levees Broke*, which focuses not just on the human suffering wrought by Katrina, but importantly on the ineptitude of the US Federal Government before and after the disaster. Lee's film poses serious questions about whose lives counted in Bush's America.

Dogville, 2003, Dir. Lars von Trier

A minimalist parable about a young woman on the run from gangsters, *Dogville* is a treatise on small-town values and perceptions of criminality. It is a story that also has much to say about both 'community justice' and ultimately revenge, as each of the 15 villagers of Dogville are faced with a moral test after they agree to give shelter to the young woman.

The Corporation, 2003, Dirs Jenifer Abbott and Mark Achbar

An insightful and entertaining documentary, *The Corporation* charts the rise to prominence of the primary institution of capitalism – the public limited company. Taking its status as a legal 'person' to the logical conclusion, the film puts the corporation on the psychiatrist's couch to ask 'What kind of person is it?' The answers are disturbing and highlight the problems associated with unchecked capitalism. See the film's excellent website (www.thecorporation.com) for some great links, information on how to study and teach the themes raised by the movie, and a number of case studies and strategies for change.

Further Reading

Hayward, K. (ed.) (2015) *Cultural Criminology.* Routledge Major Works Series. Abingdon: Routledge.
Definitive four-volume collection on cultural criminology. This edited set comprises 80 chapters grouped under the headings 'Precursor Resources', 'Core Readings, Key Themes', 'Research Methods and Critical Approaches' and 'New Directions'.

Ferrell, J. and Sanders, C. (eds) (1995) *Cultural Criminology*. Boston, MA: North eastern University Press.
An early edited collection of thirteen essays on crime and culture that includes key chapters on criminal subcultures, media representations of crime, and various criminal-ised forms of music and style. This book represents the classic early North American formulation of cultural criminology.

Hayward, K. and Young, J. (2012) 'Cultural criminology', in M. Maguire, R. Morgan and R. Reiner (eds) *The Oxford Handbook of Criminology*, 5th Edition. Oxford: Oxford University Press.
This concise chapter by two of the authors offers a good synopsis of cultural crimi-nology that is suitable for both undergraduate and postgraduate students. (See also the earlier version of this chapter in the fourth edition; useful for comparing cultural criminology's evolution as a distinct criminological perspective.)

Ferrell, J. and Hayward. K. (eds) (2011) *Cultural Criminology: Theories of Crime, The Library of Essays in Theoretical Criminology*. Farnham: Ashgate.
This volume of twenty-two previously published works consolidates classic precur-sor works with key examples of contemporary cultural criminology. A one-stop-shop for undergraduates and postgraduates alike that also includes a useful introductory essay by the editors.

Ferrell, J., Hayward, K., Morrison, W. and Presdee, M. (eds) (2004) *Cultural Criminology Unleashed*. London: GlassHouse.
Edited collection of twenty-four essays on cultural criminology that includes research into crime and culture across a variety of local, regional and national settings.

Useful Websites

Cultural Criminology website
http://blogs.kent.ac.uk/culturalcriminology/
Access a number of key publications and keep up to date with news about publications and conferences in the area at the University of Kent's cultural criminology website.

Crime, Media, Culture: An International Journal (London: SAGE)
http://cmc.sagepub.com/
Published three times a year by SAGE Publications, *Crime, Media, Culture* is an inter-national and interdisciplinary periodical dedicated to exploring the relationships between crime, criminal justice and the media.

Cultuur en Criminaliteit (Boom, The Hague, The Netherlands)
www.bjutijdschriften.nl/tijdschrift/tcc/2014/2
The cultural criminology journal of The Netherlands. Many of the papers here are published in Dutch, but this site is also home to a number of English-language articles on cultural criminology.

(Continued)

(Continued)

Critical Criminology (Springer, New York)
www.springer.com/social+sciences/criminology/journal/10612
Website of the international journal *Critical Criminology*, the longstanding home of critical analyses of crime and punishment. See also http://critcrim.org/, the home of the critical criminology division of the American Society of Criminology where you can gain free access to their newsletters.

The International Journal for Crime, Justice and Social Democracy
www.qut.edu.au/research/our-research/institutes-centres-and-research-groups/crime-and-justice-research-centre/international-journal-for-crime-justice-and-social-democracy
Run out of Queensland University of Technology in Australia, this journal covers critical research about the challenges encountered by social democratic modes of crime control and criminal justice. Register and read articles for free here: www.crimejusticejournal.com/user/register

2

THE GATHERING STORM

Sometimes you know things have to change, are going to change, but you can only feel it … Little things foreshadow what's coming, but you may not recognize them. But then something immediate happens and you're in another world … It's a reflective thing. Somebody holds the mirror up, unlocks the door – something jerks it open and you're shoved in and your head has to go into a different place. (Bob Dylan (2004: 61–2), on arriving in New York City, 1961)

Ideas do not emerge from nothingness; they occur and recur at particular times and places, in specific cultural and economic contexts. They are not concocted in the seclusion of quiet seminars, however much the scholar might think, but in the cafés and bars, in the city streets, amidst the background babble of everyday life.

In this chapter, we go backwards to go forwards. We look at the extraordinary developments in sociology and criminology in the 1960s and 1970s – developments that laid the foundation for cultural criminology and continue to animate it today. Specifically, we review some of the theoretical perspectives and ideas that have influenced and inspired cultural criminology – and note some of their limitations as well.

The cultural turn: the emergence of new deviancy theory

In a period of just over 10 years, roughly 1955–1966, a spate of books and articles published in the USA dramatically transformed our thinking about crime and deviance – and for a time placed the sociology of deviance at the centre of sociological thinking and debate. This body of work, the new deviancy theory, constituted two strands: subcultural theory and labelling theory, which developed sometimes at loggerheads and frequently in debate, but which shared in common a distinctly *cultural* approach to the explanation of crime and deviance.

It was a time of awakening. The USA had gone through an uninterrupted phase of economic growth from the late 1930s onwards. Unlike Europe, it hadn't experienced the desolation of war and the rationing and reconstruction in its aftermath. US prosperity soared to heights unknown; its cars, kitchens, super-markets and cinema were the envy of the world. Yet, just at this point, the American Dream seemed to falter. Crime rose despite prosperity, the Dream excluded many, affluence revealed great rifts within the country and the Dream itself began to seem somehow insubstantial. The blatant racial segrega-tion of the South and the stark inequalities in the North became all the more apparent in the arc light of prosperity and in a society where meritocracy was so proudly proclaimed as the American way.

The 'naturalness' of both exclusion and inclusion came into question, whether based on notions of inferior biology, inferior intelligence or cultural inadequacy. And such querying of the taken-for-granted world extended from race to the other constituencies of exclusion: women, youth, class and sexuality. The para-dox of liberal democracy was pronounced: the claim to treat all equally, to include all citizens on the basis of liberty, equality and fraternity – yet, in fact, the formal and informal exclusion of whole categories of people on the basis of biology and culture. The working class, women, youth – all, historically, fell outside the boundaries of citizenship; indeed slavery, the most despotic of all exclusions, was at its height precisely at the time that the Enlightenment proclaimed the universal nature of human rights. Demarcation disputes about the right to be included and, paradoxically, the rules of exclusion were long-standing – and the intense social conflicts which so deeply divided the USA in the 1950s and 1960s echoed this.

It was out of such struggles, and out of fundamental debates on the nature of diversity and inclusion in liberal democracy, that the revolt in criminology emerged. Binaries of inequality in terms of race, gender, age and sexuality were generalized to critically examine those designated 'normal' and those labelled 'deviant', the 'law-abiding' and the 'criminal'. This started within the sociology of deviance and then rolled out into criminology proper. The sociology of devi-ance deals with the *demi-monde*, those on the margins of society, those caricatured as lacking biologically and culturally: homosexuals, illicit drug users, the mentally ill, alcoholics. The sociology of crime and delinquency focuses even more closely on those socially and politically excluded in liberal democracies: the black, the young, the undeserving poor, the recalcitrant male. Indeed, the criminal justice system focuses precisely on those excluded from civil society. The very categories of orthodox criminology resonate with intima-tions of biological, social and cultural inferiority, from the atavism of Lombroso (2006 [1876]) and the low self-control instilled into children by 'weak' families (Gottfredson and Hirschi, 1990) to the destructive attributes of lower-class culture (Miller, 1958).

If, then, the politics of liberal democracy focus on the inclusive society yet concern themselves with criteria for exclusion, orthodox criminology has mirrored this political philosophy, focusing on the excluded and making a science of the criteria for inclusion. So it was no accident that the new deviancy theory emerged in this period, on the back of civil rights struggles, followed by women's and gay rights movements – the ever-widening politics of inclusion. For this new deviancy theory was, above all, concerned with the unfairness of social exclusion (whether political, legal or economic) and the falsity of attempting to explain such imposed deviance as the result of individual or cultural deficits. The new deviancy theory targeted three exclusionary issues: first, the notion that deviance was due to a lacking of culture, over and against a presumed cultural consensus; second, the claim that the cause of such a deficit was individual defect, as sustained by genetics, family or social inadequacy; and third, the idea that the criminal justice system and other agencies of social control rightfully imposed such interpretations on the recalcitrant – that is, rightfully labelled the deviant as an individual lacking in culture.

But the gathering storm didn't just sweep up the excluded; it caught those who were most definitely *included*, those who were the supposed success stories of the American Dream. Affluence itself, the corporate culture, the ever-bigger car and kitchen, the ideal home and family and job – all of these began to look somehow shabby, repressive, tedious. Some, then, were excluded from the Dream, some began to realize that they had been relegated to bit parts in a male drama, and others began to rail at the monotony of success and to question the very premises of the Dream, its prizes and its promises. As Betty Friedan (1963) asked in her pathbreaking feminist book, *The Feminine Mystique*: 'Is this all there is?'

The emergence of feminism, the explosive development of youth cultures, the left-leaning new bohemianism – all these spread changing attitudes through society, shaking the mostly complacent world of the early 1960s. They stressed active transformation of life and lifestyle; sensitivity to the cultural creativity of women, ethnic minorities and the poor; and critique of those presuming to represent social consensus and mainstream values. Add to such powerful cultural forces the plurality of values circulated by immigration, tourism and the mass media, and we have a 'market of worlds' (Schelsky, 1957), which profoundly influenced the new deviancy theory.

The new deviancy explosion

The new deviancy theory took shape in response to the problems of inclusion and of diversity. The shock of the plural is the jarring of lifestyles, of subcultures whose existence points to alternative worlds and tantalizing choices, all of which present troubling potentials and possibilities. The existence of pluralism immediately poses fundamental questions of inclusion: Into what social world are we being included? Does it fit our needs, satisfy our dreams? Both are questions of normality. If orthodox criminology attempted to demarcate the normal and the deviant, and posit a 'normal' consensual culture, the new deviancy theory agitated for eroding the distinction between normality and deviance, and so argued for the inherent diversity of culture. The twin problems of distinction and diversity began to confront criminological thinking.

Ultimately, a widespread crisis of legitimacy unfolded: a younger generation learnt not only of the limits of the system, of the barriers to inclusion, but of the prejudices against new ideas and cultures. They witnessed the repression of ethnic minorities and the poor as these groups fought for civil rights, and they directly experienced the backlash of police and other legal authorities against the anti-Vietnam War movement. The tear gas that hung over college campuses, the massacre of students at Kent State University by the National Guard, confirmed the worst fears of a generation. And by the early 1970s, 'the state's moral bankruptcy seemed complete with the disclosure of the Watergate scandal, which showed that corruption not simply penetrated but rather pervaded the government's highest echelons' (Lilly et al., 1989: 130).

In this historical context, the intellectual impact of the new deviancy theorists was enormous, their influence for a time seemingly irreversible. Their contribution was *to bring culture into the study of crime and deviant behaviour* – not simply by acknowledging the obvious presence of culture in social life, but by stressing the creative characteristic of culture and hence the human creation of deviance *and* the human creation of the systems attempting to control it.

For orthodox criminology, 'normal' law-abiding behaviour had been seen as conformity to the mainstream culture, crime and deviance as a *lacking* of culture, and social control as the rather automatic and mechanistic enforcement of cultural norms. In this view, crime is caused by institutions unable to transmit cultural norms or individuals unable to receive them; by social disorganization on a societal level or lack of cultural socialization on a personal level; or by some combination of the two. Such a positivist criminology seeks to explain, through factors like broken families or genetic predisposition, why such a socialization into an unquestioned consensus of cultural values has not come about. Crime is, in short, the failure of society to inculcate culture and, as such, criminological analysis can be seen as an act of othering and exclusion. It is the presumed 'well-socialized' analysing the 'under-socialized', the social viewing the asocial, the culturally evolved examining the atavistic, the meaningful world explaining 'meaningless' forms of violence and misbehaviour.

The role of the new deviancy theory, in stark contrast, was to grant criminal and deviant behaviour *cultural meaning* – and, as we will see, the power of the new labelling theory was to explain the cultural process by which othering and exclusion occurred, the process by which criminological theory, the mass media and the wider public defined deviancy, distorted and took away its meaning and so created the very stereotype they imagined. In Chapter 1, we noted two notions of 'culture' – the first conceptualizing culture as the consensual cement of society, the second seeing culture as a font of creativity, a source of creative challenges to reification, social order and acceptability. The new deviancy theorists wholeheartedly embraced the latter – culture as innovation and resistance. Yet, they also took care to expose the cultural work of the powerful, who attempt to maintain the myth of normative culture as natural, as an inevitability beyond human action. From this new view, a thoroughgoing analysis of crime and deviance must examine how human action invokes the creative generation of meaning, but also how powerful agencies attempt to steal creativity and meaning away from the deviant and the criminal – indeed, away from all those whom they subordinate. The first of these realms became the focus of subcultural theory, the second the focus of labelling theory; the first was concerned primarily with the cultural origins of deviant behaviour, the second with the social *reaction* to deviance, with social control and cultural intervention.

These new approaches didn't disavow all previous theorizing, though; like cultural criminology today, they reached back to rediscover and reinvent earlier understandings of deviance, crime and culture. Among the major influences on subcultural theory was Émile Durkheim. Durkheim's view of the relationship between human nature and society was crucial – yet it is almost invariably misconstrued. Only too frequently, criminologists take Durkheim to be saying that human nature is essentially insatiable, with the role of culture to serve as a civilizing block which can somehow hold back the potential flood of deviance (e.g. Lilly et al., 1989; Vold et al., 1998; Downes and Rock, 2007). Culture here becomes the opposite of deviance and the lack of cultural socialization its cause.

Yet, this is in reality almost the opposite of his viewpoint. For Durkheim, organic needs and animal desires are satiable and limited; it is *culturally induced* aspirations which are potentially without limit, creating incessant and interminable want, causing human beings to suffer, as he puts it, 'the sickness of infinity'. Durkheim was writing in the midst of France's rapid industrialization and he witnessed a massive transformation in social structure and social ethos – in particular, the rise of a culture of individualism and a decline in more solidaristic, traditional values. He adamantly argued that a society whose core cultural values exalted individual competition and which offered incessant, ever-retreating goals was one which would inevitably be unstable and conflict-ridden. For him, such a condition was not 'natural' but rather the cultural creation of a capitalist society – and so a society with less crime and conflict could occur if a unifying culture were developed out of trust, meritorious reward and finite achievement.

Durkheim, then, based his explanation of crime and deviance in the cultural realm, and he further insisted that deviance is a cultural product and hence a product of cultural definition. He famously noted that even in a 'society of saints' some would come to be defined as criminal (Durkheim, 1964: 68–9), and he frequently pointed out that deviance arises not from the act itself, but from the cultural rules that forbid it (e.g. Durkheim, 1965: 43).

When in 1938 Robert Merton published the most influential piece yet written on the causes of crime and deviance, 'Social structure and anomie', he drew on Durkheim to explicitly critique both individual and social positivism. Like Durkheim, he demonstrated that crime and deviance, rather than being a matter of individual pathology, are in fact 'normal' responses to particular cultural and structural circumstances. Yet, simple equations like 'poverty causes crime', Merton showed, do not hold either. Rather, the stress on the American Dream, the notion that success and social mobility is open to all, grinds against the actual structural limitations on success. Ironically, it is precisely the most legitimate of American values – the 'American Dream' – that causes deviance and disorder; as Merton puts it, 'anti-social behavior is in a sense "called forth" by certain conventional values *and* by a class structure involving differential access to the approved opportunities' (1938: 24, emphasis in original).

And Merton emphasized another criminogenic aspect of American culture: the overemphasis on success goals, rather than the means of achieving them. In combination, Merton suggested, these two elements – cultural emphasis on success at any cost and limited opportunities – create a terrible strain indeed. In his well-known typology of adaptations to this strain, Merton imagined several options, one being crime – that is, the innovative creation of new means to achieve cultural goals of success. And it is out of this insight that subcultural theory emerges, where crime and deviance are seen as cultural and material *solutions* to contradictions in wider society.

Subcultural theory

Subcultural approaches to crime and deviance have a long history, dating to vivid descriptions of criminal underworlds in the Victorian era. For all their fine detail, though, early subcultural accounts tended to omit theory. They described subcultural values, showed how these values were *transmitted* in a normal process of socialization, but did not explain their origins. It is the ability to explain both the transmission of deviant cultural values and their origins which is the hallmark of what one might term 'mature subcultural theory'. Such an approach commenced in the late 1950s and early 1960s with the pioneering work of Albert Cohen and Richard Cloward in the field of delinquency, and Gresham Sykes and Erving Goffman in their studies of total institutions.

The concept of 'subculture' in mature subcultural theory is linked to the notion of culture developed within social and cultural anthropology – that subcultural responses can be thought of as jointly elaborated solutions to collectively experienced problems. Deviant behaviour is viewed as a meaningful attempt to solve the problems faced by an isolated or marginalized group; it is necessary, therefore, to explore and understand the subjective experiences of subcultural members. Culture in this anthropological sense constitutes the innovations people have evolved in collectively confronting the problems of everyday life. These include language, dress, moral standards, myths, political ideologies, art, work norms, modes of sexuality – in sum, all creative and collective human behaviour. Finding themselves in certain shared structural positions demarcated by age, class, gender or ethnicity, people evolve shared, meaningful solutions to whatever problems such positions pose.

But, of course, these positions come alive in particular contexts – city or country, 1915 or 2015, prison, school or workplace – and so shared problems and their subcultural solutions vary tremendously, overlapping at times, diverging at others, and always evolving. As human creations, subcultures can vary as widely as the collective experience and imagination of those involved. In this sense, all people create subcultural formations; police officers, plumbers and politicians all evolve collective rituals, styles and codes. But for deviance theorists and criminologists, there is a more precise focus: the subcultures of those defined as deviant or criminal, those whom the law marginalizes and excludes.

With this focus, subculture theorists developed an insight as simple as it was important: subcultural responses are not empty, not absurd, but *meaningful*. Just think about it: in our public discourse, sometimes in orthodox criminology as well, a whole series of common terms serves to dismiss the possibility of deviant behaviour having subcultural meaning. Terms like 'mob', 'hyperactive', 'primitive', 'savage', 'mindless' and 'mad' all serve the purpose of defining deviant behaviour as simply aberrant and so lacking in any meaning or value. In contrast, subcultural theory argues that human behaviour is fundamentally meaningful – fundamentally cultural, that is – and that differences in social behaviour represent specific problems and specific solutions.

Indeed, subcultural theory from the 1950s onwards set itself the task of explaining deviant behaviours commonly assumed to be simply irrational and unproductive. Again, echoes could be heard of anthropologists' efforts to explain the meaning and purpose of seemingly bizarre cultural customs: kinship rituals, taboos and fetishes, cargo cults. Notice, though, that in this way subcultural theory quickly moved from the Mertonian claim that crime constitutes a utilitarian alternative for reaching consensual goals, and onwards to a focus on behaviour which on the face of it appeared self-defeating, if not entirely implausible.

In the classic subcultural text *Delinquent Boys: The Culture of the Gang*, Albert Cohen (1955) begins with the recognition that most delinquency is not a means to desired material goods, but rather is 'non-utilitarian, malicious and negativistic'. Stealing and then discarding goods, breaking glass, terrifying 'good' children, flouting the teacher's rules – this is 'anti-social' behaviour, at its core *transgressive*. Yet, Cohen doesn't relegate this behaviour to mindless mischievousness; he points to the locus of such delinquency low in the social structure. And what is it, he asks, about 'growing up in a class system'? Cohen's answer is well known and continues to be influential. At school, students are judged by middle-class values which lower-class children are hard-pressed to meet. The resulting experiences of status deprivation and humiliation are for these children the problem – and they can collectively, if provisionally, solve the problem by reacting strongly against these middle-class values, by negating and inverting them. Thus evolves a 'reaction formation', a process of collective energy, intensity and *cultural work*, whereby middle-class values are inverted and subcultural status is attained by this very rebellion.

Two decades later, subcultural theorist Paul Willis documented in *Learning to Labour* (1977) a similarly shared problem for lower-class kids: being asked to measure up to middle-class standards for which their background ill-prepared them, in order to achieve academic qualifications irrelevant to their future jobs. As Willis found, such kids culturally 'solve' the problem by playing up in the classroom and rejecting the teacher's discipline, while also developing a subculture that rewards manliness and physical toughness with high status. Similarly, Ken Pryce's (1979) study of young blacks in the UK found that some evolve a leisure culture which helps them survive unemployment and racism, and enables them to meaningfully reject the few menial jobs available.

Models which reduce the deviant activities of youth to the mental or physical failings of individuals are in this way rejected – since such models cannot account for the meaningful, subcultural dynamics behind such behaviour. Subcultural theorists dare to see the world and its problems through the eyes of the subculture's members; they grant subjectivity and collective agency to the subcultures they study. For them, human subjectivity and interpretation – human *culture* – is the *sine qua non* for understanding human behaviour.

Proto-subcultural theory: writing from below

Subcultural theory is an act of excavation, a delving into the depths of society to find what is bubbling underneath. Like the work of social historians, it is *writing from below*, giving voice to those that are 'hidden from history'.

The first manifestations were in Victorian London, at that time the largest city in the world, or in Manchester, the fastest-growing city of its era. Booth, Engels, Mayhew, Morrison, Dickens and others explored these 'Africas' of the city, these 'unknown continents' of the new metropolis.

The second was Chicago, the new Manchester, the city which expanded in a century from a trading post of 300 people to become, by 1910, one of the world's greatest cities with a population exceeding three million. With the immigration of

African-Americans from the South and Europeans from the Old World, it became a city of unparalleled diversity – and home of the Chicago School of sociology, where Robert Park famously exhorted his students to 'go get the seat of their pants dirty' in real research.

The third was the new deviancy theory of the 1950s and 1960s, poised between crime, delinquency and the exotic, with ethnographies of back streets and jazz clubs, of marijuana smokers and poolroom hustlers.

The fourth was represented by the trans-Atlantic shift to Britain, a transposition of subcultural theories of delinquency to spectacular youth cultures: skinheads, teddy boys, rockers, mods and punks.

The fifth, today, moves beyond classic subcultural formations and physical spaces to include new spheres of engagement associated with late modernity, a fast-changing world of global gangs and global street culture, of online cultures and virtual presence. This is the arena of today's cultural criminology, where old certainties lose their moorings amidst the mediated swirl of daily life.

Labelling theory: the constructionist revolution

Deviance ... is a creation of the public imagination ... The act's deviant character lies in the way it is defined in the public mind ... [which] has, of course, drastic consequences for the person who commits it. (Becker, 1965: 341)

This is a large turn from the older sociology which tended to rest heavily upon the idea that deviance leads to social control. I have come to believe that the reverse idea, i.e., social control leads to deviance, is equally tenable and the potentially richer premise for studying deviance in modern society. (Lemert, 1967: v)

Labelling theory revolutionized the sociology of deviance, turning the orthodox understanding of crime and deviance on its head. The lens of orthodox positivism promised to accurately reflect objective reality; labelling theory showed that there was no objective reality to reflect, only a process of ongoing action and reaction, of contested meaning changing with audience and situation. 'Deviance', labelling theorists argued, is not an objective fact, waiting to be catalogued and analysed, but rather a collective process of human creation and subjectivity. Yet, labelling theorists cautioned that not all creations, not all meanings, are of equal consequence in the construction of deviance. Some definitions and interpretations carry the imprimatur of authority and the potency of legal sanction and enforced stigma; the labelling process is one of power and marginalization. And so, as with Edwin Lemert's insight above, labelling theory stood orthodox understanding on its head once again. If dominant definitions shape what comes to be 'deviant', then it may be that mainstream social institutions don't serve to control deviance – it may well be that they *create* it. From this view, what we take to be 'deviance' results not from the failure of social control systems, but from their success.

Consider an example perhaps all too familiar to college students: drinking. As one moves from student to student, from campus to campus, from the universities of one country to those of another, the variety of labels assigned to drinking, the variety of cultural and subcultural meanings it is given, are extraordinary. Some abhor drunkenness, some insist on it as a deserved pleasure. Some see drinking as a badge of masculinity, some a crutch for the weak. Some campuses ban alcohol entirely; others sponsor a variety of student pubs and drinking clubs. Some student groups embrace drinking games and ritualized consumption; some see these as signs of social immaturity or impediments to academic success. To be 'deviant' in one subculture or on one campus is to be 'normal' in another; drinking is *simultaneously* normal, deviant, legal and illegal, depending on circumstance and perception. Certainly, it is an objective fact that some people drink – but whatever *deviancy* drinking may or may not carry cannot be inherent in their acts of drinking; it is instead a cultural construction, a shifting assignment of meaning and label.

But what of 'serious drinking'? Surely there is some unanimity about its real dangers? Well, no – and not only because 'serious' drinking is commonly labelled as fraternity tradition, successful Super Bowl party or writer's prerogative. More to the point, it's the issue of power, the cultural imposition of meaning from above. Even were we all to agree that 'serious' drinking constituted a social problem, there would still be the matter of contested definition. Various experts and organizations compete for the ownership of a problem; there are subcultures of control just as there are subcultures of deviance, and each develops its own legitimacy, language and labels. Alcohol is a prime example. If indeed serious drinking is a problem, is it a moral failure and a sin? Is it a matter of legal regulation? Or is it an illness called 'alcoholism'? And so, does the social control of serious drinking involve campus authorities, the police, Alcoholics Anonymous officials or psychotherapists?

Significantly, each of these labels creates its own deviants and deviant trajectories. Labelling a serious drinker an alcoholic invokes a particular regime of treatment, a particular set of assumptions about illness, responsibility and relapse, and so a particular set of ongoing consequences for family and career; labelling a serious drinker a criminal invokes a very different set of meanings for self and society, and so sets that person on a different course regarding career and criminal justice. And it is in precisely this sense that labelling constructs deviance – that Alcoholics Anonymous decides the meaning of alcoholism, that police and the courts construct the reality of drunk driving, that campus authorities work to define the phenomenon of student drinking.

Moreover, as this process of meaning imposition continues, the assigned label often comes to publicly signify a person's master status, and so becomes the lens through which the individual's past and future behaviour are now viewed. Whether fairly or not assigned the label of 'sex offender', for example, a person's past actions will now be unfavourably reconsidered, and future actions cast under intense suspicion. In this way, labelling not only imposes meaning but *removes* it, precluding other options for status or identity. As discussed in the previous chapter, this dynamic is exemplified in Garfinkel's (1956) notion of 'degradation ceremonies', designed to 'deculture' a person as part of imposing a new status. Witness the shaving of heads, removal of everyday clothes, verbal abuse, humiliation and rigid regulation imposed as prisons, drug rehabilitation units and military training programmes work to construct new identities (see Goffman, 1961).

Values and the lust for kicks

With the new deviancy theory, with subcultural theory and labelling theory, some of the essential foundations for cultural criminology were built: the understanding that deviance and criminality inevitably embody contested meanings and identities; the sense that all parties to crime and deviance – courts, cops, criminals, everyday citizens, media institutions – engage in cultural work as they negotiate these meanings and identities, work to assign symbolic status and attempt to find collective solutions; a sensitivity to the subcultural roots of crime and deviance, and to the meaningful process by which subcultural members confront their shared problems; and an awareness that, overarching all this, there is a web of larger societal values, carrying with them the tensions of failure and success, and the politics of inclusion and exclusion.

These foundations were laid by American theorists, but before we cross the Atlantic to find their counterparts in the UK, there is one final American contribution, one that both complements and contests ideas we've already seen. This is the contribution of David Matza, and his collaborator Gresham Sykes, to the understanding of culture, subculture and crime. In the late 1950s and early 1960s, Matza and Sykes published two groundbreaking articles on juvenile delinquency and crime (Sykes and Matza, 1957; Matza and Sykes, 1961). They argued against the orthodox notion that delinquency was a result of abnormal personality – but they also questioned the newer notion that delinquency was *necessarily* the product of distinctive deviant subcultures. Rather, they maintained that delinquents were frequently of normal personality and that they often adhered to the same values as the rest of the population. They maintained, in short, that there was no great gulf between the cultural universes of the law-abiding and the delinquent, between the 'normal' and the 'deviant'.

The 1957 article, 'Techniques of neutralization', is the best known. In it the authors argued that delinquents 'neutralize' the thrall of conventional values through a series of normative 'techniques' such as denying their own responsibility or disavowing that their acts cause injury or victimization. Such 'vocabularies of motive' (Mills, 1940) enable potential delinquents to set aside for a moment their conventional values, to temporarily loosen their bond to the moral order, and so to engage in delinquency. These techniques of neutralization, then, constitute the *cultural work* necessary to commit crimes – the creation of a narrative which particularizes and justifies a specific delinquent act while leaving larger moral prohibitions in place. A delinquent's motivation for theft, for example, likely wouldn't involve a sense that robbery should be universally accepted, but more a sense that in particular situations certain groups deserve to be targeted or can afford the loss of stolen goods. Crime and delinquency, then, are not random occurrences, but negotiated relationships, meaningful relationships, between offender and victim.

This principle has been extended fruitfully to explanations of white-collar crime, police crime and war crimes (Cohen, 2002). Likewise, Jayne Mooney (2007) has examined how domestic violence could flourish in a 'civilized' society where physical violence is held as an anathema. In answer, she found particular situations – spousal 'cheating', 'self-defence' – where male violence against women was recognized by both men and women as a likely response – not condoned, particularly by women, but normatively expected. Even the terrible question of how 'normal' people can come to commit collective genocidal atrocities has been answered in part by an understanding of these neutralizing techniques (Morrison, 2004b).

But the explanation offered by 'techniques of neutralization' has also become popular in orthodox criminology, in that it appears to confirm the existence of a single, consensual, law-abiding culture to which all belong, until such time as putative delinquents or other potential law-breakers negotiate temporary exception. In short, the thinking goes, there is no deviant culture, no criminal subculture, no alternative value system – only behaviour which on occasion deviates from the accepted norm. In this fashion, Matza and Sykes's work is seen as a useful adjunct to Travis Hirschi's (1969) control theory, for it seems to explain temporary detachments from the dominant culture.

Yet those who would co-opt Matza and Sykes into orthodox criminology fail to acknowledge the second of their two articles, 'Juvenile delinquency and subterranean values' (1961). Here, Matza and Sykes admit that their own analysis of techniques of neutralization 'leaves unanswered a serious question: What makes delinquency attractive in the first place?' In answer, they argue that it is ... fun. Delinquents, they write, 'are deeply immersed in a restless search for excitement, "thrills", or "kicks". The approved style of life, for many delinquents, is an adventurous one. Activities pervaded by displays of daring and charged with danger are highly valued ... The fact that an activity involves breaking the law is precisely the fact that often infuses it with an air of excitement' (1961: 713). Note that deviant subcultures and alternative value systems, seemingly dismissed, now return with a vengeance, with thrills and kicks and the adrenalin rush of breaking the law! All of this of course recalls Cohen's *Delinquent Boys* (1955) and their enjoyment of transgression – and like other subcultural theorists already seen, Matza and Sykes add to their list of subterranean values aggression and a disdain for work.

Table 2.1 Subterranean values

Here's a tentative list of some subterranean values – and perhaps, today, a list of ascendant cultural values under late modernity.

Formal work values	Subterranean values
Deferred gratification	Short-term hedonism
Planning future action	Spontaneity
Conformity to bureaucratic rules	Ego expressivity
Fatalism: high control over detail and little over direction	Autonomy: control of detail and direction
Routine, predictability	New experience, excitement
Instrumental attitudes to work	Activities performed as an end in themselves
Hard productive work as a virtue	Disdain for work
Avoidance of violence	Admiration of violence

So in fact, according to Matza and Sykes, a viable delinquent culture does exist – but it is here that Matza and Sykes drop their criminological bombshell: *this is the case not because this culture stands apart from dominant values, but because it is in many ways so similar to them.* Daring, adventure and the rejection of work, they argue, permeate our culture; even values of violence and aggression are rampant. Mainstream society:

> exhibits a widespread taste for violence, since fantasies of violence in books, maga-zines, movies, and television are everywhere at hand ... Furthermore, disclaimers of violence are suspect not simply because fantasies of violence are widely consumed, but also because of the actual use of aggression and violence in war, race riots, industrial conflicts, and the treatment of delinquents themselves by police. There are numerous examples of the acceptance of aggression and violence on the part of the dominant social order. Perhaps it is more important, however, to recognize that the crucial idea of aggression as a proof of toughness and masculinity is widely accepted at many points in the social system. The ability to take it and hand it out, to defend one's rights and one's reputation with force, to prove one's manhood by hardness and physical courage – all are widespread in American culture. (Matza and Sykes, 1961: 717)

Almost a half-century ago, Matza and Sykes were developing an analysis that would become central to cultural criminology: the understanding that criminal violence may at times be condemned – but also widely commodified, consumed and celebrated. And as we will show throughout the book, this is immeasurably more the case now than it was then.

Matza and Sykes were further suggesting that a fundamental cultural contradiction courses through all social strata – a set of *subterranean values* co-existing with, but also contradicting, overt or official social values. A critical example is the search for excitement, the lust for 'kicks'. Even within mainstream society, certain institutionalized situations allow such subterranean values to flourish: organized celebrations, holidays, carnivals and sports, where such values temporarily trump those of workaday existence (Presdee, 2000). In this sense, Matza and Sykes argue, this lust for kicks 'is not a deviant value, in any full sense, but must be held in abeyance until the proper moment and circumstances for its expression arrive' (1961: 716). Normally, then, such values are maintained in balance with formal values, contained in this way, and allowed expression in leisure time. For many, such values only occasionally intrude on the quiet hum of everyday life, offering little moments of respite from the drone. Other individuals and groups, though, over-accentuate these values, disdain the workaday norms of official society and so 'deviate' by breaking the balance that contains the contradiction.

Today, 50 years since Matza and Sykes, the balance is changing – or perhaps the contradiction is becoming more manifest and less containable. Late modernity, with its trajectories towards uncertain work, immediacy, short-term hedonism and mediated aggression, pushes the subterranean lust for kicks ever more to the surface. Consider, as we will more carefully in later chapters, the close symbiosis between the frustrations of those low in the social structure and the aggressive narratives of the mainstream media. In his brilliant ethnography of the Philadelphian ghetto, Carl Nightingale argues that:

> Whether the amount of violence in films and TV shows have contributed to the recent rise in homicides … is uncertain, but some of the ethical codes of aggression in [the] neighbourhood clearly have depended on the mainstream culture of violence for legitimacy … boys' efforts to compensate for humiliation and frustration owe some of their aggressive qualities to their identification with the heroes and values of the mainstream American culture of violence. (1993: 168; see also Anderson, 1999)

And, as we will see in subsequent chapters, it's not just Nightingale's ghetto kids that today over-script their lives in terms of kicks and violence – it's soldiers and students, cops and reporters, too.

The transition to late modernity: British subcultural theory

Originating in Victorian England, subcultural perspectives flourished with the emergence of the new deviancy theory in the USA of the 1950s and 1960s. Over the following decades, subcultural theory's development continued in Britain, specifically in the work of two British groups: the National Deviancy Conference (NDC), an organization of radical criminologists, and the Centre for Contemporary Cultural Studies (CCCS) of the University of Birmingham, widely known for its work on youth subcultures and its role in the development of cultural studies more generally. The timing of this shift to Britain resulted both from the later development in Europe of an affluent consumer society, and from the more general transition of all Western industrial societies to late modernity.

As already suggested, a 'Golden Age' (Hobsbawm, 1994) of general economic growth and social stability had emerged in Western industrial societies after World War II. The years that followed, though, saw a widespread restructuring of work and a rise in unemployment, growing uncertainty and insecurity, increased marital breakdown, decline in community and a wholesale contest of values. While the advent of the Golden Age had varied – with America finding prosperity earlier than did the war-torn societies of the UK and Europe – the timing of its demise was more precisely shared. From the late 1960s onwards, in the USA, Britain, France and elsewhere, both a cultural revolution and a fundamental economic restructuring were underway. These transformed the social order of the developed world; the tectonic shift into late modernity had begun (see Young, 1999), and it was at this cusp of change that an extraordinary burst of creativity occurred, this time on the British side of the Atlantic.

Over its roughly 10-year existence, the NDC became not only a major site of this intellectual tumult, but the source of an intellectual explosion that would reshape sociology and criminology – and further set the stage for what was later to become cultural criminology (see Cohen, 1981; Young, 1998). In its first five years, for example, the NDC heard from 63 British scholars, who went on to produce just under a hundred books on crime, deviance and social control. And more than crime and deviance was at issue; others developed early work in gender studies and the first flourishes of what would become 'cultural studies'. Interestingly, the basis of this work, and of the widespread interest it generated, was the early development of 'postmodern' themes. As Stan Cohen said, some 30 years later: 'After the middle of the Nineteen Sixties – well before Foucault made these subjects intellectually respectable and a long way from the Left Bank – our little corner of the human sciences was seized by a deconstructionist impulse' (1988: 101). Indeed, the arrival of Foucault's *Discipline and Punish* in an English translation in 1977 was scarcely a revelation; its themes and concepts had already been well rehearsed within the NDC.

In fact, the NDC was thoroughly deconstructionist and anti-essentialist, evoking myriad voices and viewpoints, and bent on unravelling the social construction of gender, sexual proclivity, crime, suicide, drugs and mental state. It inverted hierarchies, and saw mainstream culture from the perspective of outsiders like mods, rockers, teddy boys, hippies and skinheads. Tracing the cultural bricolage by which these new 'spectacular' youth cultures constituted themselves, it focused on their media representations and the fashion in which media stereotypes shaped social reality. And beneath it all was a critique of state intervention, of positivism and classicism; the twin meta-narratives of modernist progress, social engineering and the rule of law, were subject to ongoing criticism. Positivism was perhaps the main enemy. It drained creativity and meaning from deviant action, the NDC argued, erecting an imaginary normative consensus against which to judge and condemn outsiders. Its methodology elevated alleged experts to the role of 'scientists' discovering the 'laws' of social action, and its policy – whether in the mental hospitals, social work agencies or drug clinics – mystified human action while remaking human beings in its own narrow image.

The rule of law came under sharp scrutiny as well. The NDC saw the criminal justice system as selective and ineffective – saw that while crime occurred endemically, the justice system focused on the working class and the young, ignoring the crimes of the powerful and tolerating the deviancy of the middle class. And at the end of this justice process, the prison, brutalizing, blaming and ultimately counter-productive; in fact, two of the most blistering indictments of the prison system, *Psychological Survival* (Cohen and Taylor, 1976) and *Prisoners in Revolt* (Fitzgerald, 1977), spring from this view. Further, the NDC realized that irrational, counter-productive social reactions to crime were not limited to the institutions of the state. They also circulated in civil society, with the mass media targeting deviant groups, creating folk devils and engendering moral panics (Young, 1971; S. Cohen, 1972).

As we have seen, this critical, deconstructionist impulse had commenced in the USA, around the work of the labelling theorists. It was theoretically revolutionary in its discourse (social control generates deviance rather than deviance necessitating social control), relativistic in its analysis (deviance is not inherent but interactional) and anarchic in its inversion of orthodoxies, as it rejected the received wisdom of positivism and celebrated human diversity. In short, it was tremendously *attractive* to the young and the radical during this time of fundamental social change, in Britain and elsewhere.

At the same time that this radically deconstructionist literature was being imported to Britain, a second and more muted strand of the American new deviancy theory arrived: subcultural theory, in particular work on gangs and delinquency (Cohen, 1955; Cloward and Ohlin, 1961) and studies of prison subcultures (Clemner, 1940; Sykes, 1958). Sociologists at the London School of Economics became a major intellectual conduit for this theory, beginning with Herman Mannheim (1948), moving through Terence Morris (1957) and Terence and Pauline Morris (1963), and culminating in David Downes' influential *The Delinquent Solution* (1966). Out of this tradition there also emerged Stan Cohen's PhD thesis (1972) on mods and rockers, and related studies: Jock Young's work on drugtakers (1971), for example, and Mike Brake's (1980) research on youth culture (see Hobbs, 2007).

The British synthesis

In the debates and presentations that animated the NDC, American labelling and subcultural theories were transformed, primarily through a synthesis of the two. This synthesis was facilitated by the logic of their two foci: labelling theory focused on constructions downwards (the *reaction* against deviance) and subcultural theory on constructions upwards (deviant *actions* and responses). Moreover, the sometimes wooden tone of American subcultural theory was given a zest, a feeling of cultural creativity; top-down reactions to deviance were also invested with this sensibility. Transgressive and deviant acts were in turn given a more positive valuation. Rightly or wrongly, deviance was a sign of resistance, an effort at overcoming, a creative flourish; it was not predominantly a site of failure or grudging adaptation. The American sociology of deviance became a British sociology of transgression.

This synthesis, and these strands of energy and resistance, were transposed and interwoven in the emerging British deviancy theory. In a British society more attuned than American society to class relationships, and during this period thoroughly transfixed on the emergence of ebullient and dynamic youth cultures, class and youth emerged as the major areas of research and writing (with, unfortunately, gender and ethnicity to come only later). Bringing a synthesis of labelling theory and subcultural theory to bear, British scholars complemented labelling theory's groundbreaking analysis of social reaction/ interaction with subcultural theory's attentiveness to the dynamics of deviant behaviour. Attuned to cultural energy and excitement, they added a sense of transgressive creativity to subcultural theory's somewhat formulaic understandings of deviant behaviour.

The task of British theorization, then, was threefold: to deal with the nuances of both action and reaction, to conceptualize human actors who were neither capriciously free-willed nor stolidly over-determined, and to locate meaningful action in the context of small-scale situations as well as wider social frameworks. As regards the analysis of these larger social frameworks, the NDC sensed that both labelling theory and subcultural theory could be usefully supplemented. Labelling theory in particular was concerned very fruitfully with the immediate interaction between the actor and the labelling process, but it offered little in the way of a theory of the total society, other than a keen sense of moral entrepreneurs and their enterprise (Becker, 1963). Subcultural theory well understood the contradiction between structure and culture on a societal level, but like labelling theory did not overtly theorize the dynamics of society as a whole (see Taylor, 1971: 148).

The attempt to achieve these syntheses and supplements shaped a key text to emerge from this period: Ian Taylor, Paul Walton and Jock Young's *The New Criminology* (1973). This text proposed an explanatory framework which would serve to create 'a fully social theory of deviance'. Building on C. Wright Mills' famous exhortation in *The Sociological Imagination* (1959) – that we must situate human biography in history and in structure, and so bridge the gap between the inner life of actors and the outer dynamics of the historical and social setting – the book inquired into the wider origins of the deviant act within the structure of the total society. Yet, it also attempted to understand deviancy's immediate origins in the psychodynamics of subcultures. Further, the book attempted to develop this analysis symmetrically, to explain equally the social reaction against deviance and the subculture of deviance itself. This effort at holistic theory was also evident in *The Drugtakers* (Young, 1971), *Policing the Crisis* (Hall et al., 1978) and *The Sociology of Youth Culture* (Brake, 1980).

A final influence on the British development of cultural and subcultural theory was the work of socialist historians; this was especially the case with the Centre for Contemporary Cultural Studies under the directorship of Stuart Hall. With the influence of socialist historians like Edward Thompson, Eric Hobsbawm, Sheila Rowbotham, Christopher Hill and Stuart Cosgrove, subcultures came to be conceptualized as places of imagination and creativity rather than flatness and determinism, sites of resistance rather than retreatism. The world of leisure emerged alongside the world of school and work as a domain worth studying, and in all these worlds, human meaning trumped mechanistic malfunction (see Cohen, 1980; Downes and Rock, 2007). Critical here is the notion of 'writing from below', of history written from 'the material experiences of the common people rather than from above in the committee chambers of high office' (Pearson, 1978: 119); the goal is to reveal that which is 'hidden from history' (Rowbotham, 1973). As Chapter 8 will show, this ethos of writing from below, of writing from the streets and alleys, remains very much alive in cultural criminology.

This writing from below offered another critical advantage: by paying appreciative attention to the activities and aspirations of lowly people, social and feminist historians could discover the dynamics of the total society as well. And so for British subcultural theorists, a similar insight: subcultures could be 'read' as texts, texts that revealed the nature of power and inequality – and popular culture could be more relevant and revealing than high culture. Thus, Phil Cohen's (1972) account of 'skinheads' exposes the dynamics of urban dislocation, working-class deskilling and destruction of community. The analysis of changing youth culture forms by John Clarke and his colleagues (1976) clues us in to wider processes of embourgeoisement, mass culture and affluence. Paul Willis's (1977) attentive study of working-class lads, their intransigence and bloody-mindedness, also becomes a study of Pyrrhic resistance to wage labour and subordination.

But it was not only deviant action which was given larger meaning within this more holistic analysis; so too was the reaction against deviance. In precisely parallel fashion, labelling theory was reworked and recast as moral panic theory (S. Cohen, 1972). For if subcultural theory makes sense of the seeming irrationality of delinquency, moral panic theory offered the possibility of *making sense of* the seemingly ill-conceived and irrational reactions to deviance by authorities and the wider public. Just as delinquent vandalism appears on a superficial level negativistic and unproductive, yet becomes meaningful and understandable in its wider social context, so moral panics about crime – though disproportionate, wrongheaded and counter-productive – become understandable and 'reasonable' when considered in the context of existing societal conflicts. Of course, none of this is to say that subcultural responses are always tenable or that moral panics are ultimately justified. Rather, it is to stress, once again, that both deviant action and the reaction against it constitute *meaningful* human behaviour – beset like all human behaviour by mistake and misinterpretation, but hardly mindless or without implication.

Towards a cultural criminology

Cultural criminology is today known for its transnational character; its theories and its theorists regularly criss-cross the Atlantic in the process of research, analysis and intellectual collaboration. As must be obvious by now, this is no accident. The combined work of American and British scholars over the second half of the twentieth century in many ways established what cultural criminology was to become. The work showed that subcultural dynamics, mediated representation and collective perception are integral to the construction of crime and deviance. It found the roots of particular crimes and subcultures in larger cultural contradictions and patterns of social change, and in turn demonstrated the role of the media in masking and remaking these relationships. Ultimately, the work affirmed that the most important of issues – exclusion and inclusion, crime and control, human identity itself – cannot be understood apart from emotion, meaning and power.

As the world has moved deeper into late modernity – and as cultural criminology has emerged as a distinct criminology of the late-modern condition – this intellectual process hasn't halted. Honing the analysis already developed, theorists and researchers have further refined it by exploring ongoing tensions and contradictions.

Take, for example, the tension between affirming the cultural creativity of deviants and criminals, and on the other hand acknowledging the claustrophobic and self-destructive character of some deviant and criminal behaviour. This was of course a tension that Albert Cohen confronted with his delinquent boys – and it is one that contemporary cultural criminology continues to confront. One way of exploring this tension has been already suggested by labelling theory, and its notion of self-fulfilling social dynamics. Convicting a person of drug use may well close off legitimate avenues of work or school, negatively shape the person's self-image, and so predispose that person to ongoing drug use. Likewise, a life-time of brutalization in prison may well produce prisoners who seem little more than ... brutes. Research shows, for example, that the heavy use of solitary con-finement and disciplinary cells tends to launch an insidious ratcheting up of discipline, with prisoners who are disabled by long-term isolation acting out in such a manner as to invoke further punishment and isolation (Grassian and Friedman, 1986).

This sense of progressive alienation from society, this downward drift of increasing social reaction and increasing deviance, has also been encoded in the concept of the 'deviancy amplification theory' – a concept particularly associ-ated with the work of the NDC (e.g. Young, 1971; Cohen, 1972; Ditton, 1979). Here, spirals of social rejection are not only interpersonal but mediated, as media images, expert opinion and the workings of the criminal justice system conspire to create the very 'folk devils' that are imagined. This amplifying spiral operates even more powerfully today – and so cultural criminologists continue to explore it, and to trace the ways in which image intertwines with action (see Chapter 6).

Another significant aspect of this tension between cultural creativity and dehumanization involves, ironically, the ability of individuals and groups to cre-ate cultural practices that deny their own creativity and human agency, operating *as if* human action were merely the unfolding of destiny. Earlier, we considered Paul Willis's *Learning to Labour* (1977) and his discovery that working-class boys rebel against middle-class school standards by creating rituals of toughness and disobedience. But that's not the end of their story, as the book's subtitle – *how working-class kids get working-class jobs* – suggests. As Willis shows, working-class boys soon enough begin to realize that school offers only limited possibilities of mobility and that their attempt to 'succeed' in the educational rubric of the school is largely a charade. Yet, the subculture that they create in response – with its stress on the physical and the masculine, its rejection of intel-lectual achievement and its elevation of solidarity over social mobility – only further *prepares* the boys for a life of manual labour and hard graft. Their insight into the charade of an open-class structure is indeed a Pyrrhic victory, helping to ensure the very social immobility that they sense. This subtle, poignant analysis of the tension between subcultural creativity and social entrapment continues to be immensely influential, forming the theoretical undercurrent, for example, in Philippe Bourgois' *In Search of Respect* (1995) and Jay McLeod's *Ain't No Makin' It* (1995).

A second tension is equally important – and as we continue to explore it, we move ever closer to the contemporary realms of late modernity and cultural criminology. For British theorists, you'll recall, a subculture constituted a 'text' to be 'read' for its meanings; it was a text, a story, in which a subculture attempted to find a meaningful solution to some shared problem. The East London skinheads of the 1970s and 1980s, for example, were read as a response to the steep decline in traditional work, the beginning of gentrification and the death of small craft industries. Since all of these trends operated to remove the social and economic props of working-class masculinity, as grounded in traditional skills and physical prowess, a 'solution' was invented: the revanchist machismo of the skinheads, the shaved heads, Doc Marten boots and reactionary songs and rituals (see likewise Hamm, 1995). This shared subcultural narrative, this text, was seen as clear-cut, unified and readable for its particular meanings and implications. Distinctive subcultures were defined by precise styles and types of member; they offered signs of resistance, indicators of symbolic subversion against the hegemony of the dominant culture.

Hidden in this sense of subculture as readable text, though, is a tension – and one that has only grown under late modernity. This is the tension between the subculture and the larger culture; put differently, the tension between inclusion and exclusion, between integration and diversity. As we suggested earlier, alternative and 'subterranean' values increasingly percolate throughout late-modern culture, carried along by the media and by global migration, by mainstream advertisers as much as by subcultural adversaries. As we'll show in subsequent chapters, this shifting, uncertain cultural landscape eventually blurs even the distinction between violence and entertainment or crime and crime control. In such a swirling environment, then, the tendency can be to overstate the integrity of the subcultural 'text' and to assume too clear-cut a delineation of the subculture itself.

Perhaps in such a world subcultural identity is not so distinct, subcultural messages not always so dramatic. Increasingly, we realize that at least some subcultures must be understood, in Peter Martin's words, as 'fluid, porous, amorphous and transitory' (2004: 31), with young people capriciously adopting one subcultural role or another, playing with subcultural identities and discarding them (McRobbie, 1994) or occupying multiple subcultural worlds at once. If there remains a subculture text to be read in such cases, that text will be hybrid, plural and adulterated, borrowing from other subcultures and the mediated subterranean values of wider society, along the way 'scrambling fixed signs of identity' (Cohen, 1997: 261) and perhaps even embracing its own demonization (McRobbie and Thornton, 1995). As Ferrell has found (1998a), in such circumstances even a relatively *distinct* subculture can nonetheless define itself by dislocation, anonymity and movement. None of this discards the notion of subculture, of course; rather, it suggests that, as social, cultural and subcultural conditions change, so must our analysis of them.

And as we'll argue in the next chapter, it is under these late-modern conditions that a cultural criminology becomes essential. In late modernity, the tectonic plates of gross inequality and widespread social stigmatization continue to grind below the social surface, erupting endemically in crime and disorder, and more dramatically in riots, terrorism and the 'reconnaissance battles' (Bauman, 2005) associated with contemporary warfare. In this world of dizzying instability and insecurity, exclusionary processes continue and accelerate, pushed along by mediated representation and global fluidity. Meanwhile, subcultures of resistance, reaction and desperation flourish and fade, reminding us that something remains amiss, that the social world grows only more unstable and fissiparous. Here, crime and deviance mirror the disorder of the everyday.

Under these conditions, orthodox criminology won't suffice. The late-modern world requires a criminology that is something more than the white noise of the criminal justice system, a criminology that accounts for meaning rather than dismissing it. It demands a criminology designed to explore mass representation and collective emotion, not a criminology bent on reducing cultural complexity to atomized rational choice. If it is to be made better, this world needs not a criminological culture of control (Garland, 2001) founded in practicality and conservatism, but a criminology animated by cultural innovation and dedicated to progressive possibility.

Long gathering, the storm has now broken. There's no turning back from it.

A selection of films and documentaries illustrative of some of the themes and ideas in this chapter

Goodfellas, 1990, Dir. Martin Scorsese

Goodfellas is Scorsese's masterpiece about the true story of mobster Henry Hill and his association with the New York Mafia. The film is illustrative of a number of classic criminological theories, including the Chicago School concepts of 'differential association' and 'cultural transmission'. However, in terms of the specific relationship to this chapter, Goodfellas is interesting in that the film unknowingly evokes two of David Matza's theories – the notion of 'delinquency and drift' (the idea that individuals drift into deviance – see the opening scenes of the film which chart Hill's tentative entry into the Mafia); and his famous 'techniques of neutralization'.

This is England, 2006, Dir. Shane Meadows

Set in 1983 in a small English coastal town, *This is England* is the story of an 11-year-old boy's brief association with a group of skinheads. Set against the backdrop of Margaret Thatcher's Britain, *This is England* deals with the allure of subcultures, but also the personal, psychological differences of the group's members – differences that ultimately tear the group apart and force the film's central character to question his values.

Grin Without a Cat (original title: Le Fond de l'Air Est Rouge), 1977, Dir. Chris Marker

This is a documentary about the political upheavals of the late 1960s and early 1970s that moves from the infamous May '68 uprising of the New Left in Paris, to anti-war protests in the USA, to Chile, Cuba, Bolivia and beyond. At just shy of three hours, the film lacks coherence and an overarching narrative – not unlike the 1960s' countercultural protests themselves (see Hayward and Schuilenburg, 2014) – but is notable for the footage and interviews that catch the heady atmosphere of the times.

A Taste of Honey, 1961, Dir. Tony Richardson

Based on Shelagh Delaney's play, *A Taste of Honey*, this is a bitter sweet comedy-drama that sets out to question class and gender matters in 1960s' Britain. Like a number of other classic films produced during this period (e.g. *Look Back in Anger*, 1959, Dir. Tony Richardson, *A Kind of Loving*, 1962, Dir. John Schlesinger, and *The Loneliness of the Long Distance Runner*, 1962, Dir. Tony Richardson), *A Taste of Honey* was highly influential in the way it challenged notions of the 'nuclear family' and the class rigidities of mid-twentieth-century Britain.

Further Reading

Young, J. (2013) 'Introduction to the 40th anniversary edition', in I. Taylor, P. Walton and J. Young (eds) *The New Criminology*. Abingdon: Routledge.
An insightful and comprehensive review of the emergence of critical criminology and how cultural criminology fits into that history.

Matza, D. and Sykes, G. M. (1961) 'Juvenile delinquency and subterranean values', *American Sociological Review*, (26): 712–19.
Classic deviancy study that shows how many young people engage in delinquent acts not for the sake of physical violence or monetary gain, but for reasons of excitement, adventure, pleasure, and other cultural and existential factors.

Becker, H. S. (1963) *Outsiders: Studies in the Sociology of Deviance*. New York: The Free Press.
Definitive deviancy study that shows that laws do not emerge naturally from shared social values or spontaneous public outrage; they emerge from the enterprise of those powerful enough to mobilize support, spread particular ideologies, and eventually encode their own values and ideologies in law.

(Continued)

(Continued)

Cohen, A. (1955) *Delinquent Boys: The Culture of the Gang.* **New York: The Free Press.**
A groundbreaking work of subcultural theory that still provides valuable insights into reactive deviance and small group dynamics today (see e.g. Cottee, 2009b).

Hayward, K., Maruna, S. and Mooney, J. (eds) (2010) *Fifty Key Thinkers in Criminology.* **Abingdon: Routledge.**
Bringing the history of criminological thought alive through a collection of fascinating life stories, this book covers a range of historical and contemporary thinkers from around the world, offering a stimulating combination of biographical fact with historical and cultural context.

Morrison, W. (1995) *Theoretical Criminology: From Modernity to Postmodernism.* **London: Cavendish.**
Thoughtful and theoretically sophisticated textbook that charts the history of criminological theory, often from an intellectual position that closely resonates with thinking in cultural criminology.

Useful Websites

Jock Young's Criminology World website
www.malcolmread.co.uk/JockYoung/
Downloadable access here to a whole host of Jock Young's writings spanning over thirty years of criminological research. A veritable treasure trove of critical and cultural criminology.

Howie's Homepage
http://howardsbecker.com/
The website of the indefatigable sociologist Howard S. Becker.

Theoretical Criminology **(London: SAGE)**
http://tcr.sagepub.com/
Published four times a year since 1997, *Theoretical Criminology* is the leading international journal for the advancement of all theoretical aspects of criminology.

3

THE STORM BREAKS: CULTURAL CRIMINOLOGY NOW

In the first two chapters, we suggested that a new world is emerging – a world of 'late modernity' – and that cultural criminology is designed to resonate with this world, and so to penetrate its obfuscations and critique its injustices. This chapter develops both claims. First offering a fuller sense of the late-modern world, it next turns to cultural criminology's engagement with it.

Late modernity

In the world of late modernity, space and time compress under the forces of economic and cultural globalization, culture comes loose from locality, and material and virtual realities intermingle, with many people consequently experiencing a profound sense of disembeddedness and dislocation. Here, mass media, new media and alternative media proliferate, forming a tangled spider's web of constant, if virtual, interconnection. Here, hyper-pluralism prospers – a contested diversity of values encountered on the screen and in the street, an unprecedented plurality of cultural perspectives circulating amidst state and corporate attempts at the monopolization of meaning.

In the world of late modernity, certainties of just reward and confident identity fade away or re-present themselves chaotically. Ontological insecurity runs rampant, stereotypes scuttle around the mediated social structure in an ongoing festival of othering – and so identity politics take centre-stage while class conflicts morph into 'culture wars' against the poor and disenfranchised.

All of this anomic insecurity is cut through with gross economic and cultural inequality. While bankers drink custom cocktails at £330 a glass in trendy London bars, and undocumented workers remodel $3 million Brownstones in Brooklyn for the wealthy, others wander the streets, collecting bottles and cans in purloined supermarket carts. In the USA, the wealthiest 1 per cent of the population owns 40 per cent of the financial wealth, the poorest 80 per cent owns a mere 9 per cent – and the UK and its inequalities aren't far behind.

As these inequalities increase within the First World, they increase *between* the First World and the Third World as well. One half of the world now lives on less than $2 a day; the three richest men in the world possess wealth equal to that of the poorest 48 nations combined. With a globalized media and economy, such inequalities become all the more unbearable, all the more culturally discordant, and so in the war zones of the Middle East, the projects of East New York and the sink estates of South London, the *banlieues* of France and the poppy fields of Afghanistan, they play out. Between the global extremes of wealth and deprivation, a panicked 'middle class' remains all too ready to project its fears upon the underclass (Young, 2007) – and the disadvantaged react to their structural humiliation, sometimes righteously, sometimes terribly, and most always in ways that the authorities label crime, terrorism or immorality.

Amidst all this, in the cities and towns, the criminal justice system and the prison–industrial complex push ahead. Were all those imprisoned or supervised by the US system put together, they would constitute the second largest city in the USA, only a million short of New York City. Meanwhile, on the streets of London one is rarely beyond the scope of the CCTV (Closed Circuit Television) cameras – the average Londoner comes into view of the estimated 500,000 cameras 300 times a day. And even with crime in decline over the past decade, many in London, New York or Prague continue to clamour for more cameras, more police officers, more 'security'.

We suspect that this desire for 'security' reflects far more than simple fear of crime. Where social commentators of the 1950s and 1960s berated a complacent, comfortable, 'never had it so good' generation, today commentators talk of a risk society where social uncertainty has emerged as the constant dynamo of existence. This uncertainty pervades both production and consumption. The world of productive work has, for many, unravelled; as the primary labour market of secure employment and 'safe' careers has withered, the secondary labour market of short-term contracts, flexibility and expendability has grown, and with it an 'underclass' of the unemployed and underemployed drifting between uncertain work (Ferrell, 2012b). The world of leisure and consumption has likewise been transformed into a kaleidoscope of choice and presumed preference, turned relentlessly by the stress on immediacy, hedonism and self-actualization. And these anomic circumstances become even more precarious in light of two late-modern contradictions: the heightened demand for self-identity at a time when pervasive social disruption undermines any such self-assurance, and the heightened demand for the sorts of immediacy and excitement that a commodified culture industry is eager to promote but hard-pressed to deliver.

Little of this is inherently new. Mass migration, labour flexibility, mass media influence and social instability all presented themselves dramatically in the past;

indeed, as we've seen, the subcultural tradition emerged to make sense of precisely such disruptive developments and their consequences. What is new is the combined force of such developments today, their greater orbit and their dangerous juxtaposition. Dramatic declines in First World industry and manufacturing dissolve not only stable workplaces and reliable incomes, but stabilities of identity and community. Increased geographic mobility and hyper-individualism further disintegrate traditional human communities; growing numbers of divorced couples and single parents reflect and exacerbate this trajectory. Ultimately, these factors conspire to replace the American Dream of material comfort with a new First World Dream where meaning and expression are paramount, where finding yourself becomes an ongoing task of uncertain and often panicky reinvention.

In late modernity, this new dream is primarily scripted and marketed by way of mediated communications. Television and radio now occupy roughly half the waking hours of citizens in the UK and the USA – and of course to this must be added video games, popular films, Internet entertainment, cell phone screens and other mediated diversions. In late modernity, communications media morph and proliferate, creating and servicing a diversity of audiences, replacing weakened traditional communities with communities of virtual meaning and emotion. In this process, two social identities are created and contrasted, with one presented positively – the celebrity – and the other negatively, as embodied in various deviants, criminals and outcasts – though, as we will see, these two identities are often made to intersect. Powerful but ambiguous orientations to crime and crime control, to morality and immorality, are in this way circulated through a world hungry for just such direction. As personal identity disintegrates, virtual identity becomes more desirable, more dangerous – even more 'real'.

All the while, the labour demands of global capital and the commodified seductions of global media breach borders real and imagined, mobilizing desires and populations alike. In Europe, relatively homogeneous populations have now, for good or bad, become manifestly multicultural; in Europe and elsewhere, the sheer variety of cultures now interspersed with one another – crossing borders, contesting cultural identities, sharing mediated dreams – marks the pluralism of late modernity.

Late-modern pluralism, late-modern predicaments

For many in the Western world, late modernity's pluralism can be understood as a kind of *hyperpluralism*, a swirling proximity of discordant values that confounds the global and the local. The shock of the plural and the uncertainty of the hyperplural derive from everyday exposure to an inordinate variety of cultural meanings, subcultural styles and definitions of propriety or deviance. Here, meanings overlap, values hybridize and identities collapse into each other – to the point that 'normal' is no longer a certainty and the taken-for-granted world begins to blur. Texting a friend in Chicago, catching an email from an acquaintance in Greece, chatting with your Nigerian classmate before your class on modern French literature, watching a foreign film on your car's headrest monitor or reading the ads for Spanish language classes on the city bus that crosses a city of mixed ethnicities and contemporary subcultures, the everyday world of late modernity swarms with a plurality of meaning and value. Even for those who would escape this, by retreat to gated communities, small towns or trusted media resources, there remain the vivid television images from Iraq or the West Bank, the odd images and regular scandals of the Internet, and the ongoing moral uncertainties of marijuana, immigration, abortion, gay marriage, and more.

This shock, this *defamiliarization*, is also a regular occurrence for the immigrant, the traveller, the seasonal labourer on the move – ever-larger parts of the late-modern population. On the move, drifting between many worlds, day-to-day routines unravel and the most 'natural' of tasks becomes problematic – even 'home' loses its certainty once left behind. With mass migration and global tourism, with the ever-arriving influx of other people and other ideas, indigenous populations begin to lose their citadels of symbolic security as well. On the move, the world turns inside out, with drift becoming the only certain trajectory (Ferrell, 2012a, 2012b).

For good or bad, a sort of cultural chaos ensues. Certainties as to equality or fairness are replaced by a sense of arbitrariness; clear measures of personal worth or professional achievement or innocence and guilt, recede. People come and go, jobs come and go – the sturdy rice terraces of an earlier class structure are breached, ploughed under, replaced with a slash-and-burn economic ecology. Not surprisingly, the luck industries – casinos, online gambling, televised poker tournaments, state-sponsored lotteries – flourish. For most, insecurity, uncertainty and debt make a mockery of meritorious progress towards slow and steady accumulated wealth or secure, comfortable retirement. The sham dream of instant fame and fortune, of winning a televised talent contest or the national lottery, remains.

On one level, hyperpluralism and other late-modern dislocations create great human potential – the potential for people to cast off the heavy weight of transmitted culture, with its deference and unthinking acceptance, and its mythologizing of tradition. At another level, these late-modern uncertainties spawn great human misery, forcing into the foreground feelings of profound insecurity, social vertigo, even existential emptiness. From within this predicament, the choices are twofold: to change, reinvent and resist, or to choose to deny choice itself and instead retreat to essentialist and fundamentalist notions of oneself and others.

As regards the first choice, we will simply mention here the multitude of late-modern resistance movements, from radical post-industrial environmentalists to

Plate 3.1 Signs of uncertainty in Lexington, Kentucky and London, England

Credit: Photographs by Terry Cox, Keith Hayward and Jeff Ferrell

anti-globalization protesters, from South American political artists to African women's rights activists. We will also note, and in later chapters return to, the widening horizons of resistance within late modernity. A new generation of activists is not so much interested in older models of mass social movements as they are in mining the hyperplurality of everyday life and in launching their moments of self-determination, autonomy and cultural hybridity (Ferrell, 2001/2). These activists also understand the particular dynamics of late modernity – understand that moments of leisure and pleasure can hold radical possibilities, that the street can talk politics with the Internet, that mediated representations can be subverted and reversed, that community can be rebuilt in the contested corners of urban space or the shadows of cyberspace.

But of course, there's that second choice as well – the choice of essentializing and othering. A common salve for feelings of insubstantiality and worthlessness is to maintain that there is something essential about oneself or one's beliefs that in fact guarantees superiority. Gender, class, race, nation, religion – all can be invoked in the search for self-assessed superiority and in the creation of an outsider group that is 'naturally' inferior. All provide narratives of difference, moral castigation of the other, a neat division of an increasingly complex and confounded world into a hierarchy of innate merit. Importantly, this is not only a process of cultural dehumanization; it is a facilitator of violence. It acts as a collective technique of neutralization, promoting both the vindictive punitiveness of the master and the transgressive violence of the offender. The cruel and unusual punishments of the US prison system, the mass slaughter of *Charlie Hebdo* employees in Paris, the televised beheading of captives in the Middle East, the many everyday acts of domestic violence or racist attack – all mix essentialism and 'othering' with dehumanization and violence.

Precarious inclusion, tantalizing exclusion and social bulimia

Social exclusion is often thought of as a binary – the securely included majority on the one side, the socially and morally excluded minority on the other. Under the conditions of late modernity, we would argue, a very different dynamic applies – many of the included are discontented, insecure and disaffected, and many of those thought of as excluded are in fact only too well assimilated. In late modernity, precarious inclusion confronts tantalizing exclusion.

To remain 'included' in a late-modern world of tenuous careers and economic disarray – that is, to maintain a 'decent' standard of living, to support a 'successful' lifestyle, to allay the constant fear of failing – requires unreasonable effort, self-control and restraint. The job is insecure and the salary doesn't keep up with inflation, the work hours are long and getting longer, the weekend is short and brief moments of enjoyment arrive only with the liberal aid of alcohol. Both parents work – or the single parent works two or three jobs – and then there are the kids' schedules of school and recreation and performance. And that's not to mention the traffic jams during the long commute to and from work, the crippling cost of housing, the costs of petrol and heating – and the sense that maybe none of this is sufficient for identity or security, that none of this measures up to the last generation or the last aspirational television programme watched.

The profoundly precarious position of most of those 'included' in late-modern society in turn spawns anger, vindictiveness and a taste for exclusion. From this precarious social perch, it can all too easily seem that the underclass unfairly live on *our* taxes and commit predatory crime against *us*. It can seem that *we* are afflicted by our own hard work and decency, while *they* are free to hang about and pursue pleasure. It can seem that they are all we are not, that they are not restrained by the same late-modern inequities as are we. Such a process is, of course, not one of simple envy; the precariously included are seldom eager to swap places with the disgraced and impoverished excluded. But the very existence of the excluded, their imagined moral intransigence and unearned indulgence, makes the uncertain circumstances of the included somehow more unbearable.

Of course, late modernity creates a different set of contradictions for the excluded and the underclass. Elsewhere, we've investigated the American black underclass as a sort of test case – a test, that is, of exclusion and inclusion in late-modern society (Young, 1999) – focusing particularly on Carl Nightingale's (1993) brilliant ethnography of the Philadelphian ghetto, *On the Edge*. What Nightingale discovered confounded any simple binary of exclusion and inclusion – for the ghetto, he found, is the apotheosis of America. Here is, for many, full immersion in mainstream American culture: a world worshipping money and success, hooked on Gucci, BMW and Nike; a world of watching television 11 hours a day, sharing mainstream culture's obsession with violence, lining up outside the cinema, even embracing in some ways the racism of wider society. Likewise, in the UK, the problem of the 'sink estate' is not simple exclusion; rather, it is deep cultural inclusion confronting systematic exclusion from cultural and economic realization. It is a situation where inclusion and exclusion occur concurrently – *a bulimic world* where massive cultural inclusion is accompanied by systematic structural exclusion (see Hall et al., 2008).

In the late-modern world, then, the fundamental subject matter of criminology – crime and its causes, crime control, fear of crime, policing, punishment – is recast. Now, fear of crime may well emerge from mediated representation, and punitive attitudes from social and personal precariousness. Crimes of acquisition may now mirror the ironies of late-modern cultural inclusion, perhaps also embodying visceral reactions to particular modes of late-modern disintegration. Forms of criminality once traceable to stable locales may now be traced to individualized emotions, searches for lost identity or collisions of migratory cultures. The criminal justice system will surely respond, will certainly play its own role in exclusion and inclusion and in the policing of the image. A new sort of criminology will be needed to make sense of such a world.

A cultural criminology for late modernity

The late-modern transformations and fluctuations just outlined have been the stuff of much debate in the social sciences; in particular, the debate has been framed around epochs and eras. On one side is the view that such changes signal the demise of modernism and a transition into conditions of 'postmodernity' (e.g. Baudrillard, 1981; Lyotard, 1984; Jameson, 1991). The opposing perspective, generally associated with theorists such as Giddens (1984, 1990), Beck (1992) and Berman (1982), is more circumspect, suggesting instead that these changes don't involve anything as significant as a paradigm shift, and that current social and economic transformations remain situated in the realm of modernity. The debate turns around the knotty question of whether contemporary conditions represent a qualitative break with, or merely a quantitative intensification of, what has gone before. Whatever the case, though, we need a criminology that is not just aware of these debates (orthodox criminology generally is not), but capable of understanding, documenting and reacting to the particulars of contemporary circumstances.

Whether or not our social order is currently undergoing a period of epochal structural transformation, it is clearly beset by significant, even extraordinary, modifications to many of the taken-for-granted assumptions and modes of organization associated with classic modernity. To understand contemporary patterns of crime and crime control, these transformations must be investigated – and an 'agnostic' position as regards postmodernity/modernity enables us to do so. From this stance, we can talk of our inhabiting (or perhaps travelling through) a continuous yet discontinuous moment, an inchoate period of societal and epochal hybridity. Hence, it is our contention that the contemporary world is in fact a shifting composite of *both* modern and 'post' modern features, which, for the sake of concision and clarity, we refer to as late modernity.

As criminologists of this transitional time, we seek to identify not just the changes underway but also the important continuities, for the contemporary period is clearly constituted from both. Accordingly, we need a criminology that is at once reflexive and progressive, modern and postmodern, drawing on theories and ideas from the past, embracing contemporary concepts and methods, and inventing new hybridizations of the two. As we have argued in previous chapters, cultural criminology is just such an approach. It actively seeks to meld the best of our criminological past with newer theories and disciplines, to create a criminology that can not only situate crime and control in the context of culture, but demonstrate that contemporary cultural dynamics embody an intensification of existing trends.

What follows is a series of theoretical constellations that encapsulate some of cultural criminology's key facets. Often, they are themselves hybrid forms, responses both to existing criminological theories and newer modes of interpretation. Always they offer ways of seeing crime and criminal justice – of 'reading' it, in terms of the previous chapter – mostly absent from orthodox criminological analysis.

Emotion, expression, experience

Criminology takes as its subject matter an area of social life that is the subject of heated conversation in the workplace and at the bus stop, a primary focus of cinema and television drama, the animated stuff of video games, the staple diet of the news media and a central theme in a multitude of popular literary genres, from crime thriller to serial killer. It takes as its subject matter an act that is frequently charged with malice, thrill, shame and fear – an act which regularly galvanizes offenders, traumatizes victims and outrages the general public. Criminology takes all this … and turns it into sanitized dross. As we will explore more fully in later chapters, both the phenomenology of crime and the fascination of the spectator are lost in the theory and methods of orthodox criminology – sometimes, it seems, intentionally so. Marcus Felson (1998), for example, enjoins us to accept that the majority of crime contains precious little drama and is really 'not much of a story'. Indeed, he seems to celebrate the mundane nature of crime, reducing it to the other mass of events in everyday life. Yet, criminologists like Felson forget that everyday life is itself a site of frequent drama, tragedy and joy, and that even the dullest of habits and routines are often sites of great intensity, scuttling escapes from existential fears, places of reassurance and solace (Presdee, 2004). The human condition is very much a story of intensity, we would argue, animated by joy and fear, passion and boredom and frustration, whoever the person, whatever the life.

In contrast to Felson and other orthodox criminologists, cultural criminology seeks to unearth and capture precisely this phenomenology of social life, and this *phenomenology of crime* (Katz, 1988) – its anger and adrenaline, its pleasure and panic, its excitement and humiliation and desperation. Put in historical terms, cultural criminology is designed to attune not only to the phenomenology of crime, but also to the phenomenology of everyday life as lived in the late-modern era. The search for excitement, the retreat into tedium, the tension of conformity – as we have already seen, all become more vivid and uncertain in late modernity.

Yet we are confronted at this moment by an orthodox criminology which is denatured and desiccated. Its actors seem to inhabit some arid theoretical planet where they are either driven into crime by social and psychological deficits or left to make opportunistic choices in the marketplace of crime. They appear either miserable or mundane. They seem strange digital creatures of quantity, obeying probabilistic laws of deviancy; they can be represented by the statistical symbolism of lambda, chi and sigma, their behaviour captured in the intricacies of regression analysis and equation (see Young, 2011).

As we suggested in previous chapters and as we will confirm in the following chapters, we, on the other hand, understand human beings to be creative and culturally innovative, caught in circumstances not of their own making but making sense of these circumstances, making meaningful choices and meaningful mistakes, nonetheless. In late-modern circumstances of dislocation and structural uncertainty, such creativity and reflexivity become all the more apparent and important – and yet there is an irony: it is precisely in this culturally charged period that a fundamentalist positivism has come to dominate orthodox criminology. Put bluntly, this constitutes a dangerous ahistoricism, a dumbing down of theory and a deadening of reality – and so it is at this time that a cultural criminology stands in opposition.

Opportunity knocks: cultural criminology and the critique of rational choice theory

Currently, two approaches to crime dominate orthodox criminological theory: rational choice theory (RCT) and positivism – the first stressing the mundane, the second the measurable. Both embody simple rational/instrumental narratives. For rational choice theory, crime occurs because of rational choice(s) – it derives from the availability of opportunity and low levels of social control, particularly where individuals are impulsive and short-term oriented (e.g. Felson, 1998). Revealingly, every intellectual attempt is made to distance crime from structural inequalities or existential motivations. Instead, we are offered only calculative individuals, committing crime where possible, and on the other side the putative victims who, as likely targets, are only understood through their attempts to calculate their optimum security strategies.

In the second approach, that of sociological positivism, inequality, lack of work, community breakdown and lack of social capital are to a certain extent recognized, though the analytic bridge from deprivation to crime, particularly violent crime, is not built but assumed (see Katz, 2002a). As with RCT, we are left with a desperately thin narrative, where intensities of motivation, feelings of humiliation and rage, even moments of love and solidarity are all knowingly ignored. If rational choice theory is the criminology of neo-liberalism, sociological positivism is that of mass social democracy, but in truth there is little to choose between them. They are even similar in their determinism: RCT might be better renamed *market positivism*, for between the determinants of poor character and opportunity for crime, criminality is reduced to something akin to the decision making of a consumer's choice. Our critique of positivist social science and its attendant methodologies will be found in Chapter 7; here we'll concentrate on cultural criminology's position regarding the rational choice approach to crime.

Though they have a much longer disciplinary history, rational choice theories of crime gathered traction during the 1980s (see Cornish and Clarke, 1986). As crime and recidivism rates spiralled upwards in the 1970s, many criminologists grew tired of traditional (dispositional) theories of crime based on notions of social deprivation. Their solution was to develop theories of crime based on allegedly fundamental principles of human behaviour associated with the 'classical school' of criminology. These 'neo-classicists' combined the utilitarian ideas of Beccaria and Bentham with more recent 'deterrence' theories (Gibbs, 1968; Zimring and Hawkins, 1973) and related economic theories of crime (Becker, 1968; Hirschi, 1969).[1] The results were 'cost–benefit' constructs such as the *homo economicus* model of human action. This in turn led to the creation of a series of (deliberately) aetiologically-impoverished models of criminal behaviour where, as with classic control theory (Gottfredson and Hirschi, 1990), there is no special deviant or pathological criminality. Rather, criminal behaviour is simply understood as the result of calculative, rational strategies aimed at utility maximization. Reaching their highest forms of abstraction in sophisticated algebraic expressions, contemporary RC theorists now test the efficacy of crime-prevention initiatives by reducing the mind of the potential offender to a statistical formula: e.g. $Y_i = \alpha + \beta(XBi) + \beta2(Xci) + \varepsilon i$ (Exum, 2002). With rational choice theory, human meaning and criminal creativity are quite literally banned from the equation; criminality becomes a two-inch formula (Hayward, 2007).

Taken together with the commensurate and related rise of 'situational crime prevention' (SCP), this supply-side approach to the crime problem has achieved some notable success in combating certain forms of economic/acquisitive criminality. Yet, it has also opened the door to a new 'criminology of normality' or 'culture of control', a strategy of crime control closely attuned to the fields of risk and resource management, and to calculative governmental approaches regarding the containment and management of social problems (Garland, 1997: 190). Reducing crime and crime control to a managerial problem, reducing criminality to the rational calculation of exogenous factors, RCT forfeits any understanding of internal psychic-emotive processes, any analysis of structural inequality and injustice – and any hope of escaping the critical gaze of cultural criminology.

If the RCT of crime is characterized by instrumentality and an underlying logic that owes more to modern economic analysis than to sociology, cultural

criminology has focused attention instead on crimes that embody vivid emotional or 'expressive' elements (see Morrison, 1995; De Haan and Vos, 2003) – what
elsewhere we've referred to as the crimes of the 'irrational' actor (Hayward,
2004). Indeed, it is precisely this 'emotionally charged state' that interests cultural criminologists, who suspect that subjective emotions and textured
socio-cultural dynamics animate many crimes, and increasingly so under late-
modern conditions. Against the abstracted, mechanistic rational calculator,
cultural criminology counter-poses the naturalism of crime itself. The actual,
lived *experience* of committing crime, of concluding a criminal act, of imagining
it beforehand and re-living it after, of being victimized by crime, all bear little
relationship to the arid world envisioned by rational choice theorists. Indeed,
the adrenaline rush of crime, the pleasure and panic of all involved, are anything
but secondary to the 'crime equation'. Crime is seldom mundane and frequently
not miserable – but it is always meaningful.

Nor does acquisitive crime reduce itself to the instrumental payoffs that RCT
would suggest, nor to the deficit adjustments that sociological positivism would
pinpoint. As the ex-con John McVicar (1979) once remarked, day labourers will
always ultimately make more money than armed robbers – but of course that's
not the point. While bank robbers certainly receive 'instrumental economic pay-
off' from the completion of a successful robbery, they also reap considerable
cultural and symbolic rewards from the act – something made clear in Jack Katz's
vivid account of the visceral dynamics involved in 'doing stickup' (1988). Even
unsuccessful robbers are often fêted within the criminal fraternity and afforded
high status and respect within institutional settings. Likewise, Richard Wright
and Scott Decker (1994: 117) find that many burglars are committed not just to
property acquisition but to the 'quest for excitement' and 'illicit action', even to
the point of burglarizing occupied homes so as to amp up the excitement; one
of the adult property criminals that Ken Tunnell (1992: 45) studied similarly tells
him that 'it's exhilarating … I get off going through doors'.

These intensities of 'irrationality' and emotion extend throughout the whole
process of crime and its consequences, from the offender's momentary rage or
later shame, to the gutted despair of the victim, the adrenalin-charged thrill of
the police officer's chase, the drama of the dock and the trauma of imprisonment. And circling all this, adding their own emotional charges: the outrage of
the citizen, the moral panics of the media and the fears of those in the streets
and in their homes. We've said it before and we'll say it again: emotions 'flow
not just through the experience of criminality … but through the many capillaries connecting crime, crime victimization and criminal justice. And as these
terrors and pleasures circulate, they form an experiential and emotional current
that illuminates the everyday meanings of crime and crime control' (Ferrell,
1997: 21). This is the naturalistic, even existential, counterpoint to the de-natured
essentialism of rational choice theory and its cognate fields.

In establishing this counterpoint, cultural criminology has built a substantial body of work with an enduring focus on risky or expressive forms of crime, from the symbolic violence associated with gang membership to young girls' involvement in the pro-anorexia subculture. However, in achieving this goal, it has also played a part in reproducing the dualistic opposition between 'rationality' and 'the emotions' that endures within much philosophical and social scientific thought. (This dualism came to a head in a trenchant debate between Keith Hayward and Graham Farrell in the pages of *Social Policy and Administration* (see Hayward, 2007, 2012a; Farrell, 2010)). Importantly, cultural criminologists now recognize that there is little if anything to be gained by simply juxtaposing emotion as the opposite of reason. Instead, our goal now as cultural criminologists is to produce analyses that can help transcend this delimiting explanatory bifurcation (Hayward, 2012a: 31; see relatedly Ekblom, 2007). In this sense, an article by our colleague Majid Yar is instructive in that it seeks not only to avoid the jaws of 'these two criminological monsters' (Yar, 2009: 1) but to actively develop a 'rapprochement between economic rationalism and the kind of emotional hermeneutics developed by cultural criminology' (ibid. 6). Yar's key argument is a simple one: rather than continuing the established zero-sum game, we should instead understand emotions as reasonable (and hence rational), and reason as including important emotional elements:

> Taking such a view, the human sciences need no longer divide their subject between diametrical poles of comprehensibility (reason) and incomprehensibility (emotion). It is only in this way that the social sciences (including criminology) can proceed to develop a theory of experience and action that is adequate to the interpretive and explanatory challenges they set themselves. Readmitting rationality to the 'realm of the senses', and emotions to the realm of reason, also offers other advantages. Most especially, it enhances the explanatory power of criminology and cognate disciplines. One of the major drawbacks of the *homo economicus* model of rational action is that it cannot ground any true explanatory social science. It surrenders causation to classicist assumptions about 'free choice' and therefore cannot get 'behind' actions to their causes; it can only enumerate situational formulae that describe scenarios in which one or other 'free choice' is likely to be made by a voluntaristic subject. Similarly, thinking in terms of 'irrational' emotions renders causative explanation impossible as such, for the ability to construct an account of why things happen presupposes that they are comprehensible, which the irrational by definition is not. However, by thinking in terms of the reasons and reasonableness of actions (grounded in cognition and emotion) we can better understand their genesis. (Yar, 2009: 10)

Interestingly, this unifying process is already underway in certain areas of economics. For example, in an important recent article, the economic sociologist Milan Zafirovski (2012) actively seeks to re-examine the prevailing view that neoclassical economics is only interested in rationality. Instead, he proposes that, implicit within the classical political economy and neoclassical economics of the likes of Adam Smith and Jean-Baptiste Say, there exists a veritable 'Pandora's Box' of 'irrational choices' and 'unreasonable acts'. Moreover, according to the likes of Robert Shiller, contemporary economists are now moving away from the rational choice-driven models associated with the so-called 'efficient market hypothesis',[2] and instead following the lead of behavioural economists by exploring the micro-realities of market forces (Fox, 2010). These include the 'real world' factors that make markets less than perfectly efficient – for example, the perverse incentives banking executives have to maximize risk taking. It also involves trying to understand the mass socio-psychological factors that can lead to crowd behaviour, sometimes by harnessing diverse disciplines such as evolutionary and cell biology and hybrid fields such as neuroeconomics (Coates, 2012). At a point of intellectual crisis, financiers are currently examining everything from forest fires to immunology to try to understand how best to prevent further crises. Such an interdisciplinary emphasis, married with a less abstracted view of human action, resonates loudly with cultural criminology's goal of viewing crime through a host of alternative intellectual perspectives, whilst still prioritizing the 'lived experience' of everyday life within a 'winner–loser' consumer society.

That said, overcoming the duality between calculative rationality and expressive emotion does not mean diluting cultural criminology's critique of the various theories and preventionist strategies associated with the RCT of crime. Quite the contrary: today, we argue, far too much criminology is predicated on so-called 'evidence-based' policy and 'experimentally-proven cost-effectiveness' – most of it, not surprisingly, coming from crime preventionists, rational choice and routine activity proponents, and those who lust after a so-called 'experimental criminology'. Here, talk is always of scientific data, with many criminologists even adopting the self-styled title of 'crime scientist' (see Laycock, 2013). But as is becoming increasingly clear, much of this science is actually pseudo-science at best.

Crime prevention/reduction terminology jargon buster

Situational crime prevention: 'the use of measures directed at highly specific forms of crime which involve the management, design or manipulation of the immediate environment in which these crimes occur ... so as to reduce the opportunities for these crimes' (Hough et al., 1980: 1).

Routine activities theory (RAT): This theory asserts that there are three necessary conditions for most crime: a likely offender, a suitable target and the absence of a capable guardian, with all three coming together in time and space. In other words: for a crime to occur, a likely offender must find a suitable target with capable guardians absent.

Opportunity theory: 'An approach to explaining criminal behaviour that sees crime as a function of the characteristics of situations that offer the opportunity, to those inclined to take it, to benefit from an illegal act' (Hollin, 2013).

In recent years, crime-reduction scholar and criminological myth buster Mike Sutton has outlined a number of fundamental problems associated with the core principles of Situational Crime Prevention and the associated concept of Routine Activities Theory (RAT). In particular, he describes Opportunity Theory – the idea that so-called 'criminal opportunities' cause crime – as not a theory at all, but rather a 'simple truism' based on 'the fallacy of equivocation' (Sutton, 2012a). Sutton asserts that the RAT notion of crime opportunity ('ratortunity') is a 'post hoc fallacy' based on ambiguous definitions, and (crucially) the illogical premise that something that an offender has not yet done is the cause of his doing it! Sutton pulls no punches when it comes to bursting the perceived wisdom surrounding rational choice-driven, 'policy-oriented' models:

> Crime-as-opportunity theorists and the Crime Scientists who believe that this weird criminological notion of opportunity is a cause of crime are pseudo scholars and pseudo scientists chiefly because, whilst claiming to be either objective criminologists or else 'real' scientists, they blindly believe in their insular world of self-referential confirmation bias, anecdotes and ever more complex truisms dressed up as causal explanations. They have yet to establish a consistent definition of opportunity or guardianship. And they have yet to formulate a measurable and discoverable value for victim or target vulnerability that can be tested by empirical research … If you are happy with this RAT-based crime as opportunity notion for crime causation, then – I don't wish to be rude but – might I suggest you set up your own church for those who believe in criminological miracles. Why not call it the Church of Crime Science? Alternatively you might wish to consider the above logical arguments, which explain why the current notion of crime opportunity is both unrealistically simplistic in part and is, elsewhere in its reasoning, completely impossible as a cause of crime. (Sutton, 2012b: n.p.)

In a more recent article, Sutton (Sutton and Hodgson, 2013) in turn addresses the fundamental question of what actually constitutes 'evidence' in the evidenced-based approach by taking aim at the old criminological chestnut that a patrolling policeman in London would, on average, only pass within 100 yards of a residential burglary once every eight years (Clarke and Hough, 1984). This established maxim has been cited in countless journal articles, book chapters and research reports – as though it is a rational and logical theory – and is perceived by many crime preventionists and police departments as the very exemplar of 'evidence-based research'. The problem, as Sutton and Hodgson skilfully note, is that Clarke and Hough's much-cited article is methodologically and conceptually deeply flawed, in terms of both its shaky 'pen and paper' mathematics and its misreading of the nature of police-beat practice. By challenging three key underlying premises associated with Clarke and Hough's claim (what one might describe here as 'the robotic premise', 'the crime distribution premise' and 'the officer heuristic premise'), Sutton and Hodgson highlight the danger of oversimplifying complex criminological concerns – in this case, the diverse realities and spatial biographies that constitute everyday police-beat patrols.

All of this 'myth busting' might be seen as fun if the stakes weren't so high. But the sad truth is that criminological formulations such as Opportunity Theory and RAT are frequently viewed by governmental and private authorities as the main weapon of crime-control policy, and as a way of escaping the allegedly more abstract theorizations of critical and cultural criminology. Put another way, such models are illustrative of thinking that marries 'rational' crime 'science' with economic analysis in a bid to bring about measurable crime-reduction efficiencies. As Lucia Zedner has pointed out (2006: 155–7), in neo-liberal economies where managerialism is the mantra, it is this drive for short-term economic efficiency that trumps all other considerations. This, of course, is no way forward. No *one* criminological position can or should be valorized over all others. Rather, criminological theories have particular roles to play at particular times in particular settings and contexts. Consequently, what is needed today is a biodiversity of ideas and standpoints. Expressed differently, what is required is the restoration of Max Weber's famous assertion that explanations need to be adequate at the level of *both* meaning/interpretation *and* causal analysis. In other words, as stressed above, the way forward is clearly to foster a discussion (e.g. Hay, 2004) about the relationship between reason and emotion that is both appropriate to and critical of the particular contours of contemporary society.

Emotional metamorphoses

Acknowledging the importance of human emotions in crime, punishment and social control is a first step in countering the mechanistic clank of orthodox criminology; understanding the workings of our shared emotional lives and the sources of our emotional states is the next. Emotions are complex and mysterious – yet we must attempt to understand them, and to investigate the emotive states that contribute to criminality.

While criminology hasn't paid sustained attention to the subject of emotions, other disciplines have, among them behavioural psychology, philosophy, the sociology of law and consumer studies. Much progress has also been made by scholars in the new and diverse field of 'the sociology of emotions' (e.g. Kemper, 1990; Scheff, 1990; Barbalet, 1998; Bendelow and Williams, 1998; Williams, 2001). Yet, for all the intellectual energy, the subject of emotion within the social sciences and humanities remains enigmatic; theoretical consensus is hard to come by, even as regards fundamental questions concerning the source of emotions or the best ways to study them. That said, the social construction and social significance of the emotions is now being recognized and researchers are finally proceeding with a much clearer set of research questions. Additionally, there has been something of a convergence among scholars regarding the ontology of emotions and their amenability to individual and social mediation. Increasingly, emotions are viewed as encompassing *corporeal* dimensions (the physical body), *cognitive* dimensions (mental processes, interpretations and forms of reasoning) and *feeling* or affect dimensions (how differentially socialized and socially located individuals experience the corporeal processes occurring within their bodies). For example, while most of us might well experience a rush of adrenalin when confronted by a group of football hooligans in a train carriage (corporeal dimension), we may impart different interpretative meanings to that response (cognitive dimension), in association with how we have come to respond to such experiences (the feeling dimension).

Even here, though, the precise workings of these three elements remain poorly understood – and perhaps that's not all bad. Commencing from a default position that recognizes emotional states as complicated and diverse can help researchers avoid the pitfall of analytic reduction. Consider, for example, the way emotions are approached within emerging criminal justice policy fields. Whether it's the narrow 'diagnostic' checklist that underpins the new wave of offender 'cognitive behavioural programmes', or the deracinated concept of emotions that props up poorer incarnations of restorative justice, the tendency is to downgrade the complexity and variety of emotions. Emotional states are not one-dimensional or universal constructs, and so any approach that reduces them to a categorical listing not only fails us theoretically – it dehumanizes all involved. When it comes to the study of emotions, complexity serves as a buffer against reductionism and theoretical oversimplification.

Rather than distilling human emotion into a series of uniform 'emotive states', then, cultural criminology strives to understand the *phenomenological basis* of emotions, to locate emotions within the complexities of thought, consciousness, body, aesthetics, situation and social interaction. As we've already seen, Jack Katz's (1988) *Seductions of Crime* helped establish this phenomenological focus in cultural criminology; his later book, *How Emotions Work* (1999), can help develop this emotional dimension.[3]

Katz's starting point is unequivocal: emotions are enigmatic. At one level, they appear 'beyond our control', as when we are wracked by guilt, overwhelmed by shame or struck by something hysterically funny. On another level, emotions 'make up a part of our lives that is intimately *subjective*'. Individuals react differently to comic stimuli, for example, while we all own our particular guilt and shame. Katz (1999: 1–2) hence poses questions prescient for cultural criminology: when shame or rage flood through experience, where is the source of the inundation, where are the gates that let the rush of feelings come through, if they are not within? If we idiosyncratically own our emotions, why can't we fully own up to them?

Katz proposes a threefold answer to these questions:

1. Katz describes emotions as both *situationally-responsive* and *situationally transcendent narrative projects*: 'What is the socially visible sense that a person is trying to make in the immediate situation of his action, and what is the current sense that the situation acquires within his awareness that his life reaches beyond the current situation?' (1999: 5). Analysing a videotaped police interview with a killer, for example, Katz shows how the murderer's tears during his confession serve two purposes – aiding in his immediate dealings with the police interrogators, but also allowing him to grasp the implications of the interrogation episode for his quickly narrowing future.

2. *Interactional processes.* Katz is interested in how people shape their emotional conduct in relation to the readings and responses given to their emotions by others. At this point, Katz stresses the bodily nature of many emotive states: 'In shaping emotional conduct, the subject also exploits resources for interaction that she finds in her own body ... [we] see people creatively mining the resources they find at hand in order to shape the impressions that others take of their emotions' (1999: 6).

3. *Sensual metamorphoses.* As people move in and out of emotional states like shame, anger and rage, Katz argues, the sensual framework of their actions changes. Again, this process may be embodied. Katz takes seriously 'what might at first glance seem to be hyperbole or surreal images. For example, I treat drivers' complaints that they have been "cut off" as literal descriptions; I then look for evidence of what in their corporeal experience was amputated' (1999: 6).

Katz's tripartite typology offers a useful starting point for cultural criminology's analysis of emotions. To begin with, as Katz himself suggests, it helps us overcome simplistic distinctions between the foreground experiences of the actor, on the one hand, and other background factors like social class or education that typically pre-occupy sociological analysis. In both *How Emotions Work* and a related article (Katz, 2002a), Katz amplifies a perspective he first developed in *Seductions of Crime*: that by starting with the emotional foreground of experience, we can arrive at 'back-ground conditions such as power, gender, social class, ethnicity etc.' (2002b: 376).

Katz's analysis also helps in developing appropriate methodologies for under-standing emotions. He argues that emotions cannot and should not be studied via questionnaires or in laboratory experiments in which emotional responses are provoked or stimulated, since both methodologies distance researchers from the grounded phenomenology of emotional work. (When in Chapter 7 we dis-cuss methodology, we'll show you a particularly absurd example of just this sort of research.) Instead, Katz (1999: 17) prioritizes a more ethnographic approach, urging emotion scholars to study the way people construct their emotional behaviour in natural, everyday settings. As we'll show in this chapter's next sec-tion and in Chapter 8, cultural criminology has already developed methodologies for understanding the emotional experience of crime and crime control; Katz's work can help us refine these. As we'll also see, Katz's emphasis on the 'social interactive' dimensions of emotions, and their links to corporeality and transcendent performativity, complements existing cultural criminological perspectives on edgework and situated performance:

> It is exactly at the intersection of the situational and the transcendent that everyday life takes on its emotional force. Playwrights know this well, [and] ... often focus on (1) situations of conflictual interaction that (2) carry transcendent significance and (3) are best conveyed when the audience is drawn to focus on how actors represent the conflict in idiosyncratic corporeal ways. (Katz, 1999: 77)

Of course, the drama of emotions is not always limited to situational dynamics amenable to ethnographic methods or phenomenological analysis. Within cultural criminology, for example, interesting work on the emotions engendered by mediated images and collective representations of crime is already well underway – work that Alison Young (2004, 2007) describes as a new 'criminological aesthetics'. Still, Katz's tripartite structure provides a useful platform for taking emotions seriously and for considering criminality's emotive states.

Edgework and transgression

Crime is an act of rule breaking, an act 'against the law'. It embodies particular attitudes towards these rules, assessments of their justness and appropriateness, and motivations to break them, whether by outright transgression or momentary neutralization. Crime is not, as in positivism, a situation where actors happen to cross the rules while mechanistically propelled towards some desideratum; it is not, as in rational choice theory, a matter of actors merely seeking holes in the net of social control, then ducking their way through them. Rather, for cultural criminology, the act of transgression itself contains distinct emotions, attractions and compensations.

We would point, for example, to the way poverty is *experienced and perceived* in an affluent society as an *act of exclusion* – the ultimate humiliation in a society defined by wealth and consumption. It is an intense experience, not merely of material deprivation, but of felt injustice and personal insecurity. Exacerbating this under late modernity is a shift in consciousness such that individualism, expressivity and identity become paramount, and material deprivation, however important, is powerfully supplemented by a widespread sense of ontological deprivation. In other words, we are witnessing today a crisis *of being* in a society where self-fulfilment, expression and immediacy are paramount values, yet the possibilities of realizing such individualized dreams are strictly curtailed by the increasing bureaucratization of work, the indebtedness of everyday workers and the commodification of leisure and leisure time. In this context, crime and transgression – even crimes of economy or acquisition – can be seen as a breaking of restraints, an illicit realization of immediacy, a reassertion of identity and ontology, no matter how problematic the eventual outcome. In these and other crimes, identity and emotion are woven into the experience of rule breaking.

Within cultural criminology, this analysis of transgression, identity and emotion has been perhaps most fully developed in the research of Stephen Lyng (1990, 2005), Jeff Ferrell (2005; Ferrell et al., 2001) and others on *edgework*. In studies of individuals engaged in acts of extreme voluntary risk taking, such as advanced sky-diving, illicit motorbike racing and illegal graffiti writing, researchers have found that participants are neither dangerously 'out of control' nor possessed of some self-destructive 'death wish'. Instead, they push themselves to 'the edge' and engage there in edgework in search of 'the adrenalin rush', authentic identity and existential certainty; they lose control to take control. Edgework functions as a means of reclaiming one's life by risking it, a way of reacting against the 'unidentifiable forces that rob one of individual choice' (Lyng, 1990: 870).

Here, as suggested in Katz's analysis of emotions, the foreground of risk opens up to the background of law, power and economy. Lyng's (1990) research, for example, has emphasized especially the way in which edgework allows participants to develop the very sorts of skills that the late-modern economy of dumbed-down service work and temporary jobs takes from them. Moreover, these skills *matter* in distinctly dangerous ways, spiralling participants ever closer to an edge others can't know. After all, the more polished one's skills as a sky-diver or street racer, the more risk one can take – and the more risk one takes, the more polished those skills must become. Ferrell's (1996, 2005) research has discovered a similar dynamic, and one that links edgework directly to criminality, emotion and criminal justice: if edgework sparks an addictive 'adrenalin rush' from its explosive mix of risk and skill, then aggressive law enforcement efforts to stop edgeworkers will only heighten the risk of their edgework, force them to further hone their skills, and so *amplify* the very adrenalin rush that certain groups of participants seek to achieve and authorities seek to stop.

Notably, Ferrell (2004a) has also explored the interplay between edgework and a particular background emotion: boredom. He argues that key features of late modernity have spawned a distinctive sort of collective, organized boredom. The ongoing degradation of work, the confinement of workers to the fast food counter and the globalized factory, amplify the experience of alienation and negate the possibility of engaged or exciting occupation. Pervasive regimes of bureaucratic rationalization and risk management create an actuarial society where nothing is to be left to chance or surprise. As the Frankfurt School first began to glimpse, the cultural industry endlessly promises satisfaction or excitement with its next mediated product, and endlessly fails to deliver on that promise. The cumulative result is a vast, vacant commonality of boredom and frustration out of which, and against which, emerge both collective social and cultural movements, and subcultural moments of adrenalin-charged edgework. In this sense, moments of illicit edgework and certain other 'crimes of passion' can be understood as crimes committed not primarily against people or property, but against structural boredom. And in this sense we can see that the choice for cultural criminologists is not to focus on excitement or boredom, the exceptional or the mundane, but rather to situate all of these emotions within the defining currents of late modernity.

Nonetheless, edgework's original focus on prototypically masculine, high-risk pursuits has been criticized by a number of feminist criminologists (Howe, 2003: 279; Halsey and Young, 2006), who see it as further evidence of the essentially gendered nature of much risk research (e.g. Stanko, 1997; Walklate, 1997; Chan and Rigakos, 2002). Highlighting the extreme yet voluntary activities of street racers or graffiti writers, they argue, fails to take seriously the everyday, involuntary risks faced by women simply by virtue of being female in a patriarchal society – risks like domestic violence, sexual abuse and public assault. While these are certainly valid criticisms of early edgework research, they do suggest the sort of dichotomization we've sought throughout this chapter to avoid. Even as first formulated, for example, the concept of edgework can help us understand gender and gender dynamics, including the considerable number of crimes that produce 'hegemonic masculinity' (Connell, 1995) from a mix of risk taking and embodied masculine emotion, to the detriment of women. Moreover, subsequent research (Ferrell et al., 2001) has found that women, both individually and collectively, often constitute some of the more skilled and esteemed members of illicit edgework subcultures.

Still, the issue of edgework and gender can be approached productively from various other angles. In her thoughtful response to Lyng's (1990) early formulation of edgework, Eleanor Miller argues that the edgework model is limited because of its too narrow focus on 'activities that are engaged in primarily by white men with an attachment to the labour force' (1991: 1531). But while she is right to be deeply critical of this and other aspects of Lyng's thesis, she does not dismiss them out of hand. Instead, she explores whether or not they can have utility for her own research on the risk-taking strategies of African-American female street hustlers, especially those involved in potentially dangerous 'street missions' and 'put overs'. Revisiting once again the tension between foreground practices and background structures, Miller sees the everyday circumstances of the 'underclass women' she studies as products of wider structural inequalities and racist ideologies, but acknowledges also that particular forms of edgework practice come into play 'among those who choose especially risky hustles':

> In the case at hand, the sort of edgework engaged in by the members of these [underclass] groups should not be expected to resemble exactly the edgework

described by Lyng; the structures of oppression to which it responds are unique. The resources of the members of the groups in question are usually fewer and different. However, experientially and in terms of social psychological impact, edgework might be functionally equivalent across these groups. Or, it might be different in ways that are sociologically important and interesting. But not looking forever dooms us to not seeing. (Miller, 1991: 1533–4)

Lyng has acknowledged as much, noting that the edgework model needs 'elaboration beyond its present empirical base' (1991: 1534) – and indeed in a subsequent edited collection on edgework (Lyng, 2005), he attempts just that, with chapters exploring the relationship between edgework and drug taking, the Victorian insurance and actuarial industries, youth delinquency, even anarchy (see Banks, 2013). Most important in terms of our present concern, though, is Jenifer Lois's chapter, in which she explores the significant gender differences in edgework practices associated with voluntary mountain rescue teams. For example, she charts how trepidation and confidence emerge as gendered emotional strategies in preparation for edgework; how reactions to the 'adrenalin rush' vary by gender; and how major differences emerge in women's and men's management of fearful post-edgework emotions. She concludes that 'women's and men's gendered understanding of emotions influenced how they understood their "authentic" selves, and hence, their edgework experiences' (Lois, 2005: 150; see also Lois, 2001). Likewise, feminist criminologist Valli Rajah has developed a notion of 'edgework as resistance' in her study of poor, minority, drug-using women involved in violent intimate relationships. Rajah's work explores how 'edgework may be different across gender, class and race', and develops 'the resistance concept by specifying both when resistance is likely to occur and what the specific rewards of resistance may be' (2007: 196).[4] Jeannine Gailey (2009) has similarly employed the notion of edgework to rebut essentialist or medicalized understandings of anorexia, showing instead how anorexic women employ precise skills to accelerate their anorexia and achieve 'intense emotive reactions'.

As this body of emerging research confirms, the concept of 'edgework' constitutes a powerful intellectual model for exploring the interplay of emotion, risk, crime and identity. And as Lyng argues (2005: 5), understanding this interplay will become only more crucial as the ethos of risk taking increasingly circulates within the social and institutional structures of late modernity.

Edgework in the streets

Elsewhere, we've sought to develop the relationship between expressive crime and edgework by situating the latter within a distinctly urban context (Ferrell, 1996; Hayward, 2004). Conventional accounts of edgework often place participants on the mountain face, at the race track or aboard the sky-diving plane. But what of those denied such opportunities, as most are? For some, run-down estates or unpatrolled 'problem' neighbourhoods become 'paradoxical spaces'. While they symbolize the systematic powerlessness so often felt by individuals living in these environments, they also become sites of risk consumption that provide numerous avenues for elicit edgework. Such spaces serve as 'performance zones', places in which displays of risk, excitement and masculinity abound. In other words, 'many forms of crime frequently perpetrated within urban areas should be seen for exactly what they are, attempts to achieve a semblance of control within ontologically insecure life worlds' (Hayward, 2004: 165).

This notion applies especially to crimes with a strong 'expressive' element, crimes like joy-riding, mugging or gang violence that offer both rich excitement and an illicit means of traversing, even momentarily escaping, the socially degraded neighbourhood. We might even categorize a whole host of crimes like fire setting and football hooliganism as 'urban edgework, attempts to construct an enhanced sense of self by engaging in risk-laden practices on the metaphorical edge' (Hayward, 2004: 166).

This argument can also be extended to explain certain types of urban rioting. For example, in the August 2011 London riots, much was made of the fact that, far from a meaningful political statement, much of the violence and looting that took place during the six days of rioting was actually highly individualistic and linked to the types of personal expressivity and hedonistic self-enhancement associated with consumerism (Treadwell et al., 2013).

Green cultural criminology

Just as cultural criminology has emerged over the past two decades as an approach designed for critical engagement with the particular crimes and crises of late modernity, so too has a second approach: green criminology. Broadly, green criminology explores the interconnections between environmental harm, crime and crime control, and issues of social justice and injustice. Specifically, green criminology investigates issues including the pollution and exhaustion of natural resources, the abuse and exploitation of animals, the harms inherent in contemporary food production and the mounting harms spawned by global warming and climate change. As green criminologists take care to note, the criminology of these ecological issues and their causes in turn connects the dynamics of green or environmental harm to the core concerns of criminology as a whole: white collar crime, state crime, discriminatory enforcement and issues of personal and collective culpability. In all of this, green criminologists seek to demonstrate 'how resonant and relevant a green criminology is in terms of the local and global trends that shape our world on a daily basis' (South et al., 2013: 30).

In addition to their shared goal of creating a criminology conversant with contemporary issues, cultural criminology and green criminology share a number of striking similarities regarding the criminological enterprise itself. Both have developed from within the broad tradition of critical criminology, and so integrate their overt subject matters with an analysis of power and inequality – yet both are also openly interdisciplinary in their efforts to expand the analytic range of criminology. Likewise, both readily push past the conventional boundaries of criminological inquiry to investigate a range of social harms and cultural phenomena not traditionally defined as within the substantive orbit of criminology. Both also reject the goal of achieving the status of grand theory or meta-theory; cultural criminology's past characterization of itself as 'a loose federation of outlaw intellectual critiques' (Ferrell, 2007: 99) echoes in green criminology's disclaimer that it 'is not intended to be a unitary enterprise', but instead 'a capacious and evolving *perspective* … a loose framework or set of intellectual, empirical and political orientations' (South et al., 2013: 28, emphasis in original). This general post-disciplinary sensibility keeps the boundaries of both approaches loosely emergent as well; as per this book's subtitle, and despite criticisms (Carlen, 2011), both approaches remain openly invitational in their welcoming of new scholars and new, critical perspectives. Because of this, Rob White's (2010: 423) characterization of green criminology describes cultural criminology equally. 'Green criminology', he says, 'is a theoretical perspective that is inherently challenging – to criminology as a fairly conservative analytical and practical field of human endeavor, and to the powers that be, which would much prefer silence to dissent, obfuscation to transparency, and passivity to action'.

This undercurrent of convergence between green criminology and cultural criminology has surfaced on occasion, as with Avi Brisman's (2010) work on the criminalization of pro-environmental activities and activism, and White's (2002) linking of environmental harm to the political economy of late capitalist consumption. Similarly, green criminologists who have mined existing work in cultural criminology on consumer waste, environmental activism and related issues argue that 'cultural criminology is, at some levels, already doing green criminology' (Brisman and South, 2013: 115). Perhaps most significantly, green criminology and cultural criminology have suggested something of their foundational convergence by both invoking the 'criminological imagination' and urging its revitalization in contemporary criminology. Drawing on C. Wright Mills' (1959) classic conceptualization of the sociological imagination, we have called for the return of 'the criminological imagination', noting that 'for Mills, the key nature of the sociological imagination was to situate human biography in history and in social structure', and arguing that criminologists must connect 'personal troubles in various parts of the world with collective issues across the globe, to make the personal political' (Young, 2011: 2, 5). Likewise, Rob White (2003: 483–4), writing on 'environmental issues and the criminological imagination', has noted that green criminology requires 'an appreciation of how harm is socially and historically constructed [and] understanding and interpreting the structure of a globalized world; the direction(s) in which this world is heading; and how diverse groups' experiences are shaped by wider social, political and economic processes'. For both cultural and green criminologies, then, the criminological imagination means situating the personal in the social, cultural and historical, and linking the local and the global; as much so, it demands the sort of open, interdisciplinary approach that can keep the critical criminological gaze in focus across fields of study and between levels of human endeavour.

Of late, the confluence of these two approaches has been formalized with scholarship that directly addresses the possibilities of shared inquiry and analysis, and with the development of a distinctive 'green cultural criminology' (Brisman and South, 2013, 2014; Ferrell, 2013a). Generally, green cultural criminology seeks to link key sensibilities of cultural criminology – mediated dynamics, contested meaning, everyday crime and resistance – with the project of green criminology, on the grounds that

> Our appreciation of environmental harms and crimes is limited and incomplete without an understanding of the social construction of environmental harm and crime ... this is a process that is synergistically affected by images of environmental disaster reported in the news media and depicted in television and film; by messages that reinforce capitalist principles of conspicuous consumption, exploitation and individualism that contribute to environmental degradation ... and in response, by various forms, means and practices of resistance to such environmental harm. (Brisman and South, 2013: 117)

Appropriately for two approaches jointly committed to critical engagement with the distinct dynamics of contemporary society, early work in green cultural criminology has focused especially on the distinctly destructive dynamics of late capitalism, and on emerging forms of resistance to it. As we and others have argued, the atomized identities, manufactured insecurities and global inequities of late capitalism constitute a motor force for harms ranging from international violence to everyday crimes of production, acquisition and retribution (Young, 1999; Hall and Winlow, 2005); increasingly, these harms are understood to include environmental desecration and exhaustion as well. An essentially cultural enterprise, late capitalism manufactures insecurities and desires as a way of endlessly expanding markets for products that are themselves designed for rapid physical or cultural obsolescence. In doing so, it creates a globalized culture of consumption, ever more rapid cycles of consumption within this retail universe, and, as a result, a widening class of insatiable consumers. But if the consequences range from a First-World mania for 'lifestyle products' to Third-World child labour and factory incineration, they also include the heedless exhaustion of natural resources, the thoroughgoing commodification of the natural world and a global flood of waste as one round of consumer goods is predictably discarded in favour of the next. In turn, the advertising that initially sells these goods also operates as an ongoing, everyday 'greenwashing' campaign, hiding late capitalism's ecological destruction behind false ideologies of convenience, sanitation and even corporate ecological citizenship. Yet, despite this, as green cultural criminologists note, resistance to late capitalism and its environmental costs has arisen, with various activist and resistant groups regularly criminalized and made the focus of legal statutes and policing campaigns in the interest of protecting consumer culture and the spaces in which it flourishes (Ferrell, 2001/2, 2006a, 2013a; White, 2002, 2013; Brisman, 2010; Brisman and South, 2013).

As befits two approaches committed to emergent critiques and cross-border analysis, countless other forms of green cultural criminology can also be imagined – some already undertaken, some waiting to be developed – and all of critical importance amidst the evolving interplay of culture, crime and environmental harm in contemporary society. Among these are corporate development, corporate pollution and their environmental consequences, as documented and analysed visually in the USA by Kenneth Tunnell (2011) and in Italy by Lorenzo Natali (2013); the cultural and legal politics of water and worldwide waterfront development (Kane, 2013); and the sinister magic by which manufactured fears of crime drive people from the supposed vulnerability of their bicycles and their feet and into automobiles, while the actual, everyday criminal carnage caused by automobiles disappears behind automotive and oil company advertisements (Ferrell, 2004b; Lauer, 2005; Muzzatti, 2010). Then there's the cultural aesthetic of corporate landscaping, manicured lawns and gardens, and ever-green golf courses, as encoded in city ordinances and played out in falling water tables and toxic run-off; and the culture of excessive red meat consumption and the pervasiveness of factory farming, with laws now written to protect from exposure the systematic animal abuse which many see as inherent in such corporatized farming. Within the sort of criminological imagination embraced by green cultural criminology, these and other confluences of the cultural and the environmental exist not only as critical issues in their own right, but as part of a greater immediacy. Taken together, they confirm the broader ecological crisis that is now upon us, and now part of our daily lives, and they reinforce for green cultural criminologists a late-modern lesson taught daily by that crisis: the earth won't wait.

Cultural criminology and late modernity: reclamation and revitalization

The following three chapters explore further dimensions of late-modern life and cultural criminology's attempt to account for them. Chapter 4, 'Towards a Cultural Criminology of the Everyday', emphasizes the importance of mundane moments and everyday situations. There we suggest that day-to-day experience under late modernity is a cauldron of contested meaning and emotion, sometimes hidden, other times mediated – in large part because everyday life is increasingly the terrain in which social control is both embedded and resisted. In this sense, everyday life is also the place in which two contemporary ways of living come together and clash – one shaped by rationalization, risk management and commodification, the other by informalities of community, subculture and style (Raban, 1974; Bakhtin, 1984; De Certeau, 1984; Presdee, 2000; Muller, 2002, 2012). This chapter also draws on one of cultural criminology's foundational concepts – the analysis of urban space and its underlife (see Ferrell, 1996, 2001/2, 2006a; Hayward, 2004, 2012b; Campbell, 2013) – to explore this tension. Suffused by rule and regulation, the spaces of the everyday world nonetheless remain locations where transgression occurs, where rigidity is fudged, where the rules are by turns bent or bowed down to. It is a world in which the imaginary of the powerful confronts the life of the citizen – and is by turns negotiated, internalized and, every now and again, resisted.

Chapter 5, 'War, Terrorism and the State: A Cultural Criminological Introduction', explores cultural criminology's increasing engagement with issues of state and governmental crime, terrorism and state terrorism, and war. Taking as case studies the war in Iraq and radical Jihad, the chapter integrates structural analysis, theories of subcultural dynamics and learnt behaviour, and attentiveness to experiences and emotions to develop a holistic cultural criminology of late-modern conflict. In addition, the chapter highlights the essential role of the image in contemporary conflict, and for all involved: the state, the insurgent groups it seeks to conquer and those activist groups that would oppose the conflict as a whole. Confronting the increasingly blurry boundaries between terrorism, state criminality, crime and sub-state conflict, the chapter also argues for a soundly interdisciplinary approach, one which draws on fields like terrorism studies and international relations and methods such as visual analysis. Beyond this, we argue there that terrorism can usefully be understood as a phenomenon that is as much existential as political for its participants; we also argue for critically considering the role of the late-modern state, with its militarization of border spaces and police cultures, and its penal archipelago, in any analysis of terrorism or global conflict.

In Chapter 6, 'Media, Representation and Meaning: Inside the Hall of Mirrors', we turn to what is surely one of late modernity's defining features – a pervasive, global, 24/7 world of mediated communication – and explore the consequences of this mediascape for crime, criminal justice and everyday understanding. As we show there, images of crime and crime control are now as 'real' as crime and criminal justice itself – 'if by "real" we denote those dimensions of social life that produce consequences; shape attitudes and policy; define the effects of crime and criminal justice; generate fear, avoidance and pleasure; and alter the lives of those involved' (Ferrell et al., 2004: 4). In a world where media images of crime and deviance proliferate, where crime and control reflect off the shiny face of popular culture, cultural criminology focuses on making sense of this blurred line between the real and the virtual. And, as always, this focus is political as well as theoretical: in late modernity, with power increasingly exercised through mediated representation and symbolic production, battles over image, style and mediated meaning become essential in the contest over crime and crime control, deviance and normality, and the emerging shape of social justice.

In these three following chapters as in this one, our goal is to develop a cultural criminology that is well-equipped to understand, critique and often counter the various transformations underway in late modernity. Our ultimate goal is a progressive cultural criminology that can help shape a better, more just world. As this and the previous chapter have shown, this criminology must first *reclaim the rich historical tradition of critical, sociological criminology*, and second, *revitalize and reinvent this tradition so as to meet the challenges and inequalities thrown up by the late-modern social order.* As Chapters 7 and 8 will demonstrate, this progressive cultural criminology must also confront and overcome a suffocating irony increasingly facing sociological and criminological inquiry: at the very moment that we must engage the late-modern world and its crises, the intellectual tools that might help us with this task are under threat. Within the academy, the palpable lurch towards criminologies of control and order management and pallid opportunity has largely excluded more thoughtful and critical approaches. As a result, the distance between the late-modern world and the academy has only grown, with most criminological analysis now confined to number sets and sanitized computer printouts. Widening this gap further is the subsuming of research within bureaucratic control, such that more engaged forms of research are stifled. Between the iron cage of the university review board and the gentle pulling and pushing of government funding, the discipline changes its form, losing its critical edge and progressive direction. And it is in this context that we intend not only to develop a progressive and engaged cultural criminology, but to launch it as a criminological counter-attack on the cloistered institutional cowardice that afflicts us.

A selection of films and documentaries illustrative of some of the themes and ideas in this chapter

Minority Report, 2002, Dir. Steven Spielberg

Set aside the sci-fi hokum about the 'pre-cogs' and *Minority Report* is interesting in the way it turns around the notion of 'pre-crime'. In particular, it illustrates a shift underway from aetiological theories of crime and deviance to a control system based around risk and resource management. While we may seem a long way away from the film's Department of PreCrime, it's strange how many of the 'future' trends contained in the movie are either already with us or on the immediate horizon – everything from eye-recognition software to a virtual CCTV 'scanscape', from the erosion of trial by jury to the concept of 'digital rule' – a grid of knowledge based on digital records. Indeed, in a thoughtful article the criminologist Lucia Zedner (2007) makes the case that, as a result of the growing number of ordering practices based on pre-emptive, risk-aversive security measures, we are already moving towards a pre-crime society.

Falling Down, 1993, Dir. Joel Schumacher

At one level, a formulaic Hollywood shoot-em-up; at another level, a more problematic story of metropolitan meltdown, as Michael Douglas's character 'D-Fens' psychologically unravels during a cross-LA odyssey. Importantly, *Falling Down* should not be read only as a metaphor for late modernity or, for that matter, ontological insecurity. Rather, it is a parable of alienation and maladaption; a tale of a man out of time. D-Fens is a disillusioned and unstable man who can no longer function or make sense of a more complex, pluralized social order – as a result adopting disturbing measures to achieve his warped version of the American Dream.

Fight Club, 1999, Dir. David Fincher

'Advertising has us chasing cars and clothes, working jobs we hate so we can buy shit we don't need. We're the middle children of history, man … We've all been raised on television to believe that one day we'd all be millionaires, and movie gods, and rock stars. But we won't. And we're slowly learning that fact. And we're very, very pissed off.' So speaks Tyler Durden, the central 'character' of *Fight Club*, an anarchic and controversial tale of anti-consumerism and masculine frustration. Depending on your point of view, *Fight Club* is either 'a witless mishmash of whiny, infantile philosophizing and bone-crunching violence' (Kenneth Turan, *L.A. Times*) or 'a wild, orgiastic pop masterpiece' (Bret Easton Ellis, *Gear Magazine*). The truth lies somewhere in between, of course, but whatever your view, it's not a film that can be easily dismissed. While critics have rightly pointed to its stylized nihilism, its 'microfascism' and its glamorized hyper violence – and certainly all these problematic aspects are apparent – it also makes some interesting observations on late-modern alienation and the deadening pressure of boring, unfulfilling, precarious employment. In truth, the film is a contradiction in celluloid – for example, it's at once a critique of consumer society and a commercial Hollywood blockbuster! We include it here not because we agree with its message or support its sentiments, but because of its ability to provoke debate and pose questions. See what you make of it.

Inside Job, 2010, Dir. Charles Ferguson

This is a useful analysis of the global financial crisis of 2008, which cost over $20 trillion and nearly brought down the international banking system. Employing his usual brand of thorough research and extensive interviews with the key players,

(Continued)

(Continued)

Ferguson traces how the financial industry went rogue, corrupting politics and the financial regulation system along with it. If you're not sure about what caused the current deep, ongoing economic recession, you could do worse than start here.

The War on Democracy: A Film by John Pilger, 2007, **Dirs Christopher Martin and John Pilger**

Countering George Bush's claims about 'exporting democracy', this film shows how US foreign policy in Latin America has actually stifled its progress. The film 'explores the disenchantment with democracy, concentrating on those parts of the world where people have struggled with blood, sweat and tears to plant democracy, only to see it brutally crushed' (www.warondemocracy.net). After producing over 50 TV documentaries, the veteran Australian activist and journalist John Pilger has produced a movie that vividly shows that the enduring principles of democracy are more likely to be found among the impoverished residents of the *barrios* of Latin America than they are among the shadowy figures that stalk the corridors of the White House. See also www.johnpilger.com/videos for free access to dozens of documentaries from Pilger's TV and film career.

Spare Parts, 2003, **Dir. Damjan Kozole**

A tragic tale of illegal immigration told through the lives of two Slovenian traffickers, *Spare Parts* sheds light on the desperate world of cross-border people smuggling.

Further Reading

Young, J. (1999) *The Exclusive Society.* **London: SAGE.**
Social theoretical work documenting the transformation of the liberal democratic state in the last third of the twentieth century from an inclusive society of stability and homogeneity to an exclusive society of change and division. Requires some basic criminological knowledge prior to reading.

Young, J. (2007) *The Vertigo of Late Modernity.* **London: SAGE.**
The sequel to the above work, *The Vertigo of Late Modernity* charts how economic and social reconfigurations that took place at the end of the twentieth century gave rise to eruptions of anxiety, insecurity, tension, and 'othering' that now haunt everyday life.

Hayward, K. J. (2004) *City Limits: Crime, Consumer Culture and the Urban Experience.* **London: Glasshouse.**
A theoretical monograph in which the author puts forward the notion of the 'crime-consumerism nexus': a conceptual cultural criminological framework for thinking about certain urban crimes under the conditions of late capitalism.

Katz, J. (1988) *Seductions of Crime: Moral and Sensual Attractions in Doing Evil.* **New York: Basic Books.**
The central contention of Katz's imperious book is that there are 'moral and sensual attractions in doing evil' and that a truly inclusive account of criminal behaviour has to start from this premise. Katz asserts that deviance offers the perpetrator a means of 'self transcendence', a way of overcoming the mundanity typically associated with the banal practicalities of everyday 'regular life'.

Lyng, S. (1990) 'Edgework: A social psychological analysis of voluntary risk taking', *American Journal of Sociology,* **95: 851–86.**
Lengthy theoretical journal article exploring the concept of extreme voluntary risk-taking, or 'edgework'. Lyng shows how certain practices such as sky-diving (and by extension drug taking and other illegal activities) can be used as a means of reclaiming ones' life by risking it; a way of reacting against the 'unidentifiable forces that rob one of individual choice'.

Rajah, V. (2007) 'Resistance as edgework in violent intimate relationships of drug-involved women', *British Journal of Criminology,* **47(2): 196–213.**
An important article in which the feminist criminologist Valli Rajah develops a notion of 'edgework as resistance' in her study of poor, minority, drug-using women caught up in intimate violence.

O'Malley, P. and Mugford, S. (1994) 'Crime, excitement and modernity', in G. Barak (ed.) *Varieties of Criminology.* **Westport: Praeger, pp. 189–212.**
Early attempt to augment Katz's phenomenological analysis of crime by setting it against a wider backdrop of rationality, risk and other civilizing processes associated with modernity.

Useful Websites

Crimetalk.org
www.crimetalk.org.uk/
Originator of 'censure theory' and author of the acclaimed 1994 book *Sociology of Deviance: An Obituary,* Colin Sumner now has his own criminological website. Take a look, and while you're at it, why not think about writing something for him. He's always keen to receive well-written newsworthy criminological material.

Vice News
https://news.vice.com/
Vice is an international news channel created by and for a connected generation. The site includes written and video articles on breaking news stories, subcultural groups, and regional conflicts. Their 2014 reports from the so-called 'Islamic State' were perhaps the best example of 'gonzo journalism' this century.

(Continued)

Notes

1 'The starting point of RCT is that offenders seek advantage to themselves by their criminal behaviour. This entails making decisions among alternatives. These decisions are rational within the constraints of time, ability and the availability of relevant information' (Pease, 2006: 339).

2 This states that, thanks to millions of economic actors acting rationally, in a perfectly efficient market, prices accurately reflect all known information, and are therefore at any given point 'right'. From this observation bloomed a thousand statistical models in which were embedded the idea that historical experience, which had been acted out by rational agents, could be used to safely predict the future. The near collapse of the banking industry and the subsequent economic fallout is demonstrable evidence that the efficient markets hypothesis can be a dangerous premise – as it turned out, prices of some assets, particularly of housing, were driven far beyond rational levels by euphoric investors. This led to a crash far more extreme than models based on post-war experience had ever predicted.

3 Katz's social psychology of the emotions is not without its critics (see, for example, the extended discussion of *How Emotions Work* in the 2002 special edition of *Theoretical Criminology* on emotions [especially Scheff et al 2002: 369–74]). We hope that, just as cultural criminologists critically engaged with Katz's earlier *Seductions of Crime* and set about augmenting his analysis (Ferrell, 1992; Fenwick and Hayward, 2000; Hayward, 2001, 2004: 148–57; Young, 2003), a similar process will commence with *How Emotions Work*.

4 Rajah acknowledges, of course, that 'while edgework as a form of resistance to intimate partner violence may offer visceral rewards, it does not necessarily constitute a victory for women, and may even help to reproduce gender inequality' (2007: 210).

4

A CULTURAL CRIMINOLOGY OF
THE EVERYDAY

Everyday crimes small and large

Cultural criminologists often focus their analytic gaze on those little situations, circumstances and crimes that make up everyday life. Cultural criminology looks for evidence of globalization not only in the wide sweep of transcontinental capitalism, but amidst the most local of situations and common of transgressions. It finds the machinery of mass culture in even the most private of moments, discovers the residues of mediated meaning in even the smallest snippets of conversation. In our view, the essential subject matter of criminology – the manufacture of meaning around issues of crime, transgression and control – remains an ongoing enterprise, an often unnoticed process that seeps into commonplace perceptions and saturates day-to-day interactions.

To understand the ways in which issues of crime, transgression and control come to be animated with emotion, then, we certainly must pay attention to televised crime dramas and political campaigns – but we also must pay attention to the people around us and to their constructions of experience and understanding. Most of all, in a world where information and entertainment swirl through everyday life, emanating from countless video screens and cell phones, we can – we must – find mediated politics in personal experience. Watching people on the street, we can catch little shadows of last night's television crime drama, and all those that came before it; listening in on conversations in a pub, we can hear echoes of a politician's press conference at one table, distortions of the daily news at another. Encountering on the street or in the pub some commonplace crime, we can come to appreciate the extraordinary importance of crime itself.

Cultural criminology's critics are aware of this focus on the everyday as well, but they sometimes see in it something more insidious. For them, the focus on everyday people and everyday crimes can suggest that cultural criminologists are unwilling to take on larger, more important issues of crime and its political consequences. Martin O'Brien (2005: 610), for example, concludes his critique of cultural criminology by juxtaposing cultural criminologists' research into crimes like 'graffiti writing or riding a motorcycle recklessly' with the mercenary crimes of Mark Thatcher. The mollycoddled son of former British Prime Minister the late Margaret Thatcher, Mark Thatcher has indeed been accused of crimes ranging from racketeering and tax evasion to negligence, arms dealing and an attempted coup d'etat – crimes that critics like O'Brien assume to be objectively and self-evidently of greater significance than more mundane forms of criminality.

Yet, while we're certainly happy to judge the behaviour of a spoiled underling like Mark Thatcher to be morally odious, we're nonetheless left with a serious criminological question: By what terms can we judge his crimes to be more important, or more worthy of our analysis, than the crimes of the lesser known? Put differently, is it the exceptionality of a crime that should draw our analytic attention or the banality? Is a father's abuse of his daughter more or less troubling, more or less revealing of power and its dynamics, than the abuse of American prison inmates, or Guantanamo detainees, locked away for years in solitary confinement? Iraqi citizens killed by one daily bombing after another; African-American kids swept off the street by civil gang injunctions and stop-and-frisk procedures; British kids silenced or segregated by curfews, banning orders and Crime Prevention Injunctions; Central American children fleeing through Mexico on *el tren de los desconocidos*, the train of the unknown – are these often unnoticed, everyday occurrences more or less important to understanding and confronting injustice than the crimes of Mark Thatcher?

For cultural criminologists, *these aren't questions that can be answered definitively – they can only be interrogated culturally. The difference between one crime and another is negotiated, not innate – in the final analysis, more a matter of contested meaning than inherent magnitude.*

In fact, this negotiation of meaning, this fluid dynamic between the everyday and the exceptional, can be traced along any number of trajectories. As we and other criminologists have long documented, the criminalization process – the process by which new legal regulations are created and new enforcement strategies designed – can transform the most mundane of existing activities into major crimes and the exotica of moral panic. Trash picking, idling about in public, searching for a place to sleep, dancing with friends, getting drunk or getting high – all of these have, at various times in recent British, European and American history, been either matters of little consequence or manifestations of serious criminality. And if this criminalization process at times infuses otherwise little events with large significance, it regularly invokes larger patterns of political and cultural power as well, emerging as it does from media campaigns, staged political pronouncements and the exercise of economic and ethnic inequality. In such cases, to study everyday transgression, or more specifically to study the emergent and often amplified meaning of everyday transgression, is to study the political economy of power.

If we return to the crimes of Mark Thatcher, we can catch a different sort of trajectory and one that suggests a further dynamic linking mundane events and larger matters of meaning. A direct, cultural criminological analysis of Mark Thatcher's crimes would certainly be useful and important. Such an analysis might explore the ways in which neo-conservative values of individual responsibility and personal acquisition in fact set the stage for personal misbehaviour among those who most publicly espouse them. It might examine the ways in which the political privilege of the parent begets the cultural privileging of the offspring, opening doors to inside deals and ensuring endless irresponsibility. It might even focus on the linguistic sleight of hand offered up by expensive lawyers and top-flight public relations consultants such that the misdeeds of the powerful can, time and again, be obfuscated, reinvented, ignored – and so *not* constructed as crime.

Strategic and moral choices

To conduct this sort of analysis well, though – to actually get inside the gilded shadows that make up the world of Mark Thatcher, as opposed to relying on newspaper accounts and popular mythology – would require the sorts of money and connections that few of us have. It would perhaps require travelling in social circles that some of us find uncomfortable, if not repugnant. Most importantly, it would risk valorizing the very phenomenon we wish to analyse and critique – risk reproducing in our own research and writing, that is, the mediated gaze already fixed on the Mark Thatchers of the world – as we focus too much of our attention on those all too well positioned to capture it. Again, and despite these pitfalls, such a study could make an invaluable contribution to our understanding of political and corporate crime and its consequences – but there is, we think, another way to conduct the study.

That way is to track down Mark Thatcher in the streets and alleys of everyday life, to document his crimes and their consequences in moments more readily available to us. When, for example, wealthy entrepeneurs like Mark Thatcher engage in racketeering and tax evasion, we can effectively explore the consequences of such crimes in the growing gap between the rich and poor of our communities, in decimated local economies and shuttered factories, in underfunded local schools and inadequate healthcare (see Hedges and Sacco, 2012) – and so in street-level drug markets and untreated drug overdoses, in everyday school vandalism and violence, and in the Mertonian strain towards theft or despair encountered by unemployed or under-employed folks all around us. When a global hustler like Mark Thatcher dabbles in the arms trade and in political upheaval, we and our colleagues in other countries can catch up to him at every orphanage, can see the consequences of his actions in a severed limb or a lost life. Like the great documentary photographer W. Eugene Smith, who famously captured the horrific effects of systematic corporate mercury poisoning in the close-up deformities of one little girl, we can communicate the crimes of the powerful by way of their everyday consequences.

In this sense, cultural criminology's focus on the everyday constitutes something of a strategic choice. For some cultural criminologists, the ethnography of everyday life has offered a do-it-yourself research method kept happily independent of university grant programmes, governmental funding agencies and other outside influences likely to limit the critical scope of scholarly work. Hanging out on street corners, conducting interviews behind commercial buildings, calling up public officials or utilizing 'follow-the-money' software, researchers need ask neither for permission nor for money – and so they can follow their findings wherever they may go, unencumbered by funding concerns or official sanction. Certainly, critical scholarship can flow from any number of research strategies – but it flows with particular ease from methods that cast the researcher as an independent outsider. And if this sort of research keeps cultural criminologists outside the orbit of bureaucratic control, it also has the benefit of keeping them inside communities. Research on crime and transgression within everyday life tends to integrate the researcher into the local community, putting the researcher in touch with the lives of ordinary people and yet offering often extraordinary insights into the dynamics of those lives and communities.

In this process of human engagement, cultural criminology's focus on everyday life moves beyond strategic choice and towards moral and theoretical foundation. Attempting to understand the meaning of crime and the dynamics through which this meaning is manufactured, cultural criminology draws on a constellation of theoretical orientations attuned to everyday experience. Among these are symbolic interactionism, with its emphasis on the daily transactions by which individuals create, sustain and contest shared meaning; phenomenology, with its attentiveness to the intricate and distinctive features of everyday experience; and ethnomethodology, fine-tuned to the reflexively 'elegant knowledge' (Mehan and Wood, 1975: 117) that animates commonplace situations and events. Certainly, these rich theoretical models merit more than these few lines (Lindgren, 2005), but for present purposes we can derive from them a shared insight: *the social world cannot be understood apart from the agency of those who occupy it.* While of course working within profound limitations of political and economic exclusion, everyday people are nonetheless neither 'judgmental dopes' (Garfinkel, 1967: 67) nor calculating machines; they are agents of social reality, active interpreters of their own lives. Watching television crime news, fearing for our own safety, deciding whether to fix that broken backdoor lock, we make do as best we can – and as we do, we continue to make sense of the world around us and so to contribute to its collective construction.

Cultural criminology's focus on everyday life becomes in this way also a form of moral politics that we might call *critical humanism*. By 'humanism', we mean simply a scholarly and moral commitment to inquire into people's lived experiences, both collective and individual (see Wilkinson, 2005). By 'critical', we mean two things. First, critical humanism signifies a willingness to critique that which we study, to unpack even the most dearly held and elegantly argued of assumptions. Put differently, a commitment to engage with people on their own terms does not mean that those terms need be uncritically accepted; appreciating the human construction of meaning, we may still judge that meaning to be inadequate, not in terms of some moral absolutism, but out of concern for what harm that constructed meaning may cause others. Second, and relatedly, critical humanism denotes an inquiry into human experience within a larger project of critique and analysis. As already suggested in the case of Mark Thatcher, we intend for cultural criminology not only to give voice to everyday accounts seldom heard, but to gather those voices into a chorus of condemnation for broad structures of violence, inequality and exploitation. Again, the hope is to overcome the dualism of agency and structure, to link the ordinary and the exceptional and to discard the false dichotomy between crimes large and small.

Through this work, we hope also to affirm the possibilities for progressive social change within the practice of everyday life. Those eager to distinguish large crimes from small are often eager as well to distinguish large-scale political engagement from the less consequential politics of daily life. For them, Mark Thatcher matters more than other criminals precisely because he and his family matter more politically. And indeed they do – but sometimes they don't. Sometimes progressive social change does indeed emerge from the ballot box or the mass movement, from utilizing millions of voters or millions of marchers to confront structures of social injustice. But sometimes progressive social change percolates in the little moments of everyday experience, as one small act of resistance to the daily routine, to the micro-circuits of social control, sets the stage for the next. Our tendency, then, is to believe that the future remains unwritten, to remember that revolutions often explode when least expected, and so to celebrate progressive moments where we find them. If the everyday remains a primary site for the enforcement of injustice, it remains a place of hope and resistance, too.

A day in the life

What follows is true fiction – a compilation of everyday situations and events extant in the contemporary world, here fictionalized into a single, integrated narrative. It's also a test, of you and of us. If we've managed so far to communicate some sense of the everyday and its importance, some sense of how transgression and control animate everyday life, the following account should glow with meaning as you make your way through it. In it you should discover many little windows into the unnoticed politics of day-to-day crime and control, and more than a few clues as to what shape a cultural criminology of everyday life might take. But in case we've failed so far, or in case you're about to, we'll even provide a guide. Each time you see an italicized phrase in the following narrative, you can be sure that there's more to be said about the situation it describes – and before we do say more later, you might consider for yourself what importance some inconsequential moment, some simple situation of everyday constraint or transgression, might have for a cultural criminology of our lives.

'Ah, man', he says to himself. 'I gotta get those damned curtains fixed.'

The alarm's not set to go off for another 20 minutes and the daylight streaming in through the window where the curtains hang loose has awakened him. Waking up, it still seems more like a dream for a moment, what with the morning light coming in between the decorative *black iron burglar bars*, filling the room with long shadows like some late-modern film noir.

Hell, he figures, I'm awake. I may as well get up. Switching off the security system, he opens the front door and heads out to pick up the morning newspaper, only to find that the *ADT Security sign* planted in his front yard has been knocked over. He stoops over to get the paper, stoops again to right the sign and heads back inside.

Since the divorce, he doesn't bother much with breakfast, so after a quick bath and a cup of coffee, he gets into his business suit and heads off for a brisk walk to catch the train into the city. Arriving at the station, realizing he left his newspaper at home, *he uses his credit card to buy another paper* and a second cup of coffee and heads to the platform. Head buried in the morning paper, reading the crime news, he doesn't notice the *CCTV cameras* mounted on either end of the platform.

When he gets tired of standing and retreats to one of the few benches on the platform, though, he does notice something. *Didn't these damn benches used to be more comfortable?* Crossing and uncrossing his legs, moving from side to side, he can barely keep from sliding off as he reads the paper and waits for the train.

Once on the train, finding a seat, settling in, looking up, he notices across the aisle a young woman, half his age, maybe mid-20s. When she catches his glance he looks away, but he can't help but look back. *She's dressed in a Middle Eastern-style head scarf, sleeveless Che Guevara t-shirt over a tactical corset, long cylinder necklace, short black skirt, torn fishnet stockings and knee-high hiking boots; her arms are covered in Maori tribal tattoos. He finds her as much curious as he does attractive; now looking back at her a third time, he even finds himself a bit uneasy.* And when she catches his glance once again, frowns and shifts in her seat, he's uneasier still.

Turning to look out the train window, he's able to avoid further embarrassment, but not further discomfort. The train's getting nearer the city and the sprawl of graffiti writing on the low walls bordering the tracks is increasing. He's noticed this before, he remembers, but he still doesn't understand it: *all this wildly unreadable* graffiti along the tracks, sometimes even on the bridges and control towers above the tracks. Maybe it's the graffiti, or the girl in the odd outfit, or the crime news in the newspaper, but he's feeling unsettled, unsure of himself, even a little angry.

Turning back, he's careful not to look over at the young woman, but no need; she got off the train while he was looking out of the window, at the previous stop, the one just a quarter of a mile before his.

In fact, by now she's already made her way through the train station and out into the street. As she walks towards her job, she's a bit annoyed herself, thinking about the jerk on the train, the one who kept staring at her, but she smiles when she thinks about the cylinder necklace swinging from her neck as she walks. It's her favourite, the one her mother gave her for dealing with guys like him: the *Pepperface Palm Defender pepper spray necklace*. Really, she'd have been happy with the plain silver one, or even the 18-carat gold version, but it was her birthday, so her mother got her the top of the line: the one encrusted with Swarovski crystals – and besides, it looks cool with the Che shirt.

Since she started working at the Starbucks last year, she's walked this route hundreds of times, and to fight off the boredom and the dread of getting to work she's made a game of seeing how many different graffiti tags she can spot. She's seen some of them so many times, on so many walls and alleyways, she feels like she knows the writers who leave them. *Scanning one alley for tags as she cuts through it, she notices two broken second-floor windows and laughs to herself – side by side like that, with the big jagged holes in each one, they look like two big bloodshot eyes staring back at her.* And come to think of it, after last night's binge-drinking session down at the pub, her eyes are probably a little bloodshot, too; once she gets to work, she tells herself, she'll grab a coffee while the manager isn't looking.

She checks her watch, afraid she'll be late for work again, and picks up her pace. Problem is, she used to have a couple of shortcuts – through the park by the school and then cutting between the grocery store and the *Skeletons in the Closet shop – but now the park gate stays locked most days and somebody has planted a prickly hedge between the two shops.*

By the time she gets to work – 10 minutes late – the guy from the train has already been at his desk for 20 minutes, having grabbed a cab out front of his train station. He's hard at the first task of the day, the first task of every work day: clearing emails from his inbox. *Pornographic come-ons, African money transfers, spurious bank requests for credit card information* – the company's spam filter isn't working very well. But what the hell, he thinks, while checking out a couple of the porn websites and deleting emails, *the company monitors employee keystrokes as a way of checking up on productivity,* so for all they know I'm working. What he doesn't know is that *the company also monitors and tracks web usage,* and as the corporate data log shows, this isn't his first visit to a porn site on company time.

Not that he really cares. Since the company began downsizing operations and exporting positions overseas, he's figured it's only a matter of time until his position goes as well. It's bad enough sitting in front of a computer all day, *bored out of your mind,* without having to worry about whether you'll be back to do it tomorrow. Deep in debt as well, he's starting to feel more than a bit lost. No wife, one of these days no job, nothing but bills to pay – makes a man miss the good times, *like that*

(Continued)

last holiday they had before the divorce. His daughter had wanted to go to Walt Disney World to check out the new MyMagic+ system, but instead they decided to holiday in Spain, where the tour guides kidnapped them and marched them into the mountains of Andalusia. He enjoyed it so much he's already planning next year's holiday – even if he has to go by himself – and he has it narrowed down to the LA Gang Tour, the Guerrilla Trek in Nepal or Jonestown in Guyana.

Daydreaming about Andalusia and Guyana and deleting unsolicited emails kills off the first hour of work, filling out the online forms for the company's upcoming internal audit kills another, and now it's time for a mid-morning coffee break. Before the downsizing started, there was always a pot of coffee down in the break room; you put a few coins in the donation jar and got yourself a cup of coffee, maybe had a chat with a colleague.

These days he goes to the Starbucks across the street from the office, but just for a change he decides to walk to the Starbucks a block over. Bad decision, since the young woman in the Che t-shirt works behind the counter there – except that she too has clocked out for a quick mid-morning break. No Starbucks coffee for her – she needs something stronger. She's looking for Cocaine.

'Hey', she says to the clerk in the little convenience store in the next block, walking back towards the checkout counter from the cold case. *'Where's the Cocaine?'*

'We're out', he tells her, his accent betraying his Iraqi heritage. 'Since they had it on *The Daily Show* we can't keep it in stock. Should have some tomorrow, sorry.'

'OK, well, thanks', and she's headed back to work – may as well just sneak another cup of company coffee.

His trip to Starbucks hasn't gone any better. Sure, he got his usual – double decaff latte – and it was as good as the one he gets at the other Starbucks; identical, in fact. But then he went over to the little park across the street to sit and enjoy it, and ... damn it, another butt-buster of a bench. Is there no decent place to sit left in this city?

Then, shifting uncomfortably on the bench and slurping his latte, all hell breaks loose. *This guy in a car tosses some fast food out into the street. A female bike courier grabs the food and tosses it back in, yelling 'don't litter in my neighbourhood'. He jumps out, throws two coffees at her and now he's stomping on her bike and they start scuffling. Some guys come off the sidewalk and pull him off of her. Meanwhile, another dude with a camera just keeps shooting – but when he tries to photograph the car's licence plate, the guy from the car opens the trunk, grabs a baseball bat and charges him.*

Christ, he thinks to himself, the whole damn world is falling apart. *It's like that film with Michael Douglas, you know, where he's lost his job and people are messing with him and trying to rob him and ... what's the name of that film?*

Back at the office he Googles for a while, trying to track down the film title – more Internet misuse for the company log. Giving up, he begrudgingly gets back to the audit forms, which drag him through the afternoon in a sort of slow death march towards quitting time.

At the Starbucks, a steady stream of latte and espresso orders has dragged her through the afternoon as well, but with at least a bit of excitement. Around 3.00 pm she got suspicious of two girls lingering near the counter; one of them had an open book bag and it looked to her like they were trying to shoplift a coffee press. *So she and the assistant manager went out from behind the counter, smiling and asking the girls if they could help them with anything and then kept chatting with them until they left the store. And as the girls left, she noticed something odd: a little black orb attached to the other girl's LED-covered purse. Odd indeed – but not as odd as that day last month when a bunch of people walked in and just started taking fruit and muffins off the counter and eating them, like it was a picnic or something, without even attempting to pay.*

Work day now over, she's walking back to the train station when she notices that *the FCUK (French Connection UK) clothing store has changed its display window since she walked past this morning. It now features skinny female mannequins, dressed in the latest FCUK designs, shoving and throwing punches at each other.*

Backing away from the window to get a better look at the tableau of stylized sex and violence, she bumps into someone behind her and turns around.

Son of a bitch, it's that jerk from the train this morning! The FCUK window fresh in her mind, scared and mad that maybe he's been stalking her all day, a bit embarrassed for bumping into him, she reaches for her Pepperface pepper spray necklace, fumbles with it for a moment, gets her finger onto the spray button – but by this time he's backpedalling, arms out, palms up, saying, 'sorry, sorry' – and in a flash he's disappeared into the crowd on the sidewalk.

Plate 4.1   FCUK shop window, Canterbury, England

Credit: Photographs by Jeff Ferrell and Keith Hayward (2006)

(Continued)

(Continued)

Disappeared into the crowd indeed – he couldn't be more mortified. To be honest, yeah, he'd been fantasizing a little while looking at those sexy mannequins in the FCUK window, and then all of a sudden that girl from the train – a real girl, the real girl he had checked out on the train this morning – was right in his face. Very weird moment, very scary, very embarrassing – and it wasn't the first odd moment on the walk back to the train station from work. *There was also that bus stop shelter with the odd words and images in place of the usual advertisements.*

Calming down, getting to the train station, checking the organizer on his phone, he's reminded that Friday is his ex-wife's birthday; their daughter lives with her, so he likes to stay in touch. Early for the train, he dips into the Hallmark card shop in the arcade next door. Browsing the cards, he can't find one he likes, but then he spots a card that, well, just seems perfect for her, for their fucked-up relationship and for the day he's had. 'So, anyway, I'm standing in line to buy a freakin' birthday card', the cover of the card begins, 'and the line is like seventeen billion people long'.

After a few more verses of this, the cover concludes with 'and I just really hope you like this card'.

And then when you open the card, inside it says, 'Cause I stole it. Happy Birthday'.

That gets him laughing a little and on the train ride home he relaxes and realizes he's hungry, so he buys a prawn sandwich and a Coke – but, he thinks to himself, I'd better not let that vegan punk daughter of mine know about the sandwich. *According to her, even a prawn sandwich is a crime.*

So when he gets off the train at his local station, he's careful to toss the uneaten half of the sandwich and the Coke can into the station trash receptacle – and *not five minutes later one of the many dishevelled folks who hang around the edges of the station is just as careful to extricate from the trash the half sandwich, the Coke can – and a brand new designer scarf that someone's thrown away.*

On the walk home he's still thinking about his daughter – worrying about her, that is. It's bad enough she got arrested last year for yelling animal-rights slogans at the McDonald's assistant manager; now she's in trouble at school as well. Last month, *the school counsellor advised him and his ex-wife that their daughter seems driven to take risks, to push her own limits, to test herself and her teachers.* The counsellor even told them that the school psychologist had diagnosed his daughter as suffering from ODD, Oppositional Defiant Disorder, a pathological disregard for school and parental authority. Wait a minute, he thinks to himself, maybe that explains the girl on the train, the one who confronted him in front of the FCUK window – maybe she has ODD, too. But back to his daughter: after he heard all this from the school counsellor, he got so concerned that he bought his daughter a new cell phone, one with a GPS device so he could track her movements. But that only ended up worrying him more – one time he tracked her down across town at some sort of illegal street race. One of these days, he worries to himself, I'm going to find her with that bunch of damn 'chavs' that hangs out down at the end of the road.

Home now, he heats some leftovers and plops down in his big easy chair, surfing TV channels while he eats. *It's the same old stuff – murder mysteries, police procedurals, surveillance camera compilations –* but it keeps him occupied for a couple of hours anyway.

So, after taking two of those sleeping pills they advertise on TV, reactivating the home alarm system, setting his bedside alarm and falling into bed, he's able to drift off to sleep easily enough. But then the nightmare comes. It's not that half-awake film noir moment he had this morning; its worse – a surreal mashup of a day in the life. It's some kind of funeral, with everyone sitting around the coffin on tiny, hard benches. Fast-food wrappers and coffee cups cover the ground, cover the feet of the mourners, crawl up their legs. And there's his daughter, away from everyone else, dressed in a head scarf and a long shiny necklace. But wait a minute, now he's covered in coffee cups and he's in the coffin, his head split clean in two by the blow from a baseball bat. And the girl from the train, she's dead too, lying next to him in the coffin.

Except she's not dead. She made it home just like he did and now she's asleep next to her girlfriend. They went to bed early. Just out after doing six months on a marijuana possession charge, her girlfriend has to make an 8.00 am appointment with her parole supervisor, and she has her 9.00 am cultural criminology class at university. She's majoring in criminology and helping to pay tuition with the Starbuck's job – though she's still managing to run up one hell of a student loan debt.

In fact, she's dreaming too, her dream mixing images of her girlfriend and her major. *In the dream she's reaching for her girlfriend, trying to pull her through some sort of wall, but she can't keep her grip and she fades away, receding into the innards of the American penal gulag, disappearing into the million other prisoners for whom a day in the life is something very different indeed.*

Interrogating the everyday

Just another day in the life of two people making their way between home and work; a little unpleasantness here and there, some petty criminality – but nothing of any importance, no real violence, no crimes of politics or passion, no big police crime sweep through a dangerous neighbourhood. So to tell such a story, and to pay attention to it, is to stay safely away from the big issues of crime and social control, tucked securely inside the cultural minutiae of the mundane.

Or is it? A cultural criminology of the story – that is, an interrogation of the story in search of meaning – reveals something more. Carefully considered, this story – constructed, it will be recalled, only from existing everyday events – in fact reveals global shifts and historical trends monumental in their meaning. If we look carefully, we can see the ways in which transgression increasingly comes to be commodified and contained within late-capitalist economies. We can see something of social control and the way in which contemporary mechanisms of social control are morphed, masked, coded and reinvented. We can notice that these forms of social control, already troublesome in their insidiousness, are in turn cut and mixed with emerging patterns of legal containment and surveillance – and then, for good measure, marketed to the public under the guise of public safety, even freedom of choice. If we look carefully enough, we may even see the future – and decide, as have others, to confront and change it.

Black iron burglar bars, ADT Security sign

From the view of cultural criminology, burglar bars and home security systems provide more than a hardened home target; they offer evidence of the pervasive, politically useful late-modern fear of victimization by outsiders and invaders. They also provide everyday evidence of the billion-dollar home security industries that promote, and profit from, precisely this fear (Hayward, 2004: 128–37; Goold et al., 2010).

Home security signs, burglar bars, high fences and other domestic fortifications also become signs in another sense, constructing the home as a text to be 'read' by neighbours, passers-by and potential intruders (Pow, 2013). The 'angry lawns' and armed homesteads that Mike Davis (1990) documents betray the modernist mythology of domesticity, of the home as a pleasant refuge from the dislocated stress of everyday life.

And yet even fear and fortification are not without their aesthetics. In the USA, home security businesses seldom advertise 'burglar bars'; instead, they advertise and sell *decorative* burglar bars that can, as one real estate website notes, 'enhance, or at least not detract from, the appearance of the home' (www.real-estate-agents.com).

He uses his credit card to buy another paper

Under the coordinated corporate conditions of late modernity, the simplest of credit card purchases adds information to a massive, integrated web of databases harbouring information on consumer preferences, population movement and personal habits. Significantly, such databases not only enable corporate surveillance of individuals, but accumulate information tapped by legal authorities as part of the 'war on terror' or other social control campaigns. As Katja Franko Aas (2006) has shown, even the human body becomes a source of information and surveillance under such conditions, what with DNA databases, biometric passports and mandatory drug testing (Tunnell, 2004).

Nathan Garvis, vice president of government affairs at Target, one of America's largest retailers, has offered an unusually candid account of the logic underlying this surveillance process. Assigned by Target to explore possibilities for helping the criminal justice system become more efficient, Garvis came to realize that tracking criminals 'was really an inventory-management problem'. So, tapping into Target's already widespread affiliations with law enforcement, the company donated tracking technology and began to take 'a lead role in teaching government agencies how to fight crime by applying state-of-the-art technology used in its 1,400 stores'. The company also 'donates' its employees to law enforcement agencies, provides money to prosecutor's offices, coordinates police undercover operations and does extensive pro bono work for local, state, federal and international law enforcement agencies. Much of this work occurs at the company's own state-of-the-art forensics lab – 'one of the nation's top forensics labs', according to FBI Special Agent Paul McCabe. Target likewise runs a 'Safe City' programme that 'uses video and computer equipment to help police patrol neighbourhoods by remote control, coordinated with security workers at participating businesses' (Bridges, 2006: A1).

Seamlessly interweaving inventory control with social control, Target translates both the ideology and technology of corporate consumerism into the practice of late-modern policing. And just as distinctions between product and person are lost, so are the rights of the accused and the presumption of innocence, with Target apparently feeling no compulsion to make similar donations to defence attorneys, public defenders or databases tracking the wrongly convicted. 'Fascism' isn't a word we use lightly – but certainly this is late-modern fascism, consumer fascism, an incestuous integration of corporate control and political authority in the interest of tracking individuals and constructing cities safe for consumption.

Soon, perhaps, Target's databases will even be able to make the consumers run on time.

CCTV cameras

The UK is the undisputed leader in urban closed-circuit television provision, or CCTV, with more surveillance cameras in the UK than in the rest of Europe combined. As a result, many people in the UK accept the intrusion of panoptic camera technology into everyday life. Likewise, the small US city of Lancaster, Pennsylvania, is watched over by some 165 CCTV cameras, themselves run by a private group and monitored by civilians. 'Years ago, there's no way we could do this', says the town's police chief. 'It's just funny how Americans have softened on these issues.' Adds a local business owner: 'There's nothing wrong with instilling fear' (Drogin, 2009: A1, A11). Many US stores employ cameras to track and manipulate consumer behaviour and US cities employ gunshot-detection systems (that also pick up public conversations). Canadian airports are now equipped with microphones to record travellers' conversations, while in cities like Baltimore and San Francisco, transit authorities are quietly rolling out microphone-enabled surveillance systems on public buses that give them the ability to record and store private conversations. In Brazil, school uniforms embedded with computer chips now track students in and out of school.

With CCTV and other surveillance technologies seeping into virtually every aspect of day-to-day life, though, a cultural transformation is taking place; surveillance is becoming not just commonplace and acceptable, but at times cool, fashionable, even aspirational. CCTV is now used by everyone from artists (see the surveillance-inspired works of Julia Scher, Kyle McDonald and Marko Peljhan) to advertisers (a recent jeans promotion asked, 'You are on a video camera 10 times a day. Are you dressed for it?'), restaurant and bar designers and prime-time TV shows.

Here, we see an emerging relationship between society and surveillance that transcends sensations of safety and reassurance associated with established security products, while consigning civil liberty anxieties to the obsolescent register of early modernity. This is a world where *Big Brother* is only ironic and *Real World* just unreal, a world where non-stop surveillance becomes a source of pleasure, profit and entertainment.

Yet, while cameras may add a sense of voyeuristic or performative satisfaction to the 'lifestyle' social environment, they alone cannot build closely-knit communities or vibrant, pluralistic public spaces. On this point, it is interesting to reflect on the differing approaches to CCTV in the UK and continental Europe. In the UK, CCTV is typically the first step in attempting to 'galvanize' run-down communities, an approach that illustrates the extent to which regulation has been resituated as 'community', or more accurately a form of sanitized inclusion. Meanwhile, in countries like Italy and Spain, where community and family ties remain strong in regional towns, the demand for surveillance is almost non-existent.

Didn't these damn benches used to be more comfortable?

Yes, they did. As part of the CPTED (Crime Prevention Through Environmental Design) strategy in the USA and similar strategies of spatial crime control in the UK and elsewhere, public spaces are regularly remade as less comfortable and less welcoming to those who might linger, or loiter, or fail to consume, or commit a public offence. These strategies include rebuilding public seating in ways that disincline long-term sitting and prevent reclining, and installing ground spikes and sprinkler systems to banish homeless folks and rough sleepers. In this way, ideologies of control, surveillance and exclusion come to be built, quite literally, into the everyday environment.

She's dressed in a Middle Eastern-style head scarf, sleeveless Che Guevara t-shirt over a tactical corset, long cylinder necklace, short black skirt, torn fishnet stockings and knee-high hiking boots; her arms are covered in Maori tribal tattoos. He finds her as much curious as he does attractive; now looking back at her a third time, he even finds himself a bit uneasy

The liquidity of late modernity, the global flow of production and consumption, can be glimpsed in the bricolage of styles that constitute everyday 'fashion' and especially 'street fashion' as invented and displayed in large metropolitan areas.

Under such conditions, meaning comes loose from its original moorings; specific styles and images re-emerge as free-floating references to be re-sewn into individual and group style. Che Guevara, the 1950s Latin American revolutionary, has long since been reborn as a cultural icon and fashion accessory; along London's trendy Kensington High Street in the 1980s, the *Che* clothing shop sold the latest in mass-marketed apparel and today *The Che Store* (www.thechestore.com) markets t-shirts and berets 'for all your revolutionary needs'. The 'tactical corset' is a stylized and sexualized piece of body armour for women, one of many popular bulletproof/body armour clothing items that are now claimed to be the sartorial 'expression of a defensive mind-set intensified of late by concerns about terrorism, escalating crime rates [sic] and economic instability' (La Ferla, 2010: E7).

This late-modern mélange of meaning is not without its consequences. In what remains the definitive analysis of such stylized displays, Dick Hebdige (1979: 90) cautions us not to 'underestimate the signifying power of the spectacular subculture ... as an actual mechanism of semantic disorder: a kind of temporary blockage in the system of representation'. So while her outfit evacuates the political meaning of Latin American revolutionaries or Maori tattoos, it nonetheless retains the power to cause uneasiness, even upheaval, for those who witness it – or attempt to police it.

Still, those Maori tattoos do constitute, on closer inspection, a particularly spectacular fraud. They're actually not tattoos at all, but rather part of a line of sheer mesh tattooed shirts and sleeves, marketed by Canadian fashion designer Susan Setz, that fool the observer into thinking that their wearer is indeed tattooed.

Criminologist Wayne Morrison (2004b: 76) would be particularly amused by these ersatz Maori tattoos, dislocated from the Maori and even from the skin itself. As he has shown, Cesare Lombroso, founding father of criminological positivism, had already stolen away their meaning 125 years before, reducing them to 'the true writing of the savage' and equating them – erroneously – with common criminality.

All this wildly unreadable graffiti along the tracks, sometimes even on the bridges and control towers above the tracks

Graffiti is one of the most pervasive and visible crimes of late modernity, decorating and defacing walls, buildings and bridges throughout the USA, South America, Great Britain, Europe, the Middle East and elsewhere. Its forms are as varied as the subcultures of those who write it. Entangled on walls and buildings, these various forms of graffiti make for yet another mélange of uncertain meaning, encoding urban space with the pluralism of late-modern life. But amidst this swarm of signification, a few things are likely, though not certain:

- If our train passenger found the graffiti particularly widespread and largely unreadable, it was probably what was once called hip hop graffiti, now mostly just called 'graff', a highly stylized form of non-gang-affiliated public painting through which graffiti 'writers' compete and communicate.
- If our passenger did get a bit angry or uneasy upon seeing graffiti, that was likely mostly the result of mediated anti-graffiti campaigns that work to define the *meaning* of graffiti by intentionally confounding gang graffiti with 'graff' and other graffiti forms, and by spuriously associating graffiti with violent assault and rape.
- And if our passenger thinks that he's surely seen all the graffiti there is to see, he's surely wrong – since as the recent Underbelly Project hid and then revealed, there are whole cathedrals of unknown street art and graffiti *below* the city, too (Ferrell, 1996, 2013b; Snyder, 2009; Workhorse and PAC, 2012).

Plate 4.2 The Underbelly Project

Dazed and confused

We might hope that the authors of criminological textbooks devoted to the scholarly analysis of juvenile delinquency would clarify distinctions lost in the media-induced confusion over the types and consequences of youthful graffiti. Put differently, we might hope that students of criminology would come to know more about urban graffiti than the average train rider or newspaper reader. In most cases, that hope would be unfounded. In fact, far from addressing such issues, many juvenile delinquency textbooks perpetuate the confusion – and display their confusion on their covers for all to see.

One 1990s textbook presents on its cover what appears to be an image of early hip hop graffiti, circa 1980 or so – but it's difficult to know since hip hop graffiti doesn't appear in the table of contents, text or index (Jensen and Rojek, 1992). Bynum and Thompson's mid-1990s (1996: 288–90, 473) *Juvenile Delinquency: A Sociological Approach* likewise offers the student a cover apparently composed of computer-generated graffiti-style markings; inside is a short section dealing only with gang graffiti, and a glossary entry that defines 'graffiti' exclusively as 'the distinctive language/symbolism of street gangs'. By the seventh edition a decade later (Bynum and Thompson, 2007), a new, more stylish cover reproduces a section of a hip hop graffiti mural, the book's front page shows another sophisticated mural, chapter introductions and summaries repeat these hip hop images – and the errors of the text and glossary remain unchanged. The fifth edition of Bartollas's (2000) *Juvenile Delinquency* features as its cover an aesthetically stunning wall of multi-coloured hip hop graffiti murals and tags – and no mention whatsoever of hip hop graffiti in the table of contents, text, glossary or index. A more recent seventh edition (Bartollas, 2006: 112, 134) has replaced this cover with a drawing of a young man holding a spray can and painting a wall of non-specific graffiti. Inside, the book includes a photo of a young man painting hip hop graffiti, as an illustration of 'destruction of property' and Cohen's 'reaction formation'; another uncaptioned photo of a young Latina holding a gun in front of a wall covered in assorted tags and markings; and still, no mention of hip hop graffiti in the table of contents, text, glossary or index. Schmalleger and Bartollas's (2008) *Juvenile Delinquency* comes with a cover featuring a darkly atmospheric photograph of hip hop graffiti murals painted on trains. From the look of the trains and the graffiti, it might be New York City or Philadelphia in 1980, maybe London five years later, but we'll never know – the book omits graffiti from its table of contents, text and index. Bartollas and Schmalleger's (2011) *Juvenile Delinquency* (ninth edition) doesn't discuss graffiti in the text, either, but does wrap layered, multi-coloured graffiti markings around the front and back covers – with the graffiti's paint drips flowing upwards, apparently the result of an unnoticed upside-down image.

Other textbooks replicate this discordance between cover and content. The covers of both Struckhoff's (2006) *Annual Editions: Juvenile Delinquency and Justice* and Burfeind and Bartusch's (2006) *Juvenile Delinquency* present a young man with a spray can in front of hip hop-style graffiti, but neither manages to integrate an analysis of hip hop graffiti into the book itself. An image of non-specific graffiti adorns the cover of Regoli and Hewitt's (2006) *Delinquency in Society*, and is repeated as a background

(Continued)

(Continued)

image inside the book, yet the book neither explores nor indexes youthful graffiti. The book's eighth edition (Regoli et al., 2010) is awash in graffiti images – front and back covers, chapter introduction pages, even a 'special topics' section that begins with the same photo used on the cover of Burfeind and Bartusch (2006) – but omits graffiti from the table of contents, index and text, save for one sentence on gang graffiti and turf. While Springer and Roberts' (2011) edited collection, *Juvenile Justice and Delinquency*, superimposes on its cover dripping paint in front of a forlorn, hoodied youth sitting beneath a three-dimensional hip hop graffiti wall, none of its 21 chapters focuses on such a situation. Likewise, Bartollas and Miller's (2014) *Juvenile Justice in America* (seventh edition) superimposes the silhouettes of five young men over a wall-sized hip hop graffiti mural, but ignores this sort of phenomenon in its text.

Most dramatically, Whitehead and Lab's (2006: 125) *Juvenile Justice* wraps a spectacular example of a hip hop graffiti mural around both its front and back covers, literally encasing the book in an explosion of hip hop style and colour, and then fails spectacularly to engage with its own image. Out of its 472 pages of text, the book dedicates five lines to graffiti, under the heading 'Gang behavior and types of gangs'.[1]

We well understand that textbook cover decisions are made as much by publishers as by authors; as Burns and Katovich (2006: 111) noted in their study of melodramatic images in introductory criminal justice texts, 'the highly competitive textbook market … influences textbook design'. Yet, these graffiti covers, when affixed to books that consistently fail to address the complexity of graffiti forms – that in many cases fail to address youthful graffiti at all – constitute a form of intellectual fraud. It's not only that the books fail to deliver what their covers promise; in many cases, by juxtaposing hip hop graffiti images with discussions of gang graffiti, they reinforce the very misperceptions we might hope they would dispel. Ironically, while the repeated use of such covers tacitly acknowledges the aesthetic power of hip hop graffiti to startle and engage, the texts turn away from this engagement, ignoring the most publicly visible and aesthetically meaningful form of juvenile delinquency. Having mischaracterized graffiti in both image and analysis, Bynum and Thompson (1996: 228; 2007: 347) note that 'an understanding of graffiti is very important to law enforcement officers'.

It's very important to students, too.

Pepperface Palm Defender pepper spray necklace

'We've heard all the stats about rape and other violent attacks', writes Alyson Ward (2006: 3G) in a newspaper article breathlessly endorsing the new Pepperface Palm Defender, 'But how many of us are really carrying around a clunky canister of pepper spray?'

The solution is the Palm Defender. Its manufacturer, Ward explains, 'is turning personal safety into fashion … In fact, it hopes we'll start to think of it the way we think of our cell phones or MP3 players – as a useful *and* pretty necessity we carry everywhere'. Best of all, 'one shot will incapacitate an attacker for at least half an hour. Which gives you a chance to run, girl'.

Of course, if Ward had *really* read the stats, she'd remind her readers that the most important place to wear the Palm Defender would be around the house, since women remain far more likely to be victimized by acquaintances or intimate partners than by strangers. But no matter – the real issue here is the aesthetic consumption of crime prevention. No unsightly bulges from clunky cans of pepper spray or large concealed weapons – the stylishly hardened target prefers the Palm Defender or maybe one of the smaller, sleeker handguns that American weapons manufacturers now market to women, the 'smaller, lighter, jazzed up guns for girls' that sport fine detailing and 24-carat gold gilding (Ulrich, 2006). Twenty-four carat gold comes standard with designer Ted Noten's pistol compacts, too, which also include 'lip gloss in the muzzle, pills (including Viagra) in the loading chamber ... and a 4-gigabyte thumb drive' (Phillips, 2011: ST3) – all for just $17,000.

Coming soon to a shop near you: the new line of ultra-slender stilettos for the stylish woman – and we don't mean high heels.

You go, girl.

Scanning one alley for tags as she cuts through it, she notices two broken second-floor windows and laughs to herself – side by side like that, with the big jagged holes in each one, they look like two big bloodshot eyes staring back at her

Actually, she shouldn't be laughing – at least not according to one popular criminological model.

Perhaps the most politically prominent approach to crime over the last few decades has been Wilson and Kelling's (2003[1982]: 402–4) 'broken windows' model of crime causation. Utilized as the scholarly reference point for a range of reactionary, punitive public policing strategies since its emergence in the 1980s, 'broken windows' is often seen as a straight-ahead, no-nonsense approach to crime control. In reality, it is a deeply *aesthetic* analysis of crime's etiology – and a deeply flawed analysis as well. According to this model, broken windows and similar public displays of neglect and petty criminality function as symbolic invitations to further criminality, in that they 'signal that no one cares' or perhaps 'seem to signal that "no one cares"'. Likewise, 'such otherwise harmless displays as subway graffiti' communicate to subway riders the 'inescapable knowledge that the environment ... is uncontrolled and uncontrollable'. In such cases, Wilson and Kelling argue, 'residents will think that crime ... is on the rise', potential criminals will perceive these signs of inattention as encouragements to accelerated misbehaviour and a downward spiral of disorder will be set in motion. Claiming in this way to engage issues of image, public display and perception, 'broken windows' stands or falls on its aesthetic analysis of crime.

It falls.

A useful justification for the conservative clampdown on everyday 'quality of life' crimes like graffiti writing and panhandling, a pseudo-theoretical pretext for aggressively policing marginalized urban populations, the model is decidedly less useful as an aesthetic of crime. Imagining the contours of symbolism and perception rather than investigating them, the model constructs a series of abstract, one-dimensional meanings that it arbitrarily assigns to dislocated images and idealized audiences. In fact, as any city-dweller knows, the symbolic texture of the urban landscape is far more ambiguous and complex. To the extent that a 'broken window' functions as a symbol, for example, it may symbolize any manner of activities to any number of audiences, depending on situation and context: community resistance to absentee ownership, a personal grudge, the failure of local code enforcement, the illicit accommodation of the homeless or a nearby baseball game. Likewise, depending on particulars of content and context, gang graffiti may symbolize a neighbourhood's intergenerational history, suggest changing patterns of ethnic occupation or conflict, or even enforce a degree of community self-policing. A proliferation of stylized non-gang graffiti (a distinction ignored by Wilson and Kelling) may likewise suggest a *decline* in criminal violence – that is, it may lead some neighbourhood residents to understand that gang crime is on the decline – and in fact may harbinger a less violent social order now negotiated through the very symbols that Wilson and Kelling so tellingly misrepresent (Sanchez-Tranquilino, 1995; Ferrell, 1996; Phillips, 1999; D. Miller, 2001; Snyder, 2009).

So a man on a train may find a display of graffiti perplexing, a woman on the way to work may find broken windows amusing, and others will engage still different perceptions of the urban environment. As cultural criminologists, our job is to investigate this environment and these perceptions, to explore these various meanings – not, as with Wilson and Kelling, to impose our own constipated perceptions in the service of the state.

James Q. Wilson and the Strange Case of the Undermined Obituary

When James Q. Wilson died in 2012, his obituary made the front page of *The New York Times* (Weber, 2012: A1, B8). Not surprisingly, the lengthy obituary featured his 'best known' and most influential work: the broken windows model of crime perception and crime control. A few pages deeper into that same day's *New York Times*, another story stood in direct contradiction, its content negating the claims promulgated on the front page. It seems that graffiti in the form of stencilled red goats had begun to appear in Kingston, New York, and had quickly spread across the USA and Canada. Some citizens and city authorities in Kingston condemned the goats as vandalism; other citizens and city officials embraced them as art. Eventually, the goats became so popular that the Kingston mayor found them 'good for

Kingston's image' and the local newspaper wrote an editorial endorsing them as 'a great symbol' (Applebome, 2012: A15). But it was the article's title that perhaps most succinctly cancelled Wilson's certainty as to graffiti's singularly negative meaning and revealed the interpretive ambiguity inherent in the urban environment: 'How graffiti goats', it said, 'became a symbol of … something.'

Skeletons in the Closet shop

There exists a thriving retail market for the weapons and personal belongings of murderers and other criminals past and present, with some pieces bringing hundreds of thousands of dollars at auction; as one report notes, 'evidence of violent death does seem to increase appeal and prices' (Kahn, 2012: C24; see also Vinciguerra, 2011). Old mug shots from the 1950s are also selling well, and at the Skeletons in the Closet shop operated by the Los Angeles County Department of Coroner, toe tags can be snagged for just five dollars each, when they're not sold out (Medina, 2010; Rosen, 2011).

But now the park gate stays locked most days and somebody has planted a prickly hedge between the two shops

In the late-capitalist city, public spaces – parks, city squares, play areas – are increasingly privatized in the interest of economic development and social control; as Randall Amster (2004, 2008) has shown, even city sidewalks are made private and so made unavailable for public activity. Similarly, that new prickly hedge wasn't the gardener's idea; it was suggested by the environmental design security consultant or the neighbourhood police officer. Among today's environmental strategies for regulating human movement in urban areas is 'barrier planting' (Ferrell, 2001/2: 5–6) – the planting of shrubs and bushes with the potential to impale those who might seek out shortcuts. As it turns out, the politics of the everyday are present even in the flora.

Pornographic come-ons, African money transfers, spurious bank requests for credit card information

The sociologist Gary Marx (1995) has noted that 'new telecommunications technologies require new manners'. With each new advance in the technology of mediated communication, a new *culture* of communication must emerge as well, a new set of interactional codes and symbolic manners appropriate to the technology. The structural grammar of the written letter gives way to the casual speed of email; the expectation of response generated by the phone message differs from that of an email message; the symbolic codes of the instant message compress and abbreviate in relation to the compressed size and speed of the technology itself.

New technologies require new crimes as well, and new crime cultures. A mailed letter offering easy cash offers one kind of enticement, an email message promising an African money transfer another. With the email and its attachment, the recipient's information can be phished more deeply and more quickly – if only the sender can utilize appropriate symbols and markers so as to convince the recipient of honest intentions or emergency need. Of course, the intended victims of such crimes themselves learn new manners, new safeguards against identity theft or consumer fraud, from their own experience and from each other.

We might even say that every technology gets the crime it deserves.

The company monitors employee keystrokes as a way of checking up on productivity ... the company also monitors and tracks web usage

New technologies spawn new forms of control, too – forms of surveillance today built into advancing communication technologies as surely as spatial controls are built into the reconstructed social environment. Among these are hard-drive searches, keystroke monitors, 'spyware' and screen-view software, enabling remote viewing of home and commercial computer screens in real time. 'However, as with all forms of surveillance', Richard Jones notes, 'the more knowledgeable the person (potentially) under surveillance is about the surveillance practices likely to be used against them, the more strategies they can employ to try to evade surveillance' (2005: 484; see also 2000).

Bored out of your mind

As we've documented elsewhere (Ferrell, 2004a; see also Bengtsson, 2012), boredom seems one of the definitive experiences of late modernity; kids complain of it, workers hunker down and endure it, and activists of all sorts cite it as the condition against which they agitate and organize. Built into the assembly line and office cubicle as surely as the fast-food outlet and the school curriculum, boredom pervades the everyday operations of a rationalized social order. Even those avenues that promise an escape from the tedium of the everyday – televised entertainments, new music releases, theme parks and adventure tours – themselves quickly become routine, ultimately little more than predictable packages of commodified experience.

In this sense, boredom calibrates, second by awful second, the experience of drudgery in the late-modern world. As a cultural artifact, it likewise measures the gap between the late-modern promise of fulfilling work and the reality of a deskilled service economy, the gap between the breathless marketing of individual excitement and the delivery of fast-fried McEmotions. From a Mertonian view, boredom emerges from strain, from human expectation and experience straining against the false promises of late modernity. And as Merton (1938) would predict, this strain – this desire for desire, to paraphrase Tolstoy – can lead to all manner of illicit adaptations.

Like that last holiday they had before the divorce. His daughter had wanted to go to Walt Disney World to check out the new MyMagic+ system, but instead they decided to holiday in Spain, where the tour guides kidnapped them and marched them into the mountains of Andalusia. He enjoyed it so much he's already planning next year's holiday – even if he has to go by himself – and he has it narrowed down to three possibilities: the LA Gang Tour, the Guerrilla Trek in Nepal or a visit to Jonestown in Guyana.

With Disney's new MyMagic+ system, patrons wear MagicBand rubber bracelets encoded with credit card information and other personal data that enable Disney to 'track guest behaviour in minute detail' (Barnes, 2013: B1, B7), and that allow Disney characters, by way of hidden sensors, to offer personalized greetings to individual guests.

Playing on the romanticized mythology of the nineteenth-century Spanish *bandolero* (bandit), Spain's Bandolero Tours offer full-day or half-day kidnappings (100 or 50 euros, respectively), in which tourists pay to be kidnapped, taken into the Andalusian mountains and there 'regaled with legends about great *bandoleros*' (Abend, 2006: V2) before being returned. In Nepal, one company offers a Guerrilla Trek that allows holiday trekkers 'to follow in the steps of Maoist fighters' who fought during the country's decade-long conflict (Horton, 2011: 46). For $65 (lunch included) and a signed liability waiver, LA Gangland Tours in Los Angeles takes customers on a tour of 'high-profile gang areas and the top crime-scene locations', and even offers a graffiti workshop (SideTour in New York City also offers graffiti classes) (Archibald, 2010: A1; Harris, 2011). 'Poverty tours' and 'slum tours' likewise offer vacationers access to Brazilian favelas and South African slums (Freire-Medeiros, 2012), and 'reality adventures' provide clients interactive experiences with 'players posing as homeless people' (Weiner, 2011: 46). Mexico's Hnahnu Indians offer a *caminata nocturna* – a night-time hike – for tourists wishing to replicate the experience of illegally crossing the Rio Grande River into the USA (Healy, 2007); complete with pursuit by faux Border Patrol agents and a substitute river, a *caminata* is a bargain at just 200 pesos (US$11). But perhaps the most disturbingly haunting repackaging of historic violence as holiday entertainment is the proposed 'dark tourism' redevelopment of the decaying Jonestown, Guyana site, where more than 900 followers of Jim Jones were murdered or committed suicide in 1978. Then again, as one local hotelier noted, 'what this area really needs is a casino' (in Romero, 2010: A6).

Where's the Cocaine?

A competitor in the growing, youth-oriented 'energy drink' market, Cocaine comes in red cans with the drink's name written in what appear to be lines of white powder. Name and can alike in this way reference both the drug cocaine and the drink Coca-Cola or Coke. But whereas Coca-Cola/Coke did in its early years contain significant amounts of cocaine, Cocaine the energy drink doesn't. Instead, it contains 280 milligrams of caffeine, more than enough to contribute to the growing phenomenon that doctors label youthful 'caffeine abuse'.

We have some questions. Is the product's provocative name mostly a matter of marketing commodified transgression to kids? (Yes.) Has the controversy surrounding the drink helped promote it and cement its outlaw image? (Yes.) And how is it that Coke, a drink that in fact did once contain cocaine, is now the sanitized soft drink of choice for mid-America, and Cocaine, a drink that has never contained cocaine, is now the edgiest of drinks for the young and the restless?

In other drugs-as-image news, 'illustrious devotees' of the Morphine Generation clothing line include Brad Pitt, Scarlett Johansson and Lindsay Lohan (Vesilind, 2008), and the Internet abounds with recipes for drinks like 'liquid cocaine', 'liquid crack' and 'liquide heroine [sic]', all containing copious amounts of liquor and no cocaine, crack or heroin. Little image-covered glassine packets often do, though, and so a group of artists has staged a 'Heroin Stamp Project' show featuring hundreds of empty heroin packets picked up off the streets. Designed 'to examine the intersection of advertising and addiction' (Moynihan, 2010: C1), the show includes packets stamped with cultural references like White Fang, Last Temptation and Tango and Cash.

This guy in a car tosses some fast food out into the street. A female bike courier grabs the food and tosses it back in, yelling 'don't litter in my neighbourhood'. He jumps out, throws two coffees at her and now he's stomping on her bike and they start scuffling. Some guys come off the sidewalk and pull him off of her. Meanwhile, another dude with a camera just keeps shooting – but when he tries to photograph the car's licence plate, the guy from the car opens the trunk, grabs a baseball bat and charges him

This incidence of urban conflict exploded in Toronto's crowded Kensington Market a few years back. Happening on the scene, photographer Adam Krawesky began shooting photos of it – but that was only the first turn in a spiral of crime and culture. When he posted the photos to the CityNoise website (Krawesky, 2006; www.citynoise.org), thousands of responses began to pour in, and in no time the photos and the story had been picked up by countless other websites and blogs. Meanwhile, a daily newspaper, the *Toronto Star*, published three of the photos without Krawesky's permission as part of a feature article on the street conflict, the photos and the web responses to both (Powell, 2006). By this time, Krawesky was getting calls from national and international media, working with another daily newspaper, and, as he told us, learning about the power of mediated images to mislead and mythologize (Krawesky, 2006). After all, he emphasized, he hadn't even been able to photograph the entire incident – and yet people around the world were now sure they understood it, sure of their opinions about it, sure they could make sense of it by referencing street justice, or gender conflict, or similar scenes in the Hollywood film *Crash* (Dir. Paul Haggis, 2004).

Plate 4.3   An image of urban conflict

Credit: Adam Krawesky (2006), by permission

It's like that film with Michael Douglas, you know, where he's lost his job and people are messing with him and trying to rob him and ... what's the name of that film?

The name of that film is *Falling Down* (1993), directed by Joel Schumacher and starring Michael Douglas and Robert Duvall. Films such as these capture something of the late-modern vertigo that plagues the once-secure middle classes; perhaps they exacerbate that vertigo as well.

So she and the assistant manager went out from behind the counter, smiling and asking the girls if they could help them with anything, and chatted with them until they left the store

A while back, Jeff Ferrell scrounged a *Gap Loss Prevention Manual* from a trash bin behind a Gap clothing store. The manual emphasizes to employees that 'customer service' is the best guard against shoplifting and other theft-related 'shortage', since 'great service keeps our customers coming back and shoplifters from coming in'. The manual offers specific suggestions for customer service as crime prevention – 'extend a warm hello to customers and offer your assistance' – and even suggests scripts: 'Hello, are you shopping for yourself or for a gift?' 'How do you like our new fall colours?'

Should this preventive strategy fail, employees are advised to use 'recovery statements' to reclaim shoplifted merchandise. 'Role-play different scenarios with your managers', they're told: 'Practice using APPROPRIATE, NONACCUSATORY, SERVICE-ORIENTED Recovery Statements.' Specific statements are again suggested, including 'That dress is really cute. I bought one for my niece the other day.'

This management of verbal interaction is matched by the management of emotion (Hochschild, 2003). 'Remember to remain positive!' when making recovery statements, the manual urges; even when responding to a store alarm, 'do not accuse the customer or allow the conversation to become confrontational'. Under guidelines for the hectic holiday sales season, employees are urged to call the Loss Prevention Hotline if they suspect internal problems at the store (all calls confidential, reward of up to $500), but in the next line encouraged to 'Have fun!!! The holidays are a perfect time to "choose your attitude!!"'. Further emotional support is provided by Loss Prevention Contests, with employees rewarded with gift certificates or movie passes for knowing loss prevention procedures.

If those two girls in the store are up to nothing more than shoplifting a Starbucks CD, these sorts of soft control, customer-service-as-crime-prevention techniques may succeed. Then again, the girls may have been reverse shoplifting or 'shopdropping' – illicitly placing independent CDs or politically altered products in corporate stores (Urbina, 2007).

And if they're part of the new 'precarity' consciousness that is now confronting the precarious conditions of late modernity, then it's all but certain the store's soft controls won't work. Precarity practitioners argue that the globalized dynamics of late capitalism – 'flex scheduling', part-time service employment, outsourced work, zero-hour contracts, temporary jobs sans benefits or long-term assurances – leave more and more people, especially young people, with nothing but emotional and economic uncertainty. Yet, this very uncertainty – this very precariousness – creates a new sort of commonality, maybe a new if amorphous social class, where 'immigrants, mall workers, freelancers, waiters, squatters … an immigrant worker and a downwardly-mobile twenty-something' (Kruglanski, 2006: n.p.) together drift through the anomie of late modernity. So precarity itself replaces the job site as a place to organize the disorganized, to find some slippery common ground – and those navigating this slippery ground even invent San Precario (Saint Precarious), the playful patron saint of late-modern uncertainty.

Plate 4.4   San Precario, transgendered patron saint of the precarious and a '*detournement* of popular tradition' (Tari and Vanni, 2005)

Credit: chainworkers.org after an image by Chris Woods

After all, if for an earlier generation 'a job was an instrument for integration and social normalization', today jobs are only temporary 'instruments we use to obtain the cash we need in order to live and socialize with the least humiliation possible' (Kruglanski, 2006: n.p.). And yet the minimum-wage cash from a part-time job is never enough and the humiliation only increases – recall those young Gap workers, forced to mimic the manual. 'Smiling is working – where does my real smile begin?', Kruglanski (2006: n.p.) asks, 'whether your friendliness is tainted by the shade of networking, or shaded by "Hello, how are we today? My name is Rob and I'll be your server"'. And so, with the social contract effectively voided by the fluid predations of late capitalism, the smiling clerks and servers turn on the very situations that entrap them and think about ways to drift away from them (Ferrell, 2012a).

But wait a minute; how do these young people know so much about late capitalism? Oh, that's right – *they've been forced to read the manual.*

A little black orb attached to one girl's LED-covered purse

The black orb is ExisTech's high-fashion surveillance accessory: a sophisticated camera, not unlike the spherical ones you see scanning suspects in department stores, but here utilized by advocates of a process known as 'Sousveillance'. From the French 'sous' (below) and 'veiller' (to watch), sousveillance challenges the ubiquitous surveillance practices of late modernity. It draws on the 'detournement' practice of 'reflectionism' – that is, 'appropriating tools of social controllers and resituating these tools in a disorienting manner' (Mann et al., 2003: 333). Sousveillance not only allows the watched to do some watching of their own – as Mann and his colleagues found out in a series of Research Performances – it also greatly unsettles surveillance agents and security guards.

In one case, sousveillance practitioners donned 'invisibility suits' – wearable computer systems linked to flat-panel monitors worn as backpacks – that project images from a small head-mounted video camera. The wearer's back becomes a 'window' and gives the impression of actually seeing right through the wearer. While this type of public display brings sousveillance practitioners into conflict with security staff, 'the wearer argues that the motivation for wearing the camera is to provide protection from being seen by surveillance cameras. Thus the sur-veillance agent's objection to the sousveillance camera becomes an objection to his own surveillance camera' (Mann et al., 2003: 355).

The LED-covered purse is designed by Adam Harvey, as part of his 'stealth wear' collection; if she wishes to block unwanted photography, the purse's owner can activate the extra-bright LEDs so as to blur the photograph (Wortham, 2013).

When a bunch of people walked in and just started taking fruit and muffins off the counter and eating them, like it was a picnic or something, without even attempting to pay

In France, factory workers have recently staged a number of 'withholdings' – that is, holding bosses and managers in the factories to protest mass layoffs and plant closings. In addition, activists have staged 'wild picnics' in supermarkets – collectively eating from the shelves until thrown out by the authorities – to protest high food prices (Perelman, 2009).

The FCUK (French Connection UK) clothing store has changed its display window since she walked past this morning. It now features skinny female mannequins, dressed in the latest FCUK designs, shoving and throwing punches at each other

Unsurprisingly, a retail clothing chain whose name plays on the naughty titilla-tions of sexual slang also displays its apparel amidst a stylized tableau of female violence and victimization. Here, transgression is commodofied twice over, first 'branded' into the very identity of the retailer, then reconfirmed in the violent poses frozen in the shop window.

Meanwhile, along New York City's exclusive Madison Avenue, a dealer in fine European antiques files a $1,000,000 suit against three homeless men whose transgression consists of sitting on the sidewalk in front of his display window. According to the suit, the dealer 'spends large sums each year in carefully preparing the displays appearing in the storefront window showcases', and by their homelessness, the three men distract customers from proper appreciation (Burke et al., 2007: n.p.).

Following the lead of FCUK, he might consider instead allowing the three to set up residence just *inside* the storefront window, maybe throwing a punch or holding up one of the antiques now and then.

There was also that bus stop shelter with the odd words and images in place of the usual advertisements

Those non-commercial words and images are courtesy of Public Ad Campaign (www.publicadcampaign.com), a group that illicitly removes urban advertisements and replaces them with public art as an act of 'civil disobedience' against advertising's monopolization of public space and public perception. Public Ad Campaign operates in New York City, Madrid, Frankfurt, Paris and other cities; on the West Coast of the USA, the California Department of Corrections (www.correctionsdepartment.org) likewise 'corrects' offending advertisements without benefit of permission.

Plate 4.5   Public Ad Campaign

Permission of Public Ad Campaign

According to her, even a damn prawn sandwich is a crime
And maybe it is.

As Martin O'Brien (2006: 6) has shown, the prawns (shrimp) in that sandwich are the result of a global system of large-scale prawn production and distribution that produces at the same time 'murder, abuse, exploitation, theft and environmental destruction'. Global consumer culture not only distances the consumer from the process by which an item of consumption is produced; it distances the consumer from the criminal abuses of people, animals and the environment inherent in that process as well. From Mardi Gras beads (Redmon, 2005, 2015) to Christmas figurines (Ferrell, 2006a: 165–6), cultural criminologists attempt to traverse that distance by linking everyday consumer objects to the conditions of their globalized production. As with Dick Hebdige's (1988: 77–115) brilliant deconstruction of the Italian motor scooter, we look for the currents of meaning embedded in the materials of everyday life.

Not five minutes later, one of the many dishevelled folks who hang around the edges of the station is just as careful to extricate from the trash the half sandwich, the Coke can – and a brand new designer scarf that someone's thrown away
The vast economic inequality that haunts late modernity is confirmed each time an impoverished scrounger reaches into a trash bin, digging for survival amidst the discards; the highs and lows of late capitalism both occupy that moment.

On the high end, the hyper-consumerism that drives late-capitalist economies produces astounding amounts of waste among those privileged enough to afford the next designer suit or iphone. A century ago, the great sociologist and economist Thorstein Veblen (1953[1899]) began to notice patterns of 'conspicuous consumption' – consumption predicated not on the satisfaction of physical need but on the conspicuous attainment of status. A century later, as advertising saturates daily life with the mythology of the perpetually new and improved product, this sort of consumption is pervasive, with consumers endlessly purchasing goods for the sake of lifestyle and status. But of course these consumer goods accumulate, lose their conspicuous lustre and so are discarded to make room for the next wave of consumption. Trash bins overflow with discarded goods, many of them unused and unworn, but now unworthy (Ferrell, 2006a).

On the low end, the same economic system that spawns widespread consumption and waste also spawns widespread poverty and homelessness. The economic circumstances of those 'precarious' part-time retail clerks and flexi workers seen earlier are precarious indeed; with low wages and no guarantees of ongoing employment, they remain always on the brink of joblessness, in or near poverty, in many cases one paycheck away from homelessness. For more and more women, single parenthood or the demise of a bad marriage leaves them likewise vulnerable to loss of income or housing – and so homeless shelters fill with women and their children. Add to this the steady destruction of low-cost housing in the interest of 'urban development', and the corporate 'downsizing' and 'outsourcing' that define the late-modern global economy, and it is little wonder that more and more homeless and unemployed people – and 'under-employed' minimum-wage workers – find themselves sorting through the waste of others' consumption.

Against all odds, such folks salvage not only cans and clothes but sometimes a modicum of dignity, sharing scrounging techniques and inventing moments of do-it-yourself resourcefulness. Others mix trash with DIY political activism. The group Food Not Bombs scrounges discarded food, cooks it, and serves it free of charge to the homeless. Projecting the do-no-harm ethic of a vegan diet into the realm of consumption, 'freegans' reject retail shopping for the dumpster diving of food and clothing 'so as to give no economic power to the capitalist consumer machine' (http://freegan.info/; see Clark, 2004). Around the USA, college students also engage in activist dumpster diving, holding dumpster-diving workshops, scrounging the trash of Ivy League schools, and even making a film to serve 'as a propaganda vehicle to develop colleges' recycling programs' (Kimes, 2006: 13).

So that dishevelled scrounger digging in the train station trash bin might well be hungry and homeless, but might also be a minimum-wage worker, a political activist, a found-object artist, a train-hopping gutter punk or a committed college student. And that scrounger is hanging out of sight around the edges of the station because she or he is almost certainly a criminal as well – that is, almost certainly violating one of the many contemporary legal statutes that prohibit urban trash scrounging in particular and homeless living in general. In many cities, Food Not Bombs activists are likewise denied permits to feed the homeless, then ticketed or arrested for feeding the homeless without a permit; Las Vegas and other American cities now go further, banning any provision of food to the homeless in downtown parks. Across the USA, laws ban sitting or lying on sidewalks, 'camping' in public, even smelling of body odour in a public library; in France, the government places time restrictions on begging (Erlanger, 2011; Wollan, 2012). As urban economies come to rely increasingly on the high end of late capitalism – on upscale retail consumption within sanitized environments – urban authorities readily criminalize those who, by living off the excesses of that consumption, might somehow interrupt it (Ferrell, 2001/2, 2006a).

This dynamic of consumption and waste isn't confined to the relative affluence of the USA, the UK and Western Europe. In India, many of the destitute live from urban trash dumps, in some cases even growing vegetables in the composting waste. In the Gaza Strip, Palestinians scrounge scrap metal from abandoned Israeli settlements. Mexican peasants weave purses and belts from candy wrappers and cookie packages; Brazil's poor collect and sell trash in the tradition of the *garrafeiro* or 'bottle collector', and mine landfills for recyclables as *catadores* or 'trash pickers', as documented in the Academy Award-nominated film *Waste Land* (Walker et al., 2010). As shown in another Academy Award-nominated documentary, *Recycled Life* (Iwerks, 2006), generations of impoverished Guatemalans have likewise mined Guatemala City's landfill, the largest in Central America. The *cartoneros* ('cardboard people') who scavenge for cardboard and scrap paper in Buenos Aires, Argentina, even ride their own stripped-down 'Ghost Train' to and from their nocturnal work in the city centre. Meanwhile, in Guiyu, China, 60,000 people work amidst toxic metal and acid runoff as they disassemble old computers – a task, and risk, they share with thousands of inmates in US federal prisons, who earn as little as 23 cents an hour for disassembling electronic equipment (see Bloch, 1997; O'Brien, 2008).

The school counsellor advised him and his ex-wife that his daughter seems driven to take risks, to push her own limits, to test herself and her teachers

As you've seen in previous chapters, cultural criminological theories suggest some explanations for the daughter's behaviour and the counsellor's perception of it. Like her father, she may be responding to boredom – to the boredom that the school enforces through dress codes, attendance requirements and curricula generally drained of critical thought. Like Cohen's (1955) delinquent boys, she and her friends may be delinquent girls, inverting and resisting the standards by which they are judged. Or, as we saw in the previous chapter, she may be one of the many girls and women now engaged in edgework and so looking for the sharpened sense of self that the rationalized school denies her (see Garot, 2007b; Gailey, 2009).

It's the same old stuff – murder mysteries, police procedurals, surveillance camera compilations

So large is the market for death that it transcends death itself. 'We're really seeing the day of the zombie', says book publisher Don D'Auria. 'As a monster, it's speaking to people' (St John, 2006: 1; Boluk and Lenz, 2011). We'd guess that it's saying something about apocalyptic anxiety, and an overblown sense that danger lurks always amidst the everyday. But in any case, as zombie films, novels and video games proliferate, so do the opportunities to read of humankind stalked by a terror that doubles death back on itself, to watch as the undead eat out the brains of the soon-to-be-dead. No longer do we go gentle into that good night; now we hype the journey, and return to carry others along with us.

The roaring popularity of murder and policing programmes pushes this death culture deeper still into everyday life. Here, the long process of criminal justice is lost in the pseudo-scientific moment, and the drama of death is in the details – torn and severed flesh, flecks of blood, entry and exit wounds, all to be analysed in slow-motion close-up (Cavender and Deutsch, 2007). If mediated violence is por-nographic in its objectification of pain and victimization, these shows are hard-core pornographic snuff films: close-up shots of bullet-on-flesh action or body parts gnawed by rodents, all designed to titillate even the most satiated consumer of televised death. Indeed, it seems we're addicted to the culture of death, dancing every day with violence and morbidity, and inventing as many zombies, serial killers, terrorists and multi-fatality car wrecks as necessary to keep us, well … happy.

Can it be any surprise, then, that a society hooked on the happy indulgences of televised forensic pornography – a society that finds in televised gore and violation a sad sort of existential succour – wishes only the most painful and punitive consequences for those who traffic in actual criminality? This love/hate relationship is mostly two sides of the same titillation. The criminal must be constructed and punished as 'the other' to successfully serve the viewer's voyeuristic escape from the everyday; the escapist love of the tele-vised criminal and the punitive hatred of the actual criminal are both acts of distancing, of exclusion, and so both are necessary safeguards for the con-sumer of crime news and entertainment. A sadomasochistic marriage of fear and fascination is consumated, and with it a thin line indeed between love and hate.

And by the way: What might we think of a society where many of its most popular television shows portrayed and endorsed the tenets of fundamentalist religion? Would we be concerned about a media-abetted theocracy? If many of our most popular shows featured hardcore *sexual* pornography, might even the most liberal among us worry that citizens were just a bit preoccupied with sexual gratification, to the exclusion of other matters? So, with our most popular pro-grammes oriented towards the most graphic of death depictions, with the culture of the zombie ascending like a corpse from the grave, what now? A thanatocracy, a commercialized zombie culture consumed by its own death wish (Jarvis, 2007; Brown, 2009; Linnemann et al., 2014)?

In the dream she's reaching for her, trying to pull her through some sort of wall, but she can't keep her grip and she fades away, receding into the innards of the American penal gulag, disappearing into the crowd of two million other prisoners for whom a day in the life is something very different indeed

More and more occupants of the late-modern world find themselves extricated from the usual rhythms of the everyday, in some cases by the criminal violence they have given or received, in others by the inequitable machinery of contemporary criminal justice as embodied in mandatory and differential sentencing, racial profiling, impoverished public defender programmes, and 'wars' on drugs, gangs and terror. As we showed in Chapter 3, this incarceration machine now imprisons more than two million Americans, with millions more under the ongoing state surveillance of probation and parole.

And yet this carceral madness has spawned its own critique, has birthed a scholarly Frankenstein more than ready to turn on its creator, and in so doing to reveal the real monster. Emerging from the experiences of those who have transformed their own incarceration into informed critique, convict criminology mixes inside exposé, qualitative research and critical theory to produce a damning critique of mass incarceration. Left with little choice but to 'spend considerable amounts of time observing the culture of today's prison and their impact on staff and convicts' (Austin et al., 2001: 20), these convict criminologists likewise marshal ethnographic immersion and theoretical sophistication to construct a critical, cultural critique of 'managerial' prison research that offers 'little empathy for prisoners' and 'disregards the harm perpetrated by criminal justice processing of individuals arrested, charged, and convicted of crimes' (Richards and Ross, 2001: 177).

A collective act of intellectual courage, convict criminology might be considered the cultural criminology of the everyday life that no one cares to notice.

A selection of films and documentaries illustrative of some of the themes and ideas in this chapter

Traffic, 2001, Dir. Steven Soderbergh

Traffic is a gripping, multi-layered film that explores the intricate interconnections of the illegal drug trade in contemporary America. Broad in scope, the film's storyline cross-cuts various aspects of the drug trade, from the internal dynamics of drug cartels to the problems faced by Drug Enforcement Agency officers, from the political hypocrisy surrounding the 'war on drugs' to the drug habits of the middle classes. See also the 1990 British Channel 4 series *Traffik* (on which the Hollywood film *Traffic* was based).

Mardi Gras: Made in China, 2005, Dir. David Redmon

Vividly illustrating the inequities and ironies of global capitalism, cultural criminologist David Redmon's documentary exposes the link between the consumer excesses of the New Orleans Mardi Gras and the harsh realities of Chinese female factory workers. The film 'reveals the glaring truth about the real benefactors of the Chinese workers' hard labor and exposes the extreme contrast between women's lives and liberty in both cultures' (Meredith Lavitt, *Sundance Film Festival*). See also Redmon's related book *Beads, Bodies, and Trash* (2015).

Brick, 2006, Dir. Rian Johnson

Late-modern *film noir* for the Y Generation, *Brick* is the story of dysfunctional teenagers in an anonymous Californian high school. All the classic components of *film noir* are in evidence here – *femmes fatales*, fast-paced expositional dialogue and double-crossing – only this time they're re-energized by their location among high school drug-dealing subcultures. Of interest here is the way young people are adultized, while the actual adult world is marginalized to the point of insignificance (on this last point, see Keith Hayward's [2012c, 2013] work on life-stage dissolution and especially the processes of 'adultification' and 'infantilization' in criminology and beyond).

Recycled Life, 2006, Dir. Leslie Iwerks

Recycled Life is a sobering and ultimately touching short documentary about the generations of families who call Guatemala City's garbage dump home. Abandoned by their government, thousands of Guatemalans are today forced into a daily survival struggle as they eke out a living by recycling consumptive waste. Leslie Iwerks's film exposes this hidden world and sympathetically documents what it's like to live in the foothills of Central America's largest and most toxic landfill mountain.

Waste Land, 2010, Dirs Lucy Walker, Karen Harley and João Jardim

Waste Land records the remarkable aesthetic and social collaboration between artist Vik Muniz and the *catadores* who work to glean recyclable materials from the giant landfill outside Rio de Janeiro, Brazil.

The Greatest Movie Ever Sold, 2011, Dir. Morgan Spurlock

Super Size Me author Morgan Spurlock sets out to make a film all about product placement, marketing and advertising, where the entire film is funded by product placement, marketing and advertising. The result is a documentary that illustrates the close association between brands, artists and corporate sponsorship.

Our Currency is Information: Exposing the Invisible, 2013, Tactical Technology Collective

Part of a series of short documentaries by the Exposing the Invisible project, this 20-minute film follows Romanian activist, Paul Radu, as he uses online resources and 'follow-the-money' software to investigate financial corruption and organized crime. Available to watch free at: https://exposingtheinvisible.org.

Further Reading

Presdee, M. (2000) *Cultural Criminology and the Carnival of Crime.* **London: Routledge.**
This monograph did much to promote cultural criminology in the United Kingdom. In terms of this chapter, it is especially useful for highlighting how commodities and cultural practices are often criminalized by governments who seek to regulate forms of resistance or illicit pleasures.

Presdee, M. (2009) 'Volume crime and everyday life', in C. Hale, K. Hayward, A. Wahidin and E. Wincup (eds) *Criminology*, **2nd edition. Oxford: Oxford University Press.**
Useful textbook chapter that introduces undergraduate students to the concept of 'volume crime' – the everyday crimes that constitute the rump of the crime statistics.

Ferrell, J. and Ilan, J. (2013) 'Crime, culture, and everyday life', in C. Hale, K. Hayward, A. Wahidin and E. Wincup (eds), *Criminology*, **3rd edition. Oxford: Oxford University Press.**
Clear textbook introduction into the relationships between crime, culture, and control in contemporary Western society.

Ferrell, J. (2006) *Empire of Scrounge.* **New York: New York University Press.**
A cultural criminology-inspired ethnography in which Jeff enters a world of engorged trash piles and throwaway conspicuous consumption, as he spends a year "dumpster diving" and living off the recycled "waste" of an affluent American city to highlight consumer excess in late modern capitalism.

Miller, J. (2008) *Getting Played: African American Girls, Urban Inequality, and Gendered Violence.* **New York: New York University Press.**
An important investigation into the victimization and processes of risk negotiation experienced by disadvantaged young African American women as they go about their daily round in contemporary US society.

Garot, R. (2010) *Who You Claim: Performing Gang Identity in School and on the Streets.* **New York: New York University Press.**
An ethnographic study of how young people construct lifestyles and negotiate their gang identities in urban communities.

Hayward, K. (2012) 'Five spaces of cultural criminology', *British Journal of Criminology*, **52(3): 441–62.**
Statement article on cultural criminology and space that includes introductions and critiques of the Chicago School of sociology and more recent developments in cultural geography. See also Elaine Campbell's (2013) subsequent article on space and cultural criminology in the same journal.

Useful Websites

Carnivalesque films
http://carnivalesquefilms.com/
The website of filmmakers David Redmond and Ashley Sabin. Often inspired by the theories of cultural criminology, Redmond and Sabin's poignant documentaries tell stories about how disruption, celebration, excess, and transgression play out in everyday life.

Green Criminology website
http://greencriminology.org/
Our friend Avi Brisman's green criminology website where you can keep up to date with all the latest developments in this new field.

The Convict Criminology website
www.convictcriminology.org/
Link to Stephen Richards and Jeff Ross's Convict Criminology site. Convict criminology is a relatively new and controversial perspective in the field of corrections and the academic field of criminology.

Note

1 The publisher Jones & Bartlett Learning seems particularly enamoured of graffiti – or the image of graffiti, anyway. Of the five books on juvenile delinquency or juvenile justice listed in its 2013 Criminal Justice catalogue, four feature hip hop graffiti on their covers. Furthering the confusion, the Fall 2013 issue of the US Government-funded National Gang Center Newsletter (National Gang Center, 2013: 2) includes the article, 'Gang graffiti resources', illustrated with a photo of a young man painting a distinctly non-gang graffiti mural.

5

WAR, TERRORISM AND THE STATE: A CULTURAL CRIMINOLOGICAL INTRODUCTION

It's sometimes argued that cultural criminology has tended to conceptualize and study culture more at the levels of criminal act, subculture or media than at the level of the state. But is such a charge justified? A few years back, at an unusually lively session of the American Society of Criminology's annual conference, our colleague Mark Hamm (2008) presented a paper in which he compared three years' worth of articles published in the periodical *Crime, Media, Culture* – arguably the main journal associated with cultural criminology – with those in the more prestigious, and certainly less 'romantic', US journal, *Criminology*. The results were surprising. While each journal understandably played to its respective strengths (*Criminology* contained more articles on 'delinquency', 'policing', 'robbery' and 'life-course criminology'; *Crime, Media, Culture* more on subcultures, media representations and film/music and crime), when it came to papers associated with the rubric 'state crime' – war crimes, torture, state terrorism, capital punishment and the like – it was *Crime, Media, Culture* that included the (far) greater number of articles. This is no cause for celebration of course; the subject of state crime remains under-represented within criminology generally and it will take years of research to correct this imbalance. Instead, we mention it simply to illustrate the fact that there does already exist within cultural criminology a keen, albeit under-articulated, interest in matters relating to state crime and its associated cultural tendencies like belligerent nationalism or proactive militarism in support of economic self-interest. Likewise, the issue of terrorism and other forms of sub-state violence, as we will see, is also cropping up more and more on cultural criminology's radar screen. So, while a thoroughgoing cultural criminology of the state would require a separate book, here, in a bid to more clearly articulate our position, we sketch out two emerging lines of inquiry – as always, inviting your response and participation.

Cultural criminology and war

Do we really need 'a criminology of war' – or for that matter a sociological account of counter insurgency? Is it not the case that human rights violations or breaches of military convention that take place in conflict situations are already covered by the rigours of international humanitarian law and an array of treaties ratified by international comity? What, if anything, can criminology bring to the table? Let us attempt to answer such questions by considering the conflict of our time: the long short war in Iraq.

Among the many classified documents and reports handed to the whistle-blowing website WikiLeaks by the US soldier Bradley Manning was a digital file containing cockpit gun-sight footage from two US Army AH-64 Apache helicopters. The classified footage shows one of the helicopters opening up with a 30mm cannon on a group of (predominantly unarmed) Iraqis, including two employees of the news agency Reuters. Inevitably, all in the group are cut to pieces. Moments later, when a van arrives to assist the victims, it too is strafed by helicopter cannon fire; inside the van another three unarmed men are killed and two children seriously wounded. Although painful to watch, the video is important for any number of reasons (not the least of which is the insight it provides into the nature of communication that takes place between military personnel when assessing such situations – a mix of efficient military-speak, wisecracking and self-congratulation). For our purposes, though, what is of most interest is the public response to the video after it went viral via WikiLeaks. The incident was immediately condemned around the globe, with many commentators quickly classifying the attack as a 'war crime'. But were these impassioned claims of illegality justified? The short answer, as any military lawyer will tell you, is 'no'. Despite all the noises made in the media and elsewhere about the 'proportionality' of the attacks, or the 'reasonable certainty' of the target's hostility, from a legal perspective, there is nothing about the Al-Amin al-Thaniyah airstrike that technically contravenes the laws of war as currently configured. The following quote by the lawyer and author Chase Madar illustrates this point succinctly:

> The reaction of professional humanitarians to the gun-sight video was muted, to say the least. The big three human rights organizations – Human Rights Watch (HRW), Amnesty International, and Human Rights First – responded not with position papers and furious press releases but with silence. HRW omitted any mention of it in its report on human rights and war crimes in Iraq, published nearly a year after the video's release. Amnesty also kept mum. Gabor Rona, legal director of Human Rights First, told me there wasn't enough evidence to ascertain whether the laws of war had been violated, and that his organization had no Freedom of Information Act requests underway to uncover new evidence on the matter. This collective

non-response, it should be stressed, is not because these humanitarian groups, which do much valuable work, are cowardly or 'sell-outs'. The reason is: all three human rights groups, like human rights doctrine itself, are primarily concerned with questions of legality. And quite simply, as atrocious as the event was, there was no clear violation of the laws of war to provide a toehold for the professional humanitarians. (Madar, 2012: n.p.)

If international humanitarian law is not capable of moving beyond state-deferential definitions of criminality, or, as Madar more provocatively puts it, is 'less concerned with restraining military violence than licensing it', then how are we to make sense of the airstrike at Al-Amin al-Thaniyah – or, for that matter, drone strikes against 'enemies of the state', genocidal campaigns or the systematic regimes of torture that take place in 'dark sites' and 'off book' prisons in states the world over?

Uh Crazyhorse One–Eight request permission to uh engage.

Plate 5.1   Still from 12 July 2007, Al-Amin al-Thaniyah, airstrike, Baghdad, Iraq

Source: YouTube. (Full video available at: http://en.wikipedia.org/wiki/July_12,_2007_Baghdad_airstrike)

Such questions have concerned radical and critical criminologists for decades. For critical criminologists, the stated goal has been to extend criminology's critical ontology so that the discipline no longer relies solely on a state-deferential definition of crime (e.g. Schwendinger and Schwendinger, 1970; Chambliss, 1989;

Green and Ward, 2000, 2004; Morrison, 2006). In recent years, this position has been finessed – quite often as a result of debates surrounding the in-built political dimension of knowledge production within criminology (Hillyard et al., 2004) – by scholars associated with the 'social harm' perspective (e.g. Hillyard and Tombs, 2004; Hillyard et al., 2005; Coleman et al., 2009). Proponents of this approach argue that when national and international legalistic approaches to crime are invalid, it becomes necessary for criminology to widen its horizons beyond the legal realm and think of acts such as state violence, ecological destruction or cross-border pollution (see Chapter 3) not simply in terms of whether or not rules have been broken, but as *social and physical harms*. While it must be stressed that the social harm perspective has definitional problems of its own, it is clearly a useful tool for thinking about the state as an enabler of violence both within and beyond its own borders. Indeed, a number of critical criminologists have already undertaken studies of the state's actions during the Iraq war and subsequent military occupation (Kramer and Michalowski, 2005; Kauzarlich, 2007; Whyte, 2007, 2010).

This is useful work, but as cultural criminologists we're also aware of its limitations. Specifically, by training critical attention solely on the entity of the 'state' (either as ideological expression or overarching structural apparatus of power), these accounts have a tendency to ignore the fact that state power, whether exerted in a war zone or as part of a covert 'black operation', is in the main implemented at ground level by highly committed, indeed often zealous, individuals who are all-too-willing to undertake what military personnel or secret service operatives call the 'wet stuff' (see Goldhagen, 1996), i.e. house-to-house shakedowns, rendition, torture and search-and-destroy missions. Here, we believe cultural criminology can be very useful, not only as a better way to analyse the blurred dynamic between the laws of war and the on-the-ground realities associated with its prosecution, but as a means to provide a deeper and more meaningful understanding of the frailties of the human condition in terms of its susceptibility to perversion or corruption in extreme circumstances (Cushman, 2001: 82).

Consider again the situation in Iraq. One of the striking features of the war was the sweeping legislative upheaval enacted by the Coalition Provisional Authority (CPA) and the US Government in order to administer the occupation. By passing legislation such as Presidential Executive Order 13303 (which afforded US civilian and military personnel immunity from prosecution under Iraqi Law) and FRAGO 242 (which instructed US coalition personnel not to intervene to stop acts of violence carried out by Iraqis on Iraqis), the CPA essentially went some way toward creating what legal scholars call 'a state of exception' (Agamben, 2005). In doing so, the CPA made it extremely difficult for international humanitarian lawyers to prosecute the human rights abuses or coercive state practices undertaken during the Iraq War. At a practical level, the US government was essentially allowing its soldiers and private contractors to circumvent, if not completely divorce themselves from, key international doctrines such as the Geneva Convention governing the provisions made for civilians and detainees within international conflicts (Lepard, 2006). In some parts of Iraq, the result in effect was prosecution-free, state-sanctioned violence. But even though the state (through the guise of the CPA) had created the legal conditions by which cities like Baghdad and Fallujah essentially became 'free-fire zones', it was still human actors, functioning within small group dynamics, that were pulling triggers, kicking down doors and beating and torturing prisoners – just as it was previously under Saddam Hussein's despotic regime (Makiya, 1998) and just as it is today as members of Islamic State go about their shameful business in the Levant, destroying Christian churches and executing civilians for what they perceive to be violations of Sharia. It is here that cultural criminology can help, by stressing the importance of human experience and agency in the conduct of a war, insurgency and counter insurgency (see Morrison, 2004a; Cottee, 2011).

As has been well documented, in conflict settings and war zones, participation in mass violence and military killings is contingent upon the relationship that individuals and groups have with their immediate social and situational environment (Browning, 1992; Tanner, 2011). In post-invasion Iraq, for example, this relationship was one often highly conducive to coercive state practices and acts of brutality. Indeed, for some critical criminologists, the CPA's maladroit efforts to govern post-invasion Iraq were simply a reflection of the structural motivations for invading the country in the first place (e.g. Schwartz, 2007; Ruggiero, 2010). From the 'shock and awe' bombing strikes that started the campaign to the civic meltdown that occurred after Saddam Hussein was toppled, the chaos of post-invasion Iraq bred a culture of 'strike-first' hyper aggression that shaped the 'collective identity' and 'small group dynamics' of those tasked with prosecuting the war at street level:

> When placed in the subcultural context of actors involved in the Iraq War, we can see this process taking place, through a combination of the immunity from prosecution granted to coalition personnel, and the enemy-focussed counter insurgency. These two factors contributed to the construction of normalised deviant behaviour, such as the torture and abuse of detainees, the excessive use of force towards civilians at checkpoints and extrajudicial killings by coalition forces and PMCs [private military contractors], as acceptable conduct within the counter insurgency ... this process contributed to the capacity for those involved in this violence, to continue to conduct themselves in this manner, without seriously questioning the legitimacy of their actions, or the ramifications for their victims. (Burrows, 2013: 235–6)

Likewise, following the Syrian uprising of 2011, and the civic chaos experienced in parts of Northern Iraq following the collapse of Nouri al-Maliki's Shia government, Jihadist fighters associated first with Al-Qaeda in Iraq (AQI) and then the al-Nusra Front and the Islamic State thrived in the climate of fear and sectarian violence that characterized the surrounding environment at that time – meeting violence with violence and out-brutalizing their prior brutalizers.

And so a cultural criminology of war begins to emerge. As the above quote suggests, it draws together the macro influence of structure (in the form of governance and ideology) with more mid-level theories of subculture and 'learnt transgression' – a combination that also allows for an analysis of how state crimes and mass killings can be 'neutralized' (see Chapter 2) by both the state and the collective forces involved in human rights violations (Hamm, 2007a). However, no cultural criminological analysis would be complete unless it included the third element of the original triadic framework on which cultural criminology is founded: a micro-level understanding of the experiential and phenomenological dynamics that compel one actor to engage in transgressive violence and another in the same socio-cultural setting to desist. Here, cultural criminology draws on the small subterranean literature in sociology and military history that powerfully illuminates the sensations and emotions associated with war and combat (see Cottee, 2011, for a useful cultural criminological introduction; see also Gray, 1959; Hedges, 2002; Wright, 2004). Consider, for example, the following quote from Sebastian Junger's brilliant micro-sociological study of combat, *War* (2010), in which he attempts to explain the allure of firefights for US infantrymen serving in Afghanistan:

> War is a lot of things and it's useless to pretend that exciting isn't one of them. It's insanely exciting. The machinery of war and the sound it makes and the urgency of its use and the consequences of almost everything about it are the most exciting things anyone engaged in war will ever know. Soldiers discuss that fact with each other and eventually with their chaplains and their shrinks and maybe even their spouses, but the public will never hear about it. It's just not something that many people want acknowledged. War is supposed to feel bad because undeniably bad things happen in it, but for a nineteen-year-old at the working end of a .50 cal during a firefight that everyone comes out of okay, war is life multiplied by some number that no one has ever heard of. In some ways twenty minutes of combat is more life than you could scrape together in a lifetime of doing something else. (Junger, 2010: 144–5)

Likewise, in the following quotation by Vietnam veteran and author Phillip Caputo, the experiential 'seductions' of close-quarter combat, the adrenalin rush of life-threatening military 'edgework' are expressed in almost pure Katzian terms (see Chapter 3):

> Anyone who fought in Vietnam, if he is honest about himself, will have to admit he enjoyed the compelling attractiveness of combat. It was a peculiar enjoyment because it was mixed with a commensurate pain. Under fire, a man's powers of life heightened in proportion to the proximity of death, so that he felt an elation as extreme as his dread. His senses quickened, he attained an acuity of consciousness at once pleasurable and excruciating. It was something like the elevated state of

> awareness induced by drugs. And it could be just as addictive, for it made whatever else life offered in the way of delights or torments seem pedestrian. (Caputo, 1977: xvii)

In the next section, we will explore this synthesis of macro, meso and micro elements in more detail in relation to the debates surrounding terrorism. For now, however, let's set out in practical terms what a constitutive cultural criminology of war might look like. To help with this task, we draw upon and augment Daniel Burrows' (2013) recent multi-dimensional, cultural criminological analysis of state crime in the Iraq War.

Building on Hayward's (2011) appreciation of the interconnectivity of macro, meso and micro processes within cultural criminology, and thus mirroring the approach set out above, Burrows outlines a number of 'theoretical tropes' that he asserts are essential for constructing an integrative and interdisciplinary approach to understanding state crime (in war). Paraphrasing Burrows, they could be summarized in the following way: *first*, there is a need to situate the criminological analysis of war within *a broad historical dynamic*. For example, no analysis of the Iraq War is viable without considering Iraq's problematic history – both in terms of Saddam's reign of terror (Makiya, 1998) and the longstanding ethnic divisions that characterize the country – or the similarities between the USA's past and present counter-insurgency techniques (see Hamm, 2007a; Klein, 2007), not to mention the long history of violent US and European intervention in the affairs of the Middle East. *Second*, there is a general recognition of the limitations of international humanitarian law and the need to develop broader conceptualizations of social and personal harm that better identify and make visible the brutalities and atrocities – both big and small – which occur in war zones. *Third*, there is a readiness to engage with existing macro, structural analyses associated with the discipline of politics and international relations that view the military actions of states as expressions of national security interests and particular economic objectives. Put bluntly, as the global security scholar Doug Stokes has asked (2009: 91): would the Middle East have been subject to so many interventions, Western-backed coups and US-backed authoritarian regimes if the principal export of the region was not oil but avocados? *Fourth*, the culture underpinning military action and its aftermath must be carefully analysed, especially in cases where temporary sovereignty is established and a counter-insurgency campaign is waged. In particular, emphasis must be trained on how meso-level cultures and subcultures – be they statist or increasingly corporate (Lea and Stenson, 2007; Welch, 2009) in origin – create and valorize forms of learnt behaviour that are technically and normatively prohibited and undesirable. *Fifth*, no criminology of war can be complete without a focus on the micro-experiential attractions and emotional allures of combat and its associated 'wet' activities. In particular, we need to focus attention on how the dangers, risks and excitements of war can shape small group affinity/identity and provide individuals with a sense of meaning that transcends the norm. As Chris Hedges argues in his brilliantly insightful and disturbing book *War is a Force Which Gives Us Meaning*, this is perhaps the primary appeal of conflict:

> Even with its destruction and carnage it can give us what we long for in life. It can give us purpose, meaning, a reason for living. Only when we are in the midst of conflict does the shallowness and vapidness of much of our lives become apparent. Trivia dominates our conversations and increasingly our airwaves. And war is an enticing elixir. It gives us resolve, a cause. (2002: 3)

To this, we would add the issue of (toxic) masculinity. This can be factored into any of the six areas, but seems especially important when considering the nature of 'meaning' associated with war's emotional and experiential attractions. *Sixth*, and finally, to understand how the mainstream media frames state-sanctioned violence by, on the one hand, legitimating and celebrating narratives of war and conquest and, on the other, marginalizing other forms of state crime from popular discourse.

After the floodwater: Blackwater

In the aftermath of Hurricane Katrina, polluted floodwater, violent gangs and violent police officers were not the only toxic threats coursing through New Orleans. Patrolling the streets alongside traditional law enforcement personnel and the US National Guard (at least what was left of it after mass deployments in Iraq and Afghanistan) were members of Blackwater Security Consulting, a private military contractor. From a standing start in 2002, Blackwater and its various spin-offs (the company frequently changes its name, for obvious reasons; in 2009, it became 'Xe Services LLC' and then in 2011 it rebranded itself again, this time, hilariously, as 'Academi') quickly amassed contracts with the US government totalling in excess of half a billion dollars, largely as a result of the privatization of the 'war on terror'. While Academi, nee Blackwater, staff offer a wide range of paramilitary services, their primary role since 9/11 has been as a 'shadow army' of private mercenaries working alongside the US Army in post-invasion Iraq. During the height of the conflict, over 100,000 mercenaries were deployed in Iraq, but it was Blackwater operatives who caused the most controversy. From 2004, Blackwater contractors were involved in a series of controversial killings of Iraqi civilians, including most notably the 11 September 2007 incident in Nisoor Square, Baghdad, where, backed by their own helicopters, Blackwater staff indiscriminately opened fire on a large group of innocent Iraqis. Despite its woeful record, Blackwater has remained a nebulous target for prosecutors, both in Iraq and in the USA. Rulings by the former head of the US-led civil administration in Iraq, Paul Bremner, helped create a legal grey area surrounding privately

(Continued)

---

contracted security forces, and as a result Blackwater has gone about its business with apparent impunity (Scahill, 2007). Moreover, Blackwater/Academi has lobbied aggressively to ensure it is not subject to the same forms of military law that apply to more traditional combat forces.

Blackwater is the creation of Erik Prince, an ultra-conservative Christian bank roller of the Republican Party. Using his powerful contacts, Prince has built a small private army of ex-military and intelligence operatives that he now hires out to the US Government whenever some under-the-radar muscle is needed – hence the presence of unmarked Blackwater vehicles on the streets of New Orleans following Katrina. With their flak jackets, desert camouflage combat gear and automatic weapons at the ready, Blackwater operatives claimed to be in New Orleans to 'stop looters and criminals'. But with their lack of public accountability and their cavalier attitude to the rule of law, perhaps we should be asking ourselves: what was Blackwater actually there to stop? And who really poses the greater threat to civil liberties – the displaced population of a natural disaster or Blackwater's running dogs of neo-liberal capitalism?

This sixth dimension – the role of media, images and popular discourse – is one of particular potency and importance. In February 2003, for example, at the insistence of the Bush administration, the *Guernica* tapestry (a huge copy of Picasso's 1937 painting of the Nazi bombing of Guernica during the Spanish Civil War) was first covered, then removed, from the Security Room of the United Nations Building in New York City. Apparently, the fabric of war's horrors was no longer an appropriate backdrop for Colin Powell and other US diplomats to make media statements urging the case for the invasion of Iraq. What the neo-conservatives pulling the strings of the Bush administration knew only too well was that, when it comes to wielding power on the late-modern global stage, image management is as important as battlefield management. Or to put it another way: the play may be flawed, but there's no excuse for not properly dressing the set.

Had he been around today, Guy Debord would surely have smiled. The guiding light of the Situationist International 40 years ago, Debord declared then that, if capitalist accumulation was to continue unchallenged, it would require new forms of state control that held 'mastery over the domain of the image'. His argument was simple: as the state ramps up its involvement in the day-to-day lives of its citizenry through 'the colonization of everyday life', the control of images – especially via so-called 'perpetual emotion machines' like the television – becomes ever more vital to the maintenance of the capitalist social order. Yet, this gives rise to a paradox: the more the state relies upon the image, the more it is vulnerable to image manipulation.

So back to today's ongoing War on Terror: in an article on America's reaction to the attacks of 9/11, the Retort Collective argued that 'a state that lives more and more in and through a regime of the image does not know what to do when, for a moment, it dies by the same lights. It does not matter that "economically" or "geopolitically" the death may be an illusion. Spectacularly, it was real. And image-death – image-defeat – is not a condition that the state can endure' (Retort Collective, 2004: 20). This is not simply a retreat to Jean Baudrillard's world of 'hyper spectacle' – something that the Retort Collective is keen to avoid. Rather, it's a call for a clearer understanding of the geopolitical interaction between the symbolic and the material – a line of inquiry that, no doubt, a radical interventionist like Debord would have welcomed. As the Retort Collective makes clear, 'No one level of analysis – "economic" or "political", global or local, focusing on the means of either material or symbolic production – will do justice to the current strange mixture of chaos and grand design' (2004: 7). We must strive instead for modes of critique that merge these domains, combining images and analysis as tools to 'vulnerablize' the state and challenge its hegemony over the 'realm of the image' (Brown, 2014; Schept, 2014; Wall and Linnemann, 2014). This may sound abstract, but consider again the Apache airstrike at Al-Amin al-Thaniyah. Without the visceral gun-sight video footage, this event would surely have passed unnoticed into history. Just another anonymous US intelligence report; one of several hundred thousand reports uploaded to the Internet in the WikiLeaks 'War Logs'. This one, however, stood out. It stood out precisely because it was an image. It stood out precisely because its visual power made the event seem *real* (and note here the inversion of Jean Baudrillard's famous hypothesis in *The Gulf War Did Not Take Place* [1995]). The unexpurgated video footage did indeed therefore have the power to 'vulnerabalize the state', irrespective of what international humanitarian law ultimately had to say about it.

In an interesting article entitled 'Toward a cultural criminology of war', Josh Klein (2011) shows how 'elite military criminal action' depends on the 'partial ideological "enlistment" of the public' and thus the 'indirect involvement of otherwise law-abiding citizens in international crimes' (2011: 86–7). Klein uses public opinion data to illustrate how tendencies associated with counter-insurgency war – belligerent nationalism, chauvinism, nativism, out-group hating – are ideologically legitimated at home through various popular cultural forms manipulated by political elites and associated media bias. Yet, if public opinion can be manipulated by the propagandistic nature of television coverage, including 'embedded' journalists and officially approved war footage (Ryan and Switzer, 2009; Bonn, 2010), it can also be swayed, 'limited' and morally undermined by images that starkly highlight the disjuncture between state-centric news reporting and elite military criminality – the media criticism that followed in the wake of the scandal over the photos of Abu Ghraib prisoner abuse being perhaps the most obvious example.

And so we see the value of the image as a means of checking state power in today's multi-mediated world. It is an approach that is as viable in a war zone as it is in a commuter zone. For example, whether it's the photographing and videotaping of crowds and individuals at political demonstrations and protest marches, or the deployment of miniaturized uniform and helmet-mounted personal video cameras by beat officers, the power of the image is not something that the state and its agents can ever fully own or control (although, see relatedly McElroy, 2010). Far from it – the force of the image, the power and spectacle of the visual is simply too multidimensional. Images permeate the flow of cultural meaning in any number of ways, and just as they can be used to serve the military and other branches of the state apparatus, they can also be used to critique and undermine it. Hence, heavy-handed police arrest practices are now routinely combated by citizens with cameras, while organizers of political demonstrations often deploy their own videographers (and increasingly drones fitted with aerial cameras) to monitor potential abuses by the state. As with the case of the Al-Amin al-Thaniyah airstrike, as state agents seek to control or possess an image for its own purposes, another group can steal it and subject it to a cultural hijacking and radical reversal of meaning.

At this point, most criminologies of war, or, for that matter, most liberal-left critiques of state militarism, tend to come to an abrupt end, content simply to 'give the state a good kicking', offer some progressive suggestions and then move on. But this is not the approach of cultural criminology. To return again to the Iraq War and its aftermath – and thus to the various theoretical tropes that underpin our exploratory cultural criminology of war – we would argue that it was an intellectual failing of many commentators not to (at least) acknowledge the complexity of the events surrounding the occupation and the insurgency that followed. However badly the case for 'regime change' in Iraq was presented by the inept Bush–Cheney administration (or, for that matter, the Blair government in the UK), and irrespective of one's overarching position regarding the merits and demerits of military intervention, one must not lose sight of the fact that, after the original target was toppled – Saddam Hussein's Baathist regime – a new and very dedicated enemy emerged to combat the Coalition occupation. It was an enemy whose ranks were swollen by thousands of non-Iraqi fighters who poured across the border, not just from Syria and Jordan, but from ostensible allies of the USA/West such as Saudi Arabia and Pakistan – thousands of foreign fighters have also since travelled to Iraq from the UK and other EU states with large Muslim populations. Downplayed and even excused by certain prominent thinkers on the left (the American film-maker Michael Moore stating that the Iraqi 'resistance' was the equivalent of the Revolutionary Minutemen, while the British-Pakistani journalist Tariq Ali urged solidarity with the 'insurgents') was the fact that what groups like Al-Qaeda in Iraq were resisting was not simply the Coalition, but democratization, a new constitution and the newly acquired power of the Iraqi Shia. Moreover, the immediate intention of AQI and the Sunni insurgents was not just to destabilize Iraq, but very precisely to create the stability of a theocratic Islamic Sharia state – an ideological position that eventually spawned the Islamic State of Iraq and the Levant and ultimately Abu Bakr al-Baghdadi's repressive Islamic State (Cockburn, 2015). In a rush to critique American and British militarism, too many commentators thus misunderstood the nature of the jihadi resistance in Iraq, construing it, falsely, as an essentially anti-imperialist movement.

In sharp contrast, any emerging cultural criminology of war would recognize the plurality and complexity of motivations behind war and insurgent (and counter-insurgent) activity and importantly that these motivations must not be misconstrued for polemical-political purposes (i.e. because foreign jihadists in Iraq were, in addition to killing civilians, targeting American soldiers, they must be anti-imperialists – on the contrary, they were imperialists of the first order in their desire to recreate a global caliphate). Moreover, a cultural criminology of war needs to recognize that any comprehensive account of why men and women engage in warfare must acknowledge the non-rational or irrational aspects of war making and especially the role of religion in this (something generally played down by luminaries of the left such as Naomi Klein and Noam Chomsky). Religion must not automatically be collapsed into politics and must be recognized as a powerful shaping force in itself. Cultural criminology is uniquely attuned to capture the potent appeal and allure of religious or 'theistic violence' and the promise of transcendental bliss and heroic validation it offers (see Cottee, 2014). Indeed, it is to this very subject that we now turn.

Cultural criminology and terrorism

As the boundaries between crime, terrorism, state criminality and sub-state conflict continue to blur – with 'narco-terrorism', illegal drone-strike assassinations, international financing for terrorist organizations, organized weapon trafficking, the opaque distinction in certain regions between hard-core insurrectionists and local criminal gangs (Hamm, 2007b) – the need for criminology to improve its dialogue with disciplines such as international relations and terrorism studies becomes ever more acute. In this section, we lend weight to this process by drawing on recent developments in terrorism studies so as to develop a tentative cultural criminology of terrorism. As a stand-alone discipline, terrorism studies is not without its problems. In particular, it is blighted by longstanding ideological schisms and scrapped over by a host of competing factions, from realist to anti-realist, orthodox to post-structural. Here, we do not attempt to offer a broad overview of the field and its controversies; instead, we select a couple of key recent developments within terrorism studies that might best meet the needs of cultural criminology – and especially the type of macro, meso and micro approach outlined in the previous section.

One recent movement that has obvious application is the sub-field of 'critical terrorism studies' (CTS). Pushed forward by a small but determined group of scholars (e.g. Gunning, 2007; Jackson, 2007; Jackson et al., 2009a), CTS has carved out an impressive, if it at times controversial, niche for itself within the broader discipline of international relations.[1] Comparing CTS with cultural criminology, it's clear that there are some striking similarities. To start, both subfields have established themselves as intellectual and theoretical counterpoints to many of the traditional orientations that inform their host discipline, and both proceed from the premise that there is an *in-built political dimension to knowledge production within their master subjects*. Put another way, each subfield is concerned that mainstream approaches to terrorism/crime are simply attempts to uphold and reify the political and economic 'status quo' – that is, the existing power structures and socio-historical circumstances that constitute and define the respective problems in the first place. This challenge to what one might describe as state-centric disciplinary norms precipitates three further commonalities. First, both subfields express concern that putative 'problem-solving' approaches skew the respective discipline's research agenda by over-emphasizing obvious epiphenomena at the expense of larger, more complex issues – obvious examples being the heavy focus on the psychological motivations of Islamic suicide bombers rather than rigorous analyses of Middle Eastern history/politics/religious ideology in mainstream terrorism studies, and the prioritization of street-level surveillance by government criminologists at the expense of any substantive concern with corporate or white-collar crime. Second, both CTS scholars and cultural criminologists are highly critical of the way rational choice theory (RCT) has been taken up and utilized within their disciplines (see Chapter 3). Gunning (2009: 167), for example, worries that RCTs of terrorism overly stress the strategic ends/interests of militant groups, 'with little reference to ideology, ideas, or identity'. Third, both subfields are concerned about the way purportedly 'objective' quantitative data increasingly operate as a 'scientific' façade fronting the public presentation of their respective disciplines (see Raphael, 2009: 50–1, 56–7; Sluka, 2009: 144; and Chapter 7, this volume).

These shared lines of critique are part of the reason why both cultural criminology and CTS are keen to subject their respective fields to *multidisciplinary influence* (see Hayward, 2004: 147; Ferrell and Hayward, 2011: 10; Jackson et al., 2009b: 216, 222, 225; Ranstorp, 2009: 24, 32; Toros and Gunning, 2009: 98). Practically speaking, this manifests itself in CTS's call for terrorism studies to engage more fully with disciplines such as anthropology (Sluka, 2009), Middle East area studies (Dalacoura, 2009), media studies (Jackson, 2005), migration studies, gender studies (Sylvester and Parashar, 2009), social psychology, and social movement theory (Gunning, 2009). Cultural criminology, meanwhile, has sought to engage with inter alia cultural geography, visual sociology, media and film studies, cultural anthropology, philosophy, genocide and war studies, and cultural and youth studies. Inevitably, much of this desire for intellectual pluralism can be attributed to the emphasis both place on *meaning* and the contested (cultural) construction of their particular objects of study – a position that no doubt provides succour to critics who see both sub-disciplines as overly discursive and lacking in materialist rigour. Yet, given the evolving nature of both terrorism and criminality, a strong emphasis on meaning and definitional ambiguity is arguably a strength when developing alternative explanations and advancing new conceptual frameworks. Consider, for example, David Kilcullen's (2009) concept of the 'accidental guerrilla', a term used to describe the blurred boundaries in conflict settings between committed insurgents and self-interested local tribesmen, or the contested accounts of who (or indeed what) actually constitutes the Taliban in Afghanistan and the Federally Administered Tribal Areas. Moreover, when it comes to developing analyses of state power – or, for that matter, of terrorist organizations that wish to confront and destabilize state power – based around the type of micro, meso and macro framework outlined above, then an interdisciplinary focus is essential. Most obviously, whether it's cultural criminology's call for an enhanced visual criminology, or CTS's keenness to appropriate content analysis and other methodological modes of 'textual revelation' from media studies (Jackson, 2009: 67; see also Jackson, 2005; Altheide, 2006; Bonn, 2010), both subfields stress the *multi-level influence* of the media, whether as a tool for disseminating terroristic propaganda or as a way of averting attention from the effects of so-called 'state terrorism' (Blakeley, 2009). Similarly, a shared interest in cultural anthropology also demands that ethnographers working in this area link their 'ground up' accounts with macro- and meso-level theory. Jeffrey Sluka (2009: 153), for example, points out that 'anthropologists have made, and continue to make, a major contribution to CTS and our understanding of terrorism by studying it both as an empirical reality and political and cultural construction'. Likewise, Ranstorp asserts that 'cultural anthropology can provide a deeper granulated perspective into communicative aspects and symbolism' of terrorist action (2009: 32; see also Sluka, 2008).

But enough conceptual talk about a disciplinary fusion of CTS and cultural criminology; what might a cultural criminology of terrorism actually look like? Most importantly, as already suggested, it must be capable of functioning at the macro, meso and micro levels. It must, as Martha Crenshaw famously put it, synthesize structural factors with an analysis of group dynamics, ideological influence, and individual incentives and personal motivations (Gunning, 2009: 166). It must also, as we have already stated, be open to interdisciplinarity – because this really is the only way to ensure a truly comprehensive understanding of how macro, meso and micro explanations impact on each other. So, for example, when we look at the econometric data on structural poverty that produces Palestinian support for Hamas's Izz ad-Din al-Qassam military brigades, we must also apply visual methods to analyse how martyr posters and billboards on the streets of Gaza reproduce and cultivate a bizarre culture of street-level celebrity that aggrandizes suicide bombing and other forms of *istisha-had*. (And to think that some terrorism scholars claim there's nothing intrinsically new or distinct about terrorist activity today.) Similarly, when we (rightly, as above) pose the geo-political question about whether Iraq and other Middle Eastern countries would have been the subject of so many US-backed interventions if their primary export was not oil but avocados, we should not end our analyses there. Instead, we must embark on further anthropologically and situationally attuned forms of research into local (micro) level considerations such as the particular techniques employed by occupying forces when patrolling unfamiliar neighbourhoods and gathering dynamic intelligence, or, for that matter, the pre-existing religious/sectarian schisms that might constitute the on-the-ground spatial reality of those neighbourhoods in the first place. Such a multi-dimensional approach to the study of terrorism closely mirrors cultural criminology's approach to the study of criminality (i.e. one that conceptualizes certain transgressive behaviours as attempts to resolve internal psychic/individual conflicts that are spawned by the wider environmental or structural conditions associated with late modernity). In what follows, we offer for discussion a multi-level interpretation of contemporary Islamic Jihadism that nicely synthesizes macro-, meso- and micro-level concerns. We recognize, of course, that numerous other forms and theatres of contemporary terrorist activity exist. However, it is terrorist activity associated with radical Jihad that is overwhelmingly the most prominent and potent contemporary manifestation, and hence we have selected it for discussion here.

There is much that could be said about macro matters and terrorism. Many commentators, for example, (wrongly) account for the rise of Islamic terrorism by recourse solely to broad structural factors. It is a line of logic that has also long been a centrepiece in the US National Strategy for Combating Terrorism, which includes the adjunct programme 'War on Poverty' in an effort to reduce terrorism's pool of support and recruitment (cited in Atran, 2004). However, even though it is a fact that most Islamic terrorists are certainly not suffering from economic deprivation (Gurr, 2007), it can still be conjectured that support for radical Islamism will be especially acute among those whose legitimate opportunities for achieving personal or community fulfilment are severely limited, hence renewed support for the extremist Muslim Brotherhood in today's Egypt or the increased recruitment to the Mahdi Army in post-invasion Iraq. This line of argument is the stock-in-trade of much orthodox terrorism studies. But as the social anthropologist Scott Atran and others have pointed out, such blunt structuralism does not account for why some individuals are drawn to adopting radical positions, while others reject violence and destruction. Likewise, the recent phenomenon of the 'lone-wolf terrorist' (Spaaij, 2011;

138 | Cultural Criminology

Michael, 2012; Hamm, 2015) is also difficult to explain through a structural lens. At this point, we must augment macro analyses of Islamic terrorism by blending background problems (such as structurally imposed poverty and social exclusion) with both meso-level (subcultural and ideological) and importantly micro-level (subjective and existential) triggers. The following account of a repugnant Islamic terrorist act that took place on the streets of Holland does precisely this.

In reviewing Ian Buruma's (2007) book *Murder in Amsterdam: The Death of Theo van Gogh and the Limits of Tolerance*, the criminologist Simon Cottee (2009a) makes a number of interesting points; chief among them is the way Cottee uses subcultural criminological theory to augment Buruma's biography of Van Gogh's murderer, the 26-year-old Moroccan-Dutchman, Mohammed Bouyeri. Cottee's starting point is Al Cohen's 1955 subcultural classic, *Delinquent Boys: The Culture of the Gang* (see Chapter 2). Simply stated, Cohen's aim was to understand how the delinquent street gang functioned and why it is 'distributed as it is within our social system' (1955: 18). Among other observations, Cohen identified the 'negativistic' quality of delinquency, remarking that the values of the gang are not merely at odds with the values of 'respectable society', they are a direct 'inversion' of them: 'the delinquent subculture takes its norms from the larger culture but turns them upside down.' This 'reaction-formation' establishes 'a set of status criteria ['toughness', 'defiance' etc.] in terms of which the boy can more easily succeed … enabling him to retaliate against the norms at whose impact his ego has suffered' (1955: 168). As Cottee suggests: 'The delinquent gang, then, is created to resolve the problem of status frustration among working-class boys. It is a collective "solution" to a structurally imposed "problem"' (2009a: 1126).

Returning to *Murder in Amsterdam*, Buruma (2007) claims that Bouyeri can be understood via similar psychosocial processes, specifically those of *status-frustration* and *identity-confusion*. His ambitions and aspirations blocked at every turn, Bouyeri's life as a second-generation Muslim-immigrant in the Netherlands, was, as Buruma documents, a catalogue of failures and disappointments that made him at times resentful and angry.[2] This status-frustration was intensified by Bouyeri's identity-confusion – his double alienation from both the culture of his parents and the culture of mainstream Dutch society. Buruma's portrayal of Bouyeri – following Magnus Enzensberger – is of a 'radical loser', someone who cannot 'bear to live with themselves', and (like Cohen's gang members) wants to bring the rest of the community down with them. Yet, as Cottee infers from Buruma's biography, figures like Bouyeri 'can never entirely rid themselves of the suspicion that their predicament is self-inflicted, that they themselves are responsible for their humiliation, and they do not merit the esteem they crave' (2009a: 1127). It is at this point Cottee suggests that, like the delinquent gang for working-class Americans, the subculture of *jihadism* serves 'as a "solution" to the problems that

young second-generation Muslim immigrants face in the advanced secular societies of the West: problems specifically bound up with status and identity':

> The *jihadist* subculture not only provides a potent vocabulary for expressing out-
> right contempt for 'Western' values – values that humiliatingly scorn and mock the
> *jihadist*, since they cannot live up to them; it also confers a heroic status upon its
> members, and legitimates violent revenge against the sources of their frustration.
> Moreover, it provides them with a powerful sense of identity, and an unambiguous
> and infallible guide for negotiating their lives in the face of the vertiginous array of
> choices and possibilities and temptations that advanced Western societies have to
> offer ... Seen in this light, the roots of *jihadsim* lie not in Islam, but in how Muslim
> men respond to personal feelings of failure over who or what they are. This does
> not mean that the ideology of violent Islam is causally unimportant: on the contrary,
> it provides the justifying and exculpatory narrative that enables *jihadists* to over-
> come civilised moral constraints. Buruma clearly recognises this, and gives the ideology
> its due causal weight as a device for harnessing and unleashing murderous rage. But
> he also recognises that *jihadism* has its roots in the subjective emotional experiences
> of the actual *jihadists*. (2009a: 1127)

In this important quotation, Cottee shows us how macro-level background problems bring about meso-level subcultural and ideological reactions. But although
problematic, this relationship alone does not a terrorist make – for that, as we
have argued elsewhere (Cottce and Hayward, 2011), we must also engage in a
micro-level analysis of terrorism.

At the micro level, cultural criminology has its roots in the dynamic nature of
(individual) experience, as exemplified by the phenomenology of Jack Katz, the
subterranean naturalism of David Matza and the micro sociology of Erving
Goffman (see Chapters 2 and 3). The goal of these scholars was to unearth the
enigmatic human emotions and existential drives behind different modes of
criminality. This interest in emotional behaviour was useful because it helped
wrest the emotions back from the realm of psychopathology, but it also
cemented the notion that emotions are situationally responsive and socially
contingent; as Morrison (1995) suggests, emotions are 'stimulated by cultural
interpretation, and enjoyed or down-played in social interaction'. Cultural
criminology has continued this tradition but importantly augmented it by bal-
ancing this focus on existential motivations with a concern for essential
background factors (Ferrell, 1992: 118–19; Young, 2003; Hayward, 2004: 152–166).
Consider, for example, the following quotation by the cultural criminologist,
Wayne Morrison, and how the words might be applied to, say, Western-educated
Islamic revolutionary extremists:

> To become self-defining is the fate that the social structure of late-modernity
> imposes upon its socially created individuality. The individual is called into action;
> actions which are meant to express his/her self and enable the individual's destiny

to be created out of the contingencies of his/her past … And while resources differ, all are subjected to variations of a similar pressure as modernity moves into post-modernism, namely that of the overburdening of the self as the self becomes the ultimate source of security. The tasks asked of the late-modern person require high degrees of social and technical skills. To control the self and guide it through the disequilibrium of the journeys of late modernity is the task imposed upon the late-modern person, but what if the life experiences of the individual have not fitted him/her with this power? … Much crime is an attempt of the self to create sacred moments of control, to find ways in which the self can exercise control and power in situations where power and control are all too clearly lodged outside the self. (1995: iv)

Consider in this regard Mark Hamm's (2013) concept of 'the searcher'. Studying a number of terrorist attacks planned and instigated by ex-prisoners, Hamm became interested in a growing group of young men who had converted to radical forms of Islam whilst incarcerated in US prisons. Overwhelmingly, the prisoners in his sample had previously been involved in both street gangs and/or prison gangs. Hamm concluded that their recent conversion to radical Islam was simply the next stop on the subcultural train, and that this latest 'search for spirituality' could be explained as an attempt 'to interpret and resolve discontent'. These incarcerated jihadists, he concluded, have been 'searching for a narrative' all of their (often chaotic) lives. In other words, as Cottee outlines above in an important statement that bears repeating, 'whilst one needs to give the ideology of jihad its due causal weight as a device for harnessing and unleashing violence, one must also recognize that Western *jihadism* has its roots in the subjective emotional experiences of the actual *jihadists*'.

This line of argument can be expressed in another way. Traditional terrorism research has overwhelmingly tended to focus on two questions (1) *how terrorists act*; and (2) *how terrorists think*. In doing so, it has typically neglected a very important third question: *how do terrorists feel*? By adopting this focus, terrorism studies has prioritized ideology and instrumentality at the expense of emotionality. Thankfully, a second development in the field has emerged that prioritizes the micro-level analysis of terrorism and thus addresses this shortcoming (see Post, 2005; Cottee, 2009a,b; Wright-Neville and Smith, 2009; Atran, 2010; Cottee and Hayward, 2011; McBridge, 2011). Simon Cottee and Keith Hayward (2011) advance the possibility that terrorism is, or can be, as much an *existential* as a political phenomenon and that part of what makes it attractive as a behavioural activity is its allure as a *life mode* or *way of being*. Drawing their empirical data from a range of disciplines such as war studies, sociology, criminology and psychology, and subjects such as contract killing, street robbery, combat and terrorist biographies, they proffer three 'terrorist (e)motives' (the 'e' referring to existential): desire for excitement, desire for ultimate meaning and desire for glory.[3]

Desire for excitement

Although terrorism is indisputably a political act, we must never lose sight of the fact that it also involves violence, and as such it

> involves the deliberate infliction of physical harm or injury on human beings. To put it more strongly, terrorist acts are purposively designed to explode human bodies and tear limbs apart and shred flesh. Terrorist organizations consist of people whose primary aim is to orchestrate and carry out these acts. Terrorism is bloody, destructive and brutal; and terrorists are professional killers, the agents of physical harm and destruction. In order to properly understand terrorism, it is essential to fully recognize this – that terrorists are not just political agents, but also *violent* agents. This raises the possibility that part of the motivation behind terrorism lies in the various emotional experiences or sensual attractions associated with doing violent acts. Preeminent among these is excitement. (Cottee and Hayward, 2011: 996)

This logic was explored earlier in this chapter in relation to the allure of combat as articulated by the likes of Sebastian Junger, Philip Caputo and Chris Hedges. The question we now pose is: Are terrorists similarly enthralled and seduced by the mad excitement of violence? Drawing on Cottee and Hayward's framework, we believe that at least some of them are – something substantiated when one takes the time to read the autobiographical statements of actual terrorists.

In *Memoirs of an Italian Terrorist*, the author and former member of the Brigate Rosse,[4] who identifies himself only as 'Giorgio' (presumably his *nom de guerre*), recalls an episode in which he shot a handgun at the police during a demonstration. Giorgio describes the moment just after he discharged his revolver: 'I wasn't even slightly afraid; I was running easily, with no effort. There was something behind me that I was running away from, but it wasn't fear. My only thought was to reach the rest of the demonstration. But while I was running, one step after the other, my throat tightened with a secret, private feeling: I felt like laughing, smiling, jumping into the air' (Giorgio, 2003: 79). Similarly emotive experiences are recalled by Michael Baumann, a leading member of the German June 2nd Movement, in his autobiography *Terror or Love?*: 'We got the molotovs out of the car and threw them at the Springer trucks. That was really good … A lot of crazy shit happened that night: you got energy from it, a real high. Of course it was good too because there was a lot of humor, and that turned a lot of people on too' (Baumann, 1979: 41). Returning to contemporary Islamist terrorism, Aukai Collins, a former international jihadist and informer to the US government, is even more forthright on the pleasures of violent combat. Describing his first firefight against Russian troops in Chechnya, he writes: 'As we ran I felt the blood coursing through my veins with every heartbeat, felt every breath I took, felt the sweat run down my face. I'd never felt so alive. This was real. There wasn't any other way than this', concluding later, 'In Chechnya

I'd loved to walk point and had even lost my leg to it, but here I was again. Most fools love war until they experience it. On that day I realized that I was among the strange few who knew war and loved it nonetheless' (Collins, 2006: 72, 203). Such personal commentaries suggest that

> the excitement of violence derives in part from its emotional intensity and the heightened state of consciousness which this produces. Because of its dangers and risks, violence reawakens and arouses our senses, delivering that convulsion of adrenaline which makes it so compellingly attractive, even addictive. (Cottee and Hayward, 2011: 969)

Add to this the excitement and enhanced sense of self that stems from the clandestine activities associated with terrorism, such as recruiting willing accomplices, planning the attack, avoiding detection, gathering illegal information on bomb making or weaponry, even the drama and adventure of travelling overseas, and it's clear that terrorism provides limitless opportunities for an elevated and emotionally charged *mode of being*.

For the likes of 'Giorgio', Michael Baumann, Aukai Collins and a number of other terrorists who have left behind traces of autobiography (see, for example, the 1,500-page manifesto of the Norwegian terrorist, Anders Breivik; and Sandberg (2013) for a commentary), terrorism and excitement are inextricably linked. Moreover, and here we return to the broader social theoretical territory evoked both in the Wayne Morrison quote above and Mark Hamm's concept of 'the searcher', this search for excitement is frequently bound up with a search for ontological security. Put differently, if, as Michael Baumann suggests, terrorists are indeed 'yearning for something' (1979), then perhaps we should also consider the possibility that much terrorist ideology is simply an exculpatory narrative used by individuals to both justify their acts and provide a further sense of *existential meaning*.

Desire for ultimate meaning

> In addition to existential certainty, the terrorist group also provides its members with a sense of *ultimate meaning*: that is, the feeling that one is an active participant in a cosmic battle to defend the sacred … In defending the sacred, one experiences something larger than him- or herself, a meaning that gloriously soars above and renders insignificant one's own often frivolous and banal personal concerns. One experiences an ultimate meaning and purpose for which to live and even die. (Cottee and Hayward, 2011: 973)

Given that the vast majority of terrorists operate in groups, cells and insurgent militias, service to the sacred necessarily involves the defence of both the cause (Islam, the Nation, the Oppressed) and one's comrades. This latter concern is especially important in that it highlights the issue of group fidelity and the satisfaction derived from dedicating one's life to an ideological calling or brotherhood. Again, a parallel with military combat is instructive. We know from historical studies (such as those conducted on the Nazi soldiers who 'stubbornly fought to the end') that what typically galvanizes combat troops is not abstract notions of nationhood or political ideology, but the more personal and emotional ties that bind soldiers as friends and comrades. This sense of fierce commitment to each other has been described by Sebastian Junger in his book *War* as not just the deep affection forged in combat, but as a form of love (Junger, 2010: 239). Might this focus on the emotions of front-line combat troops also tell us something about terrorist group dynamics? (Lest we forget, countless terrorists have throughout history defined themselves as soldier combatants in a 'just war' against an evil adversary.) After all, like combat soldiers, terrorists often function as part of a tightly knit unit; on joining the organization, they are stripped of their status and asked to give up aspects of their previous lifestyle; and most importantly, they are asked to make a commitment that could result in death and destruction. Such comparisons, as Cottee and Hayward suggest, bear serious examination:

> Research on the motivations behind terrorism tends to focus on the role of the negative emotions and terrorists in this literature are commonly portrayed as pitiable figures: humiliated, frustrated, alienated, angry or hateful. These portrayals, in the specific cases to which they are applied, may well be valid. But it is also possible that in yet other cases terrorist actors may be animated by *positive* emotions, such as love, solidarity and compassion. Perhaps it is morally troubling to suggest that terrorists are activated by love, in the same way that it is morally troubling to describe them as courageous. But it may well be empirically valid in specific cases, and deserves greater exploration as a possible source of terrorist motivation. It may also help bring into focus one of the core existential attractions of terrorism: namely, violent struggle and self-sacrifice in service to the sacred. (2011: 975)[5]

Desire for glory

Contributing to an Internet forum on 7 August 2006, the American jihadi Omar Hammami, wrote: 'Where is the desire to do something amazing? Where is the urge to get up and change yourself – not to mention the world and other issues further off? Stop sticking to the earth and let your soul fly!'[6] Such statements provide a striking example of Cottee and Hayward's third 'terrorist (e)motive' – the desire for glory, or more specifically, the idea of terrorism as an *identity project*, a deeply flawed form of self-affirmation. The thinking here is that terrorists may be using violent, revengeful ideological narratives to give dramatic expression to their sense of who they are and what they aspire to be. Might it not be the case then, for example, that, 'part of what makes terrorist groups attractive is the scope they offer their members to define or remake themselves as *heroic figures*, belonging to an exalted elite' (Cottee and Hayward, 2011: 976)? In recent years, a number of terrorist scholars have begun to develop this line of argument specifically, but not exclusively, in relation to suicide bombers and Salafi-jihadists (see, for example, Oliver and Steinberg, 2005; Kruglanski et al., 2009; Sageman, 2010; and, relatedly, Juergensmeyer, 2001). Cottee and Hayward draw on such work to argue that at least some of the appeal of travelling to places such as Syria, Somalia and the Yemen in a bid to wage international jihad in the name of Allah and the restoration of the Caliphate, is the opportunity to become an elevated *righteous warrior*, a heroic figure in a cosmic struggle. Suicide bombers similarly feel a sense of ennoblement:

> From the moment they accept their mission to the moment they carry it out, the suicide bomber experiments with and actively takes on a new identity as a holy warrior and martyr-in-waiting. Thus, intriguingly and paradoxically, in doing a suicide mission the suicide bomber is simultaneously engaged in an act of self-destruction *and* an act of self-recreation. (2011: 976)

Perhaps the most important statement on such matters, though, has been made by Marc Sageman who controversially applies the label 'terrorist wannabes' to young men drawn in by jihadi propaganda:

> They dream about becoming heroes in this 'War against Islam,' modelling themselves on the seventh century Muslim warriors that conquered half the world and the Mujahedin who defeated the Soviet Union in Afghanistan in the 1980s. Many hope to emulate these predecessors by fighting in Iraq against coalition forces. Their interpretation, that the West is involved in a 'War against Islam,' is just a sound bite and has little depth to it. People bombing Western cities and volunteering for Iraq are not interested in theological debates but in *living out their heroic fantasies*. (Sageman, 2010: 31)

As Sageman suggests, the key to understanding the behaviour of many of today's jihadis is to be found not in how they think but in how they *feel* – especially about themselves and their place in the world. In other words, rather than simply repeating the approach followed by many terrorism scholars (and now many criminologists working on terrorism) and seeking to normalize the terrorist agent, the more urgent task is to *humanize* him. For as we mentioned above, at the end of the day it is *people* who plant bombs and behead prisoners, and therefore it is essential we understand the personal and interactional variables that compel individuals and groups to undertake terrorist violence. It may be an unpalatable thought, but there is a warped creativity associated with many terrorist acts (Hughes, 2011), just as there is an exuberant, carnivalesque element to systematic violence and barbarism. Not recognizing this, and instead continuing to view the perpetrators of these acts simply as cognitive ciphers, is an intelligence failing indeed.

Conclusion: possibilities and provocations

Today's world of international conflict is fast changing and complex, wracked by such problems as the unfettered development of private military power (Balko, 2014) and the dangerous revival of interest in orthodox religious doctrines that run against the grain of enlightenment and reason (Cottee, 2014). As such, it becomes all the more important that we develop a criminology capable of understanding the social havoc that such developments cause. In doing so, we must always remain vigilant when critiquing the processes by which war crimes are defined and constructed, and state power is attained and enforced (Chomsky, 2002; Blakeley, 2009). But equally we must also guard against the tendency to focus only on the existing power structures and socio-historical contingencies that constitute state power, lest our analyses become blunt or one-dimensional. On the contrary, as we have stated throughout this chapter, our approach to this field of study is constituted from the macro, micro and meso levels in an ongoing process of intellectual cross-fertilization in which each level incorporates something of the other, informs the other's development and so becomes more than any level could singly.

Thankfully, this process is already well underway, as cultural criminologists from around the world undertake their own multi-level syntheses of state, war and terrorism-related concerns – from Wayne Morrison's (2004a, 2006) use of photographs and paintings to uncover the truth behind criminology's studied neglect of genocide and state crime in modernity, to Tyler Wall's (2013; Wall and Monahan, 2011) research on drone surveillance and other M.O.U.T. (military operations in urban terrain) technologies now being used by domestic police forces; from Fahid Qurashi (2013) research on contemporary Islamic 'Radical Rudeboy' culture, a growing Western street style that employs semiotic and linguistic allusions to Jihadi terrorism as a 'revolutionary' subcultural seduction (see also Vidino, 2010, on Islamic 'hybrid street culture'), to the growing body of work on walling, rampart construction and the interlocking systems of fortification associated with today's divisive inter- and intra-state territoriality – a virulent process underway everywhere from Baghdad to Botswana, from the West Bank to West Hollywood (Caldeira, 2001; Davis, 2005; Brown, 2010; Lara, 2011; Hayward, 2012b: 453–5; Zeiderman, 2013). But these are just the opening salvos in what must be a longer and wider-ranging campaign, not least because there is so much to be studied. Torture, the systematic rape of civilian women by military personnel, the use of social media by terrorists and insurrectionists, the role of death squads in proxy wars against enemy governments, the staged perfomativity of Jihadi beheadings ... the list goes on. Only, one thing is certain, we must not shirk from the challenge, for we are most decidedly in a race against time.

A selection of films and documentaries illustrative of some of the themes and ideas in this chapter

Restrepo, 2010, Dirs Tim Hetherington and Sebastian Junger

The late photo journalist Tim Hetherington and the author Sebastian Junger spent a year with an American army platoon stationed in one of the most dangerous valleys in Afghanistan; the result is this unparalleled, extraordinary documentary that charts life on the front line as the soldiers' lives oscillate between the mundane aspects of army life and the exhilaration of firefights with the Taliban. *Restrepo* beautifully captures the camaraderie of close-knit military units. See also Sebastian Junger's 2010 book, *War*, one of the most compelling accounts of life on the battlefield ever written.

The Battle of Algiers, 1966, Dir. Gillo Pontecorvo

The winner of multiple awards, *The Battle of Algiers* uses intense realism to depict the Algerian Liberation Front's struggle against French colonial power. With scenes of violence, police torture, political assassinations and terrorist bombings, the film blends dramatic scenes and recreations of historically accurate events to show the unfolding of colonial and postcolonial violence and its role in the creation of the contemporary world order. Interestingly, it is alleged that the film was screened in the White House prior to the invasion of Iraq.

Four Hours in My Lai, 1989, Dir. Kevin Sim

Originally made by Yorkshire Television in the UK back in 1989, *Four Hours in My Lai* contains a series of fascinating and haunting interviews with surviving victims and perpetrators of the My Lai massacre of March 1968, when members of 'Charlie Company' (C Company, 1st battalion, 20th Infantry, 11th Light Infantry Brigade of the US Army) went on a killing spree in the Vietnamese village of Tu Cung. Not only are the interviews with former members of Charlie Company extremely moving, but they highlight how soldiers both 'neutralized' their behaviour and negotiated their level of involvement. (The film is available on YouTube.)

No End in Sight, 2007, Dir. Charles H. Ferguson

A no-nonsense documentary that focuses on that litany of mistakes and misjudgements made by the Bush administration in the two-year period following the invasion of Iraq. With commentary from on-the-ground Bush staffers and military personnel, the film cuts through the political spin to present a harrowing story of neo-conservative over-confidence and arrogance. *No End in Sight* makes a mockery of 'Mission Accomplished' and similar meaningless sound bites.

(Continued)

(Continued)

Poster Girl, 2010, Dir. Sara Nesson

An Oscar-nominated documentary that follows former-cheerleader-turned-US-Army-machine-gunner Robynn Murray's journey as she attempts to deal with the symptoms of post-traumatic stress disorder after facing the brutalities of war in Iraq.

The Believer, 2000, Dir. Henry Bean

A gripping feature film (starring a young Ryan Gosling) about a self-hating neo-Nazi in contemporary America and his struggle to come to terms with his ethnic heritage – a struggle that leads to a world of violence and a path of self-destruction. Useful for thinking about the existential seductions of terrorism and hate crime.

The Act of Killing, 2012, Dirs Joshua Oppenheimer, Anonymous, Christine Cynn

An amazing, almost surreal masterpiece that records the testimonies of Indonesian death-squad members responsible for slaughtering an estimated one million ethnic Chinese between 1965 and 1966. One former member, who we see walking as a free man, claims to have garrotted over a thousand victims during the carnage. A truly harrowing analysis of genocide.

Come and See, 1985, Dir. Elem Klimov

Claimed by some critics to be the most harrowing portrayal of war ever committed to film, *Come and See* is a rare Hungarian film that traces the story of a young Belorussian boy who is forced to fight alongside a hopelessly ill-equipped Soviet resistance movement against occupying German forces. As each scene of terror intensifies, the boy struggles to keep his innocence and ultimately his sanity.

The Hurt Locker, 2008, Dir. Kathryn Bigelow

An Oscar-winning movie about the lives of elite US Army bomb-disposal experts stationed in Iraq. The film offers an insight into the existential attractions of violent conflict and the toll those attractions take on soldiers' lives.

First Kill, 2001, Dir. Coco Schrijber

First-hand accounts of the highs and lows of combat by US veterans of the Vietnam War. The veterans describe how it felt to kill for the first time and how those feelings still haunt them.

Why We Fight, 2005, Dir. Eugene Jarecki

Taking as its starting point the famous speech by former US President Dwight D. Eisenhower in which he coins the term 'the military industrial complex', *Why We Fight* poses a number of important questions, such as: Is American foreign policy dominated by the idea of military supremacy? Has the military become too important in American life? Jarecki's documentary would seem to give an affirmative answer to each of these questions.

Vice News: The Islamic State, 2014, Dir. Medyan Dairieh

One of the most remarkable pieces of 'gonzo' video journalism of the twenty-first century, Medyan Dairieh spent three weeks filming alone inside the self-proclaimed

Caliphate of the Islamic State (in reality, the beleaguered strips of war-torn land formerly belonging to Iraq and Syria). This partial but nonetheless riveting documentary shows in no uncertain terms that twenty-first-century Jihad is as much about power, micro and meso fascism and masculinist violence as it is about politicized notions of Islam. This is available to watch free at: https://news.vice.com/show/the-islamic-state and www.filmsforaction.org/. Do yourself a favour: watch it.

Further Reading

Cottee, S. (2014) 'We need to talk about Mohammad: Criminology, Theistic Violence and the Murder of Theo Van Gogh, *British Journal of Criminology,* **54(6): 981–1001.**
Journal article in which Simon Cottee discusses a subject largely neglected by criminologists: the issue of jihadi violence and the broader question it raises about the relationship between religion and violent extremism.

Morrison, W. (2006) *Criminology, Civilization and the New World Order.* **London: GlassHouse.**
Theoretical monograph that examines the question of why criminology, as an academic discipline, has largely ignored issues surrounding genocide and other forms of state crime.

Bloom, M. (2014) *Bombshell: Women and Terrorism.* **Philadelphia, PA: University of Pennsylvania Press.**
One of the world's leading terrorism scholars, Mia Bloom, explores the role of women in terrorism today. Moving beyond gender stereotypes to examine the conditions that really influence female violence, Bloom argues that, while women terrorists can be just as bloodthirsty as their male counterparts, their motivations tend to be more intricate and multilayered.

Junger, S. (2010) *War.* **London: Fourth Estate.**
The book that inspired the film, *Restrepo* (see above). Junger documents everyday life for a single US infantry platoon through a 15-month tour of duty in the most dangerous outpost in Afghanistan's Korengal Valley.

Hedges, C. (2002) *War is a Force that Gives us Meaning.* **New York: Anchor Books.**
Veteran war correspondent Chris Hedges draws on his experience of combat zones to show us how war seduces not just those on the front lines but entire societies, corrupting politics, destroying culture, and perverting the most basic human desires.

Hamm, M. S. (2013) *The Spectacular Few: Prisoner Radicalization and the Evolving Terrorist Threat.* **New York: New York University Press.**
Drawing on a series of prisoner narratives, cultural criminologist and terrorism scholar Mark Hamm traces how terrorist radicalization and recruitment can take place within the prison setting.

(Continued)

(Continued)

Useful Websites

Sebastianjunger.com
www.sebastianjunger.com/
The author and filmmaker Sebastian Junger's homepage. For photos, film clips, and contact details relating to Junger's reporting and writing on combat.

Statewatch
www.statewatch.org/
Website that monitors excesses of state power and the erosion of civil liberties in Europe. Updated weekly, the site has a database of over 30,000 searchable free articles on subjects like state crime, environmental crime, surveillance, and paramilitary activity.

John Pilger's website
http://johnpilger.com/
Link to the films and journalism of veteran Australian journalist and war correspondent, John Pilger. The site includes free access to over 60 of Pilger's documentaries, including *The War on Democracy* (2007) and *The War You Don't See* (2010).

***Terrorism and Political Violence* (London: Routledge)**
www.tandfonline.com/loi/ftpv20#.VK_t2tKsV8E
Interdisciplinary academic journal interested in the political meaning of terrorist activity. *Terrorism and Political Violence* publishes work on violence by rebels and by states, and on the links between political violence and organized crime, protest, rebellion, revolution, and human rights.

Notes

1 Critical terrorism studies is not without its critics – see, for example, Horgan and Boyle (2008); Weinberg and Eubank (2008); and Joseph (2011) for thoughtful analyses.
2 See also Young (2007, Chapter 8) for a related cultural criminological analysis of terrorism, the dialectics of 'othering' and life 'inside and outside the First World'.
3 The following three sections draw closely on Cottee and Hayward (2011).
4 The Brigate Rosse, or Red Brigade, was a Marxist-Leninist paramilitary organization active in Italy during the 1970s and 1980s.
5 For example, in their research on Palestinian suicide terrorism, Ami Pedahzur, Arie Perliger and Leonard Weinberg (2003) suggest that altruism, in conjunction with fatalistic despair, is a significant motive for Palestinian suicide terrorists.
6 Quoted in Elliott (2010).

6

MEDIA, REPRESENTATION AND MEANING: INSIDE THE HALL OF MIRRORS

There is nothing more to explain … as long as words keep their meanings, and meanings their words. (*Alphaville*, dir. Jean-Luc Godard, 1965)

A priori, we were being attacked on an image level, and therefore we should have prepared and responded on an image level, on the narrative level, and we could have won that. (Einat Wilf, Member of Israeli Parliament, commenting on the media fallout after Israeli troops boarded a Turkish aid ship bound for Gaza, on BBC2's *Newsnight*, 1 June 2010)

Cultural criminology's sense that the meaning of crime and crime control is always under construction comes into especially sharp focus when we consider our contemporary world of media festival and digital spectacle (see Hayward and Presdee, 2010). For many of us, it is a rare day indeed when we don't interact with the late modern 'mediascape' (Appadurai, 1996: 35), that bundle of media that manufactures information and disseminates images via an expanding array of digital technologies. In this enveloping world of the *Mediapolis* (De Jong and Schuilenburg, 2006), meaning is made in motion. Pervasively popular forms of contemporary communications now constitute the primary gauge by which we assess the value and importance of current events – from the most serious to the most banal. Pop culture blurs with news media reportage, images of crime and war are repackaged as entertaining digital escapism, and unreal 'reality TV' moments shape moral values and social norms. In this world, the street scripts the screen and the screen scripts the street (Hayward and Young, 2004: 259); there is no clearly linear sequence, but rather a shifting interplay between the real and the virtual, the factual and the fictional. Late-modern society is saturated with collective meaning and suffused with symbolic uncertainty as media messages and cultural traces swirl, circulate and vacillate.

These are the conditions that symbolic interactionists and labelling theorists anticipated decades ago, with their sense of transgression as a sequenced negotiation of unsettled social identity (see Chapter 2); only now the situation has intensified. Enter the theorists of the so-called 'postmodern', that *Boulevard*-wise ensemble of predominantly French intellectuals who sought to understand the fluctuating socio-cultural and epistemic transformations associated with the mediascape. While Jean-François Lyotard, Michel Maffesoli and Paul Virilio have all had their say about this fluid, mediated epoch of 'disengagement, elusiveness, facile escape and hopeless chase' (Bauman, 2000: 120), it was the self-styled 'intellectual terrorist' Jean Baudrillard who was the most influential. Simply stated, Baudrillard argued that society is now constituted around reflexive 'signs' and 'codes' that have little or no referent to a 'reality' other than their own, hence his world of 'hyperreal' simulation – a media-saturated environment of 'connections, contact, contiguity, feedback and generalized interface ... a pornography of all functions and objects in their readability, their fluidity, their availability ... their performativity ... their polyvalence' (Baudrillard, 1985: 126–34; see also 1983, 1996).

Heady intellectual stuff – but if one of the goals of cultural criminology is to move beyond the insightful, yet now dated, interactionist analyses of the 1960s, it is also reluctant to embrace uncritically this post-modern sensibility; while Baudrillard may inhabit a 'void-like world of empty signs and unfilled desires', many others find crime to be painfully tangible and immediate in its impact. Yet, while many criminal acts retain their sensual immediacy, the *culture* of such acts increasingly resembles not so much static entity or domain as *flow*, a flow that carries with it the contested meanings of crime and criminality. To paraphrase Marshall McLuhan, it's this movement that in many ways is the message; this constant flow of collective meaning is itself meaningful, itself a circuitry of meaning, opening up possibilities of social control and social protest unavailable under more solid circumstances. Abuses of legal and political authority defy direct confrontation, slipping away just as we might catch them out, circulating and escaping through skilfully spun press releases and photographs lost and found. Resistance to such authority is no sure thing either, always in danger of becoming the medium through which it is carried out, or even that which it resists – and yet this very uncertainty offers new possibilities for a politics of subversion, for a 'semiotic guerrilla warfare' that fights and falls back (Umberto Eco, as quoted in Hebdige, 1979: 105). Criminals and the crimes they commit likewise often seem on the move, criss-crossing the contradictions of a globalized political economy, other times tangled up in their own mediated representations. The terms of cultural and political engagement, the meaning of crime and resistance and control, remain endlessly unsettled.

This situation is perfectly illustrated when one considers the wave of uprisings, protests and civil disturbances generally referred to as the Arab Spring. In Iran, for example, following the ballot-rigging that saw President Mahmoud Ahmadinejad controversially re-elected for a second term in June 2009, supporters of the opposition candidate Mi-Hossein Mousavi took to the streets – only this time they were carrying mobile phones and digital cameras along with their placards. Within hours, the first of a series of iconic cell phone videos of Iranian riot police beating down protestors were being uploaded to YouTube. One particular video of the collective punishment of a crowd, including violent attacks on a number of women, showed that 'the once-forlorn slogan of the anti-globalization movement had become a reality: the whole world *was* watching' (Mason, 2012: 35):

> By nightfall, that video was zipping around the global Farsi networks via blogs, YouTube, Twitter and Facebook. If it had been taken by a TV cameraman, that 58-second single shot would have won awards. It captures reality in a way you rarely see on TV news: terror, chaos, innocence, the sudden tremor in the policeman's face as he bottles out of hitting the cameraman again. But the point about the video is that it is not shot by a news crew, nor was it shown in full on any TV network. Social media's power to present unmediated reality has never been better demonstrated. (2012: 34)

But lest we forget, these same channels of communication can also be open to manipulation and exploitation.

West of Iran and another crisis of state legitimacy: this time the bloody struggle for power in civil war-torn Syria. In the early stages of the insurrection, the Assad regime banned foreign journalists from reporting on the military crackdown. So, desperate to promulgate their message to a watching world, local activist 'video journalists' (VJs) braved sniper bullets and street fighting to document the crisis. From makeshift broadcast centres, these citizen VJs overcame government attempts to jam Internet connections by using portable satellite dishes smuggled into Syria by pro-democracy campaigners. Yet, whilst their courage and innovation were not in doubt, their approach to newsgathering broke journalistic convention. Hell bent on getting across their message, VJs often carried (and discharged) weapons and used tactics such as deliberately setting fire to car tyres as a backdrop to their reports to suggest they were under direct attack from Assad's forces. In such volatile worlds, self-organized production of news media has obvious benefits, but not if truth and impartiality become just another casualty of the conflict.

If our aim is the development of a critically engaged cultural criminology, we must account for this cultural motion, must imagine ways to track meaning as it moves through the politics of crime and social control. We certainly cannot forget the experiential consequences of crime, nor surrender our critical stance to the seductions of cultural uncertainty or postmodern parlour games. But we can't forget the swirling dynamics of culture, either; a photograph, a freeze frame, can catch a moment in an emerging process, but, ultimately, neither substitutes for a moving picture of the process itself. We must conceptualize the flow of collective meaning, must immerse ourselves in it – and in immersing ourselves, perhaps discover ways to move this cultural fluidity towards progressive ends.

A key aim of this chapter, then, is to introduce and analyse some of the ways in which the meaning of crime circulates within the late-modern mediascape. After all, while notions of cultural 'motion' or 'flow' imply instabilities of collective meaning, they needn't suggest that this motion is random or that this flow is unfettered or unstructured. Far from it – political economies of contemporary culture regularly set meaning in motion and, at least initially, set the terms and parameters of its movement; just as, often, emerging technologies invent new channels through which mediated perceptions can move or be confronted. Even in motion, collective meaning leaves traces of influence and understanding, and offers up trajectories amidst all the movement.

Loops and spirals: crime as media, media as crime

For the cultural critic Paul Virilio (1986, 1991), an axiomatic feature of late-modern life is what he calls 'the logic of speed'. Virilio's various writings on so-called 'speed culture' turn on the insight that the speed at which something happens ultimately dictates its nature. Consider, as an example, 24-hour rolling news. In this hyper-competitive broadcast environment, it's obvious that 'that which moves at speed quickly comes to dominate that which is slower'. For Virilio, then, it is the speed of movement, or more accurately the velocity of circulation, that dictates what he describes as our postmodern 'logic of perception'. We agree with Virilio – at least when it comes to understanding the remarkable velocity of information in the contemporary mediascape. However, what is perhaps more important is the nature of the circulation itself – that is, the extent to which fast-moving mediated images and bits of information reverberate and bend back on themselves, creating a fluid porosity of meaning that defines late-modern life, and the nature of crime and media within it, more than does speed itself.

Fact or fiction?

A few years back, Jeff Ferrell is being interviewed for a story on urban scrounging by a friendly, decent-minded senior investigative producer for a local television station. After the interview, they're chatting amicably and the producer says, 'Hey, do let me know if you have any ideas for local crime stories. We have all those *CSI* [Crime Scene Investigation] and *Cold Case* [police detective] shows from 9 to 10 pm, and we like to use them as lead-ins to crime stories on the 10 pm newscast'.

Loops

From this view, contemporary culture can be conceptualized as a series of *loops*, an ongoing process by which everyday life recreates itself in its own image. The saturation of social situations with representation and information suggests that the linear sequencing of meaning is now mostly lost, replaced by a doppelgänger world where the ghosts of signification circle back to haunt, and revive, that which they signify. Peter Manning (1995, 1998) describes a social world of screens and reflections, and specifically a televised world of 'media loops' whereby one image becomes the content of another; elsewhere, we've described a mediated 'hall of mirrors' where 'images ... bounce endlessly one off the other' (Ferrell, 1999: 397). No matter the metaphor, each catches something of the same process: a circulating cultural fluidity that challenges any certain distinction between an event and its representation, a mediated image and its effects, a criminal moment and its ongoing construction within collective meaning. Importantly, this looping process suggests for us something more than Baudrillard's postmodern hyper-reality, his sense of an 'unreality' defined only by media images and cultural obfuscation. Quite the opposite: we mean to suggest a late-modern world in which the gritty, on-the-ground reality of crime, violence and everyday criminal justice is dangerously confounded with its own representation.

If this sense of cultural looping constitutes a starting point for making sense of contemporary meaning, it marks a starting point for cultural criminology as well. The mediated nature of contemporary culture not only carries along the meaning of crime and criminality; it circles back to amplify, distort and define the experience of crime and criminality itself. Within such circumstances, crime and culture remain hopelessly confounded – and so any criminology meant to make sense of contemporary crime and control, and to move these circumstances towards progressive possibilities, cannot do so by artificially segregating that which is intimately and inevitably intertwined. Instead, we would argue, a useful criminology of contemporary life must be, if nothing else, *culturally reflexive* – that is, self-attuned to image, symbol and meaning as dimensions that define and redefine transgression and social control.[1]

And when it comes to crime, transgression and control, this looping circularity offers up dynamics that interweave the ludicrous with the malicious. Consider, for example, *Cheaters*, an American reality TV programme (currently in its 14th season) that (allegedly) exposes extramarital affairs. In one episode, the producers contrive and film from numerous angles a confrontation between an estranged husband and his cheating wife. Stepping outside her workplace to phone police about problems with her husband, she is restrained by a *Cheaters* security guard and confronted by her husband, who, by confronting her, violates a protective order and finds himself charged with third-degree felony assault.

A domestic violence expert subsequently argues in the local newspaper that the programme has 'revictimized' the wife; the husband's lawyer counters that 'the videotape doesn't show an assault, in my opinion'. Meanwhile, more *Cheaters* videotape – this time of the wife consorting with her lover – leads to problems for the lover; he's demoted and suspended from his job ... as supervisor of the police department's criminal investigations division (Boyd, 2005a, b; Branch and Boyd, 2005).

In other news – this time from the world of celebrity – the British supermodel Kate Moss sees her career stock ebb and flow at warp speed as her cocaine proclivities are churned through the spin cycle of the world's tabloid press. The resulting interplay of shock, moral indignation, enticement and ultimate normalization says much about contemporary society's ambiguous, and mediated, relationship to drug use. Moss and her supermodel peers have long made a living pedalling corporate products that trade on edgy notions of the forbidden: perfumes like *Opium, Poison* and *Obsession*, Lolita-like sexuality, anorexic aesthetics, allusions to illicit sex and sadomasochism, and the infamous 'heroin chic' aesthetic. Yet, it's not until Moss is secretly filmed snorting cocaine that the media turn on her. With stills from the hidden camera footage splashed all over the British Sunday papers, Moss is publicly pilloried and most of her corporate sponsors drop her like a set of hot curling tongs, claiming her drug-taking image is now inconsistent with the drug-laced messages they purvey to their youthful customers. And the mediated loop of sex, drugs and commodities fizzes on. Moss enters rehab, like a waifish penitent to a late-modern nunnery – and spurred on by the newsworthiness of her publicized contrition and her 'personal battle against drugs', her flagging career is quickly regenerated. A host of multinational corporations now fall over themselves to sign the new and improved 'outlaw' Moss – an odd but marketable embodiment of edgy, street savvy and redemptive.[2]

Criminal justice likewise stumbles over its own image. For a while now, we have been treated to the spectacle of dashboard-mounted squad car camera footage – a window on crime that turns police officers into performers and traffic stops into vignettes available for the nightly news or later prime-time compilation shows such as *World's Wildest Police Videos* and *Police, Camera, Action*. Along with shows like *COPS*, this form of entertainment claims to represent the 'reality' of everyday policing, and has become so popular that it now constitutes its own genre: the so-called 'criminal vérité' format. Yet, while *COPS, Top COPS* and similar 'reality' shows have become television staples – *COPS* alone has been running on and off for over 30 years and over 700 episodes, grossing more than $250 million in the process – the reality they portray is in fact a looping process constructed in conjunction with television cameras and local police departments.

To start with, programmes like *COPS, Border Wars, Traffic Cops, Cops with Cameras, Road Wars, Sky Cops, Police Interceptors* and *Real Vice Cops Uncut* (along with bizarre celebrity-fronted versions such as *Steven Segal: Lawman*, *Vinnie Jones' Toughest Cops* and *Armed and Famous*) inevitably record the ways in which the presence of their cameras alters, and exacerbates, the reality of encounters between police and suspects. While lauding the show's supposedly unfiltered realism, the founding producer of *COPS*, for example, admits 'it's like a casting call. We look for the most proactive, interesting cops'. One cop featured on the show argues that 'what you see is what's happening out there ... [people] know exactly what we go through every day', while adding that 'the only problem I had was ... the sound guy kept giving me the signal to keep talking' (Walker, 1999; Mayhew, 2006; Woodson, 2003). Police chases likewise unfold as interactive made-for-television movies; following one deadly chase, in which a cameraman in the squad car's back seat video-records himself urging the cop to 'Go get him!', a wrongful death suit is filed based on the video-recording (Vick, 1997). More worrying still is the way these programmes shape popular views on policing, and so the mindsets of citizens, voters and police academy recruits. As Richard Rapaport (2007) suggests, both the police and the policed now believe that 'appropriate law-enforcement correlates with high-speed chases, blocking and tackling, drawn weapons, and a shoot-first, think-later mindset'.

Meanwhile, in court, American jurors increasingly expect evidence to match that fictionalized in popular *CSI* (*Crime Scene Investigation*) shows; in response, prosecutors regularly refer to television programmes in their opening statements, alter their presentation of evidence and attend acting classes (Dribben, 2006). Criminologists have even begun to investigate a specific 'CSI effect' – 'jurors who rely too heavily on scientific findings and, conversely, are sceptical about the potential for human or technical error or fraud ... jurors ... who demand that prosecution provide the same type of irrefutable evidence they see on TV' (Mopas, 2007: 111) – despite the fact that many of the forensic techniques employed on *CSI* have been dismissed as 'blatant hokum' (Roane, 2005, cited in Cavender and Deutsch, 2007). In the courtroom as elsewhere, reality and representation blur.

And it's not only jurors who get confused. For example, during the trial of the late rapper ODB (Ol' Dirty Bastard – real name Russell Tyrone Jones) on charges of illegally wearing body armour, his defence attorney argued that 'due to how famous he is, he's at risk of his life. He's been in gun battles and that's why he was wearing body armour'; the deputy district attorney countered by suggesting that ODB 'heads a street gang named Wu-Tang Clan'! Over a decade later and the confusion continues. In 2012, the attempted murder conviction of New Jersey drug dealer Vonte Skinner was overturned by an appellate court after they found that graphic rap lyrics written by Skinner (long before the alleged crime) had been used as evidence by the prosecution to establish Skinner as a violent criminal in the eyes of the jury. Following the decision of the appeal court that the lyrics were inadmissible, attorneys working on behalf of the American Civil

Liberties Union of New Jersey have written an amicus brief urging the State Supreme Court to 'adopt a more stringent set of standards to guide courts in admitting into evidence a criminal defendant's fictional, artistic expressions'. And it would seem those guidelines are sorely needed – the amicus brief identified a further 18 cases in which prosecutors had attempted to use rap lyrics against a defendant (Peters, 2013). In cases such as these, we witness yet another looping dynamic: that of 'cultural criminalization' (Ferrell, 1998a), where mediated publicity trumps legal proceedings in constructing perceptions of guilt and criminal identity.

Spirals

At times, loops such as these remain relatively self-contained, playing out as little episodes that bend back on themselves; more often, they emerge within larger processes of collective meaning, as but one twist or turn in an ongoing spiral of culture and crime. In this sense, the notion of 'loops', while certainly catching something of contemporary culture's fluid reflexivity, sometimes offers only a few frames from a longer film. The collective meaning of crime and deviance is made not once but time and again, as part of an amplifying spiral that winds its way back and forth through media accounts, situated action and public perception. Spiralling in this way, the next loop of meaning never quite comes back around, instead moving on and away to new experiences and new perceptions, all the while echoing, or at other times undermining, meanings and experiences already constructed. As with Cohen's mods and rockers, today's spirals of crime and culture continue to wind and unwind – only faster and more furiously.

Some of the loops already noted could themselves be reconsidered as spirals. When the cameras of 'reality' television programmes like *COPS* alter the very reality they record, when police officers play to the camera and producers proffer instructions and advice, when all of this is framed and edited and broadcast as the unmediated 'reality' of everyday policing, this is only the beginning. From there, 'best of' reality television programmes and for-purchase compilations are cobbled together from programmes already aired – with still other television programmes claiming, in ironic counterpoint, to expose the growing black market in fake reality video footage. As already suggested, lawsuits for wrongful death or invasion of privacy or false arrest are filed, with video footage offered up as evidence and counter-evidence, and of course full media coverage of the trials themselves. Police departments and police officers in turn utilize such programmes as recruiting tools, and as informational devices to keep up with developments in other police departments; one officer even reports that he uses *COPS* as 'a training thing. It helps me to refer to situations when I'm out on the street' (Woodson, 2003: 11F). Rapaport (2007) further documents how other popular permutations of 'criminal vérité' – police SWAT (Special Weapons And Tactics squads) shows like *Kansas City SWAT, Dallas SWAT* and *Detroit SWAT* – have served to 'culturally consecrate activities that have historically been the province of military engagements in places where the Bill of Rights do not apply'. Such shows, he argues, 'invite us to celebrate the Heckler and Koch machine pistols, Parker-Hale Model 85 sniper rifles, flash-bang grenades, armoured personnel carriers, and other paraphernalia of what is essentially infantry war-fighting transferred to American streets'. On their own, law enforcement practices that favour confrontation over consultation and risk aversion over risk assessment are bad enough, but when backed up by military-grade weaponry and army-style vehicles it's hard to imagine that police–community relations will be improved (Balko, 2014).[3] Just ask the citizens of Ferguson, Missouri.

When rappers like ODB are put on trial, when district attorneys confuse a multi-platinum selling rap group with a street gang, this is likewise no one-time collision of music and law. It is but one more turn in a now decades-old dance between rap artists, record companies, local prosecutors and moral entrepreneurs, all of whom find both problem and potential in the intermingling of 'gangsta rap', gangs and criminal history. For the record companies and the rappers, a carefully crafted outlaw image, even a criminal record, moves product; for local prosecutors and religious conservatives, high-profile public campaigns against such images move product as well, if of a somewhat different sort. For an attorney representing an accused killer, this spiral can even become a defence strategy. When Ronald Howard was convicted of killing a Texas state trooper, his defence attorney recalled his failed defence strategy: not guilty by reason of rap music. 'He grew up in the ghetto and disliked police and these were his heroes, these rappers … telling him if you're pulled over, just blast away', said attorney Allen Tanner. 'It affected him. That was a totally valid, serious defense.' And indeed, just before he shot the state trooper, Howard was listening to a Tupac Shakur rap – the one about shooting a cop and remembering the video of Rodney King (Graczyk, 2005).

Two other spirals are also worth noting for their tragic integration of mediated loops, representational spirals and concrete consequences. In the first, Andrea Yates drowns her five children in the family bathtub and at trial the prosecution, seeking to ensure a conviction, calls on psychiatrist and forensic analyst Park Dietz. A 'frequent expert witness' in such cases and a consultant on the NBC television drama *Law and Order*, Dietz is employed to bolster the prosecution's contention that Yates developed her murder scheme from watching particular episodes of *Law and Order* that fictionalized actual cases of mothers killing their children. When the defence challenges his professional credentials, Dr Deitz responds by outlining in some detail the very episode of *Law and Order* that provided Yates with the perfect script for her actions – except that such an episode never existed. As it turns out, Dietz had confounded 'the facts of three child-murder cases on which he had worked and the two *Law and Order* episodes based on them'. Because of this, Andrea Yates' murder conviction is overturned on appeal and a new trial is ordered; no word yet on whether Dr Dietz will help convert this second trial, or the first, into an episode of *Law and Order* (Wyatt, 2005).

The second tragedy is of considerably longer duration, spiralling downward for decades now. As with the criminalization of marijuana in the 1930s, the contemporary war on drugs in the USA has from its beginning spun image and ideology in such a way as to construct the very problem it claimed to address – and yet, shaped in this way, the 'problem' has continued to spiral back into the campaign that constructed it. As we noted years ago, the criminalization of drugs creates criminal consequences, consequences that call forth aggressive enforcement and further criminalization (Young, 1973). As Clinton Sanders and Eleanor Lyon (1995) have documented, police officers and prosecutors working under the pressure of contemporary anti-drug campaigns come to define almost all murders as 'drug deals gone bad', almost all assaults as fights over drugs, almost all perpetrators as drug users. As Ferrell (2004b) has shown, drug users in such circumstances sometimes do endanger the public – especially when the police are pursuing them at high speed as public dangers. And so, as the flow of drugs and drug panic becomes self-confirming, fabrications of 8-year-old heroin addicts win the Pulitzer Prize (Reinerman and Duskin, 1999), faked drug mule documentaries harvest international awards, World Health Organization officials suppress reports on marijuana's relative harmlessness, and the spiralling process so constructed continues to put people in prison and politicians in office.

To speak of such loops and spirals is to imply perhaps a certain smoothness of motion, a soft trajectory as the meaning of crime and criminal justice circulates through popular culture. But of course trajectories can change, and dramatically; spiralling movements of meaning can be made to alter course and serve new political masters. Amidst the political rubble of the 2001 World Trade Centre attacks, for example, the spiral that is the war on drugs was spun in a new direction. Playing to public fears, sensing that one war might be made to flow into another, the keepers of the drug war now engineered a cultural confluence of drugs and terror. The White House-based National Youth Anti-Drug Media Campaign produced a series of print and video ads that coupled recreational drug use with violent terrorism – creating, as Michelle Brown (2007: 13) says, 'linkages by which, semiotically, to chain individuals to the structural concerns of criminality, violence, and terror'. The spiral described by Reinerman and Duskin (1999: 85) – whereby ongoing anti-drug campaigns 'forge a public prepared to swallow the next junkie stereotype and to enlist in the next drug war' – had now been turned hard right again, this time toward a new war and a new set of stereotypes.

Loops and spirals – case study 1

Rap music and the reconstitution of reality: thinking differently about [media] signs and [street] codes

> Language, as a cultural code, relates to a world of meanings. All knowledge and language are culturally coded. Thus, knowledge or even a consciousness about delinquency is a social product. It is precisely here in the realm of knowledge that ideologies are contested, resisted, or accepted. (Visano, 1996: 92)

With its inherently transgressive dimensions, rap music is an obvious place to analyse the selling of crime and the confounding of illicit identity and consumer status. It is also an interesting place to observe the looping and spiralling processes that connect popular culture, urban violence and the war on drugs (see Bogazianos, 2012 for a more detailed cultural criminological explanation).

Since emerging out of the 'hustla' lifestyle associated with 1970s 'Blaxploitation movies', the 'retromack' pimp culture of East Oakland, and the violent street gang wars of the South Bronx, New York City and South Central Los Angeles, rap and subsequently 'hip-hop' music has gone on to become the world's best-selling musical form. Although rap music takes any number of stylistic ('party', 'mack', 'reality', etc.; see Krims, 2000) and regional ('crunk', 'bounce', 'boom-rap') forms, and is principally purchased by white youth, as a sociological phenomenon, rap music is typically analysed as a constitutive element of contemporary black urban culture. For example, in her article on the subject Charis Kubrin (2005) begins by closely associating gangsta rap with the established body of ethnographic work on the way structural conditions in black inner-city communities give rise to cultural adaptations that become embodied within a 'code of the street' (Anderson, 1999). According to this influential but now rather dated body of work, a local, hyper-masculine order develops within disadvantaged black communities, with its own codes and rituals of authenticity: a willingness to use violence in reputation building, a valorization of sexual promiscuity and conquest, conspicuous consumption as a means of establishing self-image and gaining 'respect', and a pronounced antagonism towards the police and other authorities. Building out from here, Kubrin's aim is clear: to examine the extent to which this 'code of the street' is present not only at street level but also in rap music.

Kubrin explains that standard scholarship in this field approaches gangsta rap as an expression of a classical subcultural order, with the existing street code serving as inspiration for rap lyrics, which then reflect this code. Kubrin's approach, though, is more nuanced; she views the culture/music/identity nexus from a 'constitutive' perspective. Gangsta rap, she says, should be understood as an 'interpretive resource', a way of 'organizing' or perhaps more accurately *reconstituting* reality, whereby

(Continued)

(Continued)

'rappers' accounts ... reflexively accomplish a sense of reality – for themselves and for others'. Rap in this sense 'creates cultural understandings of urban street life that render violence, danger and unpredictability normative' (Kubrin, 2005: 366, 376; see similarly Kane, 1998).

Rather than trying to isolate any pure 'media effect' (see Bandura et al., 1961, 1963; Paik and Comstock, 1994 for classic examples), Kubrin shows how media influence operates alongside related cultural and social practices in a complex process of exchange and interaction. And as regards gangsta rap, other loops and spirals abound as well. Eric Watts (1997), for example, notes the dozens of high-profile rap artists who've been perpetrators or victims of criminal activity – from Snoop Dogg's involvement with Long Beach street gangs to the murder of Tupac Shakur – and so confirms that, in gangsta rap, crime and its representation are irrevocably intertwined. But Watts is more interested in a *material* analysis of rap, exploring how consumerism functions as an interpretative schema for defining and clarifying the relations among hip-hop culture, gangsta rap narratives and the interposition of an expanding rap industrial complex.

Watts focuses on a classic 'old school' rap song/video: Ice-T's 1991 'New Jack Hustla'. Here, we are presented with a familiar slice of '90s rap imagery – Uzi-wielding rappers extolling their commitment to violence as an expression of ghetto power – and so seeming confirmation of rappers as vulgar, barbaric and nihilistic. Careful analysis, though, reveals something more and something different: clues to the close symbiosis between rap and consumer capitalism.

Superficially, 'New Jack Hustla' appears to offer a straightforward validation of Kubrin's (2005) thesis that the 'code of the street' gets integrated into rap music, with the song's lyrical boasts about instrumental violence, weapons, bitches and money. Ice-T's Hustla is justifying his way of life, clarifying his self-image, and most importantly validating his chosen 'Hustla' lifestyle. Yet, Watts argues that this portrait of 'nihilistic bravado' is not all it seems. In other moments, the song offers a peek behind the rapper's 'mask of invincibility'; in fact, a closer lyrical analysis reveals another psyche for the Hustla. Along with the drive-bys and shootouts, Ice-T is keen to articulate what he calls his 'capitalist migraine'. Not for him life working at 'Micky Ds', broke and broken, he assures us. And the solution? His own warped version of the American Dream, where 'the ends justifies the means, that's the system', where 'I had nothing and I wanted it/ you had everything and you flaunted it/ turned the needy into the greedy/ with cocaine my success came speedy'. Watts explains:

> Since the Hustler's being is constituted through the pressures of a street code, and since it seems to be a foregone conclusion that one will meet with some kind of untimely death in the ghetto, poverty represents a kind of living nothingness ... [G]angsta rap articulates an important perspective on the sad stasis of discharged personhood – the cultivated refusal by a cannibalistic consumer society to own up to its inability to meet its fabulous promises for livelihood. And so, the Hustler is a spectacular facade whose public performances both refute and sustain his status as a glamorous image (1997).

Or, as Ice-T asks, while posing the central paradox of rap and consumer society: 'Got me twisted, jammed into a paradox ... is this a nightmare or the American dream?'

Lyrics like these offer moments of 'textual revelation'. Originally, Ice-T's Hustla could only make sense of the world through an internalized code of the street. But as the song continues, a dawning awareness transcends the posturing: caught in the economic claustrophobia of mainstream materialism, the street code makes for a losing game, a trap, and some bad politics to boot.

However, by the start of the twenty-first century, as rap and hip-hop music became more commercial and more mainstream, the paradox that was so apparent in Ice-T's 1991 song all but evaporated. Old School rappers like Ice-Cube and Tim Dogg used to rap about $60 Nike trainers and 40oz bottles of Colt 45, but a decade later and the new giants of corporate hip-hop like P.Diddy and Jay-Z preferred to extol the virtues of Louis Vuitton luggage, Cristal champagne and the new Porsche Cayenne. Street-level 'grinding' had given way to suite-level commercialization. Advertising, marketing and consumerism were now displayed with a sort of knowing self-awareness, or as De Jong and Schuilenburg (2006) pointed out, so long as 'the street' and 'the urban' remain referenced for their symbolic authenticity, the rap and hip-hop industry could move high-end product, even as the genre retreated further from the impoverished lifeworlds where it originated. In the video for Snoop Dogg and Pharrell Williams' hit *Drop it Like It's Hot* (2004), for example, luxury cars and jewel-encrusted accoutrement seem intended to function as signifiers of both consumerist success and urban life, with transgressive stance and self-worth now conflated in simple commodity codes, as interpretable as a Nike 'swoosh' or a Gucci monogram.

But as rap and hip-hop culture grew in popularity, the loops and spirals of this particular fusion of crime and consumerism, transgression and popular music continued to swirl. Across the Atlantic, London's black youth began to create their own distinctive mode of urban music based on American rap, Jamaican 'dancehall' and British 'garage' and 'jungle' music. Stemming from Bow, East London and based on the early recordings of Wiley, Dizzy Rascal and Lethal Bizzle, the UK 'grime' scene began to take off in 2001. Some UK grime rappers followed their American counterparts for lyrical inspiration, referencing violent local 'postcode' feuds and 'flagging' street gang symbols and signs in their rap videos. The music quickly developed an association with street violence, stabbing and gun crime, thanks in large part to grime artists' frequent use of information and communication technology as a vehicle to disseminate their often menacing homemade music videos. Nothing new here, you might think – just another international variant of US rap music. But in recent years, parts of the UK grime scene have undergone something of a transformation. As cultural criminologist Johnny Ilan has documented (2012), high-profile grime rappers like Tinchy Stryder and Tinie Tempah have started to discard the traditional street codes of crime and violence, and instead adopt more universal themes of drinking, partying and socializing with the opposite sex. Importantly, this is not simply about embracing or validating the lush life of hyper consumerism, a la American rappers like Drake ('I get paper') or Lloyd Banks [ft Juelz Santana] ('Beamer, Benz or Bentley'). Rather, many grime artists are now championing '"respectable" entrepreneurial strategies often required to live a sustainable moderately wealthy life: gaining educational qualifications, carefully building a small business from the ground up and dutifully attending to craft' (Ilan, 2014: 74). If you think this is all a

(Continued)

(Continued)

far cry from Elijah Anderson's (1999) violent and masculine 'code of the street', it is. Just compare the following lyric by JME, the renowned underground grime MC, with the earlier stanza from Ice-T:

> I stayed in school got my degree,
>
> Even if I get a 2.2,
>
> I've done it, time waste for no-one,
>
> This year I was 22–,
>
> My dad wants me to do a masters,
>
> And my mum wants me to too.
>
> (JME, from '123', on 'Famous', Boy Better Know, 2008, cited in Ilan, 2012: 47)

With today's grime MCs advocating 'compliant behaviour' and featuring as role models in university alumni magazines, it seems that things have come a long way since Ice-T's 'capitalist migraine' paradox.

But have they really? Travel back to the USA and enter the world of the 'online gangosphere', and it's clear that elements of rap's violent past are still very much alive and kicking. The website WorldStarHipHop.com, for example, has recently emerged as the platform du jour not just for the type of DIY, homemade rap videos that propelled UK grime artists to mainstream success, but also for video uploads of inter-gang death threats and the type of violent beatdowns discussed in the next section. On WorldStarHipHop.com and similar sites, the distinction between rap, hip-hop and the 'thug' lifestyle are once again indeterminable, as youths record themselves administering beatings or denigrating rival cross-town cliques whilst shouting 'Worldstar' into the camera, all too aware that the website edits together a best-of-the-week fight compilation (Austen, 2013).

In our next case study later in this chapter, we'll delve more deeply into the relationship between crime and violence in the online world where, as we hope to show, the only thing that's certain is change. For now, we'll simply note that the media spirals associated with the signs and street codes of transgressive urban music remain as unpredictable as they are uncontrollable. Which direction they take next is anybody's guess.

The commodification of violence and the marketing of transgression

People had been working for so many years to make the world a safe, organised place. Nobody realised how boring it had become ... Nobody had left much room for adventure, except maybe the kind you could buy. On a roller coaster. At a movie. Still, it would always be that kind of faux excitement ... And because there's no possibility of real disaster, real risk, we're left with no chance for real salvation. Real elation. Real excitement ... The laws that keep us safe, these laws condemn us to boredom. (Chuck Palahniuk, 2000: 59)

There's fast, … scary fast, … and then there's 'remember this moment for the rest of your life' fast. Pursue the moment. (Advertising strapline for the Lexus IS 350)

The family board game *Monopoly* has been around for generations. Recently, however, it experienced a number of thematic makeovers. In the USA, *Ghettopoly* is a *Monopoly*-style game in which 'playas' move around from 'Tyron's Gun Shop' to 'Ling Ling's Massage Parlour', building crack houses, 'pimping' and selling guns as they go. Meanwhile, in the UK, one games company recently courted controversy with its *Chavopoly* variant. Here, properties include a 'Dealer's Flat' and 'Vandalized Bus Stop' and the traditional *Monopoly* 'Community Chest' has become a 'Community Pest'! If board games aren't your thing, how about sports and recreation? Fed up with fad diets and celebrity-endorsed fitness programmes? Then why not try an altogether more austere regime. If you're 'a workout lifer', for £10.99 you can pick up a copy of *Felon Fitness: How to Get a Hard Body Without Doing Hard Time* (Kroger and Teufel, 2011). Based on the ideal of 'the jacked-up inmate', the book is the brainchild of LA criminal attorney William 'Bill' Kroger and fitness guru Trey Teufel. When visiting his clients in prison, Kroger noticed that 'they were always in great shape', and so he enlisted Teufel to devise a workout regime based around the following rubric: 'If you're fresh meat looking to tone up, the squats, push-ups, and burpies will get you yard-ready in less than a three-month stint … Each exercise comes straight from the cellblock and the routines are those of real inmates. It's the workout of a lifetime – from guys serving twenty-five to life.' Prefer the more sedate pace of target shooting? Well, how about ordering the new gun-range target depicting a faceless hoodie-clad figure holding an iced tea and a bag of skittles. If this target sounds familiar, it's because it's meant to. The target is designed to resemble Trayvon Martin, the 17-year-old unarmed black youth gunned down by neighbourhood watch volunteer George Zimmerman in Florida in 2012. Zimmerman's acquittal may have provoked widespread protest and racial tension across America, but it also proved good for business for the anonymous Florida entrepreneur who produced the Trayvon targets: 'The response was overwhelming … We sold out in two days' (Demby, 2012: n.p.). To the untrained eye, the development of such products might not mean much. However, to cultural criminologists, it exemplifies a more widespread tendency. These examples not only reveal the relationship between criminality and consumer lifestyle, they also illustrate the broader trend towards *the commodification of violence and the marketing of transgression.*

It is a notable irony that the more Western governments attempt to control the youth crime problem by imposing a series of external controls – everything from curfews and exclusion orders in the UK, to the deployment of police patrols in schools and the so-called 'school to prison pipeline' in the USA – the more they engender within young people not compliant rationality but heightened emotionality. Hence, there is an interplay in which the 'irrational responses' of young people to state control provoke ever more punitive measures from the state, with youth culture thus becoming at once the site of excitement, contestation and experimentation. That this is the case is not surprising. The transgressive nature of youthful cultural practices has long provoked indignation among politicians keen to curry favour with the 'moral majority' by vilifying the perceived immorality of the young. Whether it's needlessly criminalizing more and more young people for minor offences or arresting young school kids for rule infractions in the classroom, Western governments are turning the screw on the young, subjecting not only their oppositional pleasures to increasing state sanction, but also their legitimate cultural practices and everyday round.

All the while, the market feeds into this dynamic, contributing to it and commodifying it. As we have seen, moral panics unfold today in a far more complex series of loops and spirals than was the case when Stan Cohen (1972) first articulated the concept. Now another twist: a decent dose of moral outrage on the part of older authorities can constitute the acid test of a truly oppositional, and therefore worthwhile, youthful endeavour. And as McRobbie and Thornton (1995) make clear, even this response is often co-opted and incorporated, as corporations use manufactured moral panic – the threat of censorship, a suggestion of sexual scandal – for their own profitable ends. In fact, panic-inducing images of crime and deviance are now prime marketing tools for selling products in the youth market. At one level, there is nothing inherently new about this; the compellingly salacious nature of certain criminal acts ensured a ready audience for crime throughout the twentieth century. What has changed, however, is the force and range of the illicit message, and the speed at which it loops and reverberates. Crime and transgression are now packaged and promoted as cool, fashionable cultural symbols, with transgression thus emerging as a desirable consumer decision (see Fenwick and Hayward, 2000). Here, within consumer culture, crime becomes an aesthetic, a style, a fashion – consider, for example, the British fashion labels *Criminal* and *Section 60*, the latter named after the police power to stop and search (see Treadwell, 2008) – and so the distinction between the representation of criminality and the pursuit of stylized excitement, especially youthful excitement, evaporates.

Today, corporations rely more and more on images of deviance as prime marketing tools for selling products, with crime and punishment featuring as regular tropes in major advertising campaigns – again, not an entirely new phenomenon, but one defined by a qualitative shift in the range and tone of advertiser-appropriated violence.[4] Consider as an example the way the automobile is often advertised in contemporary society. With cars, car culture and car chases such a prevalent staple of the entertainment industry (just think of *The Fast and the Furious* movie series, car makeover shows like *Pimp My Ride*, *Overhaulin'* and *Monster Garage*, and best-selling video games like *Grand Theft Auto* and *Carmaggedon*), it was perhaps only a matter of time before car manufacturers started to employ tropes of transgression and crime, allied with visual motifs of conspicuous disobedience, in their advertising and marketing campaigns (Hayward, 2004: 171; Muzzatti, 2010). Just look at the following list: 'joyriding' (Nissan *Shogun*), terrorist suicide bombing (Volkswagen *Polo*), extreme sports (Nissan X-Trail), reckless driving (Lexus *IS 350*), base jumping (Suzuki *Grand Vitara* and Nissan *370Z*), graffiti (Plymouth *Neon*) and urban car theft (Volkswagen *Jetta*). Even the normally conservative German manufacturer Audi got in on the act, using pyromania (a fascination with fires and fire starting)

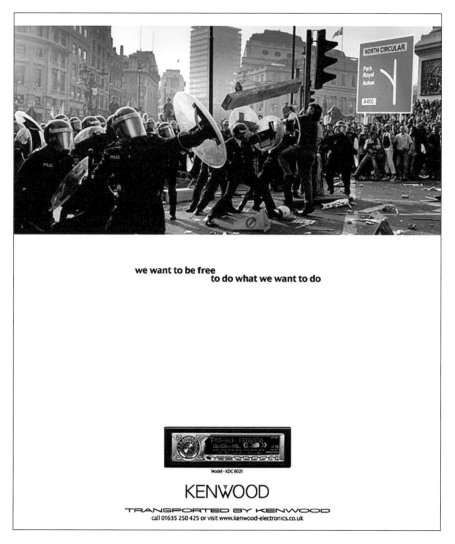

Plate 6.1 Kenwood car stereo poster: 'We want to be free – to do what we want to do'

Advertisement for Kenwood car stereos. Courtesy, Kenwood Electronics.

as a trope in a commercial for their A3 model, and employing British action movie star Jason Statham to reprise his role in car-centric movies like *The Transformer* and *Death Race* in their 2009 A6 campaign.

The advertising industry has, of course, long relied upon explicit sexuality and patriarchal gender stereotypes to move product (Berger, 1972: Ch. 7; Williamson, 1978; Goffman, 1979; Jhally, 1987) – but now women are increasingly portrayed as victims of, or passive accomplices to, crime and violence. In Chapter 4, we saw the FCUK shop window and its display of women violently victimizing one another; Kilbourne (1999) highlights similar cases of violently misogynistic marketing, with men pointing guns at women's heads, or attacking a woman in a jeans ad with the tag line 'Wear it out and make it scream'. A Baby-G watch advertisement on the side of a bus similarly depicts a naked women tied up with giant watches (Carter and Weaver, 2003: 126). More recently, über-trendy fashion house Dolce and Gabbana was forced to withdraw newspaper ads following a public outcry over their violently sexist content. In Spain, an ad showing a woman held to the ground by a half-dressed man was condemned by Labour Ministry officials as an offence to women's dignity and an 'incitement' to sexual violence. In Britain, the Advertising Standards Authority moved to ban another Dolce and Gabbana ad that featured, much like the FCUK window, bloodied women with knives (another ill-judged poster in the campaign depicted a scene that looked suspiciously like a homosexual gang rape taking place in an upscale clubhouse locker room). Such images may or may not directly 'incite' violence in the tradition of the media effects model, but they do clearly contribute to the cultural normalization of violence against women, to a sort of 'epistemic socialization' (Bennett and Ferrell, 1987) whereby viewers and consumers learn to see women as victims-in-waiting.

One final example of the deep, underlying contempt that some advertisers still have for women comes (inevitably perhaps) from the automobile industry. In 2013, the Ford Motor Company and the advertising firm WPP were forced into a series of hasty apologies after mock-up ads for the Ford Figo found their way onto the Internet (Stenovec, 2013). One of the ads featured cartoon caricatures of three women in sexually revealing costumes, with their hands and feet bound and their mouths gagged, stuffed into the back of a Ford Figo. Leering back from the driver's seat (and flashing a peace sign) is a figure that looks suspiciously like Silvio Berlusconi, the former Prime Minister of Italy, who in 2011 was embroiled in the infamous 'bunga bunga' sex party scandal involving underage prostitutes. (A second version featured Paris Hilton similarly kidnapping three members of the Kardashian family – presumably this was OK because it featured girl-on-girl violence!). According to WPP, the ads were not intended for general release, but were rather experimental mock-ups for internal discussion. Be that as it may, they are also illustrative of the willingness of mainstream corporations and their advertisers to commodify sexual violence in a bid to sell products. With dippy

fashionistas like Dolce and Gabbana ignoring the larger meaning of their advertisements, with companies making deals to place their consumer products in
misogynistic rap videos and with advertising companies inadvertently revealing
the deep-rooted sexism at the core of their industry, a particular interplay of
crime, media and profit is made manifest: the willingness of mainstream corporations and their advertisers to portray women as passive, emotionless ciphers
on the receiving end of transgressive violence.

The commodification of violence doesn't stop there, of course – far from it.
Surf late-night satellite TV and you can experience the televisual sensation of
self-styled 'extreme TV'. Here, the emphasis shifts from extreme car culture or
advertised misogyny to embodied moments of visceral transgression: broken
bones, concussions, lacerations. Unfettered by prime-time censorship restrictions, this now-established genre of youth TV constitutes a storehouse of illicit
excitement, a ready resource for the voyeuristic consumption of pain and transgression. The popular TV show and film series *Jackass*, and its many derivative
shows (e.g. Britain's *Dirty Sanchez* and the Finnish show *The Dudesons*), mix pop
nihilism, pervasive hedonism and extremes of self-destructive violence (self-
inflicted cuts, self-administered pepper spray) to create profitable mainstream
entertainment. Better yet – or worse yet – is the fusing of extreme 'reality' TV
with the *CSI* genre. Now available are explicit crime 'documentaries', such as
Bolivia's hyper-violent *Telepolicial* and the Russian prime-time offering, *Criminal
Russia*, both of which include graphic crime-scene footage of real crimes – street
and gangland slayings in the case of *Telepolicial* and infamous serial killings
(both solved and unsolved) in the case of *Criminal Russia*.

But for real extremes of mediated violence, forget television. Bubbling under
the media surface is a netherworld of uncensored websites, DVDs and Podcasts
that present brutally real crimes as illicit entertainment. From fairly innocuous
'happy slapping' compilations to hardcore 'caught on camera' schoolyard beat-
downs and street fight downloads, so much of this material now circulates that
'producers' have begun to stratify their product in a bid to meet niche demands.
Alongside standard fare like the *Agg Townz* schoolyard/street fights or the eBay
favourite *Beatdowns and Scraps*, consumers can now select DVDs or downloads
that feature fights between recently released US federal prisoners (*Felony Fights,
Volumes 1–5*), organized street gangs (*Urban Warfare: Gangs Caught on Tape*) and
'all girl' protagonists (*Spotlight Honies vs. Worldwide Honies: Good Girls Gone Bad,
Extreme Chick Flicks* and *Queen of the Hood*) (see Slater and Tomsen, 2012). And
then there are the infamous *Bumfights* – the undeniable inspiration for most, if
not all, of the above titles. Here, the premise is simple: find some homeless folks,
maybe drug addicts or alcoholics, persuade them to fight each other for booze
or cash, videotape the confrontations, synchronize the blows and pratfalls to a
cool skate punk soundtrack and package the whole thing into a series of stylish
video releases. Think consumption of this sort of staged barbarism is confined to

a few social outsiders? Think again. It's estimated that, alongside several million online views, over 600,000 hard-copy DVDs (remember them?) of the various *Bumfights* videos have been sold worldwide.

Amidst the contemporary mediascape, then, crime and violence become cheap commodities, emptied of their embodied consequences, sold as seductions of entertainment and digital spectacle. These latest transformations in mediated violence in turn reaffirm gender and class stereotypes, and highlight a mean-spirited contemporary culture of marketed aggression and hyper-violent machismo (Brent and Kraska, 2013). Along the way they obliterate old distinctions between the real and the image, between mediated cause and effect, becoming embedded in the everyday cultures of youth and consumption. And so a troubling question: How might these tendencies develop in the future, as the technology of entertainment becomes ever more sophisticated and pervasive?

Cultural criminology and 'real virtuality': crime, the Internet and the 'will-to-representation'

As the Internet and social networking have transformed society, criminology has been employed to explain and counter the myriad forms of crime, danger and deviance that quickly appeared in the wake of the digital revolution. Some useful work has emerged in the burgeoning field of Internet crime (see Jewkes and Yar, 2010 for an overview). However, whilst 'cybercrime' is now an established area of criminological attention, most research focuses either on explaining and identifying various forms of online crime (e.g. 'hacking', 'scamming', 'identity theft') or on developing ways to combat it, either through regulation and Internet law or by policing the Internet and computer forensics. This is understandable as there are major problems to solve, and moreover these problems are fluid, mutable and constantly evolving, reflecting the 'fast twitch' nature of the Internet and its attendant forms of digital technology. Yet, we would argue that so far criminology has only scratched the surface when it comes to understanding how digital communication is shaping social practice. In this section, we outline some tentative alternative (and hopefully complementary) areas of engagement that could prove useful for criminologists seeking to make better sense of cyberspace and how human beings use and abuse it.

Conceptually, ongoing criminological and legal work on cybercrime is primarily concerned with *diffusion*, whether in terms of the increased criminal opportunities afforded by decentralized networks or the potential diffusion of victimhood associated with digital crimes such as phishing scams or identity theft. Consider, for example, the legal/preventionist response to the compression and sharing of digital music files. The initial music industry panic was followed by expensive litigation and a subsequent flurry of excessive governmental legislation/prohibition that not only missed the target, but ultimately missed the point: that despite claims to the contrary, media conglomerates continue to grow and profit, largely because they have adopted new business models that work with and not against 'the download generation'.

As cultural criminologists, we're not interested in setting up rigid and ultimately false distinctions between virtual and real-world experience. Rather, as already seen in our other approaches to 'crime and the media', our line of analysis attempts to move beyond old formulae and established dualisms. Consequently, we would argue that, rather than focusing solely on models of diffusion or thinking of the Internet simply as a digital tool, we should instead focus on the *experience of the Internet* – how it functions in particular ways for particular purposes. This in turn allows us to think about digital/online (criminal) activities as a *process*, that is, as phenomena in constant dialogue and transformation with other phenomena/technologies. Here, we enter the familiar territory of Manuel Castells (1996), both in terms of his work on the networked 'space of flows' and, more importantly, his now classic notion of 'real virtuality' – the way our culture of 'embedded media' constantly impinges on physical reality, resulting in the categories of the 'real' and the 'virtual' becoming ever more hybridized. Such thinking allows us to think differently about online space and digital culture, developing concepts such as 'virtuality', 'telepresence', 'convergence' and 'presence', all of which have considerable potential criminological application.

The term 'convergence' will be well known to many cybercrime experts for at one level it describes the straightforward convergence of the technological (the networkable, compressible and manipulable features of the digital format) and regulatory processes associated with the digital media experience. Here, talk is of 'weightless money' (e.g. cash transfers), 'weightless products' (e.g. eBooks, and 'virtual goods' in online gaming platforms) and the 'weightless economy' (e.g. 'intellectual property' and 'information colonialism'). Such areas interest criminologists, of course, because they spawn criminogenic counter phenomena such as 'weightless money launderers', 'weightless counterfeiters' and 'weightless IP and bio pirates'. At another level, however, convergence is a more complex process, especially when considered in relation to the theoretical discourse surrounding *virtuality and the blurring distinction between the virtual and the actual*. Consider, for example, online crimes perpetrated against cyber profiles/identities such as game avatars. Courts in various jurisdictions have already heard numerous cases involving online theft, fraud and even cyber-bullying and assault in multi-player, online role-playing games such as *Second Life* and *World of Warcraft*. Although much-hyped, this blurring of the virtual and the actual is typically limited to monetary matters, as players find themselves out real money as a result of the theft of, for example, virtual 'goods' or 'land'. However, on occasion this blurring process is more complex and spatially interesting. Recently, Linden Lab, the company behind *Second Life*, found itself at the centre of a media storm after the German TV station ARD claimed that a *Second Life* player paid for sex with underage players or players posing as (digital) minors. Ultimately, it transpired that the players involved in the incident were a 54-year-old man and a 27-year-old woman who used their online avatars to depict a virtual sex act between a man and a child avatar. On a practical, legal level, this incident highlights issues of jurisdiction – the player involved was German and in Germany 'simulated' sex with children is punishable by up to five years in prison (in other countries it is not an offence). However, what is more interesting is how this incident highlights the nature and role of intentionality within virtual space. For some time now, intentionality has been a sufficient cause for prosecution in real-life cases involving the online 'grooming' of minors by paedophiles. However, the *Second Life* case illustrates that virtual actions/intentions can also lead to *actual* consequences. ARD passed the images to a state attorney in Halle, while Linden Lab contacted the authorities and subsequently made it abundantly clear that they would not tolerate 'erotic ageplay' on their site and would do all they could in the future to bring virtual and real-life paedophiles to justice.

Moving beyond legal questions of intentionality, these incidents raise other questions about how online space is navigated and conceived by individuals. Key here is the notion of 'telepresence' that has been used to describe the immersive experience associated with certain aspects of digital culture. Simply stated, communication technologies have the potential to alter the way we experience the sense of *being* in an environment:

> Presence is relatively unproblematic in unmediated situations, we *are* where we 'are'… However, when mediated communication or long distance interaction is introduced into the equation, things begin to change. In this situation we gain the ability to simultaneously exist in two different environments at the same time: the physical environment in which our body is located and the conceptual or interactional 'space' we are presented with through the use of the medium. (Miller, 2011: 31)

The 'interactional space' associated with telepresence has interesting criminological connotations. Most obviously, digital technology creates what one might describe as porous *spaces of subjectivity* in which moves made via the rhizomic, hyperlinked Internet appear materially or spatially insignificant, but in reality have tangible consequences. Obvious examples here include surfing for sub rosa sexual imagery (see Jenkins, 2001 on the online subcultural practices associated with child pornography) and the type of hate speech that is such a common feature of 'comment'/'message' boards. Indeed, the 'a-spatial' nature of online 'communities' actually lends itself to 'emotion dumping' and other outpourings of personal self-expression that would never be tolerated in physical space, from 'virtual revenge talk' and 'online vigilantism' (Cottee, 2010) to 'cyber bullying' and 'online stalking'.

Telepresence has been much discussed by sociologists interested in digital culture. However, what is even more relevant to criminologists (especially those concerned with the diffusion of victimization) is the growing interest in digital 'presence' (Licoppe, 2004). Of most significance here is geographer Vince Miller's recent work on how the online self is uploaded and presented via both network profiles, active and non-active forum and chatroom registrations, abandoned blogs and online shopping accounts, and what he describes as 'phatic' communication such as status updates, informationless gestures ('pokes'), microblog 'shout-outs' and other forms of digital interaction that prioritize 'connection and acknowledgement over content and dialogue' (Miller, 2011: 205). Such information, Miller argues, constitutes our digital 'presence', a quasi-private disembodied virtual 'persona' that exists at various points across the architecture of the Internet. If historically, privacy revolved around secrecy, anonymity and solitude, today there is a vast online reservoir of personal information about each and every one of us, from uploaded tagged photographs to our consumer preferences and surfing habits. In virtual space, we never sleep, we are always out there, 'alive' so to speak. What's more, digital 'personal traces', unlike 'hard copy' information, have a permanent life span. As Miller suggests, there is no more 'social forgetfulness'; our virtual 'presence' is there to be trawled, data-mined and profiled by everyone from credit and consumer agencies to anonymous dataveillance and surveillance organizations. Miller's concept of 'presence' has obvious criminological application; not just in terms of specific cybercrimes like identity theft, but in other areas such as the rehabilitation of offenders and how post-release/ prosecution identity might be affected by one's residual online presence, or in relation to other areas of digital research such as Mark Poster's (1995) notion of 'the digital superpanopticon' and connected questions about the legal dimensions of privacy and data collection.

This line of thought can be developed by drawing on the work of our colleague Majid Yar (2012) and in particular his important cultural criminological concept of 'the will-to-representation'.[5] Yar's central point, like ours, is that those interested in studying the relationship between crime and the media must move beyond the idea that the public is simply a passive internalizer of mass communication and recognize instead that large numbers of 'ordinary people' are now primary producers of self-generated mediated representations. Thanks to social networking, handheld cameras, 'webcams', blogs, vlogs and other new media forms, today's subject 'no longer interprets or attends to representations produced elsewhere, but becomes her- or himself the source of those representations' (2012: 248). Thus, we are confronted with the spectacle of individuals and groups performing, recording, sharing and publishing their acts of deviance – everything from schoolyard bullying to acts of rioting, even terrorism. In itself, this is not especially new, but what is interesting is Yar's claim that the nexus of user-generated content and the desire of individuals to mediate themselves through self-representation might *itself be a motivating factor for offending behaviour.*

> This kind of 'will to communicate' or 'will to representation' may be seen in itself as a new kind of causal inducement to law- and rule-breaking behaviour. It may be that, in the new media age, the terms of criminological questioning need to be sometimes reversed: instead of asking whether 'media' instigates crime or fear of crime, we must ask how the very possibility of mediating oneself to an audience through self-representation might be bound up with the genesis of criminal behaviour. (2012: 246)

The will-to-representation, then, becomes crucial for understanding a contemporary world where individuals 'desire to be seen, and esteemed or celebrated, by others for their criminal activities'. Consequently, we now increasingly encounter the criminogenic phenomenon of deviant and criminal acts being engineered or instigated specifically to be recorded and later shared via social networks and other Internet platforms.

This development has quickly become entrenched. For example, in the first edition of this book we discussed the case of the 2007 Virginia Tech University shooting. Our goal then was to highlight the interplay of high-speed digital communications and user-generated websites – our point being that, such was the immediacy of social networking, the students trapped in university buildings were posting digital phone footage of the shootings on the university's 45,000-member Facebook site long before even 24-hour rolling news was effectively covering the story. As a coda to the vignette, we mentioned in passing that the assailant, Seung-Hui Cho, took the step of mailing a videotape of himself outlining his intentions to the national media. Fast forward seven years to another university massacre, this time at the campus of the University of California, Santa Barbara, where 22-year-old Elliot Rodger killed six students and injured 13 others before turning the gun on himself. Rodger had a history of mental health problems, but he also had a history of blogging and posting videos about himself online. Although essentially very similar cases – both Cho and Rodger left recorded video confessions and wrote lengthy 'manifestos' explaining their motivation – it's interesting to note the extent to which the will-to-representation is more explicit in the latter case. Cho's video, albeit chilling, was recorded just prior to the shooting and has an almost perfunctory (if rambling) feel to it. Rodger, on the other hand, having grown up with social media, was far more aware of the importance of managing his self-image in the media after his suicide. Hence, he produced both a 107,000-word digital manifesto (entitled 'My Twisted World: The Story of Elliot Rodger') and a series of bizarrely compelling video blogs in which he films himself sitting in his car or by the side of the road, calmly discussing his frustration at not being able to find a girlfriend, his virginity and his hatred of ethnic minorities and interracial couples. Rodger is an abject narcissist, of course, and his videos, all carefully framed and beautifully back-lit by the fading California sun, bear testimony to his self-absorption. But they also illustrate something else – a knowing awareness of his non-degradable digital 'presence', his *eternal mediated being*. In other words, they are also a testament to his will-to-represent, both before and after his own physical death.

Rodger is an obvious candidate to illustrate the will-to-representation, but you don't have to look far to find other examples of how violent crimes are not just being committed but *enacted* for the camera. In the world of the Black US street gang, for example, you're now more likely to hear the term 'driller' – a name given to gangbangers who stir up trouble on Facebook, Twitter and Instagram – than you are old school gang labels like 'OG' (Original Gangster). The use of the Internet as a means to start 'beef', enhance 'rep' and 'call out' other cliques is now so common that a video of a gang member 'drilling' a cross-town rival uploaded to YouTube or Instagram in the morning can result in a related shooting later that same day (Austen, 2013). In fact, it has become so common for gang members to post photographs of new weapons or make claims about violent incidents or future acts of retaliation online that police departments now have special squads monitoring the 'gangosphere', looking for evidence to initiate probation revocations. Yar documents a host of other examples, including an assault that took place in the Werribee suburb of Melbourne: 'Here, a group of eight teenagers sexually assaulted a girl, urinated on her and tried to set her on fire. Not only did they film the assault, but subsequently edited the footage and created DVDs, which they proceeded to sell at a number of nearby schools for AU$5 per copy' (Yar, 2012: 253). But the most egregious example of the will-to-representation is surely found among today's Islamic terrorists and insurgents. It is something of an irony given the anti-Western, anti-modern sentiments of your average Jihadi, that Western supporters of the medieval Caliphate have become so adept at using new modes of digital communication to spread their poisonous message. Whether it's the staggered release of barbaric, if carefully choreographed, beheading videos or the more subtle propaganda of blog and vlog posts uploaded by European Muslims documenting their lives in Syria as a way of enticing others to join them (see Carr, 2014), it's clear that today's Jihad in the Levant and elsewhere relies heavily on mediated spectacle and the will-to-representation.

Loops and spirals – case study 2

Real war news, real war games

> This is not a video game. This is real war. (General Norman Schwarzkopf, press conference, First Gulf War, in De Jong and Schuilenburg, 2006: 26)

> At least one Marine seems ecstatic about being in a life-or-death gun fight. Nineteen-year-old Corporal Harold James Trombley ... has been waiting all day for permission to fire his machine gun ... Now Trombley is curled over his weapon, firing away ... Trombley is beside himself. 'I was just thinking one thing when we drove into that ambush,' he enthuses. '*Grand Theft Auto: Vice City*. I felt like I was living it when I seen the flames coming out of windows, the blown-up car in the street, guys crawling around shooting at us. It was fucking cool.' (Wright, 2004: 6–7)

In this vignette, we turn to another looping example of violence as commodified digital spectacle: the use of US military and insurgent violence as virtual entertainment in the fast-changing, dangerously creative world of digital gaming. Where better to consider the 'state of suspension' between the real and the virtual?

In *Mediapolis* (2006), Alex De Jong and Marc Schuilenburg investigate what they call the 'military–entertainment complex', showing how the US Army has converted a host of video games, from early 1980s titles like *Battlezone* and *Army Battlezone* to later offerings like *Doom* (1993), *Medal of Honor* (1999) and *Counterstrike* (2001), into simulated combat conditioning exercises for infantry soldiers. That the US Army utilizes video games for training purposes is not especially surprising, given that the majority of young military personnel have been raised in environments where video gaming was commonplace (see Wright, 2004). More surprising perhaps – and certainly more criminologically important – is the extent to which the distinction between simulated, virtual training and real-life, on-the-ground soldiering is evaporating.

This conflation is the result of two now well-established, interrelated processes. First, games industry innovations have facilitated enhanced recreation of real-world environments. Marketed with the tagline 'Real War News, Real War Games', *Kuma War* (2004), for example, incorporated downloadable TV news footage from the war zones of Afghanistan and Iraq. This allowed online gamers 'to participate in the American hunt for members of Al Qaeda in the Shah-i-Kot Valley in Eastern Afghanistan' or to experience the 'bloody happenings at the centre of Fallujah' (De Jong and Schuilenburg, 2006: 21).

Second, the US Army itself has long since experimented with a series of temporally and spatially 'authentic' first-person-shooter games. Not content with simply converting existing video-game platforms, in 2002 the US Army launched *America's Army: Operations* (followed in 2005 by *America's Army: The Rise of the Soldier*).[6] Costing over $6 million to develop, *America's Army* became one of the top five

Plate 6.2 Screenshot of 'Special Forces Extraction Alpha' from *America's Army*

Credit: De Jong and Schuilenburg (2006), by permission

online action games during the occupation of Iraq, with over 5.5 million registered users worldwide. Intended as a digital recruiting sergeant, *America's Army* didn't just recreate basic military training, from weapons instruction to rudimentary battlefield medical procedures, it reproduced actual combat scenarios in graphic detail and, importantly, in real time. The primary goal, of course, was to acculturate players to the tactics and nuances of combat. But this was no first-person-shooter free-fire fest. Indeed, one of the unwritten aims of *America's Army* was to encourage players to think more and fire less; trigger-happy gamers were discouraged. Participants were required to adhere to the same regulations that govern all Army personnel. Breaches of the rules saw players banned from the site, while those who successfully passed tests and complied with regulations proceeded to higher levels.[7]

Just one more shoot-'em-up war video game, albeit a particularly realistic one? Or an insidious international recruiting tool, designed to roll out military training and military ethos to a new generation of video gamers? Well, yes. And so another either/or dichotomy gone, as the illusory world of video games flows into the all too violently real world of contemporary warfare. This isn't the last loop in the spiral, either. Like those Internet sociologists who talk about the 'hybridized state of suspension' between real life and cyberspace (Robbins, 1996; Turkle, 1997), De Jong and Schuilenburg (2006: 13) view developments in virtual space as echoes, maybe mirror images, of still other tendencies underway in everyday life. They see *America's Army*, *Kuma War* and similar forms of real/virtual entertainment like the 2006 movie *The War Tapes* (a documentary film directed by Deborah

(Continued)

(Continued)

Scranton that drew upon hundreds of hours of real-life combat footage of the Iraq War filmed and posted on the Internet by US military personnel Sgt Steve Pink, Specialist Mike Moriarty and Sgt Zack Bazzi [Poole, 2006]) as manifestations of an increasing 'militarization of public space':

> A military control net has been thrown across the city and the mesh is being drawn tighter and tighter, leading to an altered experience of one's own identity as well as the installation of a specific regime of rules and sanctions. Renowned war games such as *America's Army* and *Full Spectrum Warrior* represent these radical changes better than the last police report or academic manuscript. These games indicate how the militarization of life has become the most important input of a culture that is oriented towards security. (De Jong and Schuilenburg, 2006: 13)

Plate 6.3 Cover of *Under Siege*

Credit: Afkar Media (2004)

In virtual space as in 'real' life, though, every action has a reaction – and so another loop or two unwinds. While the US 'military–entertainment complex' goes about its business, in other parts of the world, huddled around glowing computer screens, small teams of games-savvy programmers use similar technology to pedal their own ideological messages. Even before *America's Army* was available as a download, Palestinian supporters were releasing online video games featuring digital recreations of actual combat scenes from the ongoing Israeli–Palestinian conflict. Their goals with games like *Under Ash* (Afkar Media, 2001), *Under Siege* (Afkar Media, 2004) and *Special Force* (Hezbollah, 2003) were twofold[8]: first, to portray their own account of the struggle for Palestine, and second, to counter the worldwide hegemony of American-designed war games. In one such game – dedicated to Palestinian martyrs – players who utilize only (virtual) stones to take on Israeli soldiers are reminded to take the game out of its virtual environment and onto the streets. 'Isn't this a lesson in the continual movement from the real to the virtual world and back?' ask De Jong and Schuilenberg (2006: 67). 'The logic of the movement rests on the fact that each virtuality eventually becomes reality and that each reality sinks into a virtual world.'

All this may sound like an esoteric exercise in hyperreal theory, but one final looping development surrounding war gaming brings us back to reality with a resounding bang. In 2013, a controversy ensued when a French soldier was photographed on active duty in Mali wearing a skull facemask similar to the one worn by a character in *Modern Warfare*, a subseries of the highly successful *Call of Duty* video game. This was 'unacceptable behaviour' according to a high-ranking French colonel and French authorities quickly launched an investigation. But there was a problem. Combat soldiers have worn skull masks such as these for years; in fact, it has become something of a trend among Special Forces around the world. Moreover, as Luke Plunkett (2013: n.p.) explains: 'the mask was not invented by *Call of Duty*, or its developers Infinity Ward. Indeed, its presence in the game was inspired by the mask's use by soldiers in real life, as it's been worn by US troops – who first took to it as a fashionable alternative to regular gear (it began as a designer ski mask) at the beginning of the Iraq War – for almost a *decade* now, long before development ever began on the *Modern Warfare* series ... the mask is in *Call of Duty* because it's associated with real soldiers, not the other way around'. Just one more loop in the endless spiral by which computer-mediated and Internet-circulated communication explode the barriers between the virtual and the real.

To think critically about 'crime and the media' – to move past simple measures of media content or media effects, and on to a sense of loops and spirals, of fluidity and saturation – is not only to understand the dynamics of crime and trangression in late modernity, it is also to imagine new trajectories towards social justice. When crime policy is made in the media, when courts echo with media-made expectations, when police officers perform for their own cameras, criminologists must find ways to penetrate these dynamics if they're to humanize them. When crime collapses into commodity, war into entertainment, reality into virtuality, criminologists must find new avenues of intellectual inquiry appropriate to these confounded circumstances.

Yet, it's unlikely they'll succeed if they stick to the stale, sanitized sort of social scientific criminology that has dominated the last few decades. Instead, criminologists will need critiques that can converse with the culture at large, methods that can surf late-modern flows of meaning, knowledge that can challenge dominant understandings. Chapter 8 explores the methods by which such dangerous, fluid knowledge might be created. The book ends with an attempt to insinuate such knowledge into the flow of methodological meaning around crime and justice, and so to turn the spiral towards progressive understanding.

A selection of films and documentaries illustrative of some of the themes and ideas in this chapter

Nightcrawler, 2014, Dir. Dan Gilroy

'To capture the spirit of what we air, think of our newscast as a screaming woman running down the street with her throat cut'. So says Rene Russo's character, Nina Romina, to fledgling local news cameraman Lou Bloom (Jake Gyllenhaal) in Dan Gilroy's excoriating film about contemporary American news values. Although *Nightcrawler* has much to say about the problematic state of crime news, it is the overlapping televisual sensibilities of Romina and the borderline sociopath Bloom that is perhaps most revealing.

Network, 1976, Dir. Sidney Lumet

A searing, multi-Oscar winning satire of mainstream media, *Network* tells the story of a fictional television network, Union Broadcasting System, and how it uses morally bankrupt methods to deal with its flagging ratings. 'I'm as mad as hell and I'm not going to take this anymore', screams Peter Finch's character shortly after threatening to kill himself live on air. However, rather than sack him from his job as UBS's news anchor, the network gives him his own show!

The Pervert's Guide to Cinema, 2006, Dir. Sophie Fiennes

The entertaining philosopher Slavoj Žižek takes us on a visual journey through some of the most famous films in movie history – only this time we are asked to delve deep into the hidden language of cinema in a bid to reveal what movies actually tell us about our psychic selves. Skipping effortlessly from The Marx Brothers to Hitchcock to David Lynch, Žižek explains how fantasy, reality, sexuality, subjectivity, desire and materiality are all deeply embedded in the DNA of modern cinema. Screen all or parts of this film and you'll never view movies in the same way again.

Killing Us Softly, 1979, Dirs. Margaret Lazarus and Renner Wunderlich; *Still Killing Us Softly*, 1987, Dirs Margaret Lazarus and Renner Wunderlich; *Killing Us Softly 3*, 1999, Dir. Sut Jhally

Drawing on Jean Kilbourne's academic work on the study of gender representation in popular culture, the *Killing Us Softly* triology delves into the world of advertisements and TV commercials (hundreds are analysed) to show how, although the image of women in advertising has changed over the last 20 years, many of the underlying tendencies towards sexism and patriarchy remain the same.

Bus 174, 2002, Dir. José Padhila

Described as 'the trajectory of a tragedy', *Bus 174* is a hard-hitting documentary about the hijacking of a bus in Rio de Janeiro on St Valentine's Day 2000. It tells two parallel stories. The first describes the hijacker's life of social deprivation in Rio's shanty towns and subsequent experiences inside Brazil's brutal prison system. The second is the story of the hijack itself, which was broadcast live on TV for over four hours. Taken together, the two stories illustrate why Brazil and other countries with similar social and economic problems are so violent (see www.bus174.com).

Starsuckers, 2009, Dir. Chris Atkins

One of our favourite graffiti stencils of recent years is the one that simply states: 'Stop making stupid people famous.' The British documentary *Starsuckers* seems to agree, setting out to expose the 'shams and deceit involved in creating a pernicious celebrity culture'. If you're interested in, or fed up with, how we became so celebrity-obsessed, this film is for you.

Further Reading

Hayward, K. and Presdee, M. (eds) (2010) *Framing Crime: Cultural Criminology and the Image*. London: Routledge-Cavendish.
An edited collection of twelve cultural criminology essays aimed at helping the reader to understand the ways in which the contemporary 'story of crime' is constructed and promulgated through the image. Handily, each chapter includes a brief 'methods' section for those interested in undertaking their own media analyses.

Jewkes, Y. (2010) *Crime and the Media*, 2nd edition. London: SAGE.
Clearly set out and crisply written, Jewkes' book breaks down the barriers between media studies and criminology, offering up a series of insights into the role played by power and politics in the crime-media nexus. Highly appropriate for undergraduate students.

Ferrell, J. and Websdale, N. (eds) (1999) *Making Trouble: Cultural Constructions of Crime, Deviance and Control*. New York, NY: Aldine de Gruyter.
Leading cultural criminologists and social constructionists explore the mediated cultural dynamics surrounding a host of contemporary controversies, from tabloid TV crime to the social construction of 'stranger danger'.

(Continued)

(Continued)

Greer, C. (2009) *Crime and the Media: A Reader.* **Abingdon: Routledge.**
Easy-to-follow cultural criminologically-infused collection that offers a good starting point to get to grips with the key debates and theories relating to crime and the media.

Young, A. (2009) *The Scene of Violence: Crime, Cinema, Affect.* **London: Routledge.**
A recent text by Alison Young that stresses the *affective processes* associated with crime representation. Arguing that crime as image connects bodies, Young asks us to think about how visceral crime images affect us not only in terms of social policy or criminal justice practice, but bodily.

De Jong, A. and Schuilenburg, M. (2006) *Mediapolis.* **Rotterdam: 010 Publishers.**
More suitable for advanced students, De Jong and Schuilenburg's work suggests that developments in virtual space are being echoed in contemporary public space.

Useful Websites

Wall of Films
www.filmsforaction.org/walloffilms/
Website that provides free access to hundreds of political documentaries from some of the world's most influential filmmakers.

Mediastudies.com
www.mediastudies.com/
A website providing hundreds of links to international news media sites.

Visual and Cultural Criminology
www.facebook.com/groups/116285838427174/?fref=ts
For those of you with a Facebook account, see Chris McCormick's visual and cultural criminology page for daily postings about visual criminology, art and crime, and a host of other aspects associated with crime and its representation.

Notes

1 We acknowledge, of course, the mass of excellent existing research on the crime–media nexus. However, much of this traditional scholarship relies on relatively formulaic readings of crime's presentation in the media, or alternatively, the 'effects' of this presentation on attitudes and behaviour (see Ericson, 1995; Kidd-Hewitt and Osborne, 1995; Reiner, 2002; Carter and Weaver, 2003; Trend, 2007; Carrabine, 2008; Greer, 2009; Jewkes, 2011; Greer and Reiner, 2012 for comprehensive summaries; for a specifically cultural criminological take, see pages 125–9 of the first edition of the current text, and Yar, 2010). These established approaches (like 'content analysis', 'effects research' and 'media production observation') all have a place within cultural criminology, what with cultural criminology's concern for understanding mediated representations of

crime, their effects within individual and collective behaviour, and their connections to power, domination and injustice. Yet, none of these approaches in and of themselves seems sufficient for untangling the complex, non-linear relationships that now exist between crime and the media in our increasingly media-saturated world of global satellite television and duelling websites, Facebook and YouTube, WhatsApp and Snapchat, Tumblr and Instagram. What is required now are new modes of analysis that utilize aspects of the above approaches without reproducing their old dualisms: too much or too little media content regarding crime, effects or no effects of violent imagery, media coverage of crime that is democratic or elitist. As Carter and Weaver (2003: 16) make clear, the only way forward is to radically rethink 'the terms of a debate that has become intransigently binaristic'. The goal of cultural criminology, then, is to 'intellectually reorient' and 'radically repoliticize' the study of crime and the media, to explore the fluidities of meaning by which the crime–media dynamic 'socializes and directs our thinking and actions in a range of hierarchical, complex, nuanced, insidious, gratifying, pleasurable and largely imperceptible ways' (Carter and Weaver, 2003: 167), hence the more holistic approach to tracing the contemporary flow of meaning between crime and the media offered here.

2 Miss Moss's financial accounts certainly make interesting reading. Moss owned 100 per cent of Skate Enterprises, a company established to manage her endorsements and image rights. After the 'cocaine' incident, Skate Enterprises's turnover doubled: 'The accounts are highly significant because the financial year they cover ended five months after the publication of the photographs. They suggest that even during the depths of her brief period of disgrace Moss was prospering' (Prynn, 2007).

3 In his book, *Rise of the Warrior Cop: The Militarization of America's Police Forces*, the investigative journalist Radley Balko (2014) estimated that the number of SWAT teams in American municipalities with populations between 25,000 and 50,000 increased by some 300 per cent between 1984 and 1995.

4 While this area remains woefully under-researched within criminology, one US-based study is useful in this regard. In 2000 Maguire and associates analysed 1,699 commercials televised between 1996–7, concluding that, while violence in television advertisements was 'generally tame' and innocuous in nature, there had been a '100 per cent increase in violent content in television advertisements in 1997 compared to 1996' (cited in Carter and Weaver, 2003: 120). The limitations of this type of research not withstanding, it is interesting to note that nearly two decades after the Maguire et al. study, this tendency has accelerated, with advertisers now regularly relying upon crime and criminality as central features in their campaigns.

5 Yar's concept of 'will-to-representation' is derived from Schopenhauer's *The World as Will and Representation* (1967).

6 See also *Full Spectrum Warrior* (THQ, 2004) and its sequel *Full Spectrum Warrior: Ten Hammers* (THQ, 2006); initially developed by the US Army as sophisticated combat simulators, these training aids were also subsequently released to the general public as multi-format video games.

7 The use of military video-game simulators also extends to post-conflict rehabilitation. *Virtual Iraq* (2006) is used by US military clinics to help veterans re-experience the sounds and scenes that may have triggered painful memories of their tours of duty in Iraq. It is claimed that exposure to these simulated environments can help combat post-traumatic stress disorder (PTSD).

8 While *Special Force* and the *Afkar Media* games all hail from the same geographic region, they are very different both in terms of socio-political position and game play. While *Special Force* could be considered an Arabic reflection of *America's Army* or *Full Spectrum Warrior*, *Under Ash* and *Under Siege* are different in that they are based on real-life stories of human suffering caused by the occupation.

7

AGAINST CRIMINOLOGICAL METHOD

Mark Hamm (1998: 111) once described himself as 'a janitor for academic criminology', sweeping up and sorting through social discards – skinheads, terrorists, abusers, corrupters – other criminologists don't much care to encounter. In part, cultural criminology provides a similar sort of janitorial service. For decades, orthodox criminology consigned various cultural artifacts to the intellectual dustbin, deeming them unworthy of serious scholarly analysis. Comic books and television programmes, football matches and anti-drug campaigns, crime-scene photographs and public memorials, extremist anthems and nationalist parades – all may be entertaining or engaging enough, the thinking went, but they certainly don't merit the same serious inquiry as do murder, robbery and embezzlement. On the contrary, cultural criminologists came to understand these cultural phenomena as part of the process by which crime and crime control acquire collective meaning – and so they swept up criminology's intellectual discards and in fact attempted to position them at the heart of criminological inquiry. Can the images and storylines in comic books tell us something about juvenile crime, or moral entrepreneurs, or popular notions of justice (Nyberg, 1998; Phillips and Stroble, 2006, 2013)? Do television programmes and newspaper headlines about crime help create public perceptions that underwrite misguided criminal justice policy or at other times provide a push for social justice (Grimes, 2007; Linnemann et al., 2013)? Does the organized violence that sometimes accompanies football matches interweave with hegemonic masculinity, displaced class loyalty and the symbolic violence of the sport itself (Hopkins and Treadwell, 2014)? If so, the dustbin may hold as many answers as the textbook.

This sense of cultural criminology as a trashy counterpoint carries into methodology as well. The methods conventionally employed by orthodox criminologists may or may not tell us much about crime, but one thing is clear: they're carefully designed for neat execution and clean results. Sorting through governmental arrest statistics can be accomplished with barely a smudge to the hands or wrinkle to the blouse – and when the sorting is done, results can be presented in sets of finely ruled tables and PowerPoint slides. Likewise, victimization surveys can be constructed with precisely pre-set questions and answers, mailed to predetermined lists of respondents and then compiled into carefully cross-tabulated data sets. So pervasive is this aesthetic of academic precision, in fact, that we've begun to suspect that the appeal of orthodox criminology – an academic orientation that generally disavows the validity of emotion and style in the investigation of human experience – is precisely its own aridly fastidious style and the sanitary emotions such a style creates among those who long for certainty and assurance.

Cultural criminological research, on the other hand, tends to take place within an imprecise dynamic of method, style and emotion, and so tends to reproduce in its results the messy uncertainty of people and their problems. As the following chapter will show, cultural criminologists are less likely to find themselves sorting statistics or mailing surveys, and more likely to get caught up in the ambiguities of daily transgression, the gritty particulars of criminal acts, even the swirling referentiality of symbolic communication. In such research, straight lines and neatly pre-set arrangements are a rarity; instead, tangents are taken and back alleys travelled, all while riding the staccato rhythms of criminality and control. As we'll see, these tangents in many cases lead cultural criminologists into the frequently neglected corners of social life, into trashy situations that others – politicians, justice system officials, even other criminologists – might not wish to have explored and illuminated. And, as we'll also see, this sort of cultural criminological research regularly violates the time frames of academic criminology, flowing away from schedules and deadlines, enduring in some cases too long for efficient career advancement, in other cases sustaining itself not long enough for proper professional approval. Most of all, it stands in opposition and in counterpoint to the conventional methods of contemporary criminology.

Against method, against criminology

> For some time now, 'Saturdays' of every kind – artistic, musical, and springtime 'Saturdays', etc. – are being invented. I remind you that there is only the 'Fascist Saturday'. (Achille Starace, Italian Fascist Party Secretary during the Mussolini regime of the 1930s, cited in Sachs, 1987: 17)

In writing under the chapter heading 'Against criminological method', we intentionally put our disavowal of mainstream criminological method in the company of two dangerous treatises on orthodoxy and its consequences: Paul Feyerabend's (1975) *Against Method* and Stan Cohen's (1988) *Against Criminology*. In *Against Method*, Feyerabend demonstrates in some detail the manner in which methodological innovations in science have historically come wrapped in performance, persuasion and intrigue – tricks of the trade necessary for gaining a bit of visibility and support, and for freeing intellectual innovation from the stifling orthodoxies of the time. Significantly, he also reveals the post hoc reifications by which these tricks are forgotten – that is, the reifications by which these dicey methodological advances are later defined as purely scientific, entirely necessary … even inevitable. In this way, Feyerabend argues that the history of science resembles less a straight line towards greater and more objective scientific knowledge than it does a Fellini-esque carnival careening around the intellectual countryside, putting on little plays and seductions, occasionally falling apart and regrouping. And so for Feyerabend (1975: 23, emphasis in original) the lessons are: 'The only principle that does not inhibit progress is: *anything goes*' – and the only strategy for anyone serious about progressive knowledge is a refusal to take seriously the cannons of received wisdom.

Feyerabend's (1975: 118) passion for 'fruitful disorderliness' is equally evident in Stan Cohen's *Against Criminology*. There, Cohen carefully documents the importance of the 1960s and 1970s intellectual uprisings against orthodox criminology that we discussed in Chapter 2 – and just as carefully documents the necessity of rising up against these uprisings to the extent that they settle in as a sort of alternative, comfortable orthodoxy. Like Howard Becker (1963: 181), who never really intended for his interactionist criminology to become 'labelling theory', who then wandered away from it and into artworlds and other social milieu, Cohen was intellectually unwilling to toe the line, even one he helped draw. Instead, he understood the essential method of criminological inquiry to be not one technique or another, but the ongoing process of critique and incompletion. 'Lack of commitment to any master plan' in this way becomes an intellectual strength or maybe a disciplinary necessity – and 'the unfinished' emerges as a practical strategy for negotiating the next moment, whether it be one of normal science or intellectual negation (1988: 109, 232).

Taken together, Feyerabend and Cohen suggest a sort of anarchist understanding of method and knowledge; Feyerabend (1975: 17, 21) in fact explicitly offers an 'outline of an anarchist methodology' and argues that 'theoretical anarchism is more humanitarian and more likely to encourage progress than its law-and-order alternatives'. Said differently, both Feyerabend and Cohen invoke Dadaism as a reference point for their critiques. Looking back at the revolts against orthodox criminology in the 1960s, Cohen (1988: 11) sees them as perhaps closest to 'the products of radical art movements such as Dada and surrealism, anti-art created by artists'. Feyerabend (1975: 21) clarifies, noting that he might just as well call his work Dadaism, since

> [a] Dadaist is utterly unimpressed by any serious enterprise and he smells a rat whenever people stop smiling and assume that attitude and those facial expressions which indicate that something important is about to be said … A Dadaist is prepared to initiate joyful experiments even in those domains where change and experimentation seem to be out of the question.

And so to clarify an anarchist or Dadaist critique as it might apply to a domain like today's orthodox criminology: the more seriously a criminological method takes itself – the further it positions itself above other approaches through invocations of 'objectivity' or 'science' – the more that method is suspect of impeding understanding rather than advancing it. Methods most accepted as the disciplinary core of criminology, then, must be those most aggressively challenged, cracked open and made fun of (Ferrell, 1996: 191–2). Likewise, methodological neatness and intellectual closure suggest stasis and decay; trashy methods, methods ragged around the edges, methods not fully conceptualized or completed, suggest intellectual life and disciplinary vitality. The only way to move a discipline forward is through a healthy disrespect for the rules by which it defines itself – even for those rules by which it defines itself as moving forward. And if this is true of biology or art history, it is especially true of criminology. *The problems of crime and crime control are too serious to take criminology seriously.*[1]

Because of this, we consider it our duty and our pleasure as criminologists to stand against criminology, in particular to stand against the intellectual arrogance and assumed acceptability of orthodox criminological method. But where to start? The methodological terrain of contemporary criminology is so barren, its conventional methods so inadequate for addressing the human pathos of crime and control, so wanting in any sense of intellectual elegance and innovation, that the discipline today seems a sort of methodological kakistocracy – an upside-down world where the worst matters the most. Given this, perhaps the starting point shouldn't be the latest convenience-sampled survey of a professor's captive students or the most recent unreadable and table-turgid issue of the US journal *Criminology*, but the historical process by which we arrived at this point. Perhaps we can begin to understand something of contemporary criminology's methodological bankruptcy by tracing, if only briefly, an earlier history of intellectual fraud and methodological misappropriation.

Method past and present

Though one wouldn't know it from reading orthodox criminology journals today, many of contemporary criminology's foundational works emerged from idiosyncratic, impressionistic approaches that bore little resemblance to any sort of 'social scientific' method. When in the 1920s and 1930s Chicago School scholars conducted research – when Frederic Thrasher (1927) set out to document Chicago gang life and the 'ganglands' in which it unfolded, when Nels Anderson (1923/1961) decided to turn his own hoboing past into a study of hobos themselves – they did so largely according to their own sentiments and schedules. Thrasher (1927: xiii, 79), for example, notes that the research for his 571-page book, *The Gang*, 'occupied a period of about seven years', and in the book he not only presents in fine detail 'the thrilling street life of the gang', but includes his own *in situ* photos of gang rituals and juvenile gang life. Anderson (1923/1961: xi–xii) recalls that, in writing *The Hobo: The Sociology of the Homeless Man*, 'I found myself engaged in research without the preparation a researcher is supposed to have. I couldn't answer if asked about my "methods"'. What methodological guidance Anderson did get along the way was something less than formal as well: 'Of the guidance I received at the University of Chicago from Professors Robert E. Park and Ernest W. Burgess', Anderson remembers, 'most was indirect. The only instruction I recall from Park was, "Write down only what you see, hear, and know, like a newspaper reporter"'.

By the mid-twentieth century, though, this sort of engaged, open-ended field research had been usurped in criminology and related disciplines by a style of survey research that, as Patricia and Peter Adler (1998: xiii) note, 'has held sway within the discipline ever since'. This importation of serious and 'objective' methodologies like survey research into criminology was meant to position it as a science, or at least a social science, of crime. 'Ample funding, entrepreneurial professors and policy-makers thirsting for anything that looked like technical expertise provided a combustible mix', historian Mark Mazower (2008: 36, 42) argues:

> Huge sums of money were suddenly pouring into the universities … The social scientists who got the grants offered technical advice that simplified the world and made it governable, using behavioral science or mathematical economics models. They turned human affairs into data sets, cultural patterns into forms of behavioral response, and they replaced the messy multiplicity of words and tongues with the universal and quantifiable language of science.

Within sociology, as within criminology, the 'use of statistical instruments and the language of proof of the natural sciences was clearly a way to increase the scientific legitimacy of a discipline fully recognized neither in the university nor outside it' (Chapoulie, 1996: 11). In culture and in consequence, the effect was similar to the introduction of scientific management methods into the office and factory a few decades before. For Frederick Taylor and other early 'managerial consultants' who advocated workplace scientific management, the stop-motion camera and the key stroke counter were utilized as forms of surveillance designed to divorce mental craft from manual labour, reducing the worker to an operator within the larger organization and routinizing the work process in the interest of profit and control (Braverman, 1974). For advocates of survey research, the alleged objectivity of sample procedures and pre-set question banks was designed similarly: to divorce from the research process the human particulars of both researchers and those they studied, with the intent of positioning the researcher as an operative within the larger professional organization of state-funded scientific criminology.

Of course, as already seen here and in Chapter 2, criminologists have more than once escaped this routinized, objectified criminology. During the 1950s and 1960s – decades that the Adlers (1998: xiii–xiv) label periods of 'Renaissance' and 'Abstract Expressionism' – the ascension of social scientific methodologies was challenged by an efflorescence of vivid subcultural ethnographies. Howard Becker's (1963) participatory studies of jazz musicians and marijuana users, Ned Polsky's (1967) insider take on pool halls, hipsters and hustlers – these and other works wandered far from standards of random sampling and objective detachment, and often defiantly so. During this same period in Great Britain, equally unorthodox methods of engaged research were being used by Jock Young (1971), Stan Cohen (1972) and others. Sir Leon Radzinowicz recalls these moments of methodological abandon as something akin to the pranks of 'naughty schoolboys'; we've elsewhere characterized them more in terms of Feyerabend, or maybe Dada – as approaches that were 'hectic, irreverent, transgressive and, above all, fun' (Young, 2002).

Still, for all that, the serious business of survey research and governmental data mining today continues to dominate criminology, and now with a full range of institutional underpinnings. Joe Feagin, Tony Orum and Gideon Sjoberg (Feagin et al., 1991), for example, note that 'mainstream article sociology' – the efficient, routinized production of article-length research reports in sociology and criminology – has over time displaced the deeper intellectual, methodological and temporal commitments of 'book sociology' as the measure of professional achievement. After all, like the answer sets produced by survey research, journals can be quantitatively ranked, with each scholar's articles therein counted as an arithmetic of professional stature – and survey research can itself generate such journal articles far more quickly and easily than Frederic Thrasher and his seven years of field research or Anderson and his life of hoboing.

In the USA, the UK, Denmark, New Zealand and elsewhere, these shifts towards assembly-line research methods and objectivist measures of disciplinary productivity have been replicated in the universities themselves, with their increasing reliance on corporate management practices and a bureaucratic culture of actuarial control (see Wright et al., 2014). For US criminologists especially, this quantified academic machinery has increasingly been coupled, through criminal justice departments and federal research grants, to a parallel state machinery of surveillance, imprisonment and control – a state machinery that requires 'objective', quantifiable survey data for its operation and justification. British criminologists in addition face the demands of the national Research Excellence Framework (REF), a regular evaluation of research productivity by which scholars, programmes and universities are ranked. Like a Taylorist knowledge factory, the REF puts a premium on regular and measurable production, with the effect of bullying scholars into research methodologies (and research projects) that can produce quick and efficient results (see relatedly Walters, 2003; Hillyard et al., 2004).

Back in the USA, criminological researchers confront yet another organizational incentive for confining their work to survey research, governmental data or office-chair speculation: the Institutional Review Board (IRB). Allegedly constituted to protect the 'human subjects' of academic research, IRBs are designed to conform to the requirements of the United States Department of Health and Human Services, staffed by a mix of university bureaucrats and professors, and charged with reviewing all academic research projects involving 'the participation of humans'. At a minimum, IRBs are sources of annoyance and delay for criminologists attempting to conduct research. But like the REF and the British 'Ethics Committee' (Winlow and Hall, 2012), they are evidence as well of something more sinister: the degree to which criminological researchers are increasingly forced to forfeit scholarly independence in the interest of institutional oversight. Putting organizational risk management ahead of methodological independence, IRBs degrade the professional status of those they regulate. Even when administered with kindness and insight, even when genuinely concerned with 'human subjects' – as they sometimes are – Institutional Review Boards nonetheless embody the sort of corporate routinization that has come to define criminological inquiry.

Not surprisingly, the effects of this routinized surveillance on unconventional research methods are, to say the least, stifling. IRB guidelines peg the degree of board review to the perceived degree of risk that a research project carries for research subjects. In this context, the guidelines generally exempt from oversight methods that utilize 'existing data', that involve 'survey procedures' or that 'are conducted by or subject to the approval of department or agency heads' (TCU, 2007: 10, 11). They, on the other hand, reserve especially harsh consideration for proposed research that might put subjects 'at risk of criminal or civil liability' or for research involving 'vulnerable populations' (including prisoners) (TCU, 2007: 7, 10), and in any case they require elaborate procedures for gaining subjects' informed consent prior to research. As a result, those mailing surveys, mining existing governmental data sets or otherwise engaging in organizationally approved research face few obstacles; those wishing to conduct independent field work with criminals or cops, to interview prisoners or young people or to investigate organizational malfeasance, on the other hand, face endless impediments (Ross et al., 2000). And so in consequence there develop some dirty disciplinary secrets, secrets that have been confessed to us in confidence time and again by frustrated doctoral students and junior faculty: knowing of the IRBs, dissertation advisers dissuade their students from field research, handing them old survey data sets for dissertation analysis instead. Junior faculty wishing to do field research learn better, too, learn that this method will earn them mostly bureaucratic constipation and career delay. 'Oh, I'd love to do the sort of research you do', they tell us, 'but I just *can't*'.

Easier to get out of prison than into it?

In October 2012, Mark Hamm was awarded a grant from the United States Justice Department to research violent extremism and 'lone wolf' terrorism, in part by interviewing those imprisoned for such offenses. The grant came with one condition: that he gain IRB approval from his university and from other organizations involved before the grant would be funded.

Getting right to work, Hamm first submitted an IRB application to his home university via IRBNet, a required automated information system. Soon thereafter he received an automated email message: 'Your Application Is Not Approved.' He next met with IRB leaders, who later sent him five pages of recommendations for revisions to his application. Making the revisions and resubmitting his application, he nonetheless received an automated 'Revision Requested' response in December. In January 2013, there followed a meeting with the 12-member IRB, at which Hamm recalls, 'I was made to feel like I had done something immoral because I wanted to have face-to-face contact with human subjects – in this case, terrorists'. Worse yet, none of the IRB members seemed to be familiar with criminological fieldwork, with prisons or, for that matter, with US government regulations that should have required a prisoner representative at such a meeting.

Responding to IRB members' concerns that his interviews might cause psychological distress among prisoners, Hamm submitted a second set of revisions, to which the IRBNet again responded, 'Revision Requested'. Hamm's third set of revisions followed, with a 'Revision Requested' reply in February, and a fourth set, with a 'Revision Requested' reply in March. Following a fifth round of revisions in April, university IRB approval was granted – six painstaking months after the process began.

Hamm next turned to gaining governmental approval to interview five key prisoners housed at five different prisons – and therefore requiring five separate IRB permissions from five correctional jurisdictions. This stage also required that each prisoner be vetted by US counterintelligence officials in Washington, and by psychologists, so as to eliminate any prisoners who might be afflicted by severe mental illness. Begun in April 2013, this round of IRB submissions was successfully completed in September – leaving Hamm with two more IRB approvals to seek, one from the Justice Department itself and one from the Australian Ethics Board, since his co-investigator was a faculty member in Australia.

By October 2013, all IRB approvals had been gained, and in November 2013 – more than a year after the grant was awarded – the research funds were released. All told, Mark Hamm had been forced to pursue eight IRB approvals in order to interview five convicts. But of course, as he points out, those convicted of terrorism aren't generally eager to talk with government-sponsored researchers, and so there now followed refusals to cooperate, unreturned letters and lengthy negotiations. To put it more accurately, then, Mark Hamm had invested over a year, and had made his way through eight IRBs, for the chance to attempt five interviews (see Hamm and Spaaij, 2015).

Thrasher and Anderson, Becker and Polsky couldn't do their research either, not these days. As we've detailed elsewhere, many of criminology's most revered researchers interwove criminology and criminality in order to conduct studies now considered essential to the discipline, engaging by necessity in research that incorporated criminal conduct and 'dirty knowledge' (Ferrell, 1997). Today, such research would simply not be possible by the standards of IRBs, and so to engage in it would position the researcher as an academic outsider as well. Imagine if you will Howard Becker emailing his university IRB, requesting permission to play piano music and smoke marijuana with fellow jazz musicians *in situ*. (In fact, Becker today subversively avoids any such emails by defining his research as 'conceptual art' [in Shea, 2000: 32] that falls outside the purview of the IRB.) Imagine Ned Polsky, told he must submit to the IRB a list of questions he plans to ask pool hall hustlers, and told as well that he is required to have them sign elaborate informed consent forms before he can ask. Imagine for that matter the response of an IRB to Patti Adler (1985) as she presents her plan for in-depth participatory research among active drug users and dealers. Why, if only we'd had the foresight to put IRBs (and REFs) in place during the course of criminology's history ... well, we really wouldn't have much of a criminological history at all.

Disciplinary delusion and decay

And what sort of discipline results from this contemporary triumph of the bureaucrat and the survey statistician? What sort of discipline emerges when quantitative methodology becomes the preferred tool for satisfying the demands of professional surveillance and evaluation (Lawrence, 2007)? When methodology is defined by detachment and routinization – when it's unimaginable that the researcher might be one with the research setting, that informed consent forms and pre-approved questions might be unnecessary, not to mention impossible – what then does criminology become?

It becomes lifeless, stale and inhuman. Just as the broader inhumanity of certain aspects of modernity resulted from the reduction of human subjects to rationalized categories of work, consumption and control, the inhumanity of orthodox criminology results in large part from methodologies designed, quite explicitly, to reduce research subjects to carefully controlled categories of counting and cross-tabulation. Just as the stale redundancy of modern work stemmed from the Taylorist exhaustion of uncertainty and possibility, the thudding boredom of orthodox criminology stems from methodologies designed, again quite explicitly, to exclude ambiguity, surprise and 'human error' from the process of criminological research. Coupled with a state control apparatus organized around similar ends, these methodologies bankrupt the promise of meaningful criminological scholarship, becoming instead the foundation for the sort of 'courthouse criminology' described by Ned Polsky (1967: 136) – the criminology of the 'technologist or moral engineer' – and the bland 'so what?' criminology critiqued by Roger Matthews (2009).

In the same way that other of modernity's institutions – the public school and the reformatory, the fast-food outlet and the theme park – were designed to expunge craft and creativity from the practice of everyday life, the modern machinery of criminology functions to exhaust the idiosyncratic insights of grounded criminological inquiry. Just as the factory, the agency and the market-place were rationalized in the interest of efficiency and control, the contemporary enterprise of criminology has been so shaped towards professional efficiency that it dehumanizes both its practitioners and those it is designed to investigate or enlighten.

As a result, the great majority of mainstream criminological scholarship today can only be described as clean, safe … and thoroughly unimaginative. Like other forms of circumscribed cultural expression, this intellectual drudgery results directly from the conditions of its production, from the methodological routini-zations enforced against human beings in order to drain data sets and numeric summaries from their lives. For students in criminology classes and for readers of criminological journals, then, a shared disillusion, a disappointment – that the promise of the subject matter could be so thoroughly betrayed by the meth-ods of its presentation. The vivid experiential agony of crime victimization transmogrified into abstract empiricism, the sensuality of the criminal event tabulated and footnoted – it would be a remarkable trick of methodological sanitation if only it weren't so damaging to the discipline.

Under the methodological regime of contemporary criminology, for exam-ple, the gendered tragedy and dangerous dynamics that animate women's attempts to escape domestic abuse become 'logistic odds ratios predicting help seeking and divorce or separation for female victims of spousal violence' (Dugan and Apel, 2005: 715), and all of this statistically derived from a vic-timization survey. The wide-ranging activities and attitudes that might make up female 'political participation' are reduced to a measurement of 'female voter turnout', which is in turn reduced to a measure of 'the percentage of vot-ing age females (extracted from the Current Population Survey) who voted in the November presidential and congressional elections' (Xie et al., 2012: 119). The sneaky thrills and little moments of ritualized resistance that percolate through kids' delinquent careers are recoded as 'GLS and Tobit Random-Intercept Models Estimating Interactions Between Antisocial Propensity and Time-Varying Predictors of Delinquency' (Ousey and Wilcox, 2007: 332–3), with this recoding generating a set of survey-derived statistics so sweeping that it spans two journal pages. In one youth drug study, the actual frequency with which kids use marijuana is imagined to be measurable 'based on youths' self-reporting number of days using marijuana each year' (Murray et al., 2012: 267–8); in another, the complex and ambiguous category of 'drug use' is 'meas-ured with a dummy variable for any use of marijuana, cocaine or any "other type of illegal drug" within the past 30 days' – and the equally amorphous 'lie to parents' category is coded 'as a dummy variable where 1 indicates having lied three or more times' (Kuhl et al., 2012: 1102). The racially charged dynamics animating police stops and searches are reduced to data drawn only from 'police administrative records' of such stops – not unlike 'most research on police stops' (Rojek et al., 2012: 1002), the authors note. The relationship of racial stereotyping to perceptions of victimization risk – two intricate and situationally shifting cultural processes in their own right, much less in conjunction – is examined using samples that apparently over-represent 'females and older persons', and two telephone surveys with response rates of 39 per cent and 35 per cent. Nonetheless, the authors 'do not suspect that nonresponse bias is a serious concern in this study' (Pickett et al., 2012: 155–6). Most astoundingly for cultural criminologists, a study in which 'neighbourhood street culture' is a defining concept – or in the study's terms, a key 'independent variable' – measures the 'construct' of neighbourhood street culture by way of a 'nine-item, self-report scale' administered to individual 'primary caregivers'. All nine of the pre-set statements on the scale focus only on violence, toughness and aggression – and all nine offer pre-set responses ranging from 1 (strongly disagree) to 4 (strongly agree) (Berg et al., 2012: 371).

As noted in Daniel Nagin's Sutherland Address to the American Society of Criminology a few years back, experimental method is likewise employed to box in criminology and its concerns. Here, the exploitative dynamics of sexual crime, the dark swirl of sexual transgression, indeed the very 'interaction … between emotion and behavior', are investigated through a clinical experiment in which male undergraduates are randomly assigned to 'non-arousal' or 'arousal' conditions, with those assigned to the arousal condition then 'instructed to masturbate but not to the point of ejaculation while responding to a series of sex-related questions'. Nagin, Professor of Public Policy and Statistics at Carnegie Mellon University, speculates that the masturbators' responses may tell us something about their assessment of 'factors of long-standing interest to criminologists', and wonders also about the validity of criminological survey data derived from respondents who, unlike these student masturbators, are assumed to answer surveys 'in a "cool," non-aroused state' (Nagin, 2007: 265–6). We wonder about that last point, too, and about a few other things. First, what might Sutherland say about the uniform failure of this isolated, experimental methodology to address key criminological issues of social interaction, social learning and shared motivation? Second, assuming the masturbating undergraduates responded in writing to the 'sex-related questions' … well, did the researchers select for ambidexterity? And third, how exactly did research of this type make it past the university's IRB?

This isn't criminology, much less criminology's 'mature and well-developed methodological toolbox' (Kurlychek et al., 2012: 96). This is collective madness,

madness filling issue after issue of criminological journals that function primarily as warehouses of disciplinary delusion (see Ferrell, 2009, 2014a; Young, 2011).

And of course there is method to the madness. 'Researchers' first deploy methods designed to deny any deep understanding of, not to mention immersion in, the lives of those who are their focus; in the delinquency study, for example, 9,488 school kids were targeted and the fewer than 4,000 who eventually participated were allowed to choose only one of four simplistic, pre-set responses to statements like, 'I'm nervous or on edge' and 'My mother seems to understand me' (Ousey and Wilcox, 2007: 322–3, 351–3). Data from such surveys, little pencil marks on a response sheet or clicks on a computer screen, are then manipulated with overblown statistical packages, producing two-page tables, a distinct lack of explanatory analysis (Weisburd and Piquero, 2008) and outpourings of astoundingly obtuse intellectual gibberish. But like all good gibberish, of course, it's not really meant to make sense to those outside the delusion anyway; it's mostly for the entertainment of journal editors, tenure committees and other keepers of the discipline. Twenty-five years ago, Stan Cohen (1988: 26) asked 'who can still take seriously' this sort of criminology and argued that it should be 'relegated to the status of alchemy, astrology, and phrenology'. We would only add, 25 years hence, that this perhaps insults the astrologers.

'All figures are subject to further analysis and revision': the crime of crime statistics and the con of CompStat

Over the past two decades, police departments in the USA, the UK and elsewhere have increasingly come to define themselves, their effectiveness and their public image through the generation and presentation of statistical data. Best known in this regard is New York City's CompStat programme, introduced by Police Commissioner William Bratton in 1994 and now widely copied throughout the USA. According to the police departments that adopt them, 'data-driven management' models like CompStat institute measurable accountability and provide for rapid collection and evaluation of information, with both allegedly contributing to more efficient everyday policing. Proponents of these programmes in turn claim that this more efficient, accountable and data-driven policing has clearly led to declines in crime and to greater neighbourhood safety – as measured, of course, by the programme's own statistical data. In this sense, CompStat and similar programmes can be thought of as a quantitative methodology for defining and evaluating policing; as with other quantitative methodologies, the orientation is toward the translation of human behaviour into statistics and the precision that results from this translation (see Young, 2011: Ch. 6). No longer is there only a sense that the west side needs more foot patrols, that the south side is now safer than it was last year or that the officers on the north side should be more robust in their crime-fighting efforts; all of these can now be measured with precision, and responded to and recalibrated on a daily basis as needed.

(Continued)

(Continued)

As we have throughout this chapter, we could certainly question the epistemic assumptions underlying this sort of quantitative management methodology: Can the human complexity of daily policing really be reduced to statistical summaries? Do those statistical summaries forfeit so much situational detail as to make their precision illusory? As it turns out, though, CompStat and similar programmes have generated some more practical and politically pressing questions. In Milwaukee, Wisconsin, for example, an investigation revealed that the police had miscategorized over 500 beatings, stabbings and other violent episodes as minor assaults from 2009 to 2011 – indicating in turn that violent crime had increased during this period, rather than declining, as the police department had publicized (Poston, 2012). In Dallas, a similar police department miscategorization of violent assaults produced an 'artificial image' of police effectiveness; in addition, a new police department policy making it more difficult for retailers to report incidents of shoplifting resulted in a 75 per cent reduction in such reports – accounting for roughly a third of the city's highly publicized 11 per cent drop in crime (Thompson and Eiserer, 2009; Eiserer and Thompson, 2013). Due largely to 'officer error and software glitches', hundreds of crimes in Denver, Colorado, did not make it into FBI statistics, leading to 'vast' discrepancies between departmental and FBI data – such as the FBI's reporting of a 3.6 per cent decrease in violent crime and police statistics recording a 9.3 per cent increase (Gurman, 2013). In Chicago, where numerous police officers report being 'asked or pressured by their superiors to reclassify their incident reports' and note cases in which 'their reports were changed by some invisible hand', an officer's CompStat statistics 'are widely said to make or break a career'. In this context, even homicides are up for reclassification – as 'noncriminal death investigations'. As one officer argued, 'These days, everything is about media and public opinion. If a number makes people feel safe, then why not give it to them?' (Bernstein and Isackson, 2014a, b).

This logic seems to pervade criminal justice in the UK as well – from the questionable crime-counting methodologies of the national government (Berlinski, 2009) to local police departments like Maidstone, Kent, where five officers are arrested on suspicion of 'persuading criminals to confess to crimes they did not commit to boost detection rates' amidst a 'pressurised performance culture, a culture that is more about quantity than quality', as a Kent Police Federation official puts it (Greenwood and Nolan, 2012). But for all that, the crime of crime statistics is perhaps best understood back at the CompStat mother ship, the New York City Police Department – today helmed once again by William Bratton, returned from a stint as Los Angeles Police Chief and now also serving as advisor to the British government. There, amidst grinding departmental pressure to keep crime statistics low, officers not only reclassify felonies as misdemeanours, but try to dissuade citizens from filing crime reports in the first place – 'the newest evolution in this numbers game', as one police commander said (Baker and Goldstein, 2011: A19). A survey of retired New York City police captains reveals 'an unrelenting, often unethical pressure to manipulate crime statistics' within the department (Powell, 2012: A20; see also Eterno and Silverman, 2012). As for current city police officers who publicize this same pressure and the abuses it engenders, one of them reports to the department's Internal Affairs office his concerns about pervasive street policing practices like 'stop and frisk' designed to enhance police productivity numbers; for his trouble, he is himself charged with filing false arrest papers and subsequently surrenders his badge (Powell, 2012). Another, Adrian Schoolcraft, spends over a year collecting evidence of arrest quotas, illegal arrests and statistical manipulation. Home sick from work, his house is raided by a deputy chief and other officers who forcibly remove him and deposit him in a hospital psychiatric ward, sans judge or jury. A subsequent investigation vindicates Schoolcraft by finding 'a concerted effort to deliberately underreport crime' and leads to charges against a police commander and four officers on grounds of manipulating crime reports (Dwyer, 2012). 'All figures are subject to further analysis and revision', says a disclaimer at the bottom of the New York City Police Department's weekly CompStat summary. Indeed it would appear they are.

In light of these and other cases, a criminological analysis of CompStat and its statistics suggests some rather serious ironies and contradictions. The first of these is straightforward: crime statistics are criminogenic. An institutional reliance on statistical crime data – as decider of policing strategy, measure of institutional efficiency, determiner of individual careers and definer of public image – spawns both institutional and individual criminality in response. Official malfeasance, public intimidation, forced confessions, fraudulent reporting, even raids and abductions – all of these flow from the institutional pressure to produce crime statistics that conform to management models. Like school systems that adopt standardized testing as the measure of both student and teacher success, and then find themselves inundated by cases of leaked test questions and adulterated score sheets, police departments that adopt CompStat-style statistical management programmes spawn pervasive statistical manipulation up and down the organization. Once again, the old criminological truism holds: societies and organizations get precisely the crime they deserve. Dedicated to CompStat as a means of disciplining officers' work lives and promoting organizational crime-reduction success, departments get in return undisciplined officers and new forms of CompStat-related criminality. The problem exists at the level of institutional methodology. And the precision promised by this institutional methodology? It's not just that it's illusory, it's more that it's an institutional and methodological impossibility.

A second criminological issue might be thought of as cultural or epistemic. To put it plainly: On what possible basis might the public in general or criminologists in particular believe that crime statistics tell us anything useful – not to mention objective or precise – about crime? To begin with, it is increasingly clear that institutional pressure to produce acceptable statistics on crime and policing actually alters the realities of crime and policing themselves. In some cases, the pressure on street officers to meet individual and departmental quotas leads to arrests for otherwise ignored activities; in other cases, the pressure to keep numbers down means that officers turn away citizen complaints and resist writing reports. We know from labelling theory that crime is largely constructed by the definitions and enforcement strategies of criminal justice institutions and those that work within them; if these institutions and their employees are redefined in terms of statistical data, then so are the acts that they construct as crime and the people they construct as criminal. CompStat programmes don't record fewer citizen complaints or more arrests; they

(Continued)

(Continued)

generate fewer complaints or more arrests. They alter profoundly the very thing they claim to measure precisely. And yet this street-level self-fulfilling prophecy is only the start. Above and beyond it, on commanders' computer screens and in downtown offices, arrests and complaints are being recoded, relabelled once again, in the interest of a department's statistical politics – to the point that even a homicide can become something less. Sad enough that the resultant statistics are made the foundation of public claims as to departmental efficiency and success, and the foundation for political and budgetary campaigns, but the foundation of subsequent scholarship among quantitative criminologists as well? Rather than embracing these numbers as the basis for criminological analysis, criminologists might consider instead a further irony: crime statistics are likely to be bogus in direct proportion to the degree that criminal justice agencies and political institutions prioritize them. And if this is so, then CompStat, due precisely to its widespread contemporary adoption as a police management programme and to its sweeping claims as to efficiency and precision, is all but guaranteed to produce distinctly bad numbers.

And so, a final irony. In the midst of all this, with CompStat-style programmes in wide adoption, the United States Bureau of Justice Statistics enthusiastically promoted 2013 as the International Year of Statistics. This 'awareness campaign' was designed 'to increase public understanding of the power and impact of statistics on all aspects of society' and 'to promote greater understanding of how statistics improve quality of life and advance our global society' (BJS, 2013).

But maybe it's worse than generalized madness and delusion – maybe it's a particular form of *fundamentalist* delusion. The parallels between the fundamental, 'scientific' methods of orthodox criminology and other of the world's fundamentalisms are, it must be said, striking: a resolute unwillingness to acknowledge internal absurdities; certainty as to the innate correctness and superiority of the preferred approach; a culture of language and presentation whose incomprehensibility to outsiders matters little, since these others are in fact unqualified to understand it in the first place – in this sense, incomprehensibility becoming even a point of internal pride; denial of human agency and disavowal of ambiguity in meaning and interpretation; and most of all, claims to transcendental objectivity. And so, possessed by the spirit of social science, orthodox criminologists speak in a sort of fundamentalist glossolalia, a private prayer language of logistic odds ratios and intercept models, their tongues tied by their own ineptitude in appreciating other ways of seeing the world.

Significantly for criminology, this fundamentalism is more methodological than theoretical (see Kraska and Neuman, 2008). Discomforting as it may be to those who yearn for a unified theory of crime, most criminologists acknowledge, even embrace, the plethora of contemporary criminological theories, none of which reasonably claims determinate or comprehensive explanatory power. Method, though, is another matter. How much difference is there, after all, in the conventional claims of social scientific methodologists and Georg Lukacs' (1971: 1, emphasis in original) classic statement on Marxist orthodoxy? Orthodox Marxism, Lukacs argued, was not at all a matter of Marx's theses or his theory. Instead,

> Orthodox Marxism … refers exclusively to *method*. It is the scientific conviction that dialectical materialism is the road to truth and that its methods can be developed, expanded and deepened only along the lines laid down by its founders. It is the conviction, moreover, that all attempts to surpass or 'improve' it have led and must lead to over-simplification, triviality and eclecticism.

Few criminologists today would share Lukacs' faith in foundational Marxism – but they might well share his faith in orthodox method, his sense of 'scientific conviction', his concern for the 'triviality and eclecticism' of other methodologies. Colonizing criminals, cops, school kids, caregivers and aroused undergraduates in the interest of scientific methodology, bringing the everyday world under the imperial power of sample design and data sets, contemporary criminology attempts to colonize these other methodologies as well. In an issue of the journal *Criminology* otherwise suffused with quantitative research, for example, there appeared (at the back of the issue, mind you) a 'qualitative examination' of legal cynicism – a qualitative examination that incorporated six tables and a 'quantitative analysis' of the information gathered (Carr et al., 2007: 464).

For orthodox criminology, there may be the qualitative Saturday now and then, but ultimately there is only the quantitative Saturday. For orthodox criminology, the *method is the message*.

Methodological culture and the emperor's new clothes

The *culture* of this methodological fundamentalism confirms its consequences for the discipline. We as cultural criminologists understand symbolic meaning and stylized communication to be the animating currents of human life and so examine these cultural currents as they flow through crime and control. But if we recognize that style and representation shape the realities of those we study, then it seems only fair to consider how these same factors shape *our own* enterprise of criminology. If we claim the right to critically examine the cultural worlds of those we study, shouldn't we be willing to examine our own cultural world as well?

If so, then by the terms of its own cultural codes, the orthodox criminology of survey and experimentation seems a sadly failed project. This sort of criminology has certainly not become a 'science' in any conventional sense of analytic rigour or explanatory scope (DiCristina, 2006); a review of quantitative tests of theory in criminology, for example, finds that 'the overall level of variance explained is often very low with 80 or 90 per cent unexplained'

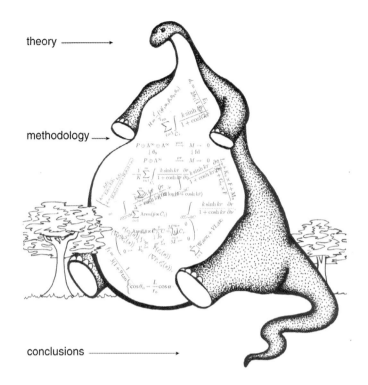

theory

methodology

conclusions

Plate 7.1 The datasoraus. Various deformities emerge amidst the madness of orthodox criminology. The 'headless chicken of an argument' (Young, 2011) is one. The Datasoraus is another – a creature with a very small theoretical brain, a huge methodological body, a Byzantine and intricate statistical gut and a tiny, inconclusive tail wagging mindlessly from database to database.

Credit: Drawing by Ellen Rose Wyatt (2007)

(Weisburd and Piquero, 2008: 453). Worse yet, the greater the effort in making criminology 'scientific', the more systematic has been the dehumanization of human subjects and the numeric abstraction of human experience. Confronting this failure, grasping for the illusion of scientific control, criminologists have turned to hyper-specialization and linguistic obfuscation, apparently on the aesthetic assumption that their work's got to be good looking if it's so hard to see. This sad pseudo-scientific trajectory has fostered a set of symbolic codes, a disciplinary culture that embodies and perpetuates the problem: passive third-person writing, interruptive in-text referencing, big tables, long equations and a general tyranny of the calculated number and the turgidly written word over the idea and the image. Note that all of these cultural codes emerge from the assumption, again, that the method is the message – that elegance and stylistic engagement are unnecessary, even inappropriate, when transmitting the objective results of scientific methodology from one researcher to another by way of the published page. Note also that the codes spawned by this assumption are distinctly arid, ugly and inhuman, devoid of any cultural markers that would distinguish a criminological article from an actuarial report.

In this sense, 'objective' or 'scientific' criminology has long operated more as anxious metaphor than accomplished reality. These cultural codes function as *symbolic performances* of scientific objectivity, as façades fronting the public presentation of criminology as a discipline. The passive voice in writing accomplishes a neat stylistic sleight of hand whereby the author's influence seems to disappear from the author's own text. Twenty-line tables and convoluted equations provide an assuring sense of precision and order, even for those uninterested in actually reading them. Pervasive in-text referencing offers the illusion of comprehensive disciplinary knowledge and the image of progression towards scientific truth as each criminologist builds on the work of those before. Together, these coded communications assure criminologists, and their audiences, that methodological rigour continues to discipline the discipline of criminology; taken as a whole, they construct a persuasive *aesthetic of authority* (Ferrell, 1996) for the presentation of criminological knowledge.

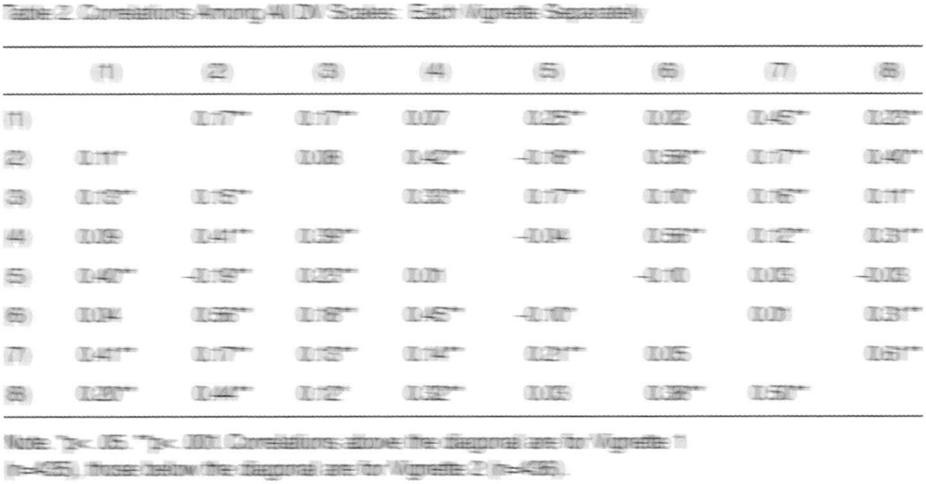

Plate 7.2 The aesthetics of authority. This table is not only out of focus, it's made up. How would you know if others were made up? And what exactly does 'made up' mean in the current criminological climate?

Credit: Table by Jeannine Gailey[2]

But, of course, this is all collective performance, academic theatre, another of Feyerabend's little carnivals where a discipline displays and deceives itself. Rationality has no more displaced emotion and personal agenda in the practice of criminology than it has in the practice of crime. Many criminological research projects go forward under less than closely controlled conditions, despite the best efforts of IRBs and other bureaucratic overseers. The 'peer review' process by which criminologists review each other's research, while certainly helpful, is certainly *not* devoid of duplicity, individual predilection and the occasional vendetta. And let's be honest: the statistical residues and objectivist protestations pulled up over criminologists' research hardly hide the pervasive obscenity of aggressive careerism and the associated practice of methodological pimping to the highest bidder.

Yet, like other cultural constructions, these codes and performances create serious consequences, feeding back into the collective work that produces them. In the case of criminology, they set the tone for a particularly inappropriate approach to human life and human society. A disciplinary fondness for a style that is off-putting and inelegant helps perpetuate the false hierarchy of content over form and helps render even the most seductive of subject matters sterile. This collection of off-putting cultural codes distances criminology from engaged public discourse, leaving it an intellectual side water with little hope of effectively confronting either the predations of criminals or the abuses of the criminal justice system (see Burawoy, 2005; Loader and Sparks, 2010). Most of all, the culture of much orthodox criminology completes what its methods begin: the dehumanization of those individuals and groups criminology allegedly seeks to understand.

'In the baseline model (model 1), no variables exert a significant effect on sexual coercion' (Piquero and Bouffard, 2007: 15); 'Results from level 2 of the HGLM demonstrated that seven of the eight life circumstances included in the model exhibited a statistically significant impact on likelihood of victimization' (Armstrong and Griffin, 2007: 91); 'As seen in table 1, the overall mean effect size for self-control on victimization (Mz) is .154 ($p < 001$), indicating that a 1 standard deviation increase in low self-control results in a .154 standard deviation increase in victimization' (Pratt et al., 2014: 99); 'Recall that a key advantage of the tobit model is that it explicitly deals with the floor-value of the summative delinquency measure' (Ousey and Wilcox, 2007: 340). Now, what kind of way is that to talk about people? We doubt that those involved in sexual coercion appreciate being reduced to baseline models and (no) variable effects. It strikes us that disassembling victims into their component parts – sentiments, self-control, life circumstances, all carved up like some intellectual butcher hard at a carcass – mostly makes them victims again. Whether delinquent youth or domestic violence victim or probation officer, it can't feel good to have words put in your mouth, to have your actions and the accounts you give of them translated into the jargon of those who claim to know you better than you know yourself. Abstract and obtuse, this sort of language is also revealing, illuminating a set of linguistic practices that systematically suck the life from those they describe.

The National Gang Survey

Since 1995, the US Department of Justice's Office of Juvenile Justice and Delinquency Prevention (OJJDP) and the National Gang Center have conducted a National Youth Gang Survey so as to 'facilitate analysis of changes and trends in the nature of youth gangs and their activities'. The 1996 survey, for example, found some 31,000 gangs with approximately 850,000 members – an important finding, since as OJJDP Administrator Shay Bilchik noted, 'sound data are essential to solving the problem of juvenile crime' (OJJDP, 1999: iii). By 2004, a decade's worth of yearly surveys allowed for the calculation of a 10-year average: 25,000 gangs with 750,000 members (National Youth Gang Center, 2007). In 2011, the estimated numbers were 30,000 gangs and 782,500 gang members (National Youth Gang Center, 2014).

But big numbers aside, the emperor's new clothes are in this case notably threadbare. The OJJDP neither surveys nor otherwise studies any gangs or gang members – its surveys are mailed only to law enforcement agencies. At the agencies, by the OJJDP's own admission, those filling out the survey are asked to base their responses on 'records or personal knowledge', though it is 'impossible to determine which'. In addition, the OJJDP for years provided 'no definition … regarding what constitutes a gang member or a gang incident', since 'little agreement has been reached on what constitutes a gang, gang member, or gang incident' (OJJDP, 1999: 7). Now, the survey offers the oddly elastic non-definition of 'a group of youths or young adults in your jurisdiction that you or other responsible persons in your agency or community are willing to identify as a "gang"' (www.nationalgangcenter.gov). Yet, none of this precludes the production of aesthetically authoritative data; an early survey summary (OJJDP, 1999), for instance, included 36 tables and 19 charts and figures, with further tables and formulae offered in Appendices A to L.

So, for governmental agencies and the criminologists who rely on them, 'sound data' apparently goes something like this: 'That which is not to be studied directly can nonetheless be surveyed definitively, based on the records, or perhaps the personal perceptions, of those whose job it is to eradicate that which they cannot define accurately'.

Honestly, though, we don't mean to make this a personal attack on our colleagues, nor to single out for special criticism those we cite; in fact, the research we note was selected by simply opening recent issues of orthodox criminology journals and, sadly, picking most any article. Further, we're aware that, were our critique to be taken seriously, academic livelihoods would be lost, grant-writing workshops evacuated, seminars in advanced statistics summarily cancelled. This is not our immediate interest either. Rather, as we've said elsewhere, 'What is of interest here is the awareness of thin ice, yet the ineluctable desire to keep on skating' (J. Young, 2004: 19). Or to put it differently: what interests us is how transparently non-existent are the criminologist's new clothes, how naked the fraud of objectivist criminology, save for everyone agreeing to agree that the clothes certainly do exist – and are damn fine clothes at that.

As Feyerabend would suggest, this fraud may be a contemporary phenomenon, but it is a long time in the making. Some criminologists, for instance, might well object to our finding contemporary criminology's foundations in the Chicago School of the early twentieth century, arguing that the real roots of criminology, its scientific roots, can be traced to the nineteenth century and the pioneering positivist work of Cesare Lombroso. We would agree – and we would add that Lombroso was a performance artist, a cultural imperialist and a scientific fraud. As Wayne Morrison demonstrates, 'positivist criminology was born amidst a dazzling and seductive spectacle' of collected skulls, catalogued tattoos, wall-mounted crime maps and gelatinized human brains, with Lombroso's collections the most dazzling of all. Designed quite literally to *display* publicly the 'scientific' methods of the new criminology, these nineteenth-century exhibits and clinical collections were part of the process by which positivist criminology emerged as a 'cultural phenomenon' (Morrison, 2004b: 68). But these showcased methods of mapping and measurement no more constituted a 'science' of crime than do today's surveys and GPS crime maps; according to Lombroso's calculations, for example, Aboriginal art was commensurate with contemporary 'criminal art' and the historic tattoos of the Maori simply evidence of atavistic criminality. The methodological imperialism by which situated meaning is stolen in the name of science – by which survey methods reduce domestic violence to a data set, by which catalogues convert local culture into crime – operates now as it did then (on this point in relation to indigenous cultures today, see Juan Tauri's powerful recent work [2012] on indigenous criminology).

As Feyerabend and Cohen would also suggest, stripping away the mythology of criminology's scientific beginnings, penetrating the cultural codes by which contemporary criminology presents itself as science, exposing the fraud of criminological fundamentalism – seeing, that is, through the criminologist's new clothes – provides just the sort of healthy disciplinary disrespect needed for intellectual progress. Freed from the collective delusion of scientific criminology, we awake to see that survey methods and statistical analysis forfeit whole areas of social and cultural life while inventing fictional social constructs out of their own methodological arrogance. Ignoring the situational and interactional dynamics of crime and crime control, missing entirely the mediated human meaning of crime and transgression, these methods imagine instead a world where data sets correlate with – indeed, somehow capture – the reality of crime and control. But of course survey methods and their resultant data sets do no such thing; they simply create that which they claim to capture.

Let's be clear on this: there exist in the lived situations of crime and crime control *no such things* as 'logistic odds ratios predicting help seeking and divorce or separation for female victims of spousal violence', *no such things* as 'interactions between antisocial propensity and time-varying predictors of delinquency', *no such things* as 'results from level 2 of the HGLM', *no such thing* as a 'standard deviation increase in low self-control'. Such phrases reference nothing more than the residues of methods that imagine such phenomena to exist and in so doing call them into existence. These are the threads of the emperor's new clothes, and to believe that these loose threads can somehow be woven into an understanding of criminal motivation or personal trauma and then generalized to 'public attitudes towards crime' or 'patterns of victimization', is to layer one imaginary garment over another. Hearing this sort of critique, concerned colleagues sometimes counter that we are asking them to give up all the facts they know: rates of vandalism in Boston, degrees of British domestic abuse, levels of personal harm in Bangalore. On the contrary: to the extent that such 'facts' derive from simplistic survey data collated and crammed through statistical grinders, then spat out and slathered with a thin sheen of science, we're asking them to give up what they *don't* know. Otherwise, we're afraid that their research, and ours, will remain mostly busy work in the service of a delusion, solving neither the problems of criminal victimization nor the abuses of state authority, and leaving us all little more than the intellectual caretakers of late modernity.

A selection of films and documentaries illustrative of some of the themes and ideas in this chapter

The Wire (TV series, 5 parts), Creator: David Simon

Perhaps the greatest TV crime series ever, *The Wire* unfolds over five series like a filmic textbook on cultural criminology: the micro-street practices of drug sellers, post-industrial urban decay, the strengths and weaknesses of contemporary police work, transnational people smuggling, corruption in the prison and criminal justice system, organized crime, money laundering and the failing US education system – the list of criminologically related themes is endless. However, in terms of this chapter, check out Season 4 in particular as it has much to say about CompStat, 'juking the stats' and the problems that arise when police forces prioritize statistical targets over community policing. (NB. Season 1 takes a few episodes to warm up, but stick with it and you will be rewarded as *The Wire's* expansive narrative gathers pace and focus.)

(Continued)

(Continued)

The Trap: What Happened to Our Dream of Freedom, 2007 (3 parts), Dir. Adam Curtis

A brilliant three-part documentary series that shows how reliance upon simplistic statistical models of human behaviour, combined with an exaggerated belief in human selfishness, has created a 'cage' for Western humans. Essential viewing for anybody who wants to understand the neo-liberal world of performance indicators, league tables and quotas constituted from dubious statistics, and ever more controlling systems of social management (available to watch for free at: www.filmsforaction.org).

Kitchen Stories, 2003, Dir. Bent Hammer

Based on a truly boring 1950s documentary about Swedish time-and-motion studies of housewives, *Kitchen Stories* is a comedy that highlights the problems that can emerge when one attempts to scientifically observe human behaviour.

Human Resources: Social Engineering in the Twentieth Century, 2010, Dir. Scott Noble

Starting from Mikhail Bakunin's assertion that 'If there is a devil in history, it is the power principle', and covering subjects such as behaviourism, scientific management and human experimentation, *Human Resources* is a visually compelling documentary about social control, mechanistic philosophy and the manipulation of human beings under hierarchical systems (available to watch for free at: http://topdocumentaryfilms.com and www.filmsforaction.org).

Brazil, 1985, Dir. Terry Gilliam

One man takes on an administrative state obsessed with terrorism and technology in Terry Gilliam's retro-future fantasy. Part surreal fantasy, part profound sci-fi satire on totalitarian bureaucracy, *Brazil* makes for interesting viewing in a post-Patriot Act world.

Sherrybaby, 2006, Dir. Laurie Collyer

Maggie Gyllenhall stars in this poignant film about a young woman (the eponymous Sherry Swanson) who tries to rebuild her life after serving a three-year sentence in a New Jersey prison. Despite good intentions, including her plans to re-establish a relationship with her young daughter, Sherry finds herself hemmed in by ever-tightening probation restrictions and a society that cares little for female ex-offenders. *Sherrybaby* illustrates a number of criminologically significant themes, but especially the distance between the bureaucratic strictures of the criminal justice system and the difficult existential choices that are the product of broken lives.

Further Reading

Young, J. (2011) *The Criminological Imagination*. Cambridge: Polity Press. Substantive critique of abstracted positivism from a cultural and critical criminological perspective.

Ferrell, J. (1997) 'Criminological *verstehen'*, *Justice Quarterly*, 14(1): 3–23.
Early cultural criminological statement on the centrality of Max Weber's concept of *verstehen* – the subjective or appreciative understanding of others' actions and motivations.

Ferrell, J. (2004) 'Boredom, crime and criminology', *Theoretical Criminology*, 8(3): 287–302.
A paper that shows how, under the dehumanizing conditions of modernity, boredom has come to pervade the experience of everyday life. Ferrell shows how this collective experience spawns not only moments of illicit criminal excitement, but also a vast machinery of abstract social scientific methodologies and analytic abstraction.

Cohen, S. (1988) *Against Criminology.* Oxford: Polity.
A collection of essays by the inimitable Stan Cohen in which he looks back on criminology's development in an attempt to point out some theoretical and methodological limitations of criminological knowledge production.

Winlow, S. and Hall, S. (2012) 'What is an "Ethics Committee?": academic governance in an epoch of belief and incredulity', *British Journal of Criminology*, 52(2): 400–416.
Winlow and Hall's article charts how risk aversion, political correctness, and the death of intellectual integrity in Western universities have resulted in ever-tightening strictures being imposed by ethics committees and institutional review boards on researchers who wish to continue studying human subjects in real world settings.

Useful Websites

Adam Curtis Films
http://adamcurtisfilms.blogspot.co.uk/
Link to the thought-provoking documentaries of BBC filmmaker Adam Curtis.

The Journal of Qualitative Criminal Justice and Criminology (JQCJC)
www.jqcjc.org/
JQCJC is an open access, bi-annual periodical publishing original qualitative research, articles that deal with qualitative research methodologies, and book reviews relevant to both qualitative research and methodology.

The International Journal of Qualitative Methods
http://ejournals.library.ualberta.ca/index.php/IJQM/index
The International Journal of Qualitative Methods is a peer reviewed journal published as an open annual volume, web-based journal by the International Institute for Qualitative Methodology at the University of Alberta, Canada.

Notes

1 An anarchist critique of knowledge need not result in the sort of extreme relativism that leaves one perspective epistemologically indistinguishable from another. Even when absolute knowledge claims are rejected – or, more accurately in the case of Feyerabend and Cohen, deconstructed – decisions can still be made and preferences expressed. As we hope to demonstrate later in this chapter and in the following chapter, it is the grounds for these preferences and decisions that are different – no longer the alleged epistemic certainty of 'truth' or 'scientific method', but rather the provisional persuasion offered by stylistic elegance, human affinity and social awareness.
2 Our thanks to Trey Williams, pioneer of the intentionally out-of-focus table.

8

DANGEROUS KNOWLEDGE: SOME METHODS OF CULTURAL CRIMINOLOGY

Seeing through the orthodox criminologist's new clothes – shaking off the delusion of social scientific criminology – we're free to imagine fresh possibilities for engaging with the problems of crime and justice. Rejecting the supercilious self-importance of orthodox method, we're able to embrace methodological possibilities that are creative, dangerous and unfinished. As before, the serious-ness of the subject matter is such that we dare not take conventional criminology seriously, lest human tragedy get lost amidst a maze of cross-tabulations. Instead, it's our disciplinary duty to move beyond the stale certainty of orthodoxy and towards approaches able to account for crime, transgression and victimization as they are lived under contemporary circumstances.

In today's world of immigration, impermanence and 'instant living', where transience trumps durability, the methods of orthodox criminology seem delu-sional indeed, and anachronistic. Set-question surveys and numeric summaries are residues of an earlier modernism, of rationalization and routinization. Such methods operate as a fixed-line knowledge factory, still churning out one widget of data at a time – and under new ownership of the IRB and the REF, the factory's assembly line becomes all the more inflexible. These methods presume, indeed require, discrete categories, fixed populations and personalities, reliability, replicability – that is, all that late modernity so often denies. Consequently, they're ill-equipped to get inside the ephemeral images and emotions that ani-mate everyday life, likewise ill-suited to surf the informational flows that shape it. A half-century ago, Martin Nicolaus (1969: 387) asked of sociology, 'What kind of science is this, which holds true only when men hold still?' A half-cen-tury later, women and men, criminals and their images, are even less likely to hold still – and so the methods of orthodox sociology and criminology are even less likely to apply.

Instead, criminology must embrace methods that can catch the subtleties of transgressive situations while locating these situations in larger currents of meaning. It must imagine methods that can capture mediated law-and-order campaigns while also accounting for the variety of audiences such campaigns hit and miss. These methods – the methods of cultural criminology – must be attuned to crime as both a phenomenon emerging from local circumstances and a commodity marketed through global networks, and must be sympathetic to contemporary identity as a source of existential stability and ongoing unease. At their best, such methods must mix instant living with long-term human commitment.

And these methods must be attuned to the image. Clearly, it's time to abandon the old social scientific hierarchy of content over form and those methods that embody it by privileging the word over the image in the investigation of crime. A world in which images of crime and justice pervade everyday life, looping and spiralling through newscasts and conversations, spawning public fear and public policy – the world described in Chapter 6 – is not a world that can be reduced to one of four survey answer options or to dry prose and numbers. Understanding this world requires researching it on its own terms, on the terms of representational dynamics, symbolic discourse and stylistic ambiguity. If our research results are to reflect this world, and to find currency in it, they themselves must become more stylish and more open to the image. A criminology of the contemporary world requires methods wired for image production and for producing styles of communication more literary or artistic than 'scientific'. Today, criminals, law makers and law enforcement agencies all make their own media, creating websites, circulating images and otherwise paying attention to the politics of communication. In studying them, we must do the same.

Much to ask of a discipline mired in methods that generally make for bad writing and ugly presentation (Ferrell, 2006b). But based on our experiences, we can promise certain benefits if the task is undertaken. The following methods demand more of researchers – but they also guarantee a good bit more intellectual adventure and experiential excitement than a survey form. Compared to orthodox criminological methods, these methods are all but certain to get researchers closer to crime and criminals – and closer to the audiences for crime, criminals and criminology. And along the way, they're likely to get researchers closer to themselves, too.

Ethnography

Fairly or not, cultural criminology is often equated with ethnography, due largely to Jeff Ferrell's (1996, 2001/2, 2006a) book-length ethnographic studies and to the collection *Ethnography at the Edge*, edited by Jeff Ferrell and Mark Hamm (1998). In a critical review of cultural criminology, for example, Martin O'Brien (2005: 600) defines cultural criminology in part by its 'ethnographic imagination' and explores in detail its ethnographic methods; in another critical overview, Craig Webber (2007) investigates and critiques the interplay between cultural criminology and culturally-informed ethnography. While arguing generally that cultural criminology 'has been easily the most exciting intellectual movement within critical criminology in the last two decades', Max Travers (2013) likewise focuses on, and at times questions, cultural criminologists' embracing of ethnography as a critical method.

As practised by Ferrell and others, ethnography denotes long-term, in-depth participation with those under study; Ferrell's (2006a) book on urban scrounging and trash picking, for example, resulted from ongoing day-in, day-out street-level research with other urban scroungers. Conducted in this way, ethnography does indeed seem a definitive method for cultural criminology, since as Paul Willis (1977: 3) says, it provides 'a sensitivity to meanings and values as well as an ability to represent and interpret symbolic articulations, practices and forms of cultural production'. Deeply immersed in the lives of criminals, crime victims or cops, the criminologist can become part of the process by which meaning is made, witnessing the ways in which such people make sense of their experiences through symbolic codes and collective conversations. Sharing with them their situations and experiences, vulnerable to their tragedies and triumphs, the criminologist can likewise learn something of the emotions that course through their experiences of crime, victimization and criminal justice.

For cultural criminologists, this goal of gaining deep cultural and emotional knowledge is embodied in the concept of *criminological verstehen* (Ferrell, 1997; Root et al., 2013). As developed by the great sociologist Max Weber, the concept of *verstehen* denotes the subjective or appreciative understanding of others' actions and motivations – a deeply felt understanding essential for fully comprehending their lives. As Weber (1978: 4–5) argued, for research that 'concern[s] itself with the interpretive understanding of social action ... empathic or appreciative accuracy is attained when, through sympathetic participation, we can adequately grasp the emotional context in which the action took place'. Here Weber, and cultural criminologists, stand orthodox criminology on its head. Rather than 'objectivity' guaranteeing accurate research results, it is in fact *emotional subjectivity* that ensures accuracy in research; without it, the researcher may observe an event or elicit information, but will have little sense of its meaning or consequences for those involved. This holds true, by the way, whether or not the researcher 'sympathizes' in a conventional sense with those being studied. In Ferrell's ethnographic work, for example, his submersion in the meaningful emotions of graffiti writers and homeless scroungers has allowed him to portray them in ways that counter their unjust demonization in the media and the criminal justice system. Mark Hamm (1997, 2002), on the other hand, has journeyed deep inside the dangerous emotional worlds of domestic terrorists with precisely the opposite intention and effect: dispelling stereotypes of them in the interest of better understanding and preventing their victimization of others. In either case, the conventional 'criminal category', as Philip Parnell (2003: 22) says, is 'a barrier worth pushing against through ethnographic practice'.

In standing the objectivism of orthodox criminology on its head, this ethnographic approach also reclaims the criminological enterprise from methodologies dependent on official records, survey data and numbers. Significantly, it is not simply that such methods aren't well equipped to take researchers inside situated emotions and meanings; it is that, by definition, they aren't *meant* to take researchers there. To engage in ethnography, to strive for criminological *verstehen*, is to humble oneself before those being studied, to seek and respect their understandings and to take note of cultural nuance *because it matters*. To mail a survey or run a data set is to miss such nuance *by intention*, to believe that meaning can be deduced by the researcher and imparted to the subject matter. Engaging in ethnography, then, cultural criminologists focus their research on their subjects, but their critique on orthodox criminology. In the current disciplinary context, ethnography exists as a subversion, as a decision to affirm and explore the human agency of those we study, whether that agency produces crime, resistance, victimization or injustice.

The disciplinary subversions of ethnographic research are temporal and existential as well. Ethnographic studies generally mix hours of tedium with explosions of surprise and moments of dangerous uncertainty. Such studies flow with the dynamics of situations, embracing the cultural meanings of others, and so carrying researchers beyond their own existential complacency and into uncomfortable ambiguities of crime and crime control. Within such studies, progress is measured not by the efficient accumulation of data, but by the abandonment of professional efficiency to the rhythms of others' temporal worlds (Ferrell, 2006a; Barrett, 2013) – rhythms that by conventional standards may seem like so much dawdle and delay. Ultimately, this do-it-yourself method generates disciplinarily dangerous knowledge, spawning human engagement, oddball insight and illicit meaning unimaginable – and unmanageable – within the sternly scheduled certainty of 'scientific' methods, IRBs and REFs.

At its extreme, ethnography suggests a process through which researchers learn to lose themselves inside a series of illicit situations – and, by losing themselves, find the meanings and emotions that those situations carry. In this way, ethnographic method comes to stand against 'methodology' itself, to the extent that methodology is conventionally conceptualized as a set of preordained procedures to be deployed as determinants of the research process. Good ethnography in contrast generally comes closer to following Feyerabend's injunction that 'anything goes', emerging as an alternative way of living for those willing to explore the uncertain nuances of transgression and control. The morality of ethnography is that of human engagement and situational decision, its politics more the do-it-yourself dynamics of anarchism than the governance of guidebooks and bureaucratic regulation.

Dangerous knowledge indeed.

Ethnography and the law

In August 2012, Bradley Garrett was arrested, handcuffed and dragged off an airplane at London's Heathrow Airport. Terrorist? No, ethnographer. Four years before, Garrett had begun a doctoral research project based on ethnographic research with 'urban explorers' or 'place hackers' in London and elsewhere. Given that contemporary urban explorers organize their leisure time around sneaking into abandoned buildings, shuttered transit stations and skyscrapers under construction, this ethnographic work necessarily pushed Garrett up against, and sometimes beyond, various legal boundaries regarding trespass and private property. For London's urban explorers, the city's many out-of-use Underground tube stations are particularly attractive, and as Garrett and his research subjects began to explore these stations, and to document and publicize their explorations in the media and elsewhere, the British Transport Police (BTP) began to take notice.

After arresting Garrett at Heathrow, the BTP battered down the front door of his house and seized his field notes and related research materials. Garrett and eight of his research subjects were subsequently charged with 'conspiracy to commit criminal damage' – a charge that carries a possible 10-year prison sentence – with the charges based in part on research materials that the BTP had taken from Garrett's computer hard drive. The authorities also took the sheer amount of field notes, photographs and videos that Garrett's ethnographic research had generated to mean that he had acted as the organizing head of this criminal conspiracy. As the case moved toward trial, the prosecution retained as its expert witness Dr Helen Kara, an 'independent social researcher' (Kara, 2014: 1). In her expert witness statement, Dr Kara argued that Garrett's lawbreaking was both unethical and unnecessary, since he could well have conducted the research legally. She also found that Garrett's ethnographic work 'brings social research into disrepute' (Kara, 2014: 9–10) and that in the course of the research he had violated the privacy, confidentiality and 'well-being' of those he studied. While admitting that she herself had 'never conducted ethnography', she nonetheless concluded that Garrett's research was soundly illegal and unethical. 'It is my unreserved opinion that many of his actions as a researcher were unethical', she wrote (Kara, 2014: 11). 'In particular, he broke the law in the course of conducting his research.'

The defence countered with its own expert witness: Jeff Ferrell. Ferrell (2014b: 10) argued that the long tradition of ethnographic research with marginal and illegal populations has made one thing 'strikingly clear: The ethnographic researcher is required to take part in interactions and situations that may be illegal if the researcher is to conduct the research fully and properly.' In contrast to Kara's finding of 'disrepute', Ferrell (2014b: 12) found Garrett's research 'to do quite the opposite: to carry on and carry forward the esteemed tradition of ethnographic field work within social

(Continued)

(Continued)

research, and by its findings and analysis to enhance significantly the repute of social research'. Ferrell likewise found Kara's concerns about violated confidentiality and privacy 'inaccurate and ironic', since it was after all 'the police and prosecution themselves [that] violated the privacy of the research subjects whom Dr Garrett had worked to protect'.

As the case unfolded, charges were dropped against all but two defendants, one of them Garrett. Garrett ultimately pleaded guilty to five counts of 'criminal damage to railway property' – including acts such as removing a wingnut and removing a board and then replacing it – for which he received not 10 years in prison, but a three-year conditional discharge and a £2,000 fine. This 'success-ful' resolution to the trial was paralleled by other successes; Garrett completed his PhD, published a book based on his research despite the BTP's legal pressure on his publisher (Garrett, 2013) and went on to employment within the British academic system.

Yet, while Garrett successfully avoided prison, he didn't succeed in escaping ongo-ing legal threats to his research. 'It is precisely the "conditional" in the "conditional discharge" I was given that continues to cause me angst', he says. 'The condition, as spelled out in law, is that I commit no further offence in the next three years, lest I be brought up on these charges again. While I'm delighted to be free again, I've also been prevented, in no uncertain terms, from doing research on any social prac-tice that may cross legal lines for the next few years, an unfortunate by-product of an already disconcerting attempt to stifle reasonable academic research' (Garrett, 2014: 39). He's also aware of the six-year ethnographic project conducted by Alice Goffman in a poor Philadelphia neighbourhood – a project, he says, that 'often brought her close to the law', while demonstrating 'the value of spending long periods of time in legally murky social contexts to learn more about marginalised members of society, people who often have less voice' (Garrett, 2014: 37). Indeed, during her research Goffman (2014) witnessed pistol-whippings, beatings, murders and 24 police raids, during one of which she was handcuffed; eventually she destroyed all her field notes to protect them from subpoena (Kotlowitz, 2014). And then there's that expert witness for Garrett's defence, who many years before had hidden away tapes of his field interviews with graffiti writers in a bank's safe deposit box and who himself had nonetheless been arrested, tried and sentenced to the confines of a year's probation (Ferrell, 1996, 1997).

For all that, though, much of what today constitutes cultural criminology was not built from classic ethnographic research in a strict sense and much of what it is to become will doubtless emerge from other approaches as well. Publication schedules and personal circumstances, REFs and IRBs, little funding, low salaries and the sorts of legal problems just noted all conspire to keep many criminolo-gists, cultural or otherwise, from deep, long-term ethnography (Adler and Adler, 1998; Webber, 2007). Put more positively, some cultural criminologists them-selves prefer other research approaches, for reasons of subject matter or style. Cultural criminology, then, is not defined, and should not be defined, by the particular methods of conventional ethnography – but it can and should be defined by an *ethnographic sensibility*. However put into play, this ethnographic sensibility orients cultural criminology to certain practices. It opens research to the meaningful worlds of others and seeks to understand the symbolic processes through which these worlds are made. It affirms the importance of emotional resonance and embraces the nuance and texture of human culture. And it humbles the arrogant 'objectivity' of orthodox methodology to the fluid ambiguities of human agency.

Thought of in this way, 'ethnography' is not a method that excludes all but the most committed researchers, but an invitation to all researchers, all criminologists to engage an attitude of attentiveness and respect. Thought of as a sensibility, ethnography can endure for months or for a moment and can be brought to bear on social situations, mediated communications or global processes.

Instant ethnography

Traditionally, the quality of ethnography has been measured in part by its duration, on the assumption that the more time a researcher spent inside a group or situation, the more deeply could its cultural dynamics be understood. This can certainly be the case, and for a researcher studying a neighbourhood's crime-prevention strategies, an urban youth gang's evolution or a white-collar criminal's emergence from corporate culture, long-term research involvement may well be invaluable. The liquid instability of late modernity, though, means that crime can just as well come and go in an instant. A neighbourhood's long-term crime-control strategy can collapse in a moment of haphazard violence; a youth gang's trajectory can change with one bad street brawl; embezzlement can emerge from ongoing corporate culture or from one moment of professional shame or workplace ridicule. As suggested in Chapter 4's excavation of everyday life, years of television viewing can spark fear of victimization, but so can a momentary misunderstanding – and crime control can be accomplished, sometimes, by little more than a gesture or a glance. With many populations increasingly cut loose from stabilities of time and space through global immigration, short-term employment and virtual communications, these little flashes of fear and transgression become all the more common and research on them all the more important.

But if crime can occur in an instant, can ethnography? Emerging work in cultural criminology and related fields suggests it can. Contrasting the tradition of tightly controlled, 'technique-driven' social science research with newer, late-modern notions of fluidity and ambiguity, Peter Manning (1995: 246) argues that this contemporary approach can usefully reorient ethnography to the 'emergent, fragile and reflexive character of modern life'. Ethnographies of such fragile circumstances, Manning (1995: 249–51, emphasis in original) notes, would account for the 'fundamental perversity and *unpredictability* of human conduct' by weaving 'fragments and shards of events' into a new sort of 'ethnography of experience'. A veteran cultural ethnographer who has spent months and years in the field, Stephanie Kane (1998: 142–3) finds similarly that moments of chaos and confusion, 'moments of extreme or unusual conditions', can themselves be interrogated as part of ethnographic work. Jarring the researcher loose from the traditional practice of ethnographic research, such moments are to be valued – maybe even engineered on occasion – for the phenomenological insights they can offer. 'Serendipity', Kane (2004: 317) says, 'can realign data' and in so doing can reveal 'empirical patterns in novel ways'.

Theoretical work in cultural criminology helps us imagine instant ethnography as well. Just as Bauman (2000) has theorized the long currents of liquid modernity, cultural criminologists have theorized the situated dynamics by which liquid *moments* are lived illicitly. For Jack Katz (1988: 7, 216), the 'seductions of crime' are such that 'the causes of crime are constructed by the offenders themselves' in moments of criminal transgression, with these causes then operating as 'lures and pressures that they experience as independently moving them toward crime'. Understanding criminal dynamics, then, means documenting these situated constructions and remaining ready to catch sight of them in 'exceptional circumstances' and moments of 'incongruent sensuality'. As conceptualized by Stephen Lyng (1990, 2005) and Jeff Ferrell (1996, 2005), transgressive experiences of 'edgework' and 'the adrenalin rush' are likewise characterized by a unity of skill and adventure that endures only as long as the transgressive moment lasts. Researching these experiences requires going 'inside the immediacy of crime' (Ferrell, 1997), inside an instant so fragile, so fleeting, that those involved consider it both ephemeral and ineffable. Katz (1988: 312) argues in this light that criminology's long-standing theoretical focus on 'background factors' rather than 'foreground' seductions has served to 'constitute the field back to front'. The same might be said of method. Perhaps conventional methods, even conventional ethnographies, have looked too long at the background and the beforehand and not enough at the moments in which background factors explode into meaning and emotion (Ferrell, 1992; Young, 2003).[1]

The ethnography of meaning's momentary construction, instant ethnography is also the ethnography of performance. Just as gender, ethnicity and other markers of identity are increasingly seen as situated accomplishments and public performances, Katz and others allow us to see crime, criminality and criminal justice as a series of contested performances undertaken in dangerous little everyday theatres. And so, just as ethnography provided Paul Willis with 'a sensitivity to meanings and values ... practices and forms of cultural production', 'performance ethnography' today offers researchers like John Warren (2006: 318) a sensitivity to 'cultural practices as living moments, enfleshed experiences, real people in real places'. Dwight Conquergood (2002) conducted ethnography in precisely this way, recording on paper and film the performative worlds of street gangs, global refugees and criminal justice practitioners, catching those moments in which the meaning of their worlds came alive. Likewise, Robert Garot (2007a: 50; 2010) has documented the dynamics of the 'Where you from!?' street challenge, showing that this bravura performance doesn't so much function to reflect stable gang membership as it does to construct it in the moment; gang identity, Garot argues, is not a 'fixed personal characteristic' but more 'a sensual response to a moment's vicissitudes'. Living as a hard-man or a 'badass' (Katz, 1988), earning respect as a police officer, surviving as a victim of assault – these are performances, too, performances meant to persuade one audience or another and one's self as well. With its close attention to the choreography of everyday life, conventional ethnography can set the stage – but an ethnography of stage presence is needed as well, a sense of those edgy, incandescent moments when the performer and the performance make the dance of transgression what it is.

Elsewhere, we've argued that moments of edgework and adrenalin embody a politics of illicit transgression, often carrying participants beyond the boundaries of law, work and safety, if fleetingly, and into new realms of subversive possibility (Ferrell, 1996, 2005). Instant ethnography confirms such political possibility in the realm of method. Manning (1995) and Kane (2004), you'll recall, talk of unpredictability and serendipity as spawning new understandings. John Warren (2006: 318), Norman Denzin (1997, 2003), Dwight Conquergood (1991) and others speak explicitly of performance ethnography as a form of political intervention, an act of transgressive insight based on 'seeing the constructed nature of our lives and then interrupting that seemingly stable process'. And, in fact, the political potential of instant ethnography recalls a long intellectual history. The *epoché* of phenomenology, the breaching procedures of ethnomethodology, the *détournement* of the Situationists – all are intellectual practices suggesting that old understandings can be undermined in an instant and new meaning made just as quickly. With instant ethnography, we likewise engage the politics of transgressive possibility and so embrace something of cultural criminology's progressive mandate. Whether committing a burglary, tackling a fleeing suspect or conducting an illicit ethnography, what Henri Cartier-Bresson (1952) called a single 'decisive moment' can mean everything – and can change everything.

Instant ethnography

Plate 8.1   BASE jumping off the New River Gorge Bridge, West Virginia, USA

Credit: Photo by Jeff Ferrell (1998a)

Jeff Ferrell, Dragan Milovanovic and Stephen Lyng (2001) conducted an instant ethnography of BASE jumpers – those who parachute from buildings and bridges. Here, the ethnography is indeed instant, as the researchers record the ephemeral experiences of BASE jumpers having only a few seconds to deploy their parachutes and negotiate a landing. Yet, even here, the loops and spirals seen in Chapter 6 appear, as BASE jumpers wear helmet-mounted video cameras, videotape jumps for later collective viewing and evaluation, and sell jump footage to mainstream media outlets in order to finance the next videotaped descent.

Liquid ethnography

If instant ethnography catches up to the speed of late modernity, liquid ethnography finds a way to flow with its swirls of meaning, representation and identity. Liquid ethnography suggests ethnography attuned to the dynamics of destabilized, transitory communities; ethnography immersed in the ongoing interplay of images; and ethnography comfortable with the shifting boundaries between research, research subjects and cultural activism. For cultural criminologists, this methodological sensitivity to ambiguity and uncertainty offers a further benefit: the ability to engage with illicit communities on their own terms, and so to explore transgression as a source of dangerous knowledge and progressive possibility. Liquid ethnography in this way follows cultural criminology's trajectory away from the 'courthouse criminology' that Polsky rightly condemned, not only by moving criminological research outside the courthouse and the court records file, but by moving it outside the codifications of crime and transgression housed there.

We might hope that some of our own ethnographic work has anticipated this sort of liquid ethnography, as with Ferrell's (1996, 2006a: 1) appreciative and illegal ethnography of graffiti writers and their images or the amorphous mix of 'field research and free-form survival' that characterized his urban trash scrounging adventures. Whatever flows we may have found, though, other cultural criminologists are now riding the currents of late modernity further still. David Brotherton, Luis Barrios and their associates have, for example, developed ethnographic approaches that are as nuanced in their cultural understandings as they are global in their scope (Kontos et al., 2003; Brotherton and Barrios, 2004; Brotherton, 2015). Immersing themselves in the cultural and political practices of the Almighty Latin King and Queen Nation and similar 'street gangs', they document the ways in which these groups in fact move beyond crime to intermingle political resistance, community empowerment and religious practice in their emerging collective identities. Global forces also intersect in these identities; both the 'gangs' and their individual members embody the liquidity of immigration, deportation and mediated communication, and broadcast this polymorphous sensibility through global alliances that they construct (Brotherton, 2007). For gang members, criminal justice operatives and ethnographers, the contested image and self-image of the 'gang' in this way constitute critical, intertwined issues. Consequently, while critiquing existing images and producing their own photographic records, these researchers also understand that the politics of the image must be investigated; as Richard Rodriguez (2003: 280) notes, the representation of gang life by gang members, cops or ethnographers 'is never an innocent practice'.

Maggie O'Neill and her associates have likewise imagined new sorts of liquid research with prostitutes, immigrants, asylum seekers and others pushed to the legal margins of the global economy. Utilizing a form of 'participatory action research' that explicitly engages researchers and researched communities in collaborative projects for progressive change, O'Neill pushes further still beyond orthodox methods by incorporating art, photography and performance in this collaborative process. Echoing the politics of the performance ethnographers, O'Neill (2004: 220) argues that this sort of 'performative praxis' can 'explore and represent the complexity of lived reality, transgressing conventional or traditional ways of presenting research data'. When staged in public settings, this performative research does indeed flow into other realms, moving criminology into popular debate and providing marginalized communities the opportunity to counter mediated demonization with their own dignified images. A research strategy perfectly attuned to the permutations of late modernity, this approach collaborates with even the most transitory and contingent communities in creating meaning and identity, developing the verstehen of shared emotional knowledge and achieving a grounded, holistic sense of social justice (O'Neill, 2001; O'Neill et al., 2004, 2008). Ultimately, this strategy flows into a 'kind of public scholarship … that deals in complexity and connects with the constructed, performative nature of our social worlds and criminological knowledge production' (O'Neill and Seal, 2012: 158–9). More liquid ethnography is emerging in cultural criminology, of course. Greg Snyder's (2006, 2009, 2016) visually charged work traces, and participates in, the uncertain trajectory of urban graffiti from illicit public painting to underground global media, for example, and likewise highlights the trajectory by which illicit street skating reconstructs constrained public space into professional opportunity. Jamie Fader's (2013) attentive ethnographic work follows young men along a different and more troubled trajectory as they make their way from the falsehoods of reform school to the precarious allures of adult life on the streets. In a particularly fluid and innovative example of ethnographic work, David Redmon (2015) not only integrates visual and textual analysis in following cultural commodities from Chinese factories to North American street rituals, but intercuts all of this with lessons on the art of video ethnography itself. Simon Hallsworth (2013) likewise integrates an autoethnography of his own street experiences with a searing critique of gang 'experts' and the gang control industry – and he then liquefies things a bit more still. Demonstrating that the positivist methods and hierarchical organizational assumptions of gang control experts distort the informal fluidity of street gang life, Hallsworth argues instead for a more nomadic approach to understanding them, a looser conceptual frame better attuned to the unstable, precarious lives of many street denizens. He recommends 'reading the street as rhizome' – understanding the street, that is, as an emergent process where people ebb and flow, boundaries are transgressed, and gang identity and gang membership remain, as with Garot (2010), always in the process of being accomplished. And he concludes with a distinctly liquid recommendation: 'Think fuzzy thoughts about fluid institutions that are only ever always interstitial', Hallsworth (2013: 124, 196) says, 'and you are halfway there'.

All of this suggests that both criminologists and those they study share a world cast increasingly adrift. Researchers, writers and videographers seeking to study the drifters that populate the contemporary world – migrants, refugees, gutter punks, sex workers, the perpetually unemployed and the college educated *sans* career – will need methods as fluid as are the lives of those they study. Ethnographers will often need to approach their subjects of study not as stable groups or communities, but more as loose federations or temporary assemblages. Writers may well need narratives that are non-linear, sentences that dissolve into fragments, chapters that float free of enumeration. Videographers may need to be concerned less with scouting locations than with exploring dislocation, may need to abandon establishing shots altogether, may need to imagine movies *sans* central characters and identifiable plots. In all of this, it is not only the medium that's the message, but the method that's the message as well; if a world adrift is the subject, it demands methods that avoid boxing it in and stopping it cold, lest it be made into something it's not. Liquid ethnography will in this sense need also to be a sort of interstitial ethnography, focused on those lost in between employment opportunities or urban spaces, and even a type of ghost ethnography, aware of those long gone or never there (see Linnemann, 2014).

For good or bad, we suspect that criminologists and other researchers will find themselves increasingly comfortable with this sort of method. The world of academic researchers is falling apart, with universities increasingly reliant on part-time faculty who piece together a course here and there while being excluded from any meaningful investment in their university, their research or their career. Major film studios are shrinking just as digital technology now makes most everyone – at least most everyone who can afford it – a potential videographer, if without salary or health benefits. Old-line media institutions continue to conglomerate, with the effect of hiring fewer writers and photographers and paying those they do hire less, while digital media runs on the work of poorly paid, or unpaid, 'content providers'. In such a world, researchers of all sorts will surely find that liquid methods not only attune them to their subjects of study but also to themselves – that is, to a world in which their circumstances may well be as uncertain as the circumstances of those who are their subjects. Perhaps such methods can even forge new sorts of shifting commonalities between those who employ them and those who are their focus; perhaps the better the next generation of criminologists under-stands those dislocated and adrift, the better they will understand their own lives as well (Ferrell, 2011, 2012a, 2012b).

Appropriately enough, then, we're happy to say that we don't know where liquid ethnographies may spill over next: across national borders alongside political refugees, against the emerging atrocities of one war or another or with some contingent community fighting to free itself from enforced misrepresenta-tion. As Stephanie Kane (2003: 293) says, it's 'a great global bricolage of deceit, revenge, and pathology' that today constitutes 'crime's ideological power', and somewhere amidst the shifting deformities of that great global remix, the next wave of liquid ethnography is no doubt breaking.

Autoethnography

Autoethnography – researchers' ethnographic explorations of themselves, their experiences and their emotions – has been a defining component of cultural criminology from the start (Ferrell, 1996, 2001/2; Presdee, 2000, 2004), and it has increasingly become a part of ethnographic research in cultural criminology and related fields. This development offers both great danger and great potential. In late-modern societies shaped by individualism and saturated with marketed self-importance, the danger is that autoethnography will resonate all too well, devolving into narcissistic self-examination on the part of the ethnographer and supplanting the ethnographic tradition of humble attentiveness to the lives of others. The great potential of autoethnography, on the other hand, lies in its ability to fully and radically incorporate the criminological researcher into the dynamics of ethnographic research and critical cultural analysis, and in this way to enrich further still the criminological imagination. Given the importance of avoiding the former and promoting the latter, it is worth considering some of the foundational issues on which autoethnography – and ethnography – rest.

The first of these foundations involves the dialectics of identity. On the one hand, ethnography by its nature always incorporates a large dose of the ethnographer's identity, and because of this a degree of autoethnography. Ethnographers inevitably become a part of those people and situations that they study, and so to do their work well, they must understand and account for their own active presence in the research process. This collaborative dynamic is confirmed by the concept of *verstehen*; in attempting to achieve empathic understanding with those under study, the ethnographer engages in a form of emotional participation that, when successful, melds subjects' emotions and perceptions with those of the ethnographer. In this sense, all good ethnography is and must be to some extent autoethnographic. But if that's the case, then so is the opposite: all good autoethnography must be essentially ethnographic. This claim comes from the heart of the sociological and criminological imagination: to explore ourselves is to explore others and our relationships with them. The self that autoethnography examines is a social self – a self shaped and continuing to be shaped by people and shared experiences, by socialization and acculturation, by patterns of gender and ethnicity, by mass media and popular culture. Moreover, particular autoethnographies emerge out of particular research settings, and in this sense come closer to being ethnographies of social settings and those who share them than to being accounts of isolated self-experience. Because of this, we would argue against any sharp distinction between ethnography and autoethnography, and certainly against any notion that autoethnography constitutes a new approach now superseding traditional ethnography. To put it more bluntly: 'first an ethnographer, and only then an autoethnographer' (Ferrell, 2012c: 219; see also Wakeman, 2014).

In our experience, a particularly useful way to keep autoethnography grounded in an ethnographic sensibility, and to steer it away from narcissistic self-indulgence, is to embrace an autoethnographic approach that in some way ruptures a researcher's existing professional identity and personal experiences. Such an approach forcefully attunes researchers to both ethnography and autoethnography, compelling them to make sense of alternative social worlds and their halting membership in them. As before, the 'self' that autoethnography studies remains always socially emergent, but in such fraught situations it seems especially malleable and emergent, often jarringly so, and because of this especially useful as a subject of reflexive criminological analysis. Sociologists sometimes talk about such situational dynamics in terms of 'status inconsistency' – the often dramatic disjunction that can emerge between the various social statuses that an individual occupies within the social order. For the ethnographer and autoethnographer, the disjunction between two such statuses – that of academic scholar and that of participant in a new or marginal situation – can indeed be jarring, and because of this can open space for critically analysing situations, statuses, the assumptions underlying them and the broader social patterns that they embody. Dangerous and disturbing as they may be, these status ruptures nonetheless provide one of the primary means by which autoethnography and ethnography can be integrated into critical criminological analysis.

As with autoethnography generally, this focus on status inconsistency and its heuristic value has long been a part of cultural criminological work. Ferrell and Hamm's (1998) *Ethnography at the Edge* gathered the accounts of experienced criminological ethnographers as they reflected on their own research experiences and considered how these experiences had contributed to the research itself. In doing so, it revealed time and again the critical insights that emerged from moments of ethnographic status inconsistency. For Christine Mattley (1998), the disjunction between her ethnographic research among phone sex workers and her usual professional status among academics revealed gender expectations and gendered stigma in both domains. Twice misperceived and denigrated while undertaking ethnographic work among sex workers, Stephanie Kane (1998: 140) likewise learned a double lesson. 'Twice glanced', she says:

> I was shown that my identity as a middle-class white woman is so loosely bound to my body that if I am inhabiting a social space in which white middle class-ness is not evident through context, if I do not fulfill the conditions required to represent white middle class-ness, the privileges will be immediately withdrawn … In fieldwork, such a glance thus blurs the lines between personal and professional, causing the ethnographer a certain amount of productive turmoil. The glance, repeated, keyed me to the importance of determining the particular ways in which race structures the organization of sex work.

More recent work in and around cultural criminology continues this approach. Hallsworth's (2013) autoethnographic account of sometimes violent encounters with street gangs not only offers a sanguine counterpoint to the bloodless analytics of the gang control industry, but in turn buttresses his critique of their inflated factual claims. On the other side of the law, Carl Root (Root et al., 2013) turns the 'brutal serendipity' of his own violent encounter with the local police into a critical rumination on silence, privilege and social control. Approaching a researcher's status disjunctions from yet another direction, Stephen Wakeman (2014: 705) makes the case for criminological autoethnography by noting both the great potential and great danger of the 'biographical congruence' between his former status as a drug user and dealer, and his current status as an ethnographer of illegal drug use.

At least since James Clifford and George Marcus's *Writing Culture* (1986), scholars have also understood that ethnography inevitably intertwines a researcher's field experiences with the forms of communication by which such experiences are crafted, categorized and disseminated. If in this sense all ethnography is story-telling, then autoethnography offers a new sort of story – one in which ethnographers include themselves as characters in their ethnographic narratives. Appropriately enough for cultural criminology, this requires understanding autoethnography as both ethnographic strategy and alternative form of ethnographic communication, and requires also considering a question: How can autoethnography operate as a narrative device within cultural criminology (Aspden and Hayward, 2015)? At their best, autoethnographic accounts seem to provide a surrogate presence for the reader; moving the reader a narrative step closer to the ethnographic action, they close some of the distance separating subject matter, author and reader. Moments of dramatic tension or personal pathos provide a type of narrative *verstehen* that can pull readers into emotional and analytic involvement with the ethnographer, the ethnographic project and the larger social issues with which the project engages. This notion of autoethnography as narrative persuasion suggests in turn that ethnographers and autoethnographers might well learn from traditions long conversant with the power of first-person narrative – autobiography, playwriting, documentary film making – and from techniques of character development, plot continuity and foreshadowing that keep human actors connected to the bigger story. Continuing to develop as method and as discursive strategy, autoethnography can contribute significantly to the larger development of cultural criminology as an alternative form of critical inquiry; it can also put cultural criminology and its autoethnographic work in conversation with other alternative criminologies such as the 'lyrical criminology' advocated by Wakeman (2014: 714) and the newly forming 'narrative criminology' that argues for the centrality of narrative as sense making (Presser and Sandberg, 2015).

As an alternative methodological orientation and a communicative strategy, autoethnography also becomes a potent form of disciplinary politics. If cultural criminology and its ethnographic orientation challenge the positivist assumption that criminologists can remain emotionally detached from their research, as well as the positivist claim that methods can operate apart from those who employ them, then autoethnography pushes this challenge further still. Overcoming the 'coyness of criminology' (Jewkes, 2012: 63, 69) by which the researcher's humanity and emotions are considered modestly unmentionable, autoethnography instead recasts a researcher's emotions as an 'intellectual resource' and defines the emotional subjectivity of *verstehen* as a research standard. As Yvonne Jewkes (2012: 69) says of prisons and research on them, 'reflexively informed prison ethnography is a vital counterpoint both to the positivist, quantitative agenda of governmental research agencies and to the growing popularity of prison tourism whereby the "researcher" is escorted on heavily scripted carceral tours by the prison governor or other authority'.[2] The power of this autoethnographic counterpoint and the dangerous potency of its challenge to positivist criminology can be glimpsed in the 'paralyzing', years-long delays between the emotional experiences of Jewkes and other prison ethnographers and their decisions to dare publishing considerations of them; in Wakeman's (2014: 705) noting of 'one last factor that impedes the further use of autoethnography in criminology – fear'; and in the Bradley Garrett court case, where the prosecution's expert witness argued that Garrett's autoethnographic admissions of uncertainty and concern constituted evidence of improper research. Yet, despite this, the challenge posed by autoethnography seems likely to grow. Students and faculty from marginalized or criminalized backgrounds who are now finding their way into criminology seem, in our experience, often unwilling to discard these backgrounds in the interest of professional success, and in fact increasingly willing to embrace them for the critical perspectives they can bring to crime, criminal justice practices and criminology. Here, it is a distinct sort of status inconsistency – the disjunction between prior lived experience and current immersion in criminological claims and practices – that opens avenues for autoethnography and critical analysis; those who were once the focus of criminological examination and state control now turn their experiences back on criminology itself. Considered as a whole, autoethnography in its many forms even begins to suggest the possibility of a post-methodological criminology pushed beyond method as a formal procedure and toward more fluid, holistic and humanistic forms of inquiry (Ferrell, 2009).

Ethnographic content analysis

Exploring in Chapter 5 the looping dynamics of contemporary media, we noted that conventional content analysis – the method of measuring static content categories within media texts – was ill-equipped to account for the fluid uncertainty of late-modern media. Multiple audiences, shifting meanings, sampling, mashups, media consumers doubling as media producers – very few of the forces that drive the contemporary interplay between media, crime and criminal justice can be captured in quantitative summaries of textual word frequency or source type. Yet, much of criminology's recent movement into the analysis of crime and the media has relied on precisely this methodological framework – and with predictably constipated results. Certainly, content analysis can function as a useful tool for suggesting patterns of presentation; utilized as a free-standing method of inquiry, though, it can't catch the fluid, *cultural* dynamics of crime and the media.

Numeric summaries of discrete textual categories miss the larger aesthetic within which a text takes shape and ignore the structural frames that shape a text's flow of meaning. The methodological myth of objectivity that traditionally accompanies content analysis reproduces the old notion that we can free content from its hiding place behind the façade of stylized presentation; in this way, it likewise denies the sensual and aesthetic experiences by which texts come to have meaning for their audiences (A. Young, 2004, 2010). Moreover, content analysis is regularly utilized with the intent of proving the degree of divergence between the 'real' nature of a crime issue and a 'biased' media representation of it. This approach misfires in multiple ways, missing the essentially symbolic construction of crime, justice and social issues; the looping and spiralling dynamics by which this construction occurs; and the multiplicity of audiences, audience interpretations and public debates that will continue to confound the real and the representational as an issue runs its course.

Confronting these problems, David Altheide (1987: 68; 1996) has developed the method of *ethnographic content analysis*, an approach that situates textual analysis within 'the communication of meaning', and conceptualizes such analysis as a process of ongoing intellectual give and take. Rejecting the myth of content analysis as objective textual measurement, he instead acknowledges the importance of deep involvement with the text, such that the researcher is able to develop a thickly descriptive account of the text in all its complexities of 'information exchange, format, rhythm, and style'. Rather than seeing the text as a unitary entity to be analysed, he likewise understands the text and its meanings to be a cultural process, and so embraces emergent concepts and categories that develop from the interplay of text and researcher or text and text. Here once again we see the value of conceptualizing ethnography not as a single method of field research, but as a methodological sensibility open to subtleties of meaning and the orientations of others – even if those others are textual in nature. We also see a style of content analysis appropriate to a criminology of late modernity – one that retains the power of such analysis to identify textual patterns while recognizing the fluid dynamics of inter-textuality and inter-subjectivity within which such patterns take shape.

Utilizing this approach as a method of cultural criminological analysis, Jennifer Grimes (2007) has untangled the complex process by which the 'three strikes and you're out' policy emerged as part of punitive criminal justice politics in the USA. As she shows, existing criminal justice policies were ramped up and reinvented as 'three strikes' approaches amidst the hysteria of a high-profile murder case, with various mass media outlets providing both emotional cues for the hysteria and a set of imagined remedies for it. Overriding individual reservations – even on the part of the murder victim's father and grandfather – this mutually reinforcing interplay of crime, criminal justice policy and public perception flowed from one media source to another, from one state legislature to another, as 'three strikes' came to define the mediated debate over crime and punishment – and continued to do so off and on for a decade. By employing ethnographic content analysis, Grimes (2007: 97) goes deep inside 'the intersection of symbolism created within the mass media, and collective behavior which results in cultural change'; said differently, she investigates moral panic as a cultural process and so traces the life history of a panic and its consequences (see Chancer, 2005). Similarly, Michael Coyle (2013) has utilized Altheide's ethnographic content analysis and 'tracking discourse' approaches to deconstruct a host of linguistic constructions, from 'innocent victim' to 'tough on crime'. In so doing, he has shown how the coded language of moral entrepreneurs shapes crime discourse into a machinery of insidious social control and subconscious social reproduction. With his careful ethnographies of criminal justice discourse across a variety of settings, Coyle reveals the cultural process by which powerful ideologies insinuate themselves into everyday language and conversation. As with others (see e.g. Mayer and Machin, 2012), Grimes and Coyle also confirm that to critically analyse the content of what is said is to begin to hear what has not been said, and what else might be.

Charles Acland (1995: 19) has argued that 'the appraisal of a cultural phenomenon involves following traces of cultural forms, activities, and histories' and ethnographic content analysis offers a sophisticated tool for just such cultural tracking. Moving beyond the quantitative analysis of fixed, discrete textual categories, ethnographic content analysis attunes us to the rhythm and style of cultural texts, to their dissemination or disappearance over time, to their traces and residues in everyday life and to the possibilities of what they omit. In this sense, ethnographic content analysis is the textual equivalent of liquid ethnography. Both are forms of ethnographic analysis oriented to the disorienting flows of meaning that drift through the late-modern world, to the spaces that open and close within and between texts, and to the cultural ghosts that such processes leave behind.

Visual criminology

Peter Manning (1999) once suggested that contemporary surveillance, transgression and control couldn't be understood without a sharp sense of the visual and an awareness of the many screens on which visual information is circulated and displayed. Nearly two decades later, the screens have morphed and multiplied, the flow of visual information has accelerated and Manning's point is all the more important. The everyday experience of late modernity may or may not be suffused with crime, but it is certainly suffused with images, and with images of crime. Television offers an avalanche of crime imagery, from local news reports to prime-time crime dramas. On the movie screen, clouded images of crime, enforcement (Brown, 2007) and imprisonment (Fiddler, 2007) are layered into the latest release. Images of transgression, victimization and vigilante justice punctuate the Internet, popping up on computer screens and cell phone displays. Criminals record their crimes, protesters photograph their protests, police shoot far more images than they do people, security agents scrutinize the image making of criminals and protestors – and a million surveillance monitors keep pace (Biber, 2007; Parks, 2007). All the while, the liquidity of these images leaks them from one medium to another, with downloads, cross-postings and video clips cutting illicit images loose from their origins, freeing them to drift from screen to street to phone, freeing them to become part of the collective consciousness by which we make sense of crime and control (see Hayward and Presdee, 2010). How, today, can there be a viable criminology that is not also a visual criminology?

Some might argue that a visual criminology has long since emerged. After all, phrases like 'images of' and 'media constructions of' are now common, and commonly accepted, prefixes to conventional criminological categories such as domestic violence or policing, and even orthodox criminology's own books and journals today include analyses of representation, even photographic illustrations. Yet this disciplinary move into the realm of the image hardly constitutes an adequate visual criminology; unless coupled to a concomitant methodological reorientation, it's likely to create more confusion than clarity. Simply importing images into a discipline defined by words and numbers is in fact likely to *retard* the development of a visual criminology, since it will leave in place the ugly notion that written or numeric analysis can somehow penetrate the obfuscation and conquer the opaqueness of the image. Images relegated to the status of illustration likewise simply reinforce this tyranny of word and number, and as seen in Chapter 4's critique of juvenile delinquency textbook covers, generally hide more than they reveal.

Put bluntly, the tradition of positivistic social scientific criminology is no foundation on which to build a late-modern visual criminology. But there are other foundations. We can usefully turn to the long tradition of documentary photography, to Walker Evans, whose photographs were 'not illustrative [but] coequal, mutually dependent, and fully collaborative' with the text, or to W. Eugene Smith, who described his approach as 'photographic penetration deriving from study and awareness and participation' (Agee and Evans, 1960: xiv–xv; Miller, 1997: 150; see also Ferrell and Van de Voorde, 2010; Carrabine, 2012). We can recall the early work of the Birmingham School and the National Deviancy Conference, whose members drew on critical theorists, literary writers and image makers to develop what Tony Jefferson (1976: 86) called a 'grammar' for decoding cultural symbols, a grammar that could 'discern the hidden messages inscribed in code on the glossy surfaces of style' (Hebdige, 1979: 18). We can look around and beyond criminology today, to visual research methods and visual sociology (Harper, 2001; A. Young, 2004; Stanczak, 2007) or to the new generation of street gang scholars already noted, whose deep understanding of visual politics substantiates the primacy of photography in their work. And we can certainly look to the work of those who have developed the very sort of visual grammar that Jefferson embraced: Camilo José Vergara (1995), for example, who shot 9,000 images of urban space over 18 years and developed from them thematic 'pictorial networks' of social change, or Heitor Alvelos (2004),

Plate 8.2 Graffiti? Or corporate advertising? Graffiti palimpsest, including tags, advertisements and political messages, London, England

Credit: Heitor Alvelos (1999)

who, through an intricate, long-term photographic study of urban graffiti, was able to reveal subtly shifting patterns in the production of illicit urban meaning.

If collectively this work suggests a foundation on which to build a contemporary visual criminology, this foundation offers us less a series of answers than 'a set of dialectical *questions*, a series of *creative tensions*' between objectivity and subjectivity, immersion and immediacy (Ferrell and Van de Voorde, 2010: 40, emphasis in original) – or as Eamonn Carabbine (2012: 486) puts it, a consideration of 'different and difficult subjectivities (between photographer, criminal, victim, spectator, torturer and artist)'. Among these tensions is one particularly salient to cultural criminology and its critical, ethnographic orientation: the tension between precise visual attentiveness and politically charged visual analysis. At times, cultural and visual criminologists embrace this tension by engaging in a close, contextualized analysis of existing images in the hope of drawing insights into larger issues of justice and injustice. Wayne Morrison (2004b: 341; see also 2010), for example, 'uses as data for cultural criminology' an album of photographs taken by German soldiers and policemen involved in the Holocaust in order to understand the links between 'genocidal tourism' and crime. Reproducing and reconsidering a series of four blurry photographs surreptitiously taken inside Auschwitz and then smuggled out to the Polish resistance, Carrabine (2014: 154; see also 2011) likewise considers the hellish context of their production, the morality of their later contextual use and the larger issues around 'archival practices' and collective memory. Through a detailed deconstruction of torture photographs taken at Iraq's Abu Ghraib prison, Mark Hamm (2007a) documents patterns of physical abuse that transcend the actions of individual US soldiers and trace to the highest levels of the US political system. In these and other cases, important critiques of the largest sorts of crimes – transnational torture, human rights abuses, genocide – develop not only from a visual criminology, but from detailed attention to the smallest particulars of images, their production and the charged circumstances of their use.

Others concerned with crime and justice build this tension into their *own* photography, producing images attentive both to little moments of human pathos and to larger patterns of social harm. Here, Henri Cartier-Bresson's notion of the 'decisive moment' can usefully be recalled. One of the great documentary photographers, Cartier-Bresson conceptualized the decisive moment as 'the simultaneous recognition, in a fraction of a second, of the significance of an event as well as a precise organization of forms which give that event its proper expression' (in Miller, 1997: 102). With the well-timed click of the shutter, then, a moment of *instant visual ethnography* – and an image whose particular subject matter and composition say something significant about the world the image encapsulates. At just the moment a homeless woman crosses in front of a 'No Loitering' sign, a decisive image of law and social exclusion; at just the moment an intoxicated husband turns angrily to his wife, a decisive image of domestic violence and its antecedents; at the very moment an interracial police stop explodes into violence, a decisive image of selective enforcement and systemic injustice. Here, of course, the tension between the visual moment and the larger lesson is particularly fragile, particularly fleeting, and the skill of the visual criminologist most rigorously tested. Even in a world suffused with such decisive moments, most will elude us – yet those caught will create criminological insights few other methods can match.

Plate 8.3 The decisive moment

Photograph by Hughes Leglise-Bataille

At its best, then, visual criminology is becoming an essential method in cultural criminology's attempt to account for meaning, situation and representation, and to confront the harms of injustice and inequality (Ferrell, 2006b; Hayward and Presdee, 2010). Exemplars abound, though unsurprisingly, often outside the box of orthodox criminology: photographer Taryn Simon and her shocking images of the wrongly convicted, photographed at the scenes of the crimes they didn't commit, sometimes accompanied by those who falsely accused them (Courtney and Lyng, 2007); documentary film makers and cultural criminologists David Redmon and Ashley Sabin, their films on Mardi Gras and post-Katrina New Orleans intercutting do-it-yourself hope with damning indictments of global injustice; activist artists like Seth Tobocman (1999) and Peter Kuper

(Lovell, 2006), whose condemnatory images of capital punishment and inter-personal violence are graphic indeed. As visual sociologist Emmanuel David (2007: 251) says, work of this sort functions as a form of 'visual resistance', not only to the powerful and their officially promulgated imagery, but to 'the milieu of social researchers who choose not to look at the world'.

The panoptic gaze of digital citizenry

Plate 8.4 Two wheels bad for Officer Pogan

Source: YouTube.com

It's 28 July 2008 and Times Square, New York City is deluged by hundreds of bicy-clists as the activist group Critical Mass holds one of its monthly rides. During the ride, committed urban cyclist Christopher Long, 29, is involved in a collision with Rookie NYPD officer Patrick Pogan. Tension has been running high between the NYPD and Critical Mass since 2004, when 250 riders were arrested for parading without a permit during a protest rally against the Republican Party National Convention. Perhaps no surprise, then, that Long was arrested on charges of 'Attempted Assault in the Third Degree', 'Resisting Arrest' and 'Disorderly Conduct'. However, within days of the incident, a video of the collision (shot by a tourist) surfaced (see Plate 8.4). It revealed that, far from being Long's fault, the 'collision' had been caused deliberately by Officer Pogan, who violently body slammed Long off his bike and onto the pavement (Eligon and Moynihan, 2008). Within days, the story was taken up and publicized by video activists such as the Glass Bead Collective, the TIMES UP Video Collective and *I-Witness Video*, all groups who know more than a thing or two about using images in defence of civil liberties. This small collision became big news (at the time of writing, over 1.6 million people have viewed the YouTube footage of the incident) – and ultimately big trouble for Officer Pogan. In an incredible volte-face by the NYPD, Pogan was first suspended and later indicted by a Manhattan grand jury for falsifying a police report and assault. In the words of *I-Witness's* Eileen Clancy, 'This indictment is a signal event for video activists. Despite the abundance of video showing that police officers have fabricated charges against people arrested at demonstrations, in New York City at least, we have never before achieved an indictment of a police officer for lying in a sworn statement' (Clancy, 2008).

In this regard, we'd return to the documentary photography tradition and suggest especially the work of W. Eugene Smith. Smith was there at the birth of modern jazz in the 1950s, catching on film the furious creativity of Charles Mingus and Thelonious Monk. He was there in Pittsburgh in the 1950s – there too long, in fact, sent on assignment for a couple of weeks, defiantly staying to study and photograph for a couple of years. And he was there at Minamata in the early 1970s. A Japanese fishing village, Minamata had seen its citizens poisoned and killed, its children grossly deformed, by the Chiso Corporation's pervasive dumping of toxic mercury, and Smith went to their aid. Existing for three years on a diet of 'home-grown vegetables, rice and whiskey', beaten almost blind by company thugs, Smith produced a series of searing photographs that became an early visual criminology, dare we say a cultural criminology, of corporate crime. 'Each time I pressed the shutter', he said, 'it was a shouted condemnation' (Hubbard, 1994; Miller, 1997: 140, 156; Smith, 1998; Ferrell, 2001/2).

Beyond this, we'd recommend the growing body of work in visual criminology and cultural criminology that explores yet another essential tension: that between visibility and invisibility. As this work shows, the dialectic between visibility and invisibility is regularly animated by the exercise of power: the power of the state to mandate visibility in some venues while demanding invisibility in others or the power of economic institutions to render invisible that which is not profitable. Notably, this work is going forward not only in urban areas – often the focus of visual documentation and analysis – but amidst the changing legal and economic environments of rural domains. Kenneth Tunnell's (2011: 41) book-length photographic study of rural Kentucky, for example, documents the profound social disorganization visited upon rural areas and their small communities by a globalized corporate economy – the 'Wal-marting of rural America', as he calls it. Photographing boarded-up small town stores and abandoned farms, Tunnell makes visible the consequences of this late-modern economy; for that matter, he makes visible social disorganization theory itself. Yet, at the same time, he photographs absence and disappearance, documenting that which is no longer there as it decays into ultimate invisibility. In the USA, the economy of small farms and local stores has been replaced not just by Walmarts, of course, but by the economics of proliferating rural prisons, and it is here that Judah Schept (2014: 198–9) documents rural ghosts of another sort. 'While prisons proliferate in the rural landscape and sites of penal tourism expand', he argues, 'the carceral state structures the available visual and analytic vantages through which to perceive this growing visibility'. As he discovered first-hand in his photographic fieldwork, 'only authorized personnel could look with anything other than a fleeting gaze at the embodiment of state power and violence that is a prison' – with this enforced invisibility not only serving to hide the rural prison in plain sight, but to hide 'the ghosts of racialized regimes past' and other carceral consequences. Similarly, Tyler Wall and Travis Linnemann (2014) show how policing and security agencies, though their efforts to squelch citizen photography, attempt to construct a particular sort of social order by controlling what is to be seen and not seen. In counterpoint, as Michelle Brown (2014: 176, emphasis in original) shows, prisoners, organizers and others produce and disseminate their own images in an attempt to make mass incarceration and its victims politically visible. Beyond simply documenting these efforts, though, Brown explores 'how a visual criminology might reveal *and* participate in the contestations and interventions that increasingly challenge the project of mass incarceration' – and Schept (2014: 217) argues for a 'counter-visual ethnography' equipped to 'intervene in the visuality of mass incarceration' (see Van de Voorde, 2012). Shouted condemnation or visual intervention, this form of research offers cultural criminologists a tight focus on the economic and political arrangements of the late-modern world.

Towards a cultural victimology

Victimology – the scholarly concern for crime victims and victimization – often reduces crime victims to sets of aggregate victimization data, or worse, takes them hostage to a mean-spirited politics of retributive justice. In light of the methods discussed in this chapter, we might imagine a different sort of *cultural victimology* – a victimology attuned to human agency, symbolic display and shared emotion. Such a victimology would consider performances of victimization and enactments of grief through which the meaning of victimization is constructed. It would explore the symbolic environments created by victims, their families and their friends as they come to terms with their experiences. And it would trace the path of personal pain as it moves through the mass media and the criminal justice system, and so re-emerges as a collective accomplishment.

In this task, as W. Eugene Smith showed, methods of visual criminology would be essential for exposing the often hidden victims of corporate and governmental crime. Visual methods could also record the many displays of emotion and remembrance that emerge around victimization: roadside shrines (Ferrell, 2004b), 9/11 memorials and tattoos (A. Young, 2007), graffiti 'rest in pieces', commemorative T-shirts, online communities of grief (Greer, 2004) – even the body's own scar tissue. Instant ethnographies

Plate 8.5   Roadside shrine, New Mexico, USA

Credit: Jeff Ferrell (2005)

could go inside those decisive moments when a robbery goes bad, when a woman finally flees ongoing domestic abuse or when grief unexpectedly overwhelms an earnest effort to forget; long-term ethnographies might explore a family's slow process of recuperation from victimization or the parallel course of trial, appeals and imprisonment for the perpetrator. Here, liquid ethnography would also be of help, watching for the ambiguous reconstruction of personal victimization as a criminal justice category or media phenomenon; autoethnography can help us understand how a newly embraced status as victim can recast the meaning of one's social life prior to victimization as well; and through ethnographic content analysis, we might well find a high-profile victim made eventually into a mediated *cause célèbre* or transformed yet again into social policy. Most importantly perhaps, a sense of *verstehen* would attune our research to the human agency of those victimized – might even aid in some small way as they work to regain human dignity – and would remind us to look for signs of resistance and survival amidst the emotional scar tissue of misfortune (Mawby and Walklate, 1994; Root et al., 2013). This approach might even suggest a sort of historical victimology, as with labour organizer Joe Hill, murdered by firing squad in 1915, and offering to his fellow workers a rousing benediction: 'Don't mourn – organize.'[3]

Conclusions: methodological and political engagement

Cultural criminology has come to be known, at least in part, for what some consider its sensational subject matter: skinheads and domestic terrorists, underground graffiti writers, skydivers and BASE jumpers, outlaw motorcycle racers, prostitutes, drug users, dumpster divers, street buskers and urban radicals. Critics of cultural criminology fear that this sensationalism, this 'adrenaline-pumping, here-and-now quality of cultural criminology' (Webber, 2007: 154) constitutes a sort of cheap intellectual trick. By picking amidst the cultural detritus for oddities and titillations, they say, cultural criminology draws attention to itself. By then dressing up this degraded subject matter in stylish language and presentation – by offering 'a gilded invitation to readers to revel pruriently and voyeuristically in the exotica of ... deviant doings' (O'Brien, 2005: 610) – cultural criminology manages to generate easy public interest and fraudulent intellectual excitement.

Such criticisms, we would argue, mistake subject matter for method. Sparks of dangerous sensuality may sometimes fly from bikers or street buskers, or from their flinty clashes with the authorities – but as such groups and situations become the subject matter of criminology, those sparks are snuffed out or fanned into flame, by method. As we demonstrated in the previous chapter, even the most sensational of subject matters can be reduced to tedious abstraction with the proper methodology. Think about it: the orthodox criminology we explored there had as its subject matter some truly sensational issues – sexual assault, escape from domestic abuse, anti-social juvenile crime – and yet the criminology of these issues, as produced by survey research and statistic, couldn't have been less engaging. With those same methods, the alleged sensationalism of cultural criminology could quite easily be extinguished as well: skydivers drained of adrenaline, dumpster divers imbued with standard deviations of low self-control, terrorists brought to heal by tobit models and time-varying predictors. The contemporary enterprise of orthodox criminology, as played out in its own journals and conferences, confirms it: nothing kills good criminology like bad method.

Whatever intellectual vigour cultural criminology may offer, then, comes mostly from its *methodological engagement* with its subjects of study. In actuality, attentive ethnography, sharp-eyed visual criminology and crisp cultural analysis don't require BASE jumpers or drug users for intellectual excitement; as we hope cultural criminologists have already shown, such methods can find vivid insight and critique in historical photos, old motel rooms, new legal regulations ... even in boredom itself (Hamm, 1998, 2004; Ferrell, 2004a; Morrison, 2004a). From such situations – from any such everyday situation – these methods can generate genuinely dangerous knowledge as well (see Miller and Tewkesbury, 2000). Critics contend that this focus on motorcycles and motel rooms prevents cultural criminology from addressing deeper structures of injustice and so from posing any real political danger to the powers that be. On the contrary, cultural criminology is designed to be dangerous and to draw that danger directly from everyday situations. As we noted in Chapters 1 and 4, structures of inequality and injustice permeate the situations of everyday life and everyday crime – it is precisely their presence there that gives them such great power. Cultural criminology's goal is to expose that presence to those who might not notice it, thereby helping us and others to understand and confront the

everyday reality of injustice – with the *tools* for accomplishing this liberatory communication to be found in methods of attentive observation and compassionate
analysis. Exposing injustice, unpacking ideologies of crime and victimization, giving
voice to those unheard and unnamed, such methods if done well can make for some
decidedly dangerous knowledge.

And for cultural criminology that's just the question: How best can we endanger existing arrangements of predatory crime, corporate malfeasance, punitive
criminal justice and pervasive late-modern exclusion? The stale methods of
orthodox criminology offer neither the analytic insight nor the invitational edge
necessary for constructing a collective counter-assault; similarly unhelpful and
unappealing is the disavowal of human meaning in the interest of calculated
abstraction. Methods of inquiry attuned to the swirling cultural dynamics of late
modernity, open to the human construction of collective meaning, attentive to
both the harm and the hope of transgression – now those methods, on the other
hand, promise real problems for those invested in the status quo.

Because what good is knowledge, really, if it's not a danger to those who would
deny it?

A selection of films and documentaries illustrative of some of the themes and ideas in this chapter

All Watched Over by Machines of Love and Grace, 2011, Dir. Adam Curtis

A three-part BBC documentary series that focuses on our relationship with
machines, especially computers, and how this relationship now shapes the way we
relate to the world and each other. In terms of this chapter, *All Watched Over by
Machines of Love and Grace* is interesting in that it illustrates the problems associated
with technological and statistical determinism when applied to natural environments (available to watch for free at: www.filmsforaction.org).

Heart Broken in Half: Chicago's Street Gangs, 1990, Producers Taggart Siegel and
Dwight Conquergood

An intimate documentary that goes behind the headlines to confront the human
reality and complexity of street gangs in urban America. Based on Conquergood's
groundbreaking ethnographic research and drawing on personal interviews, *Heart
Broken in Half* debunks stereotypes and reveals the reality of gang life: 'Here is an
intricate web of symbols and passions, territory and brotherhood, honour and, all
too often, death.'

(Continued)

(Continued)

From My Point of View: Exposing the Invisible (2013) Dir. Tactical Technology Collective

Another short documentary from the Exposing the Invisible team, this time activist researchers use innovative digital methods, from the analysis of YouTube videos to DIY aerial mapping, to launch their own investigations into weapon supply routes in Syria, urban land-grabbing in Beirut, and power relations in Jerusalem. This documentary shows what's possible when individuals look beyond the standard research methods of sociology and criminology. Available to watch free at: https://exposingtheinvisible.org.

Special Flight, 2011, Dir. Fernand Melgar

An emotional documentary portrait of Switzerland's highly bureaucratic and increasingly carceral immigration system, a process that can culminate in special deportation flights for immigrants whose permission to stay is withdrawn. The film is interesting both as a visual ethnography and as an expression of Michel Foucault's notion of governmentality and the triumph of bio power over humanity.

Who is Bozo Texino?, 2005, Dir. Bill Daniel

Like *Recycled Life* and *Kamp Katrina* (see earlier film links), *Who is Bozo Texino?* takes us inside the sort of off-the-radar world that would never appear in a social scientific survey. Bill Daniel's film is a rolling, rail-clacking account of one man's search for a legendary and elusive freight train graffiti artist.

18 with a Bullet, 2006, Dir. Ricardo Pollack

A captivating insight into the everyday lives and practices of 18th Street, a street gang with members in Los Angeles and San Salvador, El Salvador. From the harrowing first scene, where a young girl is initiated into the gang by being kicked repeatedly on the ground by fellow gang members, it's clear that the world depicted in *18 with a Bullet* is something that could never be captured by a quantitative gang survey.

Further Reading

Ferrell, J. and Hamm, M. (eds) (1998) *Ethnography at the Edge*. Boston: Northeastern University Press.
The classic cultural criminology work on ethnography. A methodological *tour de force* that excites from the first pages of Patricia and Peter Adler's Foreword to the editors' final thoughts on 'dangerous methods'.

Altheide, D. (1996) *Qualitative Media Analysis*. Thousand Oaks, CA: SAGE.
Clear-sighted and engaging introduction to the main research methods associated with media analysis.

Manning, P. (1995) 'The challenge of Postmodernism', in J. Van Maanen (ed.) *Representation in Ethnography*. Thousand Oaks, CA: SAGE.
Book chapter offering a series of reflections on the need for ethnography to adapt to the changes in community composition, individual experience, and group

dynamics brought on by the more fluid and heterogeneous conditions of late modernity.

Ferrell, J. (1999) 'Cultural criminology', *Annual Review of Sociology,* **25: 395–418.**
A lengthy journal article that develops some of the putative ideas set out in Ferrell and Sanders' 1995 collection *Cultural Criminology*. As in that text, the emphasis here is very much on subcultural and media analyses of crime. The author also provides a useful introduction to some of the core research methods employed by cultural criminologists.

Root, C., Ferrell, J. and Palacios, W. (2013) 'Brutal serendipity: criminological
verstehen **and victimization',** *Critical Criminology,* **21(2): 141–155.**
Interesting example of autoethnography in practice based on one author's own phenomenological encounter with police brutality.

Useful Websites

Visual Studies **(London: Routledge)**
www.tandfonline.com/toc/rvst20/current#.VK_0-tKsV8E
The house journal of the International Visual Sociology Association publishing scholarly articles on all aspects of visual methodology, from digital ethnography to photo elicitation.

Visual Ethnography
www.vejournal.org/?journal=vejournal
Online peer-reviewed journal dedicated to the production and the use of images and audiovisual media in the socio-cultural sciences.

Narrative Criminology Research Network
www.jus.uio.no/ikrs/english/research/projects/networkfornarrativecrim/
Coordinated by Sveinung Sandberg and Thomas Ugelvik of the University of Oslo, Norway, this site provides information about narrative criminology, an emergent theoretical framework for the study of stories in criminology.

Notes

1 From this view, even long-term ethnography can be seen as an elongated moment, a temporal slice of something more – with the question for ethnographers, then: how big the slice, how long the moment?
2 See the special section of the journal *Qualitative Inquiry* (20(4), 2014) on 'Doing prison research differently', edited by Yvonne Jewkes, for more on these issues.
3 See, similarly, the final passage of John Steinbeck's (1972[1936]) *In Dubious Battle* and Mythen (2007) for a different sense of 'cultural victimology'.

9
Conclusions

The issue of meaning makes a question mark of orthodox criminology and criminal justice – and as an orientation designed especially for critical engagement with the politics of meaning surrounding crime and crime control, cultural criminology is intended to facilitate just such punctuation. As scholars and as citizens, our lives are littered with 'facts' about crime: crime statistics, fear-of-crime percentages, gang member head counts. Knowing something of meaning and representation, though, we can see these 'facts' for what they are: myopic snapshots of a moving world, more deserving of critical interrogation than unthinking acceptance. Reconsidered through the lens of cultural criminology, crime statistics appear mostly as political accomplishments – embodiments of police discretion and governmental agenda, certainly – but just as certainly not representations of crime's lived reality. The percentage of the population reported to be 'somewhat afraid' of crime is shown to be a double duplicity, a fiction of conceptualization and of method, as survey researchers imagine the shifting contours of collective fear to be a measurable category of individual emotion and then imagine they can capture this category with little answer sets. An always shifting and ambiguous entity, even within gang life itself, 'the number of gang members' currently residing in Birmingham or Boston, as announced by criminal justice agencies or the mass media, is seen to be mostly a projection of prejudiced perception and racial anxiety.

Re-encoded in this way, the valences of orthodox criminology and criminal justice are reversed. The taken-for-granted authority of policing agencies and government-funded researchers is questioned. The assumed hierarchy of credibility that situates agency reports and media accounts at the forefront of our understanding of crime is inverted. Instead, the experience and everyday meaning of crime for those involved in it come to the front – and issues of representation and power are not far behind.

The rate of domestic violence in India declined in the last year by 34 per cent? We hope so – but whose numbers are these? In what way might they reflect women's fear of reporting domestic violence, or police officers' disinclination to code it, or perhaps new laws narrowing the legal definition of domestic violence?

Three out of five UK citizens say that they are afraid of crime? To whom do they say it and in what way? Are they afraid of crime or afraid of what the media presents as crime? And what does 'afraid of crime' mean for their lives, for the choices they make when no researcher or reporter is present?

Gang membership is on the increase in large urban areas in the USA? Who decides when a young person is 'in' or 'out' of a gang? How can such a fluid identity be counted with any certainty? How and why is the media reporting this 'fact'? And most importantly, is there governmental grant money riding on this asserted increase, or maybe someone's political career?

In counterpoint to orthodox assertions about crime, cultural criminology una-shamedly offers more questions than it does answers – or maybe it provides some new answers by questioning the old ones.

Notice also that the politics of cultural criminology is no after-the-fact overlay; it's inherent in the approach itself. To concern oneself with the collective human construction of meaning is to undermine those who claim authoritative knowl-edge of crime and to confront those who make meaning disappear inside mazes of numbers and jargon. Likewise, to understand the power of representation is to appreciate the loops and spirals by which image and experience intertwine – and to realize that those who claim otherwise, who claim to present the unmediated truth about crime, are mostly marketing delusion, diversion or ide-ology. Cultural criminology is in this sense innately subversive; by paying attention to meaning and representation, it undermines the authority of politi-cians, police commissioners and orthodox criminologists, looking instead to discover perspectives less noticed or less understood.

In the complex, contested and ambiguous late-modern world seen throughout this book, this subversion of epistemic authority seems all the more necessary and appropriate. In a world animated by morphing identities and increasing human migration, in a world awash in new meanings and new media, stern truth claims about 'crime' or 'criminal justice' seem downright ludicrous – sad attempts to measure precisely how many criminals can be incarcerated on the point of some punitive pin. As we argued in previous chapters, such claims seem dangerous as well, suggesting a longing for surety at any cost, a fondness for an epistemic orderliness that can somehow staunch the flow of late-modern uncer-tainty. When politicians launch 'zero tolerance' drug campaigns or promise to simply 'eliminate' anti-social behaviour, when criminologists present statistical summaries as self-evident factual statements, their reports reveal a reactionary recoil against the world they inhabit, an echo of dinosaurs dying hard. Now is no time not to notice these reductionist absurdities and their effects.

About those effects let us be clear. Social worlds saturated with surveillance technologies today drain freedoms of movement and identity from the practice of everyday life. American anti-gang injunctions and anti-homeless laws, British shopping centre bans and ankle tags to monitor offenders' alcohol consumption, add their repressive weight, further criminalizing the minutiae of personal movement and public presence. In the USA, Britain, France and elsewhere, expanding police states continue to pass themselves off as democratic systems of criminal justice; elsewhere, absurdly anachronistic, fundamentalist 'justice' systems continue to demean and destroy the lives of girls, women and non-believers. Reactionary American criminal justice policies such as determinant sentencing and 'life in prison without parole' disenfranchise millions while stretching institutionalized hopelessness over a slow accumulation of decades. And for the thousands of Americans now serving such sentences for crimes committed before their 18th birthdays, an additional existential ache: the more life you have left, the longer your sentence. Meanwhile, from Mexico to Malaysia, international trade laws and local legal corruption protect a global economy that destroys other young lives and that pollutes the lived environments of young and old as well.

We can do better than this. We can create a world in which late-modern fluidities of people and meaning are cause for polymorphous celebration, sparks for cultural invention, not reasons for official reaction. We can create a world in which the ambiguities of late modernity usefully call into question rigid categories of race and medieval forms of religion, rather than calling forth their vengeful return (J. Young, 2007). We can imagine something better for millions of the world's citizens than predatory victimization amidst environmental degradation or deadening work intercut with imprisonment. To do so, though, we must have a criminology that is effective, persuasive, meaningful and unafraid. If orthodox criminologists and criminal justice practitioners insist on certainty and essentialism, insist on reducing people to quantifiable categories and their cultures to dangerous abstractions, then we must have a criminology that can leverage up the very intellectual foundations of their work. If late-modern political orders find it increasingly effective to 'govern through crime' (Simon, 2007) – that is, to recast social issues as crime issues, to define crime and victimization as the essential dynamic of social life, and so to govern through fear and exclusion – then we must have a criminology that can confront this political transformation and define the meaning of social life in other, more progressive terms.

Cultural criminology and critical criminology

Having argued that cultural criminology constitutes a distinct type of critical criminology due to its focus on the meaning of crime, we'd now like to argue the opposite: that both historically and in its contemporary manifestations, the larger project of critical criminology has likewise been defined by its engagement with the politics of meaning. This is by no means an attempt at colonization – not, that is, some grandiose attempt to claim that all of critical criminology can be subsumed under the logic of cultural criminology. Actually, it's quite the opposite: a claim that the roots of cultural criminology were there all along in the broad enterprise of critical criminology, and continue to be there, not only in specific US and British antecedents, but in the critical ethos of critical criminology itself. In making this argument, we'll not undertake a systematic survey of critical criminology past and present; we'll only highlight some examples that suggest an ongoing conversation between cultural criminology and other critical criminologies. For those critical approaches that we may omit, we offer apologies and an invitation to join the conversation.

Certainly one of the central foundations of critical criminology has been a Marxist, or more broadly conflict-oriented, analysis of crime and justice. This approach is sometimes taken to be a hard-nosed economic critique of crime and its causes, with issues of culture, ideology and meaning relegated to a secondary, super-structural position. In reality, it strikes us that Marxist or conflict-oriented approaches have offered from the first a searing cultural assault on the accepted meanings of crime, law and justice (Ferrell, 2007). To propose that the law operates as the hammer of the ruling class is not only to link law and economy, but to put forth an epistemic challenge – a challenge to conventionally constructed understandings of law. It is to suggest that, in its formation and in its everyday practice, the law means not justice but the perpetuation of injustice and the protection of privilege. This Marxist critique also confronts the elaborate ideologies by which law and criminal justice are defined as forces of social containment and social good, and at its best inaugurates a praxis for undermining the meanings that such ideologies promote. Further, this view of law and criminal justice promotes a reconsideration of the past and its ideological edifices as well. Are we to understand vagrancy laws as protecting the agreed upon social order from ne'er-do-wells or as protecting the shifting interests of the ruling powers (Chambliss, 1960)? Was the emergent juvenile justice system in fact designed for the betterment of children or to control marginal populations and socialize immigrant children into dominant work and gender roles (Platt, 1977)?

This critical reappraisal of law and justice continues in two contemporary approaches. Convict criminology has been invaluable in giving voice to those imprisoned by various wars on drugs and crime, and so in transforming the silenced objects of criminal justice into the critical conscience of criminology (Richards and Ross, 2001; Ross and Richards, 2002). In this liberatory work, convict criminology has also had the effect – the quite intentional effect – of subverting the conventional meaning and practice of criminal justice. The very presence of ex-convict scholars within academic criminology exacts a lovely sort of intellectual retribution, giving lie to stereotypical constructions of criminals, prisoners and punishment. In addition, their inside-out critique of the criminal justice system brings with it a hard-earned epistemic authenticity that further undermines the truth claims of Justice Department statistics or recidivism rates. Convict criminology, then,

> challenges the way in which crime and correctional problems are traditionally represented and discussed by researchers, policy makers, and politicians … [it] also challenges commonly held beliefs; thus, it is coterminous with many of the episte-mological approaches found in critical criminology, which tries to deconstruct myths and look for deeper meanings. (Jones et al., 2009: 152, 156)

Deeper meanings are likewise at issue for peacemaking criminology, which undertakes a similarly thoroughgoing critique, if at a different philosophical pitch. For peacemaking criminologists, the goal of this critique is not simply a critical re-evaluation of criminal justice, but ultimately a profound reconceptu-alization of justice itself. As they argue, any approach that links justice to violence or punishment has already undermined justice itself, in both its mean-ing and its practice. And so, radically reimagining the meaning of justice along the lines of Buddhist, Gandhian, indigenous and socialist humanist philoso-phies, peacemaking criminologists conceive of justice as a process designed to 'heal rifts in the social fabric and weave all members back into accepted, responsible, safe social relations' (Pepinsky and Quinney, 1997: 109).

Similarly radical reconceptualizations of crime and justice are undertaken by two other critical approaches – the first one obviously so, the second perhaps less so. With its focus on the cultural and linguistic construction of crime, postmodern/ constitutive criminology is a critical enterprise founded in issues of meaning. First, this approach argues that there exists no reality of crime preceding its legal and linguistic construction; discursive categories and legal practices not only shape public perceptions, but constitute crime as meaningful activity in the first place. Not unlike labelling theory, 'the goal' then becomes 'working on the production of meaning in the area of crime' – meaning that is 'co-produced by those who engage in crime, those who try to control it, and those who study it' (DeKeseredy, 2011: 49–50). To do this work, a second analytic move must be made – one like that which cultural criminologists employ in exploring everyday situations of crime control: deconstructing or decoding existing linguistic constructions so as to problematize their taken-for-granted acceptance and thereby expose their power. As Bruce Arrigo (2003: 48) says, deconstruction 'entails reading between the lines to ascertain the meanings (i.e. ideology) given preferred status in a par-ticular language system'. Finally, postmodern and constitutive criminologists argue that criminologists, media workers and others must disseminate a 'replacement discourse' that can reconstitute the meaning of crime and justice in the interest of progressive social change (Henry and Milovanovic, 1996).

A second critical approach has, it seems to us, been among the most successful in accomplishing just this task. This is feminist criminology. Certainly, feminist criminology has exposed the gendered dynamics of crime and justice and has confronted the social harms visited on women by way of these dynamics. In this work, though, feminist criminology has also constructed a deeper and more systematic critique of meaning – a critique demanded by the very depths at which gendered assumptions are embedded in the everyday practice of crime and justice. As feminist criminologists have shown, confronting intimate partner violence against women necessitates confronting the ideologies that keep such violence invisible, and likewise means constructing domestic violence as a meaningful category of law and human experience. As recent legal changes have shown, confronting sexual assault demands deconstructing and reconstructing the assumptions encoded in the legal definition of rape. Likewise, confronting the public demonization of young women necessitates not only supporting young women's own efforts, but also decoding the everyday meanings about them that are manufactured by crime statistics and the mass media (Chesney-Lind and Irwin, 2008). Perhaps more than any other critical approach, feminist criminology has demonstrated that progressive scholarship and activism demands engagement with the existing politics of meaning. For feminist criminologists and other critical criminologists, imagining a better future begins with dismantling the meaningful limitations of the present.

And, as we might hope, other critical dismantlings of meaning continue to emerge – queer criminology among them. Substantively, queer criminology confronts the crimes committed against lesbian, gay, trans-sexual, bisexual and queer populations, and highlights their mistreatment and miscategorization within the criminal justice system. But as its theorists are keen to point out, queer criminology is as much a confrontation with the sorts of everyday meanings and understandings, both within academia and the world outside it, that undergird such violence. Matthew Ball (2014: 22) argues that 'many queer theorists … seek to challenge identities, forms of regulation, and what they might argue is the foundational normativity of many disciplines' – and that in this sense 'critical criminologies and queer theories share a common attitude of pushing against orthodox knowledges, politics, and ways of thinking – whether regarding crime and justice matters, or sexuality and gender issues'. Salo Carvalho (2013: 5) in fact places queer criminology in the context of similar criminological 'rupture movements' like labelling theory, feminist criminology, critical criminology and cultural criminology. Indeed, in the earliest days of cultural criminology, Ferrell and Sanders (1995: 319) called for just such a rupture, arguing that

> if the criminality and criminalization of women and girls, lesbians and gays tend to be overshadowed by the coincidence of masculinity and crime, we must develop

a cultural criminology that highlights these alternative processes and the gendered politics within which they occur.

In the intervening two decades, cultural criminology has not done enough to make 'queer criminology ... part of any cultural criminology that sets out to explore in depth the politics of culture and crime', but now queer criminology is well underway, within cultural criminology and beyond.

Meaningful work

For cultural and critical criminologists, the necessary attentiveness to various theatres of meaning is complemented by another imperative: intervention in these theatres on the side of social justice and progressive social change. Across the range of cultural and critical criminology, activism takes many forms, from union and community organizing to advocacy on behalf of criminalized groups and social justice campaigns. In whatever we do, though, it seems that we are, if nothing else, well-practised cultural workers; after all, our careers in teaching and scholarship are founded in a particular facility at offering critical interpretations and creating persuasive forms of performance and communication. Put differently, our scholarly careers require that we be skilled not only at ferreting out encoded ideologies and exposing hidden meanings, but at producing our own critical meanings and alternative understandings in the classroom and on the page. Thinking about our work in this way, drawing on and expanding the skills that make it possible, we can imagine any number of possibilities for critical intervention in the politics of meaning – and with these possibilities the potential also for a critical public criminology.

Situations

In the same way that we pay attention to the dynamics by which the meaning of crime and crime control is negotiated in others' everyday lives, we can productively notice these dynamics in the situations that make up our own lives as well. Bringing an ethnographic/autoethnographic sensibility to bear, we can usefully politicize our own lives by critically examining the meanings that shape them. In this sense, every traffic ticket, every encounter with a police officer or airport security screener, every court case or legal dispute or fleeting moment of fear opens a window into the ongoing construction of crime and justice – if only we can learn to be attentive to them. In this sense also, every such situation offers an opportunity for critical intervention – that is, for converting the mundane meanings of everyday crime and crime control into a meaningful analysis of larger criminological issues. This is certainly the case in dramatic situations where a criminologist is the victim of police brutality (Root et al., 2013), for example, or comes to be arrested in the course of field research (Ferrell, 1997). But significantly, it is just as much the case when no punches are thrown or arrests made. Just as critical criminologists have made important contributions by investigating the power relations by which the social harms of economic or state elites are *not* constructed as criminal, we can usefully investigate, write and teach about the relations through which crime is not constructed in our own lives. If we know that young black men in the USA and the UK are regularly stopped and searched on the street, but we haven't been stopped for years, by what valences of our own power and privilege is this so? If for many people the sight of a police car invokes apprehension, but for some of us suggests a sense of safety, what do these divergent meanings reveal about our own participation in everyday inequalities of ethnicity, social class, age and location?

Notice that these sorts of critical intellectual interventions into our own everyday situations offer in turn two distinct advantages: they require no research grants or IRB approvals and they transform the always-useful awareness of our own privilege into critical criminological analysis (Ferrell, 2012c). A similarly accessible sort of critical intervention is suggested by another set of situational meanings: the pervasive encoding of surveillance technologies and social control ideologies into the built environments of everyday life. We can confront and expose these insidious systems of control by writing and teaching about them; we can also confront and expose them through individual or collective civil disobedience against them. Groups like Food Not Bombs have responded to statutes prohibiting the feeding of the homeless in public spaces by feeding the homeless in public spaces; critical and cultural criminologists have organized sit-ins in the middle of sidewalks governed by discriminatory no-sitting ordinances (Amster, 2008) and have staged student flash mobs as pedagogic performances in regulated public space (Landry, 2013). Such interventions seem near-perfect examples of Marxian praxis or anarchist direct action; they accomplish practical, progressive goals while at the same time forcing into view the hidden meanings and hidden inequities of the social control mechanisms that would prevent them. Put in different terms – the terms of the Situationists – they seem just the sorts of situated interventions to promote a progressive revolution of everyday life (Vaneigem, 2001[1967]).

Media and popular culture

Chapter 6 explored the many dynamics through which media and popular culture make meaning around issues of crime and justice, and explored also opportunities for intervening in these dynamics; we'll not rehearse those here. Instead, we'll simply recall some possibilities. The proliferation of alternative and digital media allows cultural criminologists and others to develop podcasts and websites (e.g. http://blogs.kent.ac.uk/culturalcriminology/, www.convictcriminology.org, www.artcrimearchive.org, http://antiblogdecriminologia.blogspot.com/), give and record TED talks and otherwise disseminate alternative understandings. The looping and spiralling nature of mediated meaning invites us into those loops, as in the first edition of this book, where we showed that the provocative phrase 'pretty girls make graves' could be made to illuminate Zen celibacy, gay identity, Riot Girl empowerment, sexual allure or, in our hands, the violent objectification of women (Ferrell et al., 2008: 206–10). The courageous work of groups like Public Ad Campaign, noted in Chapter 4, reminds us that mediated popular culture is now deeply encoded in public space itself and raises a question: If the Public Ad Campaign illicitly replaces public space advertising with art, what should we do? Paint over 'No Loitering' signs with street poetry? Reposition CCTV cameras so that they point at the police station? Most of all, the media-saturated environments of late modernity remind us that as critical scholars we can write books *and* make documentary films (Redmon, 2005, 2015; Yuen Thompson, 2014); that we can write, film and photograph in ways that are both erudite and accessible; and that we can and must create a criminology that operates less as a social science and more as a poetic (Jacobsen, 2014) – a criminology attuned to elegance and communication in its effort to put forth a critical analysis of crime and justice.

Policy

It is sometimes suggested that cultural criminology is uninterested in or inapplicable to policy. Certainly cultural criminology is, in David Matza's (1969) terms, largely a 'naturalistic' and 'appreciative' approach which eschews conventional notions of 'correctionalism'. But to be appreciative does not inevitably mean to romanticize or to valorize, and to disdain the correctionalism of conventional criminology and criminal justice doesn't necessitate a wholly non-interventionist approach to crime (see Hayward and Young, 2012). While there are many activities needlessly criminalized and punished – more every day, in fact – there are many others necessitating some form of control or correction, from domestic violence and street assaults to war crimes and corporate malfeasance. And it is in this area of crime control policy that cultural and critical criminology, and the larger issue of meaning, seem applicable indeed, and for a particular reason: failure to understand the cultural meanings of crime and responses to it all but guarantees the failure of policy and the interventions it promotes.

To begin with, any appropriate response to crime must be founded on an understanding of the social predicaments and cultural responses out of which that crime emerges. A useful policy regarding 'gangs' or 'white-collar crime' cannot begin with gangsters or corporate greedheads, but must instead burrow into the structural strains and cultural milieu that spawn gangsters and greedheads in the first place – and that situate their actions within shared meaning and experience. Likewise, those who are the focus of policy initiatives cannot be reduced, as they often are in establishment criminology, to abstract embodiments of misguided theoretical categories: economic robots, rational actors, human variables devoid of cultural context and human emotion (Hayward, 2007, 2012a). Otherwise, all that remains for policy are the blunt instruments of force and containment, the arid options of punishment and prevention, the concomitants of deterrence theory or rational choice logic. This failure to ground policy in the meanings of crime leads in turn to a second failure, as those who are its recipients demonstrate to policy makers that they are assuredly *not* robots or rational machines by creatively subverting the intended meanings of the policy itself. The same measure of punishment can become a matter of shame and social embarrassment, a weighty deterrent, a badge of subcultural honour or an inducement to escalating transgression – with the latter two all the more likely if the culture of those punished has been misunderstood or ignored. Policy that disregards human culture will be disregarded by those human cultures it targets; or, as Dick Hebdige (1988: 8) says, those cultures will 'convert the fact of being under surveillance into the pleasure of being watched'. Either way, culturally insensitive policy gets in return the sort of crime that it deserves.

Useful policy requires another sort of cultural sensitivity as well: a sensitivity to the larger cultural dynamics within which any sort of policy and its enforcement become meaningful. Social responses to crime are never merely technical matters; they are inevitably collectively contested normative statements, drawing on and reinventing conceptions of penalty, safety and justice that circulate within the larger culture (Melossi, 2001). This foundational notion within cultural criminology – that the meaning of crime policy is always mixed up with moral rectitude and moral panic, with folk wisdom and folk devils, with policing the crises of social order and social change – not only provides an essential critique of discriminatory policy and its enforcement, it also suggests the role that the cultural and critical criminologist can take in policy development. In the media, in the courts – in an advisory role to policy makers, when possible – cultural and critical criminologists can work to shape policy that resonates with progressive cultural currents and that avoids the regressive cultural references of, for example, 'wars' on crime or 'crusades' against terror. In a late-modern world of global migration and cultural relocation, they can provide especially important correctives to policies that force one sort of cultural practice through the filter of another. Here, method matters again as well. The ethnographic methods favoured by cultural criminologists will never produce the sorts of numeric summaries of which policy makers are fond, but they will produce the sorts of nuanced insights essential to understanding the cultural meanings of both policy and the lives of those who are its focus. At its best, we might even imagine crime policy that emerges as a collaboration between policy makers, cultural and critical criminologists and those affected by it – policy that, by addressing both immediate problems and underlying social predicaments, helps eliminate over time the very problems that necessitate it.

In all this we're reminded of the African-American practice of signifying – surely an exemplar of the human capacity for cultural creativity and resistance amidst the most brutal of circumstances (Gates, 1988; Potter, 1995). Signifying suggests an especially fluid facility for communicating multiple meanings to multiple audiences. For African-Americans, this facility emerged as an essential survival skill amidst the predations of enslavement and racial bigotry; an ability to talk in ways that hid subversive understandings in the vocabulary of convention, to slip alternative meanings into the gaps of language and perception, to layer messages into lyric and beat, meant that oppression could be at the same time accommodated as necessary and resisted as possible. As contemporary critical and cultural criminologists, our privileges preclude any such stakes – but the lesson holds. Recognizing the politics of meaning and working to intervene in them, the question is not whether we will function as scholars or activists, whether we will examine our own lives or those of others, whether we will operate at the level of subculture or social media or social policy. The question is how we can best embody all of these endeavours as public intellectuals, moving fluidly within and between various theatres of meaning, comfortable with the multiple forms of understanding and communication that the multiple audiences of late modernity mandate. The question is how to make cultural criminology, and criminology more broadly, a meaningful enterprise in a world shaped by meaning – how to craft a criminology that through its mix of critique and compassion, scholarship and social engagement can confront the contemporary politics of meaning as they circulate in the realms of crime and justice.

BIBLIOGRAPHY

Aas, K.F. (2006) 'The body does not lie', *Crime, Media, Culture*, 2(2): 143–58.

Aas, K.F. (2012) 'The earth is one but the world is not', *Theoretical Criminology*, 16(1): 5–20.

Abend, L. (2006) 'Paying to be kidnapped', *The New York Times* (15 January): V2.

Acland, C. (1995) *Youth, Murder, Spectacle*. Boulder, CO: Westview.

Adler, P. (1985) *Wheeling and Dealing*. New York: Columbia.

Adler, P. and Adler, P. (1998) 'Foreword', in J. Ferrell and M. Hamm (eds) *Ethnography at the Edge*. Boston: Northeastern.

Agamben, G. (2005) *State of Exception*. Chicago: University of Chicago Press.

Agee, J. and Evans, W. (1960) *Let Us Now Praise Famous Men*. New York: Ballantine.

Alkemade, R. (2013) 'Outsiders amongst outsiders'. Available at: www.japansubcul ture.com/outsiders-amongst-outsiders-a-cultural-criminological-perspective-on-the-sub-subcultural-world-of-women-in-the-yakuza-underworld/

Altheide, D. (1987) 'Ethnographic content analysis', *Qualitative Sociology*, 10(1): 65–77.

Altheide, D. (1996) *Qualitative Media Analysis*. Thousand Oaks, CA: SAGE.

Altheide, D. (2006) *Terrorism and the Politics of Fear*. Blue Ridge Summit, PA: AltaMira Press.

Alvelos, H. (2004) 'The desert of imagination in the city of signs', in J. Ferrell, K. Hayward, W. Morrison and M. Presdee (eds) *Cultural Criminology Unleashed*. London: GlassHouse.

Alvelos, H. (2005) 'The glamour of grime', *Crime, Media, Culture*, 1(2): 215–24.

Amster, R. (2004) *Street People and the Contested Realms of Public Space*. New York: LFB.

Amster, R. (2008) *Lost in Space*. New York: LFB.

Anderson, E. (1999) *Code of the Street*. New York: W.W. Norton & Co.

Anderson, N. (1923/1961) *The Hobo*. Chicago: University of Chicago Press/Phoenix Books.

Appadurai, A. (1996) *Modernity at Large*. Minneapolis: University of Minnesota Press.

Applebome, P. (2012) 'How graffiti goats became a symbol of ... something', *The New York Times* (3 March): A15.

Archibald, R. (2010) 'A gangland bus tour, with lunch and a waiver', *The New York Times* (16 January): A1, A11.

Armstrong, G. and Griffin, M. (2007) 'The effect of local life circumstances on victimization of drug-involved women', *Justice Quarterly*, 24(1): 80–104.

Arrigo, B. (2003) 'Postmodern justice and critical criminology', in M. Schwartz and S. Hatty (eds) *Controversies in Critical Criminology*. Cincinnati, OH: Anderson.

Aspden, K. and Hayward, K. (2015) 'Cultural criminology and narrative criminology', in L. Presser and S. Sandberg (eds) *Crime as Story*. New York: New York University Press.

Atran, S. (2004) 'Mishandling suicide terrorism', *The Washington Quarterly*, 27(3): 67–90.

Atran, S. (2010) *Talking to the Enemy*. London: Allen Lane.

Austen, B. (2013) 'Public enemies: social media is fueling gang wars in Chicago', 17 September. Available at www.wired.com/2013/09/gangs-of-social-media/all/ (accessed 25 October 2013).

Austin, J., Marino, B., Carroll, L., McCall, P. and Richards, S. (2001) 'The use of incarceration in the United States', *Critical Criminology*, 10(1): 17–24.

Baker, A. and Goldstein, J. (2011) 'Offenses left unrecorded, to keep city's crime rates down', *The New York Times* (31 December): A19.

Bakhtin, M. (1984) *Rabelais and this World*. Bloomington: Indiana University Press.

Balko, R. (2014) *Rise of the Warrior Cop*. New York: Public Affairs.

Ball, M. (2014) 'Queer criminology, critique, and the "art of not being governed"', *Critical Criminology*, 22(1): 21–34.

Bandura, A., Ross, D. and Ross, S. (1961) 'Transmission of aggression through imitation of aggressive models', *Journal of Abnormal and Social Psychology*, 63: 575–82.

Bandura, A., Ross, D. and Ross, S. (1963) 'Imitation of film-mediated aggressive models', *Journal of Abnormal and Social Psychology*, 66: 3–11.

Banks, C. (2000) *Developing Cultural Criminology*. Sydney: Sydney Institute of Criminology.

Banks, J. (2013) 'Edging your bets', *Crime Media Culture*, 9(2): 171–87.

Barbalet, J. (1998) *Emotion, Social Theory and Social Structure*. Cambridge: Cambridge University Press.

Barnes, B. (2013) 'The digital kingdom', *The New York Times* (7 January): B1, B7.

Barrett, C. (2013) *Courting Kids*. New York: New York University Press.

Bartollas, C. (2000) *Juvenile Delinquency*, 5th edition. Boston: Pearson.

Bartollas, C. (2006) *Juvenile Delinquency*, 7th edition. Boston: Pearson.

Bartollas, C. and Miller, S. (2014) *Juvenile Justice in America*, 7th edition. Boston: Pearson.

Bartollas, C. and Schmalleger, F. (2011) *Juvenile Delinquency*, 9th edition. Boston: Pearson.

Baudrillard, J. (1981) *For a Critique of the Political Economy of the Sign*. St Louis, OH: Telos.

Baudrillard, J. (1983) *Simulations*. New York: Semiotext(e).

Baudrillard, J. (1985) 'The ecstasy of communication', in H. Foster (ed.) *Postmodern Culture*. London: Pluto.

Baudrillard, J. (1995) *The Gulf War Did Not Take Place*. Bloomington: Indiana University Press.

Baudrillard, J. (1996) *The System of Objects*. London: Verso.

Bauman, Z. (1999) *Culture as Praxis*. London: SAGE.

Bauman, Z. (2000) *Liquid Modernity*. Cambridge: Polity.

Bauman, Z. (2005) 'Living and occasionally dying in an urban world', in S. Graham (ed.) *Cities, War and Terrorism*. Oxford: Blackwell.

Baumann, M. (1979) *Terror or Love?* London: John Calder.

BBC (2010) *Newsnight*, broadcast 1 June on BBC2.

Beck, U. (1992) *Risk Society*. London: SAGE.

Becker, G. (1968) 'Crime and punishment: an economic approach', *Journal of Political Economy*, 76: 169–217.

Becker, H. (1963) *Outsiders*. New York: Free Press.

Becker, H. (1965) 'Deviance and deviates', in D. Boroff (ed.) *The State of the Nation*. Englewood Cliffs, NJ: Prentice Hall. (Reprinted in H.S. Becker (1971) *Sociological Work*. London: Allen Lane.)

Bendelow, G. and Williams, S. (1998) *Emotions in Social Life*. London: Routledge.

Bengtsson, T. (2012) 'Boredom and action: experiences from youth confinement', *Journal of Contemporary Ethnography*, 41(5): 526–53.

Bennett, H. and Ferrell, J. (1987) 'Music videos and epistemic socialization', *Youth and Society*, 18(4): 344–62.

Berg, M., Stewart, E., Schreck, C. and Simons, R. (2012) 'The victim–offender overlap in context', *Criminology*, 50(2): 359–89.

Berger, P. (1972) *Ways of Seeing*. Harmondsworth: Pelican.

Berlinski, C. (2009) 'The dark figure of British crime', *City Journal*, 19(2). Available at: www.city-journal.org/2009/19_2_british-crime.html (accessed 8 July 2014).

Berman, M. (1982) *All that is Solid Melts into Air*. London: Verso.

Bernstein, D. and Isackson, N. (2014a) 'The truth about Chicago's crime rates', *Chicago* magazine (May). Available at: www.chicagomag.com/Chicago-Magazine/May-2014/Chicago-crime-rates/

Bernstein, D. and Isackson, N. (2014b) 'The truth about Chicago's crime rates: part 2', *Chicago* magazine (June). Available at: www.chicagomag.com/Chicago-Magazine/June-2014/Chicago-crime-statistics/

Biber, K. (2007) *Captive Images*. London: Routledge.

Bilton, N. (2011) 'Masked protestors aid Time-Warner's bottom line', *The New York Times* (28 August).

Blakeley, R. (2009) *State Terrorism and Neo-Liberalism*. Abingdon: Routledge.

Bloch, S. (1997) *Donkey Without a Tail* (documentary film). New York: Filmmakers Library.

Bogazianos, D. (2012) *5 Grams*. New York: New York University Press.

Boluk, S. and Lenz, W. (2011) *Generation Zombie*. Jefferson, NC: McFarland & Co.

Bonn, S. (2010) *Mass Deception*. New York: Vintage Books.

Bourgois, P. (1995) *In Search of Respect*. Cambridge: Cambridge University Press.

Bovenkerk, F. and Yesilgoz, Y. (2004) 'Crime, ethnicity, and the multicultural administration of justice', in J. Ferrell, K. Hayward, W. Morrison and M. Presdee (eds) *Cultural Criminology Unleashed*. London: GlassHouse.

Bovenkerk, F., Siegel, D. and Zaitch, D. (2003) 'Organized crime and ethnic reputation manipulation', *Crime, Law and Social Change*, 39: 23–38.

Boyd, D. (2005a) '"Ambush" for TV backfires for husband', *Ft Worth Star-Telegram* (12 May): 1B, 8B.

Boyd, D. (2005b) 'Reality TV show "revictimized" wife, expert says', *Ft Worth Star-Telegram* (14 May): 4B.

Brake, M. (1980) *The Sociology of Youth Culture*. London: Routledge & Kegan Paul.

Branch, A. and Boyd, D. (2005) 'Officer suspended for 90 days over affair in park', *Ft Worth Star-Telegram* (23 September): 3B.

Braverman, H. (1974) *Labor and Monopoly Capital*. New York: Monthly Review.

Brent, J. and Kraska, P. (2013) 'Fighting is the real and most honest thing', *British Journal of Criminology*, 53(3): 357–77.

Bridges, S. (2006) 'Retailer target branches out into police work', *The Washington Post* (January 29): A1.

Brisman, A. (2010) 'The indiscriminate criminalisation of environmentally beneficial activities', in R. White (ed.) *Global Environmental Harm*. Cullompton: Willan, pp. 161–92.

Brisman, A. and South, N. (2013) 'A green-cultural criminology', *Crime, Media, Culture*, 9(2).

Brisman, A. and South, N. (2014) *Green Cultural Criminology*. London: Routledge.

Brotherton, D. (2007) 'Proceedings from the transnational street/organisation seminar', *Crime, Media, Culture*, 3(3): 372–81.

Brotherton, D. (2011) 'The Latin kings and the global process', *Journal of Studi Sulla Questione Criminale*, 4(1): 7–46.

Brotherton, D. (2015) *Youth Street Gangs: A Critical Appraisal*. London: Routledge.

Brotherton, D. and Barrios, L. (2004) *The Almighty Latin King and Queen Nation*. New York: Columbia University Press.

Brown, M. (2007) 'Mapping discursive closings in the war on drugs', *Crime, Media, Culture*, 3(1): 11–29.

Brown, M. (2009) *The Culture of Punishment*. New York: New York University Press.

Brown, M. (2014) 'Visual criminology and carceral studies', *Theoretical Criminology*, 18(2): 176–97.

Brown, W. (2010) *Walled States, Waning Sovereignty*. New York: Zone Books.

Browning, C. (1992) *Ordinary Men*. New York: Harper Perennial.

Burawoy, M. (2005) 'The critical turn to public sociology', *Critical Sociology*, 31(3): 313–26.

Bureau of Justice Statistics (BJS) (2013) 'BJS promotes the International Year of Statistics – 2013', NewsFromBJS@ncjrs.gov (email alert, 6 August).

Burfeind, J. and Bartusch, D. (2006) *Juvenile Delinquency*. Boston: Jones & Bartlett.

Burke, K., Fox, A. and Martinez, J. (2007) 'Hobo madness hits Madison Ave', *New York Daily News*, 18 January.

Burns, R. and Katovich, M. (2006) 'Melodramatic and consentient images in introductory criminal justice textbooks', *Journal of Criminal Justice*, 34: 101–14.

Burrows, D. (2013) 'Framing the Iraq war', PhD thesis, University of Kent.

Buruma, I. (2007) *Murder in Amsterdam: The Death of Theo van Gogh and the Limits of Tolerance*. London: Atlantic Books.

Butler, J. (1999) *Gender Trouble*. New York: Routledge.

Bynum, J. and Thompson, W. (1996) *Juvenile Delinquency*. Boston: Allyn & Bacon.

Bynum, J. and Thompson, W. (2007) *Juvenile Delinquency*. Boston: Pearson.

Caldeira, T. (2001) *City of Walls*. Berkeley: University of California Press.

Campbell, E. (2013) 'Transgression, affect and performance', *British Journal of Criminology*, 53: 18–40.

Caputo, P. (1977) *A Rumor of War*. London: Pimlico.

Carlen, P. (2011) 'Against evangelism in academic criminology', in M. Bosworth and C. Hoyle (eds) *What is Criminology?* Oxford: Oxford University Press.

Carr, D. (2014) 'With videos of killings, ISIS sends medieval message by modern method', *The New York Times*, 7 September.

Carr, P., Napolitano, L. and Keating, J. (2007) 'We never call the cops and here is why', *Criminology*, 45(2): 445–80.

Carrabine, E. (2008) *Crime, Culture and the Media*. Oxford: Polity.

Carrabine, E. (2011) 'Images of torture', *Crime, Media, Culture*, 7(1): 5–30.

Carrabine, E. (2012) 'Just images', *British Journal of Criminology*, 52(3): 463–89.

Carrabine, E. (2014) 'Seeing things', *Theoretical Criminology*, 18(2): 134–58.

Carter, C. and Weaver, C.K. (2003) *Violence and the Media*. Buckingham: Open University Press.

Cartier-Bresson, H. (1952) *The Decisive Moment*. New York: Simon & Schuster.

Carvalho, S. (2013) 'On the possibilities of a queer criminology', at SSRN: http://ssrn. com/abstract=2268168 or http://dx.doi.org/10.2139/ssrn.2268168

Carvalho, S., Neto, M., Mayora, M. and Linck, J. (2011) *Criminologia Cultural e Rock*. Rio de Janeiro: Editora Luman Juris.

Castells, M. (1996) *The Information Age, Vol. 1*. Oxford: Blackwell.

Cave, D. (2011) 'Mexico turns to social media for information and survival', *The New York Times* (24 September): 5.

Cavender, G. and Deutsch, S. (2007) 'CSI and moral authority', *Crime, Media, Culture*, 3(1): 67–81.

Chambliss, W. (1960) 'A sociological analysis of the law of vagrancy', *Social Problems*, 12(1): 67–77.

Chambliss, W. (1989) 'State organised crime', The American Society of Criminology Presidential Address, 1988, *Criminology*, 27(2): 183–208.

Chan, W. and Rigakos, G.S. (2002) 'Risk, crime and gender', *The British Journal of Criminology*, 42: 743–61.

Chancer, L. (2005) *High-Profile Crimes*. Chicago: Chicago University Press.

Chapoulie, J.-M. (1996) 'Everett Hughes and the Chicago tradition', *Sociological Theory*, 14(1): 3–29.

Chesney-Lind, M. and Irwin, K. (2008) *Beyond Bad Girls*. New York: Routledge.

Chomsky, N. (2002) 'What anthropologists should know about the concept of terrorism: a response to David Price', *Anthropology Today*, 18(2): 22–3.

Clancy, E. (2008) 'Indicted! NYPD officer who tackled cyclist', http://lists.indymedia. org/pipermail/imc-rochester/2008-December/1216-rw.html (accessed 22 January 2015).

Clark, D. (2004) 'The raw and the rotten', *Ethnology*, 43(1): 19–31.

Clarke, J., Hall, S., Jefferson, T. and Roberts, B. (1976) 'Subcultures, cultures and class', in S. Hall and T. Jefferson (eds) *Resistance through Ritual*. London: HarperCollins.

Clarke, R.V.G. and Hough, M. (1984) Crime and Police Effectiveness, Home Office Research Study No 79. London: HMSO.

Clear, T. (2007) *Imprisoning Communities*. Oxford: Oxford University Press.

Clemner, D. (1940) *The Prison Community*. New York: Holt, Rinehart, Winston.

Clifford, J. and Marcus, G. (1986) *Writing Culture*. Berkeley: University of California Press.

Cloward, R. and Ohlin, L. (1961) *Delinquency and Opportunity*. New York: Free Press.

Coates, J. (2012) *The Hour Between Dog and Wolf*. New York: Penguin.

Cockburn, P. (2015) *The Rise of the Islamic State*. London: Verso.

Cohen, A. (1955) *Delinquent Boys*. New York: Free Press.

Cohen, P. (1972) 'Subcultural conflict and working-class community', *CCCS Working Papers*, 2: 5–53.

Cohen, S. (1972) *Folk Devils and Moral Panics*. London: MacGibbon and Kee.

Cohen, S. (1980) 'Symbols of trouble', Introduction to the 2nd edition of *Folk Devils and Moral Panics*. Oxford: Martin Robertson.

Cohen, S. (1981) 'Footprints in the sand', in M. Fitzgerald, G. McLennan and J. Pawson (eds) *Crime and Society*. London: RKP.

Cohen, S. (1988) *Against Criminology*. Oxford: Transaction.

Cohen, S (1997) 'Intellectual scepticism and political commitment', in P. Walton and J. Young (eds) *The New Criminology Revisted*. London: Macmillan.

Cohen, S. (2002) *States of Denial*. Cambridge: Polity.

Cohen, S. and Taylor, L. (1976) *Psychological Survival*. Harmondsworth: Penguin.

Coleman, R., Sim, J., Tombs, S. and Whyte, D. (2009) *State, Power, Crime*. London: SAGE.

Collins, A. (2006) *My Jihad*. New Delhi: Manas.

Connell, R. (1995) *Masculinities*. Cambridge: Polity.

Conquergood, D. (1991) 'Rethinking ethnography', *Communications Monographs*, 58: 179–94.

Conquergood, D. (2002) 'Lethal theatre', *Theatre Journal*, 54(3): 339–67.

Cornish, D. and Clarke, R. (1986) *The Reasoning Criminal*. New York: Springer-Verlag.

CorpWatch Report (2007) *Goodbye Houston*, www.corpwatch.org

Cottee, S. (2009a) 'A murder in Amsterdam', *Democratiya*, 16/Spring–Summer: 64–80. Available at: www.ignaciodarnaude.com/ufologia/Rev.Democratiya,Spring-Summer%20 2009.pdf (republished in *Dissent*).

Cottee, S. (2009b) 'The Jihadist solution', *Studies in Conflict and Terrorism*, 32(12): 1117–34.

Cottee, S. (2010) 'A grammar of everyday justice talk', paper presented at the annual meeting of the the Law and Society Association, Chicago, IL, 27–30 May.

Cottee, S. (2011) 'Fear, boredom and joy', *Studies in Conflict and Terrorism*, 34(5): 439–59.

Cottee, S. (2014) 'We need to talk about Mohammad', *British Journal of Criminology*, 54(6): 981–1001.

Cottee, S. and Hayward, K. (2011) 'Terrorist (e)motives: the existential attractions of terrorism', *Studies in Conflict and Terrorism*, 34(12): 963–86.

Courtney, D. and Lyng, S. (2007) 'Taryn Simon and the Innocence Project', *Crime, Media, Culture*, 3(2): 175–91.

Coyle, M. (2013) *Talking Criminal Justice*. London: Routledge.

Cunneen, C. and Stubbs, J. (2004) 'Cultural criminology and engagement with race, gender and post-colonial identities', in J. Ferrell, K. Hayward, W. Morrison and M. Presdee (eds) *Cultural Criminology Unleashed*. London: GlassHouse.

Cushman, T. (2001) 'The reflexivity of evil', in J.L. Geddes (ed.) *Evil*. London: Routledge.

Dalacoura, K. (2009) 'Middle East area studies and terrorism studies', in R. Jackson, M. Breen Smyth and J. Gunning (eds) *Critical Terrorism Studies*. Abingdon: Routledge.

David, E. (2007) 'Signs of resistance', in G. Stanczak (ed.) *Visual Research Methods*. Los Angeles: SAGE.

Davis, M. (1990) *City of Quartz*. London: Verso.

Davis, M. (2005) 'The great wall of capital', in M. Sorkin (ed.) *Against the Wall*. New York: New Press.

De Certeau, M. (1984) *The Practice of Everyday Life*. Berkeley: University of California Press.

De Haan, W. and Vos, J. (2003) 'A crying shame', *Theoretical Criminology*, 7(1): 29–54.

De Jong, A. and Schuilenburg, M. (2006) *Mediapolis*. Rotterdam: 010 Publishers.

DeKeseredy, W. (2011) *Contemporary Critical Criminology*. London: Routledge.

Demby, G. (2012) 'Seller offers gun range target meant to resemble Trayvon Martin', *The Huffington Post*, 11 May.

Denzin, N. (1997) *Interpretative Ethnography*. Thousand Oaks, CA: SAGE.

Denzin, N. (2003) *Performance Ethnography*. Thousand Oaks, CA: SAGE.

DiCristina, B. (2006) 'The epistemology of theory testing in criminology', in B. Arrigo and C. Williams (eds) *Philosophy, Crime and Criminology*. Urbana, IL: University of Illinois Press.

Ditton, J. (1979) *Contrology*. Basingstoke: Macmillan.

Downes, D. (1966) *The Delinquent Solution*. London: Routledge & Kegan Paul.

Downes, D. and Rock, P. (2007) *Understanding Deviance*. Oxford: Oxford University Press.

Dribben, M. (2006) '"CSI" effect has jurors expecting more evidence', *Ft Worth Star-Telegram* (2 March): 4E.

Drogin, B. (2009) 'Keeping a close eye on itself', *Los Angeles Times* (21 June): A1, A11.

Dugan, L. and Apel, R. (2005) 'The differential risk of retaliation by relational distance', *Criminology*, 43(3): 697–726.

Durkheim, E. (1964) *The Rules of Sociological Method*. New York: Free Press.

Durkheim, E. (1965) *Essays in Sociology and Philosophy* (ed. K. Wolff). New York: Harper & Row.

Dwyer, J. (2012) 'Telling the truth like crazy', *The New York Times* (9 March): A18.

Dylan, B. (2004) *Chronicles, Volume One*. New York: Simon & Schuster.

Eisenstein, H. (2010) *Feminism Seduced*. Boulder, CO: Paradigm.

Eiserer, T. and Thompson, S. (2013) 'Dallas policy change leads to 75% decline in reported petty shoplifting cases', *The Dallas Morning News*, 23 March.

Ekblom, P. (2007) 'Enriching the offender', in G. Farrell, K. Bowers, S. Johnson and M. Townsley (eds) *Imagination for Crime Prevention: Essays in Honour of Ken Pease*. Cullompton: Willan.

Eligon, J. and Moynihan, C. (2008) 'Police officer seen on tape is indicted', *The New York Times*, 15 December.

Elliott, A. (2010) 'The jihadist next door', *The New York Times*, 27 January. Available at: www.nytimes.com/2010/01/31/magazine/31Jihadist-t.html (accessed 10 January 2011).

Ericson, R. (1995) *Crime and the Media*. Aldershot: Dartmouth.

Erlanger, S. (2011) 'France: time limits on begging', *The New York Times* (16 September): A5.

Eterno, J. and Silverman, E. (2012) *The Crime Numbers Game*. Boca Raton, FL: CRC Press.

Exum, M.L. (2002) 'The application and robustness of the rational choice perspective in the study of intoxicated and angry intentions to aggress', *Criminology*, 40(4): 933–66.

Fader, J. (2013) *Falling Back*. New Brunswick, NJ: Rutgers University Press.

Farrell, G. (2010) 'Situational crime prevention and its discontents', *Social Policy and Administration*, 44(1): 40–66.

Feagin, J., Orum, A. and Sjoberg, G. (1991) *A Case for the Case Study*. Chapel Hill, NC: UNC Press.

Felson, M. (1998) *Crime and Everyday Life*. Thousand Oaks, CA: Pine Forge Press.

Fenwick, M. and Hayward, K. (2000) 'Youth crime, excitement and consumer culture', in J. Pickford (ed.) *Youth Justice*. London: Cavendish.

Ferrell, J. (1992) 'Making sense of crime', *Social Justice*, 19(2): 110–23.

Ferrell, J. (1996) *Crimes of Style*. Boston: Northeastern.

Ferrell, J. (1997) 'Criminological *verstehen*', *Justice Quarterly*, 14(1): 3–23.

Ferrell, J. (1998a) 'Criminalizing popular culture', in F. Bailey and D. Hale (eds) *Popular Culture, Crime and Justice*. Belmont, CA: West/Wadsworth.

Ferrell, J. (1998b) 'Freight train graffiti', *Justice Quarterly*, 15(4): 587–608.

Ferrell, J. (1999) 'Cultural criminology', *Annual Review of Sociology*, 25: 395–418.

Ferrell, J. (2001/2) *Tearing Down the Streets*. New York: St Martins/Palgrave.

Ferrell, J. (2004a) 'Boredom, crime, and criminology', *Theoretical Criminology*, 8(3): 287–302.

Ferrell, J. (2004b) 'Speed kills', in J. Ferrell, K. Hayward, W. Morrison and M. Presdee (eds) *Cultural Criminology Unleashed*. London: GlassHouse.

Ferrell, J. (2005) 'The only possible adventure', in S. Lyng (ed.) *Edgework*. New York: Routledge.

Ferrell, J. (2006a) *Empire of Scrounge*. New York: New York University Press.

Ferrell, J. (2006b) 'The aesthetics of cultural criminology', in B. Arrigo and C. Williams (eds) *Philosophy, Crime, and Criminology*. Urbana, IL: University of Illinois Press.

Ferrell, J. (2007) 'For a ruthless cultural criticism of everything existing', *Crime, Media, Culture*, 3(1): 91–100.

Ferrell, J. (2009) 'Kill method', *Journal of Theoretical and Philosophical Criminology*, 1(1): 1–22.

Ferrell, J. (2011) 'Disciplinarity and drift', in M. Bosworth and C. Hoyle (eds) *What is Criminology?* Oxford: Oxford University Press.

Ferrell, J. (2012a) 'Anarchy, geography and drift', *Antipode*, 44(5): 1687–704.

Ferrell, J. (2012b) 'Outline of a criminology of drift', in S. Hall and S. Winlow (eds) *New Directions in Criminological Theory*. London: Routledge.

Ferrell, J. (2012c) 'Autoethnography', in D. Gadd, S. Karstedt and S. Messner (eds) *The SAGE Handbook of Criminological Research Methods*. London: SAGE.

Ferrell, J. (2013a) 'Tangled up in green', in N. South and A. Brisman (eds) *Routledge International Handbook of Green Criminology*. London: Routledge.

Ferrell, J. (2013b) 'The Underbelly Project', *Rhizomes* 25, at www.rhizomes.net/issue25/ferrell/

Ferrell, J. (2014a) 'Manifesto for a criminology beyond method', in M.H. Jacobsen (ed.) *The Poetics of Crime*. London: Ashgate.

Ferrell, J. (2014b) Statement of Witness (C.J.Act, 1967, S.9; M.C. Act, 1980, S.102; M.C. Rules, 1981, r. 70), 23 April (Re: Bradley Garrett).

Ferrell, J. and Hamm, M. (1998) *Ethnography at the Edge*. Boston: Northeastern.

Ferrell, J. and Hayward, K. (2011) 'Cultural criminology', in J. Ferrell and K. Hayward (eds) *Cultural Criminology: Collected Papers*. Farnham: Ashgate.

Ferrell, J. and Sanders, C. (1995) *Cultural Criminology*. Boston: Northeastern.

Ferrell, J. and Van de Voorde, C. (2010) 'The decisive moment', in K. Hayward and M. Presdee (eds) *Framing Crime*. London: Routledge.

Ferrell, J. and Websdale, N. (1999) *Making Trouble*. New York: de Gruyter.

Ferrell, J., Greer, C. and Jewkes, Y. (2005) 'Hip hop graffiti, mexican murals, and the war on terror', *Crime, Media, Culture*, 1(1): 5–9.

Ferrell, J., Hayward, K., Morrison, W. and Presdee M. (eds) (2004) *Cultural Criminology Unleashed*. London: GlassHouse.

Ferrell, J., Hayward, K. and Young, J. (2008) *Cultural Criminology: An Invitation*, 1st edition. London: SAGE.

Ferrell, J., Milovanovic, D. and Lyng, S. (2001) 'Edgework, media practices, and the elongation of meaning', *Theoretical Criminology*, 5(2): 177–202.

Feyerabend, P. (1975) *Against Method*. London: Verso.

Fiddler, M. (2007) 'Projecting the prison', *Crime, Media, Culture*, 3(2): 192–206.

Fitzgerald, M. (1977) *Prisoners in Revolt*. Harmondsworth: Penguin.

Fleetwood, J. (2014) *Drug Mules*. London: Palgrave Macmillan.

Fonow, M. and Cook, J. (eds) (1991) *Beyond Methodology*. Bloomington: Indiana University Press.

Foucault, M. (1977) *Discipline and Punish*. London: Penguin.

Fox, J. (2010) *The Myth of the Rational Market*. Petersfield, Hampshire: Harriman House.

Freire-Medeiros, B. (2012) *Touring Poverty*. New York: Routledge.

Friedan, B. (1963) *The Feminine Mystique*. Harmondsworth: Penguin.

Gadd, D. and Jefferson, T. (2007) *Psychosocial Criminology*. London: SAGE.

Gailey, J. (2009) 'Starving is the most fun a girl can have', *Critical Criminology*, 17: 93–108.

Garfinkel, H. (1956) 'Conditions of successful degradation ceremonies', *American Journal of Sociology*, 61: 420–4.

Garfinkel, H. (1967) *Studies in Ethnomethodology*. Englewood Cliffs, NJ: Prentice-Hall.

Garland, D. (1997) '"Governmentality" and the problem of crime', *Theoretical Criminology*, 1(2): 173–214.

Garland, D. (2001) *The Culture of Control*. Oxford: Oxford University Press.

Garot, R. (2007a) 'Where you from!?', *Journal of Contemporary Ethnography*, 36(1): 50–84.

Garot, R. (2007b) 'Classroom resistance as edgework', paper presented at the On the Edge: Transgression and the Dangerous Other Conference, New York City, 9–10 August.

Garot, R. (2010) *Who You Claim*. New York: New York University Press.

Garrett, B. (2013) *Explore Everything*. London: Verso.

Garrett, B. (2014) 'Access denied', *Times Higher Education* (5 June): 35–9.

Gates, H.L. (1988) *The Signifying Monkey*. New York: Oxford University Press.

Gelsthorpe, L. (1990) 'Feminist methodologies in criminology', in L. Gelsthorpe and A. Morris (eds) *Feminist Perspectives in Criminology*. Milton Keynes: Open University Press.

Gibbs, J. (1968) 'Crime, punishment and deterrence', *Southwestern Social Science Quarterly*, 48: 515–30.

Giddens, A. (1984) *The Constitution of Society*. Cambridge: Polity.

Giddens, A. (1990) *The Consequences of Modernity*. Cambridge: Polity.

Giorgio (2003) *Memoirs of an Italian Terrorist* (trans. A. Shugaar). New York: Carroll and Graf.

Goffman, A. (2014) *On the Run*. Chicago: University of Chicago Press.

Goffman, E. (1961) *Asylums*. New York: Doubleday.

Goffman, E. (1979) *Gender Advertisements*. New York: Harper & Row.

Goldhagen, D. (1996) *Hitler's Willing Executioners*. London: Little Brown & Co.

Goold, B., Loader, I. and Thumala, A. (2010) 'Consuming security', *Theoretical Criminology*, 14(3): 3–30.

Gottfredson, M. and Hirschi, T. (1990) *Positive Criminology*. London: SAGE.

Graczyk, M. (2005) 'Killer whose attorneys blamed rap lyrics is executed', *Ft Worth Star-Telegram* (7 October): 5B.

Grassian, S. and Friedman, N. (1986) 'Effects of sensory deprivation in psychiatric seclusion and solitary confinement', *International Journal of Law and Psychiatry*, 8: 49–65.

Gray, G.J. (1959) *The Warriors*. Lincoln, NE: University of Nebraska Press.

Green, P. and Ward, T. (2000) 'State crime, human rights and the limits of criminology', *Social Justice*, 27: 101–20.

Green, P. and Ward, T. (2004) *State Crime*. London: Pluto.

Greenwood, C. and Nolan, S. (2012) 'Five police arrested for persuading criminals to confess to crimes they did not commit to boost detection rates', *Daily Mail*, 14 November.

Greer, C. (2004) 'Crime, media and community', in J. Ferrell, K. Hayward, W. Morrison and M. Presdee (eds) *Cultural Criminology Unleashed*. London: GlassHouse.

Greer, C. (2005) 'Crime and the media', in C. Hale, K. Hayward, A. Wahidin and E. Wincup (eds) *Criminology*. Oxford: Oxford University Press.

Greer, C. (2009) *Crime and the Media: A Reader*. London: Routledge.

Greer, C. and Reiner, R. (2012) 'Mediated mayhem', in M. Maguire, R. Morgan and R. Reiner (eds) *The Oxford Handbook of Criminology*, 5th edition. Oxford: Oxford University Press.

Grimes, J. (2007) 'Crime, media, and public policy', PhD dissertation, Arizona State University.

Gunning, J. (2007) 'A case for critical terrorism studies?' *Government and Opposition*, 17(37): 363–93.

Gunning, J. (2009) 'Social movement theory and the study of terrorism', in R. Jackson, M. Breen Smyth and J. Gunning (eds) *Critical Terrorism Studies*. Abingdon: Routledge.

Gurman, S. (2013) 'Officer error, software trouble skewed Denver crime stats', *The Denver Post*, 24 July.

Gurr, T.R. (2007) 'Economic factors', in L. Richardson (ed.) *The Roots of Terrorism*. London: Routledge.

Hall, S. and Winlow, S. (2005) 'Anti-nirvana', *Crime, Media, Culture*, 1(1): 31–48.

Hall, S. and Winlow, S. (2007) 'Cultural criminology and primitive accumulation', *Crime, Media, Culture*, 3(1): 82–90.

Hall, S., Critcher, C., Jefferson, T., Clarke, J. and Roberts, B. (eds) (1978) *Policing the Crisis*. London: Macmillan.

Hall, S., Winlow, S. and Ancrum, C. (2008) *Criminal Identities and Consumer Culture*. Cullompton: Willan.

Hallsworth, S. (2013) *The Gang and Beyond*. Houndsmills, UK: Palgrave Macmillan.

Halsey, M. and Young, A. (2006) 'Our desires are ungovernable', *Theoretical Criminology*, 10(3): 275–306.

Hamm, M. (1995) *American Skinheads*. New York: Greenwood.

Hamm, M. (1997) *Apocalypse in Oklahoma*. Boston: Northeastern.

Hamm, M. (1998) 'The ethnography of terror', in J. Ferrell and M. Hamm (eds) *Ethnography at the Edge*. Boston: Northeastern.

Hamm, M. (2002) *In Bad Company*. Boston: Northeastern.

Hamm, M. (2004) 'The USA Patriot Act and the politics of fear', in J. Ferrell, K. Hayward, W. Morrison and M. Presdee (eds) *Cultural Criminology Unleashed*. London: GlassHouse.

Hamm, M. (2007a) 'High crimes and misdemeanours', *Crime, Media, Culture*, 3(3): 259–84.

Hamm, M. (2007b) *Terrorism as Crime*. New York: New York University Press.

Hamm, M. (2008) 'Bicycles to genocide', paper presented at the 60th Annual Meeting of the American Society of Criminology, St Louis, Missouri, 1–4 November.

Hamm, M. (2013) *The Spectacular Few*. New York: New York University Press.

Hamm, M. (2015) *Lone Wolf Terrorism in America*. Washington, DC: National Institute of Justice.

Hamm, M. and Ferrell, J. (1994) 'Rap, cops and crime', *ACJS Today*, 13(1): 3, 29.

Hamm, M. and Spaaij, R. (2015) 'Paradigmatic case studies and prison ethnography in terrorism research', in G. LaFree and J. Froelich (eds) *Handbook on the Criminology of Terrorism*. New York: Wiley.

Harper, D. (2001) *Changing Works*. Chicago: University of Chicago Press.

Harris, R. (2011) 'Enlightenment by way of adventure', *The New York Times* (18 November): C31.

Harvey, D. (1990) *The Condition of Postmodernity*. Cambridge, MA: Blackwell.

Hay, C. (2004) 'Theory, stylized heuristic or self-fulfilling prophecy?' *Public Administration*, 82(1): 39–62.

Hayward, K.J. (2001) 'Crime, consumerism and the urban experience', PhD thesis, University of East London.

Hayward, K.J. (2004) *City Limits*. London: GlassHouse.

Hayward, K.J. (2007) 'Situational crime prevention and its discontents', *Social Policy and Administration*, 41(3): 232–50.

Hayward, K.J. (2011) 'The critical terrorism studies – cultural criminology nexus', *Critical Studies on Terrorism*, 4(1): 57–73.

Hayward, K.J. (2012a) 'A response to Farrell', *Social Policy and Administration*, 46(1): 21–34.

Hayward, K.J. (2012b) 'Five spaces of cultural criminology', *The British Journal of Criminology*, 52(3): 441–62.

Hayward, K.J. (2012c) 'Pantomime justice', *Crime, Media, Culture*, 8(2): 213–29.

Hayward, K.J. (2013) '"Life stage dissolution" in Anglo-American advertising and popular culture', *The Sociological Review*, 61(3): 525–48.

Hayward, K.J. and Presdee, M. (eds) (2010) *Framing Crime*. London: Routledge.

Hayward, K.J. and Schuilenburg, M. (2014) 'To resist = to create?' *Tijdschrift over Cultuur en Criminaliteit*, 4(1): 22–36.

Hayward, K.J. and Yar, M. (2006) 'The "Chav" phenomenon', *Crime, Media, Culture*, 2(1): 9–28.

Hayward, K.J. and Young, J. (2004) 'Cultural criminology: some notes on the script', *Theoretical Criminology*, 8(3): 259–72.

Hayward, K.J. and Young, J. (2012) 'Cultural Criminology' in M. Maguire, M. Morgan and R. Reiner (eds) *The Oxford Handbook of Criminology*. Oxford: Oxford University Press.

Healy, P. (2007) 'Hikes pay homage to path taken by illegal immigrants', *Ft Worth Star-Telegram* (February 4): 5H.

Heath, J. and Potter, A. (2006) *The Rebel Sell*. Toronto: HarperCollins.

Hebdige, D. (1979) *Subculture*. London: Methuen.

Hebdige, D. (1988) *Hiding in the Light*. London: Comedia.

Hedges, C. (2002) *War is a Force That Gives Us Meaning*. New York: Anchor Books.

Hedges, C. (2009) *Empire of Illusion: The End of Literacy and the Triumph of Spectacle*. New York: Nation Books.

Hedges, C. and Sacco, J. (2012) *Days of Destruction, Days of Revolt*. New York: Nation Books.

Heidonsohn, F. (2012) 'The future of feminist criminology'. *Crime, Media, Culture*, 8(2): 123–34.

Henry, S. and Milovanovic, D. (1996) *Constitutive Criminology*. London: SAGE.

Herman, E. and Chomsky, N. (1994) *Manufacturing Consent*. New York: Pantheon.

Herzog, L. and Hayward, K.J. (2015) Special edition of *Global Society* on the US–Mexican Border, forthcoming.

Hillyard, P. and Tombs, S. (2004) 'Beyond criminology?' in P. Hillyard, S. Pantazis and D. Tombs (eds) *Beyond Criminology*. London: Pluto Press.

Hillyard, P., Pantazis, C., Tombs, S., Gordon, D. and Dorling, D. (eds) (2005) *Criminal Obsessions*. London: Crime and Society Foundation.

Hillyard, P., Sim, J., Tombs, S. and Whyte, D. (2004) 'Leaving a "stain upon the silence"', *British Journal of Criminology*, 44(3): 369–90.

Hirschi, T. (1969) *Causes of Delinquency*. Berkeley: University of California Press.

Hobbs, D. (2007) 'East ending', in T. Newburn and P. Rock (eds) *Politics of Crime Control*. Oxford: Clarendon Press.

Hobsbawm, E. (1994) *The Age of Extremes*. London: Michael Joseph.

Hochschild, A. (2003) *The Managed Heart*. Berkeley: University of California Press.

Hollin, C. (2013) 'Opportunity theory', in E. McLaughlin and J. Muncie (eds) *The SAGE Dictionary of Criminology*. London: SAGE.

Hopkins, M. and Treadwell, J. (2014) *Football Hooliganism, Fan Behaviour and Crime*. Basingstoke: Palgrave Macmillan.

Horgan, J. and Boyle, M. (2008) 'A case against critical terrorism studies', *Critical Studies on Terrorism*, 1(1): 51–64.

Horkheimer, M. and Adorno, T.W. (2002) *Dialectic of Enlightenment*. Stanford, CA: Standford University Press.

Horton, J. (2011) 'Trekking with the guerrillas', *The Guardian Weekly* (4 March): 46.

Hough, J.M., Clarke, R.V.G. and Mayhew, P. (1980) 'Introduction', in R.V.G. Clarke and P. Mayhew (eds) *Designing Out Crime*. London: HMSO.

Howe, A. (2003) 'Managing men's violence in the criminological arena', in C. Sumner (ed.) *The Blackwell Companion to Criminology*. Oxford: Blackwell.

Hubbard, J. (1994) *Shooting Back from the Reservation*. New York: New Press.

Hughes, J. (2011) *Performance in a Time of Terror*. Manchester: Manchester University Press.

Ilan, J. (2012) 'The industry's the new road', *Crime, Media, Culture*, 8(1): 39–55.

Ilan, J. (2014) 'Commodifying compliance?' *Tijdscrift over Cultuur & Criminaliteit*, 4(1): 67–79.

Jackson, R. (2005) *Writing the War on Terrorism*. Manchester: Manchester University Press.

Jackson, R. (2007) 'The core commitments of critical terrorism studies', *European Political Science*, 6(3): 244–51.

Jackson, R. (2009) 'Knowledge, power and politics in the study of political terrorism', in R. Jackson, M. Breen Smyth and J. Gunning (eds) *Critical Terrorism Studies*. Abingdon: Routledge.

Jackson, R., Breen Smyth, M. and Gunning, J. (2009a) *Critical Terrorism Studies*. Abingdon: Routledge.

Jackson, R., Breen Smyth, M. and Gunning, J. (2009b) 'Critical terrorism studies', in R. Jackson, M. Breen Smyth and J. Gunning (eds) *Critical Terrorism Studies*. Abingdon: Routledge.

Jacobsen, M.H. (2014) *The Poetics of Crime*. London: Ashgate.

Jameson, F. (1991) *Postmodernism, or the Cultural Logic of Late Capitalism*. London: Verso.

Jarvis, B. (2007) 'Monsters Inc.', *Crime, Media, Culture*, 3(3): 326–44.

Jefferson, T. (1976) 'Cultural responses of the teds', in S. Hall and T. Jefferson (eds) *Resistance through Rituals*. London: Hutchinson.

Jenkins, P. (1999) 'Fighting terrorism as if women mattered', in J. Ferrell and N. Websdale (eds) *Making Trouble*. New York: Aldine.

Jenkins, P. (2001) *Beyond Tolerance*. New York: New York University Press.

Jensen, G. and Rojek, D. (1992) *Delinquency and Youth Crime*. Chicago: Waveland.

Jewkes, Y. (2004) *Media and Crime*. London: SAGE.

Jewkes, Y. (2011) *Media and Crime*, 2nd edition. London: SAGE.

Jewkes, Y. (2012) 'Autoethnography and emotion as intellectual resources', *Qualitative Inquiry*, 18(1): 63–75.

Jewkes, Y. and Yar, M. (2010) *Handbook of Internet Crime*. London: SAGE.

Jhally, S. (1987) *The Codes of Advertising*. New York: Routledge.

Jones, R. (2000) 'Digital rule', *Punishment and Society*, 2(1): 5–22.

Jones, R. (2005) 'Surveillance', in C. Hale, K. Hayward, A. Wahidin and E. Wincup (eds) *Criminology*. Oxford: Oxford University Press.

Jones, R., Ross, J.I., Richards S. and Murphy, D. (2009) 'The first dime', *Prison Journal*, 89(2): 151–71.

Joseph, J. (2011) 'Terrorism as a social relation within capitalism', *Critical Studies on Terrorism*, 4(1): 23–37.

Juergensmeyer, M. (2001) *Terror in the Mind of God*. Berkeley: University of California Press.

Junger, S. (2010) *War*. London: Fourth Estate.

Kahn, E. (2012) 'Bloodstains with a story', *The New York Times* (14 September): C24.

Kane, S. (1998) 'Reversing the ethnographic gaze', in J. Ferrell and M. Hamm (eds) *Ethnography at the Edge*. Boston: Northeastern.

Kane, S. (2003) 'Epilogue', in P. Parnell and S. Kane (eds) *Crime's Power*. New York: Palgrave MacMillan.

Kane, S. (2004) 'The unconventional methods of cultural criminology', *Theoretical Criminology*, 8(3): 303–21.

Kane, S. (2013) *Where Rivers Meet the Sea*. Philadelphia, PA: Temple.

Kara, H. (2014) Witness Statement (Criminal Procedure Rules, r27.2; Criminal Justice Act 1967, s.9; Magistrates' Courts Act 1980, s.5B), 13 April (Re: Bradley Garrett).

Katz, J. (1988) *Seductions of Crime*. New York: Basic Books.

Katz, J. (1999) *How Emotions Work*. Chicago: Chicago University Press.

Katz, J. (2002a) 'Start here: social ontology and research strategy', *Theoretical Criminology*, 6(3): 255–78.

Katz, J. (2002b) 'Response to commentators', *Theoretical Criminology*, 6(3): 375–80.

Kauzarlich, D. (2007) 'Seeing war as criminal', *Contemporary Criminal Justice*, 10(1): 67–85.

Kemper, T.D. (1990) *Research Agendas in the Sociology of Emotions*. New York: SUNY Press.

Kidd-Hewitt, D. and Osborne, R. (1995) *Crime and the Media*. London: Pluto.

Kilbourne, J. (1999) *Deadly Persausions*. New York: Free Press.

Kilcullen, D. (2009) *Accidental Guerrilla*. London: Hurst.

Kimes, M. (2006) 'Garbage pail kids', *The New Journal* (October): 11–17.

Klein, N. (2007*) The Shock Doctrine*. London: Penguin.

Klein, J.R. (2011) 'Toward a cultural criminology of war', *Social Justice*, 38(3): 86–103.

Kontos, L., Brotherton, D. and Barrios, L. (2003) *Gangs and Society*. New York: Columbia.

Kotlowitz, A. (2014) 'Deep cover', *The New York Times* (29 June): 34–5.

Kramer, R. and Michalowski, R. (2005) 'War, aggression and state crime', *British Journal of Criminology*, 45(4): 446–69.

Kraska, P. (2001) *Militarizing the American Criminal Justice System*. Boston: Northeastern.

Kraska, P. and Neuman, W. (2008) *Criminal Justice and Criminology Research Methods*. Boston: Pearson.

Krawesky, A. (2006) 'Motorist vs. courier', *City Noise* (Toronto) at: www.citynoise.org

Krims, A. (2000) *Rap Music and the Poetics of Identity*. Cambridge: Cambridge University Press.

Kroger, W. and Teufel, T. (2011) *Felon Fitness*. Avon, MA: Adams Media.

Kruglanski, A. (2006) 'Precarity explained to kids', *Journal of Aesthetics and Protest* 4, at: www.journalofaesheticsandprotest.org

Kruglanski, A., Chen, X., Dechesne, M., Fishman, S. and Orehek, E. (2009) 'Fully committed', *Political Psychology*, 30(3): 331–57.

Kubrin, C.E. (2005) 'Gangstas, thugs and hustlas', *Social Problems*, 52(3): 360–78.

Kuhl, D., Warner, D. and Wilczak, A. (2012) 'Adolescent violent victimization and precocious union formation', *Criminology*, 50(4): 1089–127.

Kurlychek, M., Bushway, S. and Brame, R. (2012) 'Long-term crime desistance and recidivism patterns', *Criminology*, 50(1): 71–103.

La Ferla, R. (2010) 'A look that's bulletproof', *The New York Times* (21 January): E1, E7.

Landry, D. (2013) 'Are we human?' *Critical Criminology*, 21(1): 1–14.

Lara, F.L. (2011) 'New (sub)urbanism and old inequalities in Brazilian gated communities', *Journal of Urban Design*, 16(3): 369–80.

Lauer, J. (2005) 'Driven to extremes', *Crime, Media, Culture*, 1(2): 149–68.

Lawrence, P. (2007) 'The mismeasurement of science', *Current Biology*, 17(15): 583–5.

Laycock, G. (2013) 'Defining crime science', in M. Smith and N. Tilly (eds) *Crime Science*. London: Routledge.

Lea, J. and Stenson, K. (2007) 'Security, sovereignty and non-state governance "from below"', *The Canadian Journal of Law and Society*, 22(2): 9–28.

Lemert, E. (1967) *Human Deviance, Social Problems and Social Control*. Englewood Cliffs, NJ: Prentice Hall.

Lepard, B.D. (2006) 'Iraq, fundamental ethical principles and the future of human rights', *Journal of Human Rights*, 4(1): 53–9.

Levy, A. (2006) *Female Chauvinist Pigs*. London: Pocket Books.

Licoppe, C. (2004) '"Connected" presence', *Environment and Planning D*, 22(1): 135–56.

Lilly, J.R., Cullen, F. and Ball, R. (1989) *Criminological Theory*. Thousand Oaks, CA: SAGE.

Lindgren, S. (2005) 'Social constructionism and criminology', *Journal of Scandinavian Studies in Criminology and Crime Prevention*, 6: 4–22.

Linnemann, T. (2014) 'Capote's Ghosts: Violence, Media and the Spectre of Suspicion', *British Journal of Criminology* (Advance Access publication, 29 December).

Linnemann, T., Hanson, L. and Williams, L.S. (2013) 'With scenes of blood and pain', *British Journal of Criminology*, 53(4): 605–23.

Linnemann, T., Wall, T. and Green, E. (2014) 'The Walking Dead and the Killing State', *Theoretical Criminology*, 18(4): 506–27.

Lippman, L. (2005) 'The Queen of the South', *Crime, Media, Culture*, 1(2): 209–13.

Loader, I. and Sparks, R. (2010) *Public Criminology*. Abingdon: Routledge.

Lois, J. (2001) 'Peaks and valleys', *Gender & Society*, 15(3): 381–406.

Lois, J. (2005) 'Gender and emotion management in the stages of edgework', in S. Lyng (ed.) *Edgework*. New York: Routledge.

Lombroso, C. (2006 [1876]) *The Criminal Man* (trans. M. Gibson and N. Rafter). Durham, NC: Duke.

Lovell, J. (2006) 'This is not a comic book', *Crime, Media, Culture*, 2(1): 75–83.

Lukacs, G. (1971) *History and Class Consciousness*. Cambridge, MA: MIT Press.

Lyng, S. (1990) 'Edgework', *American Journal of Sociology*, 95(4): 851–86.

Lyng, S. (1991) 'Edgework revisited', *American Journal of Sociology*, 96: 1534–9.

Lyng, S. (ed.) (2005) *Edgework*. New York: Routledge.

Lyng, S. and Bracey, M. (1995) 'Squaring the one percent', in J. Ferrell and C. Sanders (eds) *Cultural Criminology*. Boston: Northeastern.

Lyotard, J.F. (1984) *The Postmodern Condition*. Manchester: Manchester University Press.

McBridge, M. (2011) 'The logic of terrorism', *Terrorism and Political Violence*, 23(4): 560–81.

McElroy, W. (2010) 'Are cameras the new guns?' Available at: http://gizmodo.com/5553765/are-cameras-the-new-guns, 6 February.

McLeod, J. (1995) *Ain't No Makin' It*. Boulder, CO: Westview.

McRobbie, A. (1994) *Postmoderism and Popular Culture*. London: Routledge.

McRobbie, A. and Thornton, S. (1995) 'Rethinking "moral panic" for multi-mediated social worlds', *British Journal of Sociology*, 46(4): 245–59.

McVicar, J. (1979) *McVicar*. London: Arrow.

Madar, C. (2012) 'What the laws of war allow', at: www.aljazeera.com (accessed 26 April 2012).

Maguire, M., Morgan, R. and Reiner, R. (eds) (2000) *The Oxford Handbook of Criminology*, 3rd edition. Oxford: Oxford University Press.

Makiya, K. (1998) *Republic of Fear*. Berkeley: University of California Press.

Mann, S., Nolan, J. and Wellman, B. (2003) 'Sousveillance', *Surveillance and Society*, 1(3): 331–55.

Mannheim, H. (1948) *Juvenile Delinquency in an English Middletown*. London: RKP.

Manning, P. (1995) 'The challenge of postmodernism', in J. Van Maanen (ed.) *Representation in Ethnography*. Thousand Oaks, CA: SAGE.

Manning, P. (1998) 'Media loops', in F. Bailey and D. Hale (eds) *Popular Culture, Crime and Justice*. Belmont, CA: Wadsworth.

Manning, P. (1999) 'Reflections', in J. Ferrell and N. Websdale (eds) *Making Trouble*. New York: Aldine de Gruyter.

Martin, P. (2004) 'Culture, subculture and social organization', in A. Bennettt and K. Khahn Harris (eds) *After Subculture*. Basingstoke: Palgrave.

Marx, G.T. (1995) 'New telecommunications technologies require new manners', *Cybernews* 1(1). Available at: https://papyrus.bib.umontreal.ca/xmlui/bitstream/handle/1866/9307/articles_210.html?sequence=1

Mason, P. (2012) *Why It's Kicking Off Everywhere*. London: Verso.

Matthews, R. (2009) 'Beyond "so what?" criminology', *Theoretical Criminology*, 13(3): 341–62.

Mattley, C. (1998) '(Dis)courtesy stigma', in J. Ferrell and M. Hamm (eds) *Ethnography at the Edge*. Boston: Northeastern.

Matza, D. (1969) *Becoming Deviant*. Englewood Cliffs, NJ: Prentice Hall.

Matza, D. and Sykes, G. (1961) 'Juvenile delinquency and subterranean values', *American Sociological Review*, 26: 712–19.

Mawby, R. and Walklate, S. (1994) *Critical Victimology*. London: SAGE.

Mayer, A. and Machin, D. (2012) *The Language of Crime and Deviance*. London: Continuum.

Mayhew, M. (2006) 'Some like it swat' Ft. Worth Star-Telegram (4 January), pp. 1F, 7F.

Mazower, M. (2008) 'Mandarins, guns and money', *The Nation*, 287(10) (6 October): 36–42.

Measham, F. (2004) 'Play space', *International Journal of Drug Policy*, 15: 337–45.

Medina, J. (2010) 'Dealing in death, and trying to make a living', *The New York Times* (26 December): 16.

Mehan, H. and Wood, H. (1975) *The Reality of Ethnomethodology*. New York: Wiley.

Melossi, D. (2001) 'The cultural embeddness of social control', *Theoretical Criminology*, 5(4): 403–24.

Merton, R.K. (1938) 'Social structure and anomie', *American Sociological Review*, 3: 672–82.

Michael, G. (2012) *Lone Wolf Terror and the Rise of Leaderless Resistance*. Nashville, TN: Vanderbilt.

Miller, D. (2001) 'Poking holes in the theory of "broken windows"', *The Chronicle of Higher Education*, 47(22) (9 February): A14–A16.

Miller, E.M. (1991) 'Assessing the risk inattention to class, race/ethnicity and gender', *American Journal of Sociology*, 96: 1530–4.

Miller, J. (2001) *One of the Guys*. Oxford: Oxford University Press.

Miller, J.M. and Tewkesbury, R. (2000) *Extreme Methods*. London: Allyn & Bacon.

Miller, R. (1997) *Magnum*. New York: Grove Press.

Miller, V. (2011) *Understanding Digital Culture*. London: SAGE.

Miller, W. (1958) 'Lower class culture as a generating milieu of gang delinquency', *Journal of Social Issues*, 14: 5–19.

Mills, C.W. (1940) 'Situated actions and vocabularies of motives', *American Sociological Review*, 5(6): 904–13.

Mills, C.W. (1959) *The Sociological Imagination*. Oxford: Oxford University Press.

Mooney, J. (2007) 'Shadow values, shadow figures, real violence', *Critical Criminology*, 15(2): 59–70.

Mopas, M. (2007) 'Examining the "CSI *effect*" through an ANT lens', *Crime, Media, Culture*, 3(1): 110–17.

Morris, T. (1957) *The Criminal Area*. London: Routledge & Kegan Paul.

Morris, T. and Morris, P. (1963) *Pentonville*. London: RKP.

Morrison, W. (1995) *Theoretical Criminology*. London: Cavendish.

Morrison, W. (2004a) 'Reflections with memories', *Theoretical Criminology*, 8(3): 341–58.

Morrison, W. (2004b) 'Lombroso and the birth of criminological positivism', in J. Ferrell, K. Hayward, W. Morrison and M. Presdee (eds) *Cultural Criminology Unleashed*. London: GlassHouse.

Morrison, W. (2006) *Criminology, Civilization and the New World Order*. London: GlassHouse.

Morrison, W. (2010) 'A reflected gaze of humanity', in K. Hayward and M. Presdee (eds) *Framing Crime*. London: Routledge, pp. 289–307.

Moynihan, C. (2010) 'The art of the potentially deadly deal', *The New York Times* (23 June): C1, C5.

Muller, T. (2002) *De warme stad: betrokkenheid bij het publieke domein*. Utrecht: Jan van Arkel.

Muller, T. (2012) 'The empire of scrounge meets the warm city', *Critical Criminology*, 20(4): 447–61.

Murray, J., Loeber, R. and Pardini, D. (2012) 'Parental involvement in the criminal justice system and the development of youth theft, marijuana use, depression and academic performance', *Criminology*, 50(1): 255–302.

Muzzatti, S. (2006) 'Cultural criminology', in W. DeKeseredy and B. Perry (eds) *Advancing Critical Criminology*. Lanham, MD: Rowan & Littlefield, pp. 63–81.

Muzzatti, S. (2010) 'Drive it like you stole it', in K. Hayward and M. Presdee (eds) *Framing Crime*. London: Routledge.

Mythen, G. (2007) 'Cultural victimology', in S. Walklate (ed.) *Handbook on Victims and Victimology*. Cullompton: Willan.

Nagin, D. (2007) 'Moving choice to center stage in criminological research and theory', *Criminology*, 45(2): 259–72.

Natali, L. (2013) 'Exploring environmental activism', *CRIMSOC: The Journal of Social Criminology*, 'Green Criminology' Special Issue, autumn/winter: 64–100.

National Gang Center (2013) *National Gang Center Newsletter* (Fall, Vol. 2). Washington, DC: National Gang Center.

National Youth Gang Center (2007) National Youth Gang Survey Analysis. Available at: www.iir.com/nygc/nygsa/

National Youth Gang Center (2014) National Youth Gang Survey Analysis. Available at: www.nationalgangcenter.gov/survey-analysis

Nicolaus, M. (1969) 'The professional organization of sociology', *Antioch Review* (Fall): 375–87.

Nightingale, C. (1993) *On the Edge*. New York: Basic Books.

Nyberg, A. (1998) 'Comic books and juvenile delinquency', in F. Bailey and D. Hale (eds) *Popular Culture, Crime, and Justice*. Belmont, CA: West/Wadsworth.

O'Brien, M. (2005) 'What is *cultural* about cultural criminology?' *British Journal of Criminology*, 45: 599–612.

O'Brien, M. (2006) 'Not Keane on prawn sandwiches: criminal impoverishments of consumer culture', paper presented at the Second International Conference on Cultural Criminology, London, May.

O'Brien, M. (2008) *A Crisis of Waste?* New York: Routledge.

O'Conner, S. (1990) *The Emperor's New Clothes*. New York: Golden.

O'Malley, P. and Mugford, S. (1994) 'Crime, excitement and modernity', in G. Barak (ed.) *Varieties of Criminology*. Westport, CT: Praeger.

O'Neill, M. (2001) *Prostitution and Feminism*. Cambridge: Polity Press.

O'Neill, M. (2004) 'Crime, culture and visual methodologies', in J. Ferrell, K. Hayward, W. Morrison and M. Presdee (eds) *Cultural Criminology Unleashed*. London: GlassHouse.

O'Neill, M. (2010) 'Cultural criminology and sex work', *Journal of Law and Society*, 37(1): 210–32.

O'Neill, M. and Seal, L. (2012) *Transgressive Imaginations*. London: Palgrave Macmillan.

O'Neill, M., Campbell, R., Hubbard, P., Pitcher, J. and Scoular, J. (2008) 'Living with the other', *Crime, Media, Culture*, 4(1): 73–93.

O'Neill, M., Woods, P. and Webster, M. (2004) 'New arrivals', *Social Justice*, 32(1): 75–89.

Office of Juvenile Justice and Delinquency Prevention (OJJDP) (1999) *1996 National Youth Gang Survey*. Washington, DC: US Department of Justice.

Oliver, A.M. and Steinberg, P. (2005) *The Road to Martyrs' Square*. New York: Oxford University Press.

Ortiz Uribe, M. (2011) '"Narco culture" becoming popular north of the border', KPBS, 26 May. Available online at: www.kpbs.org/news/2011/may/26/narco-culture-becoming-popular-north-border/ (accessed on 11 March 2015).

Ousey, G. and Wilcox, P. (2007) 'The interaction of antisocial propensity and life-course varying predictors of delinquent behavior', *Criminology*, 45(2): 313–54.

Paik, H. and Comstock, G. (1994) 'The effects of television violence on antisocial behaviour', *Communications Research*, 21(4): 516–46.

Palahniuk, C. (2000) *Choke*. London: Vintage.

Panfil, V. and Miller, J. (2014) 'Beyond straight and narrow', *The Criminologist*, 39(4): 1, 3–8.

Parks, L. (2007) 'Points of departure', *Journal of Visual Culture*, 6(2): 183–200.

Parnell, P. (2003) 'Introduction: crime's power', in P. Parnell and S. Kane (eds) *Crime's Power*. New York: Palgrave Macmillan.

Pearson, G. (1978) 'Goths and vandals', *Contemporary Crises*, 2(2): 119–40.

Pease, K. (2006) 'Rational choice theory', in E. McLaughlin and J. Muncie (eds) *The Sage Dictionary of Criminology*. London: SAGE.

Pedahzur, A., Perliger, A. and Weinberg, L. (2003) 'Altruism and fatalism', *Deviant Behavior*, 24: 405–23.

Pepinsky, H. and Quinney, R. (1997) 'Thinking critically about peacemaking', in B. MacLean and D. Milovanovic (eds) *Thinking Critically about Crime*. Vancouver: Collective Press.

Perelman, M. (2009) 'Vive la Revolution?' *The Nation* (18 May): 22–4.

Peters, J. (2013) 'A shameful prosecutorial act', at www.slate.com

Peterson, A. (1997) 'Review of the times of the tribes', *Acta Sociologica*, 40(3): 323–7.

Peterson, V. and Runyan, A. (2010) *Global Gender Issues in the New Millennium*. Boulder, CO: Westview.

Phillips, L. (2011) 'Go out with a bang', *The New York Times* (3 July): ST3.

Phillips, N. and Stroble, S. (2006) 'Cultural criminology and kryptonite', *Crime, Media, Culture*, 2(3): 304–31.

Phillips, N. and Stroble, S. (2013) *Comic Book Crime*. New York: New York University Press.

Phillips, S. (1999) *Wallbangin'*. Chicago: University of Chicago Press.

Pickett, J.T., Chiricos, T., Golden, K.M. and Gertz, M. (2012) 'Reconsidering the relationship between perceived neighborhood racial composition and whites' perceptions of victimization risk', *Criminology*, 50(1): 145–86.

Piquero, A. and Bouffard, J. (2007) 'Something old, something new', *Justice Quarterly*, 24(1): 1–27.

Platt, A. (1977) *The Child Savers*. Chicago: University of Chicago Press.

Plunkett, L. (2013) 'The silly outrage over a soldier wearing a *Call of Duty* mask', 22 January. Available at: http://kotaku.com/5978161/photo-of-call-of-duty-mask-on-real-soldier-causes-outrage (accessed 8 September 2014).

Polsky, N. (1967) *Hustlers, Beats and Others*. New York: Anchor.

Poole, O. (2006) 'Pentagon declares war on internet combat videos', *The Daily Telegraph*, 26 July.

Post, J.M. (2005) 'When hatred is bred in the bone', *Political Psychology*, 26(4): 615–36.

Poster, M. (1995) *Second Media Age*. Cambridge: Polity.

Poston, B. (2012) 'Hundreds of assault cases misreported by Milwaukee Police Department', *Milwaukee Journal Sentinel*, 22 May.

Potter, R. (1995) *Spectacular Vernaculars*. Albany, NY: SUNY Press.

Pow, C.-P. (2013) 'Consuming private security', *Theoretical Criminology*, 17(2): 179–96.

Powell, B. (2006) 'Many wade into Toronto brawl online', *Toronto Star* (31 January): A8.

Powell, M. (2012) 'No room for dissent in a police department consumed by numbers', *The New York Times* (8 May): A20.

Power, N. (2009) *One Dimensional Woman*. Winchester: Zero.

Pratt, T., Turanovic, J., Fox, K. and Wright, K. (2014) 'Self-control and victimization', *Criminology*, 52(1): 87–116.

Presdee, M. (2000) *Cultural Criminology and the Carnival of Crime*. London: Routledge.

Presdee, M. (2004) 'The story of crime', in J. Ferrell, K. Hayward, W. Morrison and M. Presdee (eds) *Cultural Criminology Unleashed*. London: Glasshouse.

Presser, L. and Sandberg, S. (eds) (2015) *Narrative Criminology*. New York: New York University Press.

Price, D. (2011) *Weaponizing Anthropology*. Oakland, CA: AK Press.

Pryce, K. (1979) *Endless Pressure*. Harmondsworth: Penguin.

Prynn, J. (2007) 'Moss doubles her money after "Cocaine Kate" scandal', *London Evening Standard* (12 June).

Qurashi, F. (2013) 'An ethnographic study of British Muslim radicalism', PhD thesis, University of Kent, UK.

Quinones, S. (1998) 'In celebration of drug smugglers' "narcoculture"', *The Baltimore Sun* (21 September). Available at: http://articles.baltimoresun.com/1998-09-21/news/1998264026_1_smugglers-jesus-malverde-silk-shirts

Raban, J. (1974) *Soft City*. London: Hamilton.

Rafter, N. and Brown, M. (2011) *Criminology Goes to the Movies*. New York: New York University Press.

Rajah, V. (2007) 'Resistance as edgework in violent intimate relationships of drug-involved women', *British Journal of Criminology*, 47: 196–213.

Ranstorp, M. (2009) 'Mapping terrorism studies after 9/11', in R. Jackson, M. Breen Smyth and J. Gunning (eds) *Critical Terrorism Studies*. Abingdon: Routledge.

Rapaport, R. (2007) 'Dying and living in "COPS" America', *San Francisco Chronicle*, 7 January.

Raphael, S. (2009) 'In the service of power', in R. Jackson, M. Breen Smyth and J. Gunning (eds) *Critical Terrorism Studies*. Abingdon: Routledge.

Redmon, D. (2015) *Beads, Bodies, and Trash*. New York: Routledge.

Regoli, R. and Hewitt, J. (2006) *Delinquency in Society*. Boston: McGraw-Hill.

Regoli, R., Hewitt, J. and Delisi, M. (2010) *Delinquency in Society*, 8th edition. Boston: Jones & Bartlett.

Reiner, R. (2002) 'Media made criminality', in M. Maguire, R. Morgan and R. Reiner (eds) *The Oxford Handbook of Criminology*. Oxford: Oxford University Press.

Reinerman, C. and Duskin, C. (1999) 'Dominant ideology and drugs in the media', in J. Ferrell and N. Websdale (eds) *Making Trouble*. New York: de Gruyter.

Retort Collective (2004) 'Afflicted powers', *New Left Review*, 27(May/June): 5–21.

Richards, S. and Ross, J. (2001) 'Introducing the New School of Convict Criminology', *Social Justice*, 28(1): 177–90.

Robbins, K. (1996) 'Cyberspace and the world we live in', in J. Dovey (ed.) *Fractual Dreams*. London: Lawrence & Wishart.

Rodriguez, R. (2003) 'On the subject of gang photography', in L. Kontos, D. Brotherton and L. Barrios (eds) *Gangs and Society*. New York: Columbia University Press.

Rojek, J., Rosenfeld, R. and Decker, S. (2012) 'Policing race', *Criminology*, 50(4): 993–1024.

Romero, S. (2010) 'Can ghosts bring life to old cult compound?' *The New York Times* (3 May): A6.

Root, C., Ferrell, J. and Palacios, W. (2013) 'Brutal serendipity', *Critical Criminology*, 21(2): 141–55.

Rosen, S. (2011) 'Old mug shots fuel art, and a debate on privacy', *The New York Times* (28 August): 21.

Ross, J. and Richards, S. (2002) *Convict Criminology*. Belmont, CA: Wadsworth.

Ross, J., Ferrell, J., Presdee, M. and Matthews, R. (2000) 'IRBs and state crime: a reply to Dr Niemonen', *Humanity and Society*, 24(2): 210–12.

Rowbotham, S. (1973) *Hidden from History*. London: Pluto.

Ruggiero, V. (2005) 'Review: city limits', *Theoretical Criminology*, 9(4): 497–9.

Ruggiero, V. (2010) 'War as corporate crime', in W. Chambliss, R. Michalowski and R.C. Kramer (eds) *State Crime in the Global Age*. Cullompton: Willan.

Ryan, M. and Switzer, L. (2009) 'Propaganda and the subversion of objectivity', *Critical Studies on Terrorism*, 2: 45–64.

Sachs, H. (1987) *Music in Fascist Italy*. New York: W.W. Norton.

Sageman, M. (2010) 'Small group dynamics', in S. Canna (ed.) *Protecting the Homeland from International and Domestic Terrorism Threats*. Available at: www.start.umd.edu/start/publications/U_Counter_Terrorism_White_Paper_Final_January_2010.pdf

St John, W. (2006) 'Market for zombies?' *The New York Times* (26 March): 1, 13.

Sanchez-Tranquilino, M. (1995) 'Space, power and youth culture', in B. Bright and L. Bakewell (eds) *Looking High and Low*. Tucson: University of Arizona Press.

Sandberg, S. (2013) 'Are self-narratives unified or fragmented, strategic or determined?' *Acta Sociologica*, 56(1): 65–79.

Sanders, C. and Lyon, E. (1995) 'Repetitive retribution', in J. Ferrell and C. Sanders (eds) *Cultural Criminology*. Boston: Northeastern.

Saur, B. and Wöhl, S. (2011) 'Feminist perspectives on the internationalization of the state', *Antipode*, 43(1): 108–28.

Sauter, M. (2012) Guy Fawkes Mask-ology, *HiLobrow*, 30 April, at: http://hilobrow.com/2012/04/30/mask/

Scahill, J. (2007) *Blackwater*. London: Serpent's Tail.

Scheff, T. (1990) *Microsociology*. Chicago: Chicago University Press.

Scheff, T., Stanko, E. A., Wouters, C. and Katz, J. (2002) 'How Emotions Work', *Theoretical Criminology*, 6: 361–380.

Schelsky, H. (1957) 'Ist die Dauerreflektion Institutionalisierbar?', *Zeitschrift für Evangelische Ethik*, 1: 153–74.

Schept, J. (2014) '(Un)seeing like a prison', *Theoretical Criminology*, 18(4): 198–223.

Schmalleger, F. and Bartollas, C. (2008) *Juvenile Delinquency*. Boston: Pearson.

Schopenhauer, A. (1967) *The World as Will and Representation, Vol. 1*. New York: Dover.

Schwartz, M. (2007) 'Neo-liberalism on crack', *City*, 11(1): 21–69.

Schwendinger, H. and Schwendinger, J. (1970) 'Defenders of order or guardians of human rights', *Issues in Criminology*, 7: 72–81.

Seal, L. (2013) 'Pussy Riot and feminist cultural criminology', *Contemporary Justice Review*, 16(2): 293–303.

Sellin, T. (1938) *Culture, Conflict and Crime*. New York: Social Science Research Council.

Shea, C. (2000) 'Don't talk to the humans', *Lingua Franca* (September): 27–34.

Simon, J. (2007) *Governing through Crime*. Oxford: Oxford University Press.

Slater, M. and Tomsen, S. (2012) 'Violence and carceral masculinities in *Felony Fights*', *British Journal of Criminology*, 52(2): 309–23.

Sluka, J. (2008) 'Terrorism and taboo', *Critical Studies on Terrorism*, 1(2): 1–17.

Sluka, J. (2009) 'The contribution of anthropology to critical terrorism studies', in R. Jackson, M. Breen Smyth and J. Gunning (eds) *Critical Terrorism Studies*. Abingdon: Routledge.

Smith, W.E. (1998) *W. Eugene Smith* (G. Mora and J.T. Hill, eds). New York: Harry Abrams.

Snyder, G. (2006) 'Graffiti media and the perpetuation of an illegal subculture', *Crime, Media, Culture*, 2(1): 93–101.

Snyder, G. (2009) *Graffiti Lives*. New York: New York University Press.

Snyder, G. (2016) *The Grind: Professional Street Skateboarding in an Age of Spatial Constraint*. New York: New York University Press.

South, N., Brisman, A. and Beirne, P. (2013) 'A guide to green criminology', in N. South and A. Brisman (eds) *Routledge International Handbook of Green Criminology*. London: Routledge.

Spaaij, R. (2011) *Understanding Lone Wolf Terrorism*. Springer Briefs in Criminology. Berlin: Springer.

Spencer, D. (2011) 'Cultural criminology: an invitation … to what?' *Critical Criminology*, 19: 197–212.

Springer, D. and Roberts, A. (eds) (2011) *Juvenile Justice and Delinquency*. Boston: Jones & Bartlett.

Stanczak, G. (2007) *Visual Research Methods*. Los Angeles: SAGE.

Stanko, E. (1997) 'Conceptualizing women's risk assessment as a "technology of the soul"', *Theoretical Criminology*, 1(4): 479–99.

Steinbeck, J. (1972[1936]) *In Dubious Battle*. New York: Viking.

Steinmetz, K. (2015) 'Craft(y)ness', *British Journal of Criminology*, 55(1): 125–45.

Stenovec, T. (2013) 'Ford India ad', *The Huffington Post*, 14 March.

Stokes, D. (2009) 'Ideas and avocados', *International Relations*, 23(1): 85–92.

Struckhoff, D. (2006) *Annual Editions: Juvenile Delinquency and Justice*. New York: McGraw-Hill.

Sutton, M. (2012a) 'On Opportunity and Crime'. Dysology.org: http://dysology.org/page8.html

Sutton, M. (2012b) 'Opportunity does not make the thief: busting the myth that opportunity is a cause of crime', *BestThinking*, at: www.bestthinking.com/articles/science/social_sciences/sociology/opportunity-does-not-make-the-thief-busting-the-myth-that-opportunity-is-a-cause-of-crime

Sutton, M. and Hodgson, P. (2013) 'The problem of zombie cops in voodoo criminology', *Internet Journal of Criminology*, May. Available at: www.internetjournalofcriminology.com/Sutton_Hodgson_The_Problem_of_Zombie_Cops_in_Voodoo_Criminology_IJC_May_2013.pdf

Sykes, G. (1958) *The Society of Captives*. Princeton, NJ: Princeton University Press.

Sykes, G. and Matza, D. (1957) 'Techniques of neutralization', *American Sociological Review*, 22: 664–70.

Sylvester, C. and Parashar, S. (2009) 'The contemporary Mahabharata and the many Draupadis', in R. Jackson, M. Breen Smyth and J. Gunning (eds) *Critical Terrorism Studies*. Abingdon: Routledge.

Tanner, S. (2011) 'Towards a pattern in mass violence participation?' *Global Crime*, 12(4): 266–89.

Tari, M. and Vanni, I. (2005) 'On the life and deeds of San Precario, Patron Saint of Precarious Workers and Lives', Fibre Culture 5, at http://journal.fibreculture.org

Tauri, J.M. (2012) 'Indigenous critique of authoritarian criminology', in K. Carrington, M. Ball, E. O'Brien and J. Tauri (eds) *Crime, Justice and Social Democracy: International Perspectives*. London: Palgrave Macmillan.

Taylor, I., Walton, P. and Young, J. (1973) *New Criminology*. London: Routledge & Kegan Paul.

Taylor, L. (1971) *Deviance and Society*. London: Michael Joseph.

TCU (2007) *Faculty Handbook*. Ft Worth, Texas: TCU.

Thompson, H.S. (1971) *Fear and Loathing in Las Vegas*. New York: Popular Library.

Thompson, S. and Eiserer, T. (2009) 'Experts: Dallas undercount of assaults builds "artificial image"', *The Dallas Morning News*, 15 December.

Thrasher, F. (1927) *The Gang*. Chicago: University of Chicago Press.

Tobocman, S. (1999) *You Don't Have to Fuck People Over to Survive*. New York: Soft Skull.

Toros, H. and Gunning, J. (2009) 'Exploring a critical theory approach to terrorism studies', in R. Jackson, M. Breen Smyth and J. Gunning (eds) *Critical Terrorism Studies*. Abingdon: Routledge.

Travers, M. (2013) 'Ethnography and cultural criminology', in I. Bartkowiak-Théron and M. Travers (eds) *6th Annual Australian and New Zealand Critical Criminology Conference Proceedings 2012*. Tasmania: University of Tasmania, pp. 119–26.

Treadwell, J. (2008) 'Call the (fashion) police', *Papers from the British Criminology Conference*, 8(1): 117–33.

Treadwell, J., Briggs, D., Winlow, S. and Hall, S. (2013) 'Shopocalypse Now: Consumer Culture and the English Riots of 2011', *British Journal of Criminology*, 53(1): 1–17.

Trend, D. (2007) *The Myth of Media Violence*. Oxford: Blackwell.

Tunnell, K. (1992) *Choosing Crime*. Chicago: Nelson-Hall.

Tunnell, K. (2004) *Pissing on Demand*. New York: New York University Press.

Tunnell, K. (2011) *Once Upon a Place*. Bloomington, IN: Xlibris.

Turkle, S. (1997) *Life on the Screen*. London: Phoenix.

Ulrich, E. (2006) 'Gun makers focus on what women want', *Medill News Service* (24 May), at: cbs2chicago.com

Urbina, I. (2007) 'Anarchists in the aisles?' *The New York Times* (24 December): C24.

Van de Voorde, C. (2012) 'Ethnographic photography in criminological research', in D. Gadd, S. Karstedt and S. Messner (eds) *The SAGE Handbook of Criminological Research Methods*. London: SAGE.

Vaneigem, R. (2001[1967]) *The Revolution of Everyday Life*. London: Rebel Press.

Van Hoorebeeck, B. (1997) 'Prospects of reconstructing aetiology', *Theoretical Criminology*, 1(4): 501–18.

Veblen, T. (1953[1899]) *The Theory of the Leisure Class*. New York: Viking.

Vergara, C.J. (1995) *The New American Ghetto*. New Brunswick, NJ: Rutgers.

Vesilind, E. (2008) 'Morphine clothing designer tries higher-end line', *Ft Worth Star-Telegram* (19 October): 9F.

Vick, K. (1997) '"Real TV" at heart of lawsuit over fatal crash', *The Arizona Republic* (12 December): A4.

Vidino, L. (2010) *The New Muslim Brotherhood in the West*. New York: Colombia University Press.

Vinciguerra, T. (2011) 'The "murderabilia" market', *The New York Times* (5 June): 2.

Virilio, P. (1986) *Speed and Politics*. New York: Semiotext(e).

Virilio, P. (1991) *The Aesthetics of Disappearance*. New York: Semiotext(e).

Visano, L. (1996) 'What do "they" know?' in G. O'Bireck (ed.) *Not a Kid Anymore*. Scarborough, Ontario: Thompson.

Vold, G., Bernard, T. and Snipes, J. (1998) *Theoretical Criminology*. Oxford: Oxford University Press.

Wakeman, S. (2014) 'Fieldwork, biography and emotion', *British Journal of Criminology*, 54(5): 705–21.

Walby, S. (1997) *Gender Transformations*. London: Routledge.

Walker, D. (1999) 'Hands up! COPS hits valley for 400th show' *The Arizona Republic* (30 April), pp. D11, D12.

Walklate, S. (1997) 'Risk and criminal victimization', *British Journal of Criminology*, 37(1): 35–45.

Wall, T. (2013) 'Unmanning the police manhunt: vertical security as pacification', *Socialist Studies/Études socialistes*, 9(2): 32–56.

Wall, T. and Linnemann, T. (2014) 'Staring down the state', *Crime, Media, Culture*, 10(2): 115–32.

Wall, T. and Monahan, T. (2011) 'Surveillance and violence from afar', *Theoretical Criminology*, 15(3): 239–54.

Walters, R. (2003) *Deviant Knowledge*. Cullompton: Willan.

Ward, A. (2006) 'Defend yourself', *Ft Worth Star-Telegram* (16 July): 3G.

Warren, J. (2006) 'Introduction: performance ethnography', *Text and Performance Quarterly*, 26(4): 317–19.

Watts, E.K. (1997) 'An exploration of spectacular consumption', *Communication Studies*, 48: 42–58.

Webber, C. (2007) 'Background, foreground, foresight', *Crime, Media, Culture*, 3(2): 139–57.

Weber, B. (2012) 'Originated "broken windows" policing strategy', *The New York Times* (3 March): A1, B8.

Weber, M. (1978) *Economy and Society*. Berkeley: University of California Press.

Weinberg, L. and Eubank, W. (2008) 'Problems with the critical studies approach to the study of terrorism', *Critical Studies on Terrorism*, 1(2): 185–95.

Weiner, J. (2011) 'If your life were a movie', *The New York Times Magazine* (23 January): 45–9.

Weisburd, D. and Piquero, A. (2008) 'How well do criminologists explain crime?' *Crime and Justice*, 37(1): 453–502.

Welch, M. (2009) 'Fragmented power and state-corporate killings', *Crime, Law and Social Change*, 51: 351–64.

White, R. (2002) 'Environmental harm and the political economy of consumption', *Social Justice*, 29(1–2): 82–102.

White, R. (2003) 'Environmental issues and the criminological imagination', *Theoretical Criminology*, 7(4): 483–506.

White, R. (2010) 'A green criminology perspective', in E. McLaughlin and T. Newburn (eds) *The SAGE Handbook of Criminological Theory*. London: SAGE.

White, R. (2013) 'Eco-global criminology and the political economy of environmental harm', in N. South and A. Brisman (eds) *Routledge International Handbook of Green Criminology*. London: Routledge.

Whitehead, J. and Lab, S. (2006) *Juvenile Justice*. New York: LexisNexis.

Whyte, D. (2007) 'The crimes of neo-liberal rule in occupied Iraq', *British Journal of Criminology*, 47: 177–95.

Whyte, D. (2010) 'The neo-liberal state of exception in occupied Iraq', in W. Chambliss, R.J. Michalowski and R.C. Kramer (eds) *State Crime in the Global Age*. Cullompton: Willan.

Wilkinson, I. (2005) *Suffering*. Cambridge: Polity.

Williams, S. (2001) *Emotion and Social Theory*. London: SAGE.

Williamson, J. (1978) *Decoding Advertisements*. London: Marian Boyars.

Willis, P. (1977) *Learning to Labour*. New York: Columbia.

Willis, P. (2000) *The Ethnographic Imagination*. Cambridge: Polity.

Wilson, J.Q. and Kelling, G. (2003[1982]) 'Broken windows', reprinted in J. Muncie, E. McLaughlin and M. Langan (eds) *Criminological Perspectives: A Reader*, 2nd edition. London: SAGE/Open University.

Winlow, S. and Hall, S. (2006) *Violent Night*. Oxford: Berg.

Winlow, S. and Hall, S. (2012) 'What is an "ethics committee"?', *British Journal of Criminology*, 52(2): 400–16.

Wollan, M. (2012) 'Free speech is one thing, vagrants, another', *The New York Times* (20 October): A16.

Wonders, N. (2013) 'Globalization, gender projects, and feminist futures', paper presented at the Second Crime, Justice and Social Democracy International Conference, Brisbane, 8–11 July.

Woodson, P. (2003) '"COPS" still rocks', *Ft Worth Star-Telegram* (22 February): 1F, 11F.

Workhorse and PAC (2012) *We Own the Night*. New York: Rizzoli.

Wortham, J. (2013) 'The better not to see you with, my dear', *The New York Times* (30 June): BU4.

Wright, E. (2004) *Generation Kill*. New York: Berkley Caliber.

Wright, R. and Decker, S. (1994) *Burglars on the Job*. Boston: Northeastern.

Wright, S., Curtis, B., Lucas, L. and Robertson, S. (2014) 'Research assessment systems and their impacts on academic work in New Zealand, the UK and Denmark.' Summative Working Paper for URGE Work Package 5. Copenhagen: EPOKE, Department of Education, Aarhus University.

Wright-Neville, D. and Smith, D. (2009) 'Political rage', *Global Change, Peace & Security*, 21(1): 87–8.

Wyatt, E. (2005) 'Even for an expert, blurred TV images became a false reality', *The New York Times*, 8 January.

Xie, M., Heimer, K. and Lauritsen, J. (2012) 'Violence against women in US metropolitan areas', *Criminology*, 50(1): 105–43.

Yar, M. (2005) 'The global "epidemic" of movie "piracy"', *Media, Culture & Society*, 27(5): 677–96.

Yar, M. (2009) 'Neither *Scylla* nor *Charybdis*', *Internet Journal of Criminology*, January. Available at: www.internetjournalofcriminology.com/Majid%20-%20Neither%20Scylla%20nor%20Charybdis.pdf

Yar, M. (2010) 'Screening crime: cultural criminology goes to the movies', in K.J. Hayward and M. Presdee (eds) *Framing Crime: Cultural Criminology and the Image*. London: Routledge.

Yar, M. (2012) 'Crime, media and the will-to-representation', *Crime, Media, Culture*, 8(3): 245–60.

Young, A. (2004) *Judging the Image*. London: Routledge.

Young, A. (2007) 'Images in the aftermath of trauma', *Crime, Media, Culture*, 3(1): 30–48.

Young, A. (2010) *The Scene of Violence*. London: Routledge Cavendish.

Young, J. (1971) *The Drugtakers*. London: Paladin.

Young, J. (1973) 'The amplification of drug use', in S. Cohen and J. Young (eds) *The Manufacture of News*. Thousand Oaks, CA: SAGE.

Young, J. (1998) 'Breaking windows', in P. Walton and J. Young (eds) *The New Criminology Revisited*. London: Palgrave Macmillan.

Young, J. (1999) *The Exclusive Society*. London: SAGE.

Young, J. (2002) 'Critical criminology in the twenty-first century', in R. Hogg and K. Carrington (eds) *Critical Criminology*. Cullompton: Willan.

Young, J. (2003) 'Merton with energy, Katz with structure', *Theoretical Criminology*, 7(3): 389–414.

Young, J. (2004) 'Voodoo criminology and the numbers game', in J. Ferrell, K. Hayward, W. Morrison and M. Presdee (eds) *Cultural Criminology Unleashed*. London: GlassHouse.

Young, J. (2007) *The Vertigo of Late Modernity*. London: SAGE.

Young, J. (2011) *The Criminological Imagination*. Cambridge: Polity.

Yuen Thompson, B. (2014) *Covered Women*. New York: New York University Press.

Zafirovski, M. (2012) 'Beneath rational choice', *Current Sociology*, 6(1): 3–21.

Zedner, L. (2006) 'Opportunity makes the thief-taker', in T. Newburn and P. Rock (eds) *The Politics of Crime Control*. Oxford: Oxford University Press.

Zedner, L. (2007) 'Pre-crime and post-criminology', *Theoretical Criminology*, 11(2): 261–82.

Zeiderman, A. (2013) 'Living dangerously', *American Ethnologist*, 40(1): 71–87.

Zimring, F. and Hawkins, G.J. (1973) *Deterrence*. Chicago: University of Chicago Press.

FILMOGRAPHY

18 With a Bullet (2006)	Dir. Ricardo Pollack
The Act of Killing (2012)	Dirs Joshua Oppenheimer, Anonymous, Christine Cynn
All Watched Over by Machines of Love and Grace (2011)	Dir. Adam Curtis
Alphaville (1965)	Dir. Jean-Luc Godard
The Battle of Algiers (1966)	Dir. Gillo Pontecorvo
The Believer (2000)	Dir. Henry Bean
Brazil (1985)	Dir. Terry Gilliam
Brick (2006)	Dir. Rian Johnson
Bus 174 (2002)	Dir. José Padhila
A Clockwork Orange (1971)	Dir. Stanley Kubrick
The Corporation (2003)	Dirs Jenifer Abbott and Mark Achbar
Come and See (1985)	Dir. Elem Klimov
Covered: Women and Tattoos (2010)	Dir. Beverly Yuen Thompson
Crash (2004)	Dir. Paul Haggis
Dogville (2003)	Dir. Lars von Trier
Donkey Without a Tail (1997)	Dir. Sergio Bloch
Falling Down (1993)	Dir. Joel Schumacher
Fatal Attraction (1987)	Dir. Adrian Lyne
Fight Club (1999)	Dir. David Fincher

First Kill (2001)	Dir. Coco Schrijber
Four Hours in My Lai (1989)	Dir. Kevin Sim
From My Point of View: Exposing the Invisible (2013)	Dir. Tactical Technology Collective
Girl Model (2010)	Dirs David Redmon and Ashley Sabin
Goodfellas (1990)	Dir. Martin Scorsese
The Greatest Movie Ever Sold (2011)	Dir. Morgan Spurlock
Grin Without a Cat (Le Fond de l'Air Est Rouge) (1977)	Dir. Chris Marker
Heart Broken in Half: Chicago's Street Gangs (1990)	Producers Taggart Siegel and Dwight Conquergood
Human Resources: Social Engineering in the Twentieth Century (2010)	Dir. Scott Noble
The Hurt Locker (2008)	Dir. Kathryn Bigelow
Inside Job (2010)	Dir. Charles Ferguson
Kamp Katrina (2007)	Dirs David Redmon and Ashley Sabin
Killing Us Softly (1979)	Dirs Margaret Lazarus and Renner Wunderlich
Killing Us Softly 3 (1999)	Dir. Sut Jhally
A Kind of Loving (1962)	Dir. John Schlesinger
Kitchen Stories (2003)	Dir. Bent Hammer
Look Back in Anger (1959)	Dir. Tony Richardson
The Loneliness of the Long Distance Runner (1962)	Dir. Tony Richardson
Mardi Gras: Made in China (2005)	Dir. David Redmon
Minority Report (2002)	Dir. Steven Spielberg
Network (1976)	Dir. Sidney Lumet
Nightcrawler (2014)	Dir. Dan Gilroy

No End in Sight (2007)	Dir. Charles H. Ferguson
Our Currency is Information: Exposing the Invisible (2013)	Dir. Tactical Technology Collective
The Pervert's Guide to Cinema (2006)	Dir. Sophie Fiennes
The Pervert's Guide to Ideology (2012)	Dir. Sophie Fiennes
Poster Girl (2010)	Dir. Sara Nesson
Recycled Life (2006)	Dir. Leslie Iwerks
Restrepo (2006)	Dirs Tim Hetherington and Sebastian Junger
Sherrybaby (2006)	Dir. Laurie Collyer
The Sound of Music (1965)	Dir. Robert Wise
Spare Parts (2003)	Dir. Damjan Kozole
Special Flight (2011)	Dir. Fernand Melgar
Starsuckers (2009)	Dir. Chris Atkins
Still Killing Us Softly (1987)	Dirs Margaret Lazarus and Renner Wunderlich
A Taste of Honey (1961)	Dir. Tony Richardson
Taxi Driver (1976)	Dir. Martin Scorsese
This is England (2006)	Dir. Shane Meadows
Traffic (2001)	Dir. Steven Soderbergh
The Trap: What Happened to Our Dream of Freedom (2007)	Dir. Adam Curtis
V For Vendetta (2005)	Dir. James McTeigue
Vice News: The Islamic State (2014)	Dir. Medyan Dairieh
The War on Democracy: A Film by John Pilger (2007)	Dirs Christopher Martin and John Pilger
The War Tapes (2006)	Dir. Deborah Scranton
The War You Don't See (2010)	Dirs Alan Lowry and John Pilger
Waste Land (2010)	Dirs Lucy Walker, Karen Harley and João Jardim

We Steal Secrets: The Story of WikiLeaks (2013) Dir. Alex Gibney

When the Levees Broke (2006) Dir. Spike Lee

Who is Bozo Texino? (2005) Dir. Bill Daniel

Why We Fight (2005) Dir. Eugene Jarecki

The Wire (series, 5 parts) (2002–2008) Creator: David Simon

INDEX

Madar, C., 125–126
Making Trouble, 24
Malverde, Jesus, 1–2
Mannheim, H., 46
Manning, B., 125
Manning, P., 155, 215, 228
Marcus, G., 224
Maori tattoos, 100–101, 204
Mardi Gras: Made in China, 120
Martin, P., 51
Martin, T., 165
Marx and Marxism, 4, 199, 243
Marx, G., 107
masculinity, 131, 184
hegemonic masculinity, 75
Matthews, R., 192
Mattley, C., 24, 223
Matza, D., 7, 41–44, 140, 248
Mazower, M., 188
McDonald, K., 100
McIntosh, M.,
McLeod, J., 50
McLuhan, M., 152
McRobbie, A.,
McVicar, J., 66
meaning, 2, 15, 34–35, 37, 49, 97, 102, 137,
    141–145, 151–154, 226, 231, 240–250
flow of, 151–154
politics of, 240–250
Measham, F., 24
media, 57, 81–82, 137, 151–180, 247–248
experience of the internet, 171–173
loops and spirals, 154–164, 176–179, 248
military entertainment complex, 176–177
speed of, 154
will-to-representation, 173–175
    see also advertising; internet; video
    games
Mediapolis, 151, 176
Memoirs of an Italian Terrorist, 142
Merton, R.K., 36, 109
methods/methodology, 180, 184–237, 249
anarchist/Dadaist understanding of,
    186–187
critique of orthodox methods, 184–205
culture of, 184–185, 193, 199–205
    as symbolic performance, 201–202
of cultural criminology, 209–239
autoethnography, 220, 222–225
ethnographic content analysis, 225–227
ethnography, 210–215
instant ethnography, 215–218
liquid ethnography, 218–221
visual criminology, 210, 220, 228–234

methods/methodology *cont.*
of emotions, 72–73
of everyday life, 90
feminist methodology, 23–24
history of, 187–192
impact on discipline, 192–199
methodological engagement, 236–237
methodological fundamentalism,
    198–199, 204
participatory action research, 219–220
militarization of public space, 178
military entertainment complex, 176–177
Miller, E., 75
Miller, V., 173
Miller,W., 5
Mills, C.W., 48, 78
Milovanovic, D., 218
Minamata, 233
Minority Report, 82
mods and rockers, 39, 45–46
Mooney, J., 42
moral entrepreneurs, 11, 159, 184, 227
moral panic theory, 49
moral panics, 46, 49, 66, 88, 166, 227
Morris, P. 46
Morris, T. 46
Morrison,W., 14, 101, 140, 146, 204, 230
Moss, K., 156
mountain rescue teams, 76
Murder in Amsterdam, 139
MyMagic+ system, 109

Nagin, D., 194
narco culture, 2
narrative criminology, 224
Natalie, L., 80
National Deviancy Conference (NDC),
    45–47, 50, 229
National Gang Survey, 203
naturalism, 140
Network, 180
New Criminology, The, 47–48
new deviancy theory, 31–36
labelling theory, 39–41
subcultural theory, 36–39
'New Jack Hustla', 162
Nicolaus, M., 209
Nightcrawler, 181
Nightingale, C., 44, 61
Nike, 163
No End in Sight, 147

O'Brien, M., 88, 116, 210
O'Neill, M., 24, 219–220